S OF EASTERN HYBRIDIZERS

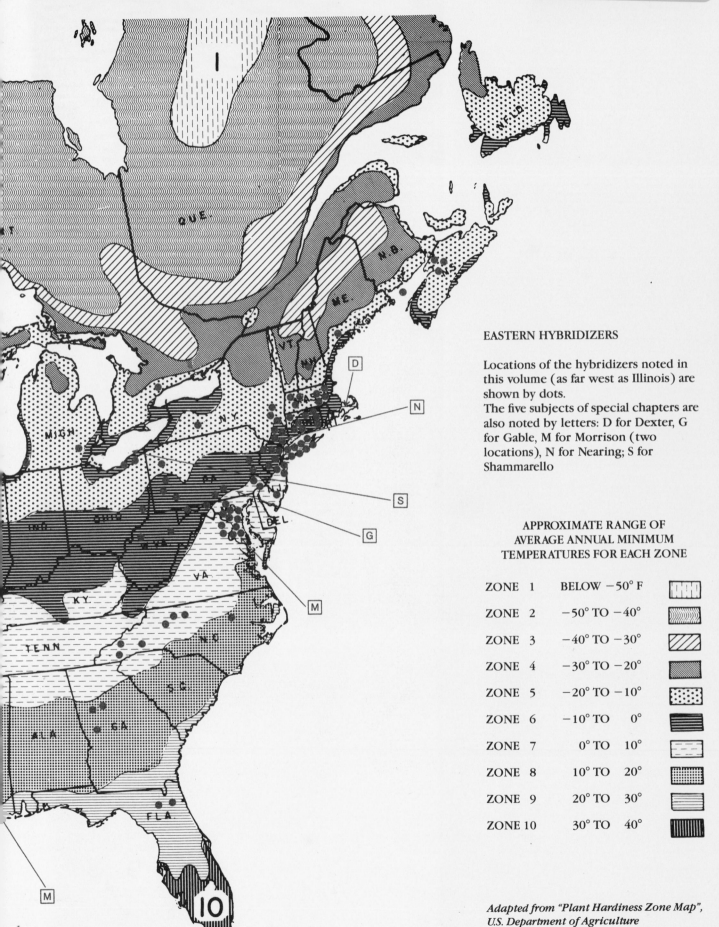

EASTERN HYBRIDIZERS

Locations of the hybridizers noted in this volume (as far west as Illinois) are shown by dots.
The five subjects of special chapters are also noted by letters: D for Dexter, G for Gable, M for Morrison (two locations), N for Nearing; S for Shammarello

**APPROXIMATE RANGE OF
AVERAGE ANNUAL MINIMUM
TEMPERATURES FOR EACH ZONE**

ZONE 1	BELOW −50° F	
ZONE 2	−50° TO −40°	
ZONE 3	−40° TO −30°	
ZONE 4	−30° TO −20°	
ZONE 5	−20° TO −10°	
ZONE 6	−10° TO 0°	
ZONE 7	0° TO 10°	
ZONE 8	10° TO 20°	
ZONE 9	20° TO 30°	
ZONE 10	30° TO 40°	

*Adapted from "Plant Hardiness Zone Map",
U.S. Department of Agriculture
Miscellaneous Publication No. 814.*

HYBRIDS AND HYBRIDIZERS

SPONSORED BY THE AMERICAN RHODODENDRON SOCIETY

HYBRIDS
AND
HYBRIDIZERS

Rhododendrons and Azaleas for
Eastern North America

Edited by
Philip A. Livingston and Franklin H. West

Introduction by
David Goheen Leach

HARROWOOD BOOKS
NEWTOWN SQUARE, PENNSYLVANIA

Library of Congress Cataloging in Publication Data

Hybrids and Hybridizers, rhododendrons and azaleas
    for Eastern North America

    Bibliography: p.
    Includes index
    1. Rhododendron—Breeding   2. Azalea—
Breeding.   3. Plant breeders—United States—
Biography.   4. Rhododendron—Varieties.
5. Azalea—Varieties.   6. Hybridization,
Vegetable.   I. Livingston, Philip A., 1901-
II. West, Franklin H., 1921-
SB413.R47H9   635.9′33′62   77-16822
ISBN 0-915180-04-9

10 9 8 7 6 5 4 3 2 1

Harrowood Books
3943 North Providence Road
Newtown Square, Pennsylvania 19096

To John C. Wister

Without his encouraging support and special contributions, this book would not have come into being. He gave words to its substance, but more importantly, for fifty years was responsible for gathering and sharing rhododendron information and plant material throughout the East.

His generosity great, his enthusiasm boundless, his encouragement gentle, his friendship unstinting, Dr. John Caspar Wister deserves far more than this dedication in appreciation of his devoted service to horticulture and the genus rhododendron.

CONTENTS

COLOR PLATES

PREFACE

A century ago, rhododendrons and azaleas were rarely grown in the gardens of North America. If anyone wished to plant some, there were only a few native species and a small group of ironclad hybrids from which to choose.

The ironclads had been hybridized in England by the Waterers who had based their work on *Rhododendron catawbiense* of our southern Appalachians. This parentage endowed these hybrids with adaptive capabilities to the climate of the Atlantic Coast. Their introduction at the 1876 Centennial Exposition heralded the beginning of the extensive use of these plants in eastern gardens.

During the next fifty years, the work of creating new rhododendron varieties was done mostly in England, Belgium, Holland, and Japan. With the exception of the Mollis and Ghent deciduous azaleas and some of the Belgian Indian evergreen azaleas, most of these new hybrids were not able to adapt to the same region that so hospitably welcomed the ironclads.

The genetic endowment of rhododendrons is so climate-specific that they lack the general adaptability of other garden flowers such as the rose and marigold. Successfully adaptable new varieties would have to come from those bred and raised in the same region where they were to be grown. Thus it fell to eastern breeders to produce hybrids that could perform well in their region. For parent stock they used the hardy species and hybrids introduced by plant explorers, brought principally from the East Coast of the Asian continent.

Only seedlings with the right genes can survive the three to seven year exposure to the local climate between their germination and first flowering. Natural selection eliminates the unfit, and the hybridizer selects the most beautiful. The fruits of this process produced a major garden miracle in eastern America during the past sixty years.

The planners of this book have long felt that the hybridizers who produced this miracle deserved appreciative recognition through a permanent record commemorating their lives and their plants. Each of our contributors gave with generous enthusiasm to help achieve this goal.

This book focuses major attention on five eastern hybridizers—Dexter, Gable, Morrison, Nearing, and Shammarello—and their hybrids. Others currently following the example set by the pioneering five are described in Chapter six. To discover the current preferences of rhododendron growers, we conducted a survey of all eastern members of the American Rhododendron Society. From this our compiler developed ratings and lists of recommended varieties for each of seven eastern growing regions, presented in Chapter seven.

The information published here gives the reader what he needs to know when dipping into the treasure trove of over one thousand new azaleas and rhododendrons—all perfectly at home in eastern gardens. It also equips anyone who chooses to apply the hybridizers' know-how in developing beautiful new hybrids for future gardeners to enjoy, wherever they may be needed.

The Editors have followed *Rhododendron Information,* published by The American Rhododendron Society, 1967, in matters of spelling, capitalization, and italicizing of varietal names, except when journals and correspondence are quoted. In these cases the style of the writer (usually that of Bowers, 1960) is followed. *Yakusimanum* is used instead of its alternate spelling and a few other arbitrary choices have been made.

There are many people to thank. This book represents a major contribution of time and effort on the part of a group of knowledgeable (and busy) people who have written the material, gathered the text illustrations and contributed the many color slides from which our selection was made. They are identified in the contributors' section following Chapter Seven. This book owes much to the Heritage Plantation of Sandwich, Massachusetts. Through their Horticulturist, Heman Howard, they participated in the early planning, and furnished encouragement and financial assistance.

The Editors are particularly grateful to Pamela Foley, Ann Gross, Paul Harris, Wendy Harris, Daniel Layman, Robert Heden, Dinah Ramey, Hazel Richmond and Maureen Turzo, who assisted in many ways to make a book out of a thousand pieces.

INTRODUCTION

Charles Dexter, the patrician New England industrialist; Joe Gable, the devout farmer; Guy Nearing, the brilliant, nonconforming intellectual; Tony Shammarello, the inner city kid who made good; Ben Morrison, the scientist-aesthete: it would be hard to assemble a more incongruous lot, with so little in common. Among them, however, they will have given a new lilt and grace to eastern gardens through the phenomenal rhododendron and azalea hybrids they have produced. Their names are the wave of the future, their greatest renown yet to come. The rhododendrons of present commerce in cold climates were produced a century ago; the newcomers are unlikely to attain similar celebrity until well after the beginning of the third millenium.

Their hybrids, with appraisals of both quality and hardiness, and how they were produced, their thoughts on promising prospects for improvements, and much more are all here for the hobbyist to read and relish. This book has no parallel in its interest for both the novice and the knowledgeable. Over a hundred color plates offer a dazzling panorama of the biographees' achievements. It is an invaluable record of the transformation of garden rhododendrons and azaleas in the eastern United States.

The chapter on the beloved Joe Gable is an evocative profile of a man whose incisive mind was disguised by a simple demeanor. Written from fond familiarity with his life's history, it is cunningly couched in terms which revive the ambience of rural life much earlier in the century. The kindly man of steely principles is portrayed as I remember him: homely in manner, Christian in outlook, essentially sophisticated in the true sense, erudite, generous, and humorous.

Even his faults had their virtues. Next to the renowned British hybridizer, the late Edward Magor, no breeder concocted less imaginative or more startling names for his plants. They ranged from "Stump", for an admired hybrid, to "Rattlesnake" for a form of *R. bakeri*. Horrors, coined from combinations of parents' names, such as "Amath", "Camich", "Brachdis" and "Cathaem" confounded the uninitiated and produced the most dissonant human utterances since the invention of Esperanto. But the names remained embedded in the memory.

I worked with Milton Lehman on the production of an article for *The Saturday Evening Post* which bore the flamboyant title, "The Flowering Forest of Joe Gable." It focused national notability on its deserving subject, but I have speculated more than once whether its consequences were more bane or benefit to a man so modest and retiring.

The Gable chapter includes an account by George Ring, of the origin of the best known rhododendrons most often associated with their creator. It is followed by a descriptive listing, with quality and hardiness of ratings, of the named clones, the parentages of the crosses which produced seedlings that were sold, and the species that Gable grew. More detailed descriptions, with ratings, are given for the cultivars that have achieved wider distribution. Similar listings are provided for the persistent leaved azalea hybrids, for which Gable was perhaps even better known.

Jane Goodrich has contributed a transcription of Gable's later notebooks and file cards, which detail most of the crosses he made, the species and hybrids which he grew, and in many cases his observations of their adaptability and ornamental value. It is an invaluable record for the hybridizer and the hobbyist in zone 7a climates, and for the horticultural historian.

Breeders in the cold Northeast usually regard Joseph Benson Gable as the dean of American hybridizers. His output was astonishing but his experience with, and knowledge of rhododendrons were overwhelming. Years ago I had his original notebooks copied. They occupy three volumes in my library. They contain wryly humorous comments, many deleted in later versions, about the incredible number of different species and hybrids he grew. Describing the unattractive progeny of a cross which particularly disappointed him, he called the seedlings "a rather disreputable lot." That was the harshest judgement, of plants or people, of which Joe Gable was capable. He loved them both.

The account of the achievements in rhododendron hybridizing by Charles Owen Dexter is more historical than personal, but perhaps all the more valuable for that reason. The stern, aristocratic New Englander, tall, hawk-nosed, with strong, striking features, was not the flashing personality that makes for easy character portrayal. But in his later years, plants were his life; he bred rhododendrons on a Lucullan scale, and produced more hybrids more widely grown than any other American hybridizer.

Dexter's output is realistically evaluated in this useful chapter; his unjust reputation for having produced legions of gross growing rhododendrons with undistinguished flower colors, none too hardy at that, is set to rights.

Hobbyists will find here the clonal names for the innumerable Dexter cultivars which have been floating through the trade under number for decades, and a candid appraisal of their ornamental merit by John Wister, the leading authority on these rhododendrons. A listing of sources of supply completes the best available information on the Dexter hybrids, familiar in the name of their originator but not in their origin.

Many who have no great knowledge of rhododendrons are aware of the name "Scintillation". It is a Dexter hybrid. His own great favorite, which he always showed to visitors, was his number 9, with apricot colored flowers, subsequently called "Skyglow" by the Baldsiefen Nursery. They are only two of many worthy clones, mostly anonymous, the yield from hundreds of thousands of seedlings grown by this dedicated gentleman in one of the largest breeding programs for woody plants in the history of the United States.

An anthology of the correspondence of men of letters is commonplace; an anthology of a horticulturist's writing is a rarity; but an anthology of a literary horticulturist's exchanges with a kindred spirit is unique.

Guy Nearing's name is nearly always associated uncomfortably with superlatives: scholarly, brilliant, creative, intellectual, intuitive, talented, wise, gifted, resourceful, profound, perceptive—the descriptions usually add up to one word: genius.

Paul Sleezer introduces the letters written by Nearing to his great, good friend, Joseph Gable, with an affectionate memoir. The remarkable correspondent emerges through self-revelation in the letters spanning many years which have been preserved by the Gable family. Magnanimous, honorable, unpretentious, prophetic, the product of this luminous intelligence discloses the author's foibles as well as his shrewd deductions.

When I first visited the nursery which Nearing was laboring to establish, I was astounded to find him presiding over an unpromising patch of land strewn with rocks of all sizes. As we picked our way along the paths, I inquired how the deep storage pits had been excavated through the huge buried boulders. The seemingly frail, gray haired man diffidently replied that he had done it himself, using a principle of Archimedes.

One of the most phenomenal Nearing traits is his capacity to endure. Now 87, his life has been ravaged by disasters: blindness, an inconstant patron, ill health, privation, devastating flood and finally, after the chapter in this book was written, the one affliction he had seemed to escape: fire, which utterly destroyed his home.

The reader of the Nearing letters will need an acquaintance with the Asian rhododendron species to fully understand them, but there is much to be gleaned by those more casually interested. Some conclusions seem a bit hasty, perhaps based on insufficient evidence, but they derive from later observation.

The human interest is compelling. The letters are often buoyantly optimistic and totally committed, as when he writes that, despite the lack of future financial return, "the work seemed so tremendously worthwhile that we had to go ahead with it." Or, "Rhododendron breeding is a sort of religion with us." After his appalling afflictions, including the destruction of his nursery, only 20 months after a second start with the help of his close friend, Gable, he was writing, "I really feel encouraged."

Then there are the dark moods. At 66, Nearing wrote, "I'm beginning to feel my age. It looks as if my hybridizing has nearly come to an end." He was still doing strenuous folk dancing at 87. Then, "After nearly 15 years of breeding, I have fewer than a dozen plants kept for observation, and most of those will pretty surely be thrown away." Or, later, "And now, after . . . years of work, I still haven't raised a first class seedling." After the flood came despair: "I have sold off . . . my nursery, and closed the place for keeps . . . there is small likelihood that I can ever take up . . . hybridizing . . . again." But the resolute spirit always regains ascendancy: "It is likely that none of the crosses I make now will ever do me any good. However, as you may guess, I intend to go right on crossing as though I had 200 years to live. I want to go ahead with all that give promise." Or, "By the time next year's seed is turned into flowering plants, we'll be old men . . . however, if I were not interested in this work for its own sake, I wouldn't be in it at all."

The Nearing letters are a rewarding resource for the rhododendron breeder; the final outcome is often unknown, yet the hybridizer learns the prospects that a brilliant, informed mind considered promising. The comments on the commercial marketing of novel rhododendron hybrids have been proven all too true.

Nearing was the originator of an entire, new system of propagating rhododendrons; he pioneered methods which are in universal use today. Perhaps a single sentence best summarizes the approach of this singular man: "My microscopic measurements . . . show that (rhododendron) leaves grown in the sun are 20% thicker."

The chapter on Nearing concludes with a descriptive listing of the best known hybrids that somehow survived the calamities which were visited upon his efforts.

Plantsman, hybridist, painter, composer, musician, landscape designer, editor and writer, winner of seven major horticultural awards, Benjamin Yeo Morrison was renowned as an azalea breeder, but all of his talents were quite a little larger than life. The Glenn Dale hybrid azaleas which he created, and later the Back Acres hybrids, are household words among nurserymen and gardeners nearly everywhere that these plants can be grown. Their creator was as extraordinary as his creations, a complex, volatile man whose splintered facets were rarely seen as the handsome prism from which they sprang.

He was invariably courteous, even charming, to me; but I was a little afraid of him in the early days. His acid tongue, devastatingly witty observations, and corrosive letters were famous. They were the product of a quick brain with friction brakes that worked in reverse. Friction, especially of mindless origin, loosened the rolling tongue. Ben Morrison was the Terrible Tempered Mr. Bang in the memory of many a singed horticulturist.

His goal in creating the persistent leaved Glenn Dale hybrids was simple, he said. He wanted to produce the spectacular southern Indian azaleas in versions which would be hardy at Washington, D.C. He did much more, of course. His hybrids bloom at both earlier and later seasons; additional flower colors, statures and other useful attributes were added. The breeding method was as old as man-made efforts to improve cultivated plants. All of the plausible combinations of parents were tried, 75,000 seedlings were grown, and from the survivors in the Washington climate 454 selections were named. Morrison disdained the theoretical geneticists, but he wrote knowingly of the interpretation of his results.

He justified the introduction of 454 Glenn Dale cultivars by his expectation that they would find niches in varying climates for gardeners with diverse preferences in color, stature, and season of bloom. Some, he thought, would quietly disappear as sister clones proved to be more adaptable under the differing conditions of growth to be found south of the Mason and Dixon Line. Unhappily, it did not work that way. The trade found the legions of Glenn Dales so bewildering that they were generally shunned by nurserymen. Only two large growers propagated them in any assortment representative of their splendid multiformity. Had he known the outcome, it would not have deterred Morrison in the least. It was a worthy challenge; it was a contribution. Today, one or two hobby nurseries offer good assortments of the Glenn Dale hybrids, but many sources would be needed to assemble a comprehensive collection.

The authors of the chapter on Ben Morrison wisely allow a talented pen to speak for itself. There are extensive extracts from *The Glenn Dale Azaleas,* published just 25 years

ago as Monograph #20 by the U.S. Department of Agriculture. Its information is still valid, and of interest to the azalea breeder. There are quotations from Morrison's work sheets and perhaps best of all, his lively, lucent letters to his friends. His replies to a budding nurseryman are the horticultural equivalent of G. K. Chesterton's letters to his son. Morrison was scholarly and accomplished, but his ivory tower was firmly anchored in the earth; he was fully aware of the commercial facts of life. He referred to descriptions of some of his hybrids as obituaries.

There are many helpful bits of information in this chapter: Morrison's own selection of his best hybrids; his comments on the inheritance of flower color patterns; the indicators of the derivation of azalea hybrids without known pedigree; his methods of gathering and sowing seeds and growing seedlings, now in widespread use; and much more.

Roy Magruder offers an admirable selection of Glenn Dale hybrids for use in small gardens in the Washington area, with a rare emphasis on autumn and winter leaf colors. It is followed by an equally useful listing of all of the Glenn Dales arranged conveniently by season of bloom, height, and flower color and form. Those which are especially desirable are so marked.

Frances Patteson-Knight has contributed a graphic memoir of Morrison after his retirement to Mississippi, where he produced the Back Acres hybrid azaleas. Fifty-three cultivars were registered with the Royal Horticultural Society in 1964 and 1965. Just before his death in 1966 he named seven more. Prolific to the end, Morrison steadfastly maintained a cadence of his own. Little is known about the garden performance of the Back Acres hybrids; Art Frazer, a specialist nurseryman in Virginia who has championed their attractions, finds them to be as hardy and adaptable as the Glenn Dales.

The Morrison Azalea Garden in the United State National Arboretum, which contains virtually all of the Glenn Dale hybrid azaleas, was established in 1954 as a tribute to its first Director. The world "memorial" was carefully avoided; Ben wouldn't have liked that.

A penny probably led Tony Shammarello into rhododendron hybridizing. His immigrant father, earning 18¢ an hour as boss of a three-man maintenance crew in Cleveland's Lakeview Cemetery, was promoted to head an eight-man squad, but without pay increase. The management considered for two months his suggestion that he should receive a wage boost commensurate with his increased responsibility, and then advanced him to 19¢ an hour. Mr. Shammarello had confidently expected 20¢ so he quit, and started the landscape business that eventually led to his son's national reputation as a breeder of rhododendrons and azaleas.

Tony had grown up in Little Italy, one of Cleveland's toughest neighborhoods. Many of his friends were young hoodlums; some of them ended up in prison. Few escaped the trap of the inner city, but Tony and his family were different.

Young Shammarello had always been impressed by his father's work at the cemetery, famed then, as now, for its floral displays. He thought it was a great feat to put small magnolias and flowering cherries into the ground, and have them produce in a few years the springtime showers of flowers staged by the older trees. When he was 17, Tony met Michael Horvath, the owner of Mentor Nurseries, who knew the Latin names of plants and was willing to take the time to explain their meaning to an eager teenager. Tony was so impressed that he offered to work without pay in Horvath's greenhouse, for the knowledge and experience to be gained from the distinguished older Hungarian. Came Christmas, and Mr. Horvath presented his helper with a cash gift. It was immediately refused. The obligation lay in the other direction. Tony's father directed him to take a gallon of wine as a holiday gift to Mr. Horvath.

The father's little landscaping business prospered, but the rootballs of the shrubs and trees bought from nurseries in the sandy Mentor soil fell apart. Father and son decided to grow their own, once more a link in the chain of circumstances.

Then the depression devastated the nursery industry; plants and like frills were dispensable. However the Shammarellos noticed that their competitors were concentrating on junipers and arborvitae. There seemed to be not quite enough rhododendrons and azaleas, more difficult to produce, to fill even the reduced demand. They decided to specialize in them—yet another circumstance.

Finally, the terrible winter of 1938 swept down upon northeastern Ohio. When the dejected father and son surveyed their browned fields the following spring, they found 90 percent of their rhododendrons dead. It was the fourth key circumstance.

Tony decided to use the survivors as parents to create a race of rhododendron hybrids which would fill their special needs as landscaper-nurserymen. Always perceptive, with the Latin aesthetic talent, he despised the ungainly, bare based, grafted hybrids of the day. He thought there should be rhododendrons of modest size available which would be handsome foliage plants the year around.

So began the evolution of the Shammarello hybrids, described by Alfred Martin in Chapter V. No theory was involved, no study of wild forebears, or of the work of others. The self-instructing breeder knew his goals and set out to achieve them by trial and error.

I remember two things about my first visit to Tony's many years ago: it was the first, and still the only, nursery I had seen with the edges of the fields landscaped; and he was clearly breaking the rules. He didn't seem to know that the literature invariably cautioned the breeder against crossing complex hybrids of unknown derivation.The breeding program was untainted by theory, pragmatic in its objectives, and self-sustaining in its operation.

As a group, the Shammarello rhododendron hybrids are compact, well furnished with foliage, free blooming and precocious about it, sturdy and easily propagated. They are "commercial" in the best sense, meaning that they present no problems to either the professional grower or the consumer. His azalea hybrids, some of them patented, have been successful for the same reasons.

Chapter V concludes with a descriptive listing of all of the azalea and rhododendron hybrids introduced by Tony Shammarello, their hardiness, seasons of bloom, and the original numbers under which they were first grown. Quality ratings are also given for the azaleas. At 74, Tony has been married recently for the first time. The affable, immensely knowledgeable plantsman is turning out new *yakusimanum* hybrids, now as a hobby nurseryman, which are finding a place in the affection of gardeners as did their originator with his colleagues long ago.

The chapter captioned "Contemporary Hybridizers", contains capsule descriptions of the work of 45 later, or at least younger, hybridizers in the eastern United States. All breeders can find here an account of those with similar goals, and the parents others have chosen to achieve them. A listing by climatic zones gives the azalea and rhododendron hybrids produced by the biographees. There follows a register, with parentages, of the new cultivars released, year by year, between 1959 and 1975, as recorded by The American Rhododendron Society. An index, by climatic zones, of eastern azalea and rhododendron breeders, with their addresses, completes a reference source unobtainable elsewhere.

The book concludes with a section designed to aid the hobbyist who is not necessarily a hybridizer. Tables give the eastern quality and hardiness ratings of a selection of the rhododendron and azalea cultivars introduced by each of the five principals, and of the species, ironclads and miscellaneous commercial hybrids in the trade. This helpful information has been assembled for the first time from a widely representative sampling of eastern growers.

The last pages of information are probably controversial, but interesting nonetheless. A selection of "favorite" azaleas and rhododendrons, in the order of the number of nominations which are received for each, is provided by hobbyists who responded to a questionnaire. Resumes of results in the various geographical regions of the East include recommendations of both species and hybrid cultivars for each.

This book constitutes a unique record of hybridizing rhododendrons in the eastern United States. Its like is not to be found for this or any other genus, at any other time, in any other place, in the history of horticulture. In the scope of its concept and the comprehensiveness of its execution, it stands alone. It is an enduring account of an American revolution in garden rhododendrons designed to replace the mid-nineteenth century hybrids of the British, and of the evolution of hybrid azaleas which more fully reflect the best qualities of their wild forebears.

David G. Leach
Madison, Ohio

Color plate, following page
Dexter Rhododendron "Scintillation" from the watercolor by J.D. Scott

J. P. Scott

CHAPTER I

Charles Owen Dexter 1862-1943

1921, Shawme Farm

When rhododendron growers in eastern North America undertook the task of creating a group of plants suited to the gardens of the Atlantic states and provinces, the best-known series in mid-century were the Dexters. Charles O. Dexter was one of the first to undertake a massive breeding program; his new hybrids were hardy, attractive and unfortunately widely dispersed before they had been properly evaluated. This scattering of the Dexters led to a dramatic rescue operation after his death—a rescue of both his plants and his reputation—with a plot that had enough elements of drama and detective work to constitute a horticultural mystery story.

As outstanding plants were discovered and given code numbers or registered names, rhododendron lovers entered into the excitement. Large collections were found, including one at Heritage Plantation, formerly Dexter's Shawme Farm, where Heman Howard has sought out and "brought home" what is now a nearly complete collection of the superior varieties.

The history of the Dexters begins in 1921, when Charles O. Dexter, a prosperous New Bedford textile manufacturer—and a descendant of

Shawme Farm. circa 1921

John Alden and Richard Warren, members of the original Mayflower group—bought an abandoned farm in Sandwich, Massachusetts, overlooking Shawme Pond. He planned to restore the property, over a hundred acres of rolling terrain, with a fine colonial house, for a retirement home. Paul Frost, a Cambridge landscape architect, was engaged, and Shawme Farm, a beautiful and most remarkable country estate, was the result.

Paul Frost had an unusual interest in, and knowledge of, rhododendrons. Naturally, comprehensive collections of the Ironclads (catawbiense hybrids) available in the New England nurseries of that era were planted. However, Charles Dexter was persuaded to try some special plants that Frost had seen in a new nursery his friend, Boston seedsman R. J. Farquhar, had started in the mild climate of

Cape Cod in nearby Barnstable. The plants, imported from the famous Robert Veitch Nursery in Exeter, England, apparently had not been tried before in New England.

The following spring, the blooms from those British imports were so different from the Ironclads—the colors clear and vivid, the flowers strikingly beautiful—that they fascinated Charles Dexter. Whether indeed the impetus that started Dexter on his hybridizing came from those rhododendrons is a tantalizing question, which will remain to tease horticulturists. However, the fact remains that for the next several decades, Dexter undertook his breeding work on a monumental scale.

Encouraged, advised, and assisted by the world renowned Ernest H. "Chinese" Wilson and Professor Charles Sprague Sargent (the latter was then director of the Arnold Arboretum in Jamaica Plain, near Boston) Dexter began the experiment that became his chief hobby, if not indeed his chief occupation, for the rest of his life: to make crosses in an effort to produce more varieties of rhododendrons hardy in his climate. Soon he was working on such a vast scale that for more than fifteen years hybrid seedlings were produced at the rate of over 10,000 a year.

No records have been found of the names of the Ironclads Mr. Frost planted or of the names of the plants from the Farquhar Nursery. It is known, however, that Mr. Dexter gave the designations #1 – #9 to either the first of the Farquhar plants he received, or the first of them to bloom and interest him. Of these, only #8 (now called Wellfleet) and #9 (Skyglow) have survived. Dexter considered #8 to be the species *fortunei*, however, authorities of the 1970s state it is not the pure species. It is evidently closely related to or a hybrid of the species *fortunei,* or of the closely related species *decorum.* This is probably true also of #9.

Dexter may have continued to designate some of the other Farquhar plants with numbers up to #25. Of these, two, #16 (Sagamore Bayside) and #23 (Chatham), have survived. It is believed that all the higher number designations given to the plants by Mr. Dexter were for his own hybrid seedlings.

In addition to the rhododendrons already mentioned, it is believed that he received other species and varieties from the Arnold Arboretum or other sources. About 1928, Mr. Wilson secured pollen from British friends to give to Mr. Dexter. The exact names or sources of the pollen are not known, and obviously, pollens may have come directly from other places. Dexter also received seeds from the Edinburgh Botanic Gardens about 1933.[1]

Labels on surviving plants indicate that in breeding, Dexter used—either as seed or pollen parents—at least the following species:

decorum, discolor, fortunei[2]*, griersonianum, haematodes;* and the following varieties: the Dutch introductions Britannia and Earl of Athlone, the British introduction Pygmalion, all then new, and the British varieties Lady Eleanor Cathcart of 1850, and Cornubia.

The breeding work Charles Dexter undertook with such enthusiasm was only begun when he was in his early sixties, what people familiar with horticulture would call quite old. Nevertheless, he must have produced at least 150,000 to 200,000 hybrid seedlings. Most were planted out in the fields or open woods bordering Shawme Pond. Many hundreds—probably thousands—were given to friends and public botanical collections, and perhaps some were sold to nurserymen.[3] Some of these were plants or propagations from plants that he had selected and numbered, but most were unbloomed seedlings in flats. Survivors have been found with numbers as high as #221.

Charles Owen Dexter The Man

What kind of man was C. O. Dexter? Interviews with members of his family reveal a man of broad interests and many talents; a man active in business and civic affairs—a trustee of the New Bedford Textile School, director of several institutions, and chairman of the Norristown Hosiery Mills. He was also an accomplished violinist, photographer, and yachtsman who had, finally, to disqualify the boat he had designed and built . . . otherwise it won every race! A tragedy ended his photographic career in the 1930s. Dexter tripped in his office and struck his eye on a desk corner.

---

[1] See Appendix B.

[2] *Fortunei* types are so tremendously predominant in all surviving plants that the term "Fortunei Hybrids" is used by the rhododendron public for all widely distributed Dexter hybrids.

[3] For complete lists, see Appendix H.

The eye was lost, and from then on he wore a glass one.

The first Dexter of this family line came to the New World in 1664 with Roger Williams, settled in Rhode Island, and served as a minister of the First Baptist Church in Providence. One branch of the family later settled in Nyatt, Rhode Island, where they became interrelated with the Owens, Sharpes, and Starkweathers. There, C. O. Dexter's grandfather married an Owen and prospered as one of the owners of the Gorham Silver Company. His son, Lewis Dexter raised four sons in Nyatt: Lewis, George Owen, Charles Owen (born August 26, 1862 in Providence), and Smith Owen. After the silver crash of the 1800s, Lewis senior went to England as a United States Consul. All the Dexter sons went to Brown University. Charles Owen studied engineering there, prepared himself for a career in textile manufacturing, and was graduated in 1885. Soon after graduating, Dexter married Alice Elizabeth Wadsworth.

In 1887, he took his bride to Milltown, New Brunswick, where he managed the St. Croix Cotton Mill until 1892, then moved on to the Canadian Colored Cotton Company in Ontario until 1904. Their four children, Alice Elizabeth, John, Mary, and Charles O., Jr., were born in Canada. When their oldest child, Alice Elizabeth, was eighteen, the Dexters returned to Massachusetts. With his uncle and cousin, C. O. Dexter had chosen New Bedford as the location of their new joint venture, the Beacon Manufacturing Company, which became one of the largest manufacturers of cotton blankets in the United States.

Ludwig Schierenbeck Recalls

C. O. Dexter made his home at 150 Orchard Street, in New Bedford, on such a small piece of ground that it did not allow for any significant indulgence in horticulture. He always regretted that he could do so little with this garden. His son-in-law, Ludwig Schierenbeck, recalls first meeting C. O. Dexter in 1913 when

Charles Owen Dexter as a young man

Ludwig was courting Alice Elizabeth. He felt somewhat awed by the big house, the many fine antique furnishings and clocks inside, the family, and by the person of his father-in-law to be.

"He impressed you right away. He was very tall, very slim—there was not a visible ounce of fat on him ever! He was of the old aristocratic New England types. Mr. Dexter was very easy to get to know and could converse about a thousand different subjects; it didn't make any difference what topic came up."

Dexter had been thinking of a retirement place for a long time. After the blanket factory was moved to North Carolina, he began his search in earnest. He wanted a large piece of land to farm and garden, and it had to be on the Cape, which he loved. The purchase of Shawme Farm was made in 1921, when Dexter at fifty-nine had just been told that he had a bad heart and could not expect a long life. In fact, he had twenty-two productive years ahead of him. Shawme Farm, as he called it, was mostly wooded, but had some acreage suitable for fulfilling his long-smoldering

Alice Elizabeth Wadsworth Dexter

desire to move closer to nature and become a farmer and plantsman. The Dexters wintered in New Bedford until 1935, when they took up permanent residence at Sandwich, although Mr. Dexter continued commuting until the end of his life.

Dexter was aware that the Cape soil was very much on the acid side. His first plantings were blueberries, set out in a hollow near the house. Later, he grew peaches and apples. He planted a formal garden in the area enclosed by the newly constructed wing of the house; put in a sunken hothouse heated by a coal furnace; and hybridized a Dexter strain of Golden Bantam corn in the extensive flower and vegetable garden in a vale below the house. To add minerals to the sandy soil, Dexter imported tons of "stone meal" (ground rock) which he believed helped in growing especially fine potatoes. (The Heritage Plantation has had much difficulty in growing anything on this site except grass. Perhaps some long delayed toxicity from the slowly dissolving stone meal could explain this mystery.) In all these efforts, Dexter had the help of a Mr. Kelly, who supervised four Italian and Portuguese groundsmen. Mrs. Kelly was the cook.

Dexter spent nearly all of the day outdoors on the farm. His wife would have to summon him to dinner with a loud call, and it might take her husband ten minutes to make it to the table. Although Alice Dexter admired his gardening efforts, she was not personally involved in his outdoor activities.

One of Charles Dexter's most characteristic traits was his perfectionism. It served him well in many ways: in maintaining the high quality of his cotton blankets, in the care and upkeep of the beautiful clocks and furnishings of his impeccably kept home, in his meticulous attention to detail in his landscape photography, in the careful packing of his white peaches, which he trucked in his four-door Buick and sold to Tabor's Market, his New Bedford grocer. (His daughter Mary deMaCarty, recalled that he would not let anyone else pack the peaches for market until one year when he asked her to help and she acquitted herself admirably.) He tested each new fruit tree for his orchard by removing all the fruits but one, and then deciding the fate of that variety by the quality of that single survivor.

How Charles O. Dexter actually became involved with rhododendrons no one knows for certain. Was he intrigued by the selection the landscape architect planted? Perhaps his eye had noticed these glowing perennials—different from and superior to the Ironclads—on those many business and personal trips to Europe or the southern United States. He may have been influenced by Ward, the Long Island nurseryman, during their summers together in New Hampshire. Whatever the stimulus, he began hybridizing right from the start at Shawme Farm. As Ludwig Schierenbeck recalled it:

"I remember the first time I visited Shawme Farm in May. The plants were in full bloom, and it was a magnificent sight. He mentioned a desire to go further with the rhododendrons to see what the results would be. He had no definite goals other than improving what he had on hand. Dexter personally numbered his acquisitions and kept the record in his little black book. I can still see him tie the paper bag over the flowers to keep the bees away. He carried camels hair brushes in his pockets, along with that little notebook. Native rhododendrons and other evergreens were ordered from Asheville. Later, Dexter sent some of his hybrid seedlings to Asheville, and these were planted at his cousin Charles Owen's place in Biltmore Forest." (Years later the Dexter Study Committee saw these plants but found none of exceptional merit.)

Dexter and du Pont

Dexter dug deeply and thoroughly into his rhododendron hobby, and the plants not available from nurserymen he grew from seed. The following correspondence came to light through the courtesy of the Eleutherian Mills Historical Library, Greenville, Delaware.

On October 21, 1927, E. H. Wilson of the Arnold Arboretum wrote to Pierre S. du Pont:

A few years ago the Arnold Arboretum obtained from its friends in England seeds of a number of rhododendrons for Mr. Charles O. Dexter of Sandwich, Mass., who had become keenly interested in these notable evergreens. Mr. Dexter has been extraordinarily successful in raising rhododendrons from seeds and in getting rapid growth of them afterwards. Of the seeds received from England he has raised more plants than he has room for so I told him that Arnold Arboretum would be very glad of a set of these plants to send on to Mr. P. S. du Pont.

A list followed:

4	Rhododendron	*aucklandii*	
5	"	*burmanicum*	
3	"	*campanulatum*	
2	"	"	Wallichii
4	"	*campylocarpum*	

3	Rhododendron	*campylocarpum x aucklandii*	
		(seedlings from x)	
3	"	*cinnabarinum* Roylei	
3	"	*diaprepes*	
4	"	*fortunei,* good variety	
3	"	*fulgens*	
5	"	*griffithianum*	.
3	"	*irivecum*	
4	"	*leptoturium*	
4	"	*pachtrichum*	
3	"	sp. (Penjerrick, fine yellow)	
2	"	loderi, seedling from	
4	"	shilsonnii	
4	"	sp. Forrest #	
5	"	*thompsonii*	
4		*triflorum*	

74 plants

Mr. du Pont promptly sent his thanks to both Wilson and Dexter; he received the following letter on October 27, 1927, from Charles Dexter in New Bedford in response:

My dear Mr. du Pont:

I received your letter on October 24 and was only too glad to be able to send you the rhododendrons which Mr. Wilson of the Arnold Arboretum wanted you to have.

I might mention that I have a few other varieties planted this year that are coming along nicely—some of which may be available next year, if you would like to have them. They are among the choicest rhododendrons known and include Edgworthii and Maddenii. Both of these are tender plants which will grow only in the most favored locations in Great Britain and therefore would be greenhouse plants with us but both have very beautiful flowers and they are very fragrant. If you would like to have two or three of each next year, and will advise me, I would hold them for you.

In a letter written the next day, Pierre du Pont gladly accepted the offer of additional plants and repeated his earlier invitation "to visit my house and see the collection, which I hope might be of interest to you, especially in the spring when the rhododendrons and azaleas are in bloom." Dexter replied October 31, 1927:

My dear Mr. du Pont:

I have your letter of October 28th. I have heard a great deal about your azalea and rhododendron houses and have been very anxious to see them and have looked forward to the day when I could do so.

I am interested in a hosiery mill at Lansdale, Pa., and I had intended, some time on one of my trips down there, to drive over to your place and shall plan to do so next spring, if you will let me know the proper time to see the houses at their best.

Dexter visited Longwood Gardens several times with his son-in-law and exchanged views with du Pont, who, like Dexter, kept a lively interest in every individual plant he had growing on his estate.

Dexter and one of his hybrids

The Operation Grows

Ludwig Schierenbeck recalled that Dexter raised his own hybrid seedlings by the thousands!

"Nursery beds were scattered all over the estate. He prided himself in being able to bloom a plant in four or five years, instead of the usual six or seven. Plants not hardy through their first winter outdoors were discarded. After blooming them, a further selection was made by throwing away all the unattractive ones. The one color he disliked was mauve. He made layers of the most beautiful plants to give to friends. Hundreds of cuttings went to C. S. Sargent at Arnold Arboretum, as well as many others. Many flats of seedlings were given away before they had bloomed. Yet, all this rhododendron work was done in the twenty-two years after Charles Dexter moved to Sandwich in 1921.

Favorites were brought into the house and the blossoms floated in a big crystal bowl on the dining room table: white, a light pink, two deep pink ones, and one deep red. As far as I can remember, these were not named but only referred to by number. I do recall that a carload of his hybrids was sent to the University of Washington Arboretum in Seattle."

Dexter did a little hybridizing of deciduous azaleas and planted them across the pond and along the walks in the woods. (Many of these were crosses of Ghent hybrids and arborescens.) A large planting of Kurume azaleas could be seen from the house, but I do not believe he hybridized those.

On April 14, 1943, while searching for a water valve by Shawme Pond, death came to C. O. Dexter at the age of 81. He was survived by his wife Alice Elizabeth, his daughter Mary, and his son Charles O., Jr.

Mrs. Dexter, who felt her loneliness keenly at Shawme Farm, wrote this poetic essay several years after becoming a widow:

Glimpses

I knew a garden on Old Cape Cod, where the gates were never closed. Where friends and strangers from far and near strolled the winding paths—absorbed in admiration of the peace and beauty anchored there. It was off the noisy high-way, in calm seclusion sheltered. Its heights looked out to Cape Cod Bay, in tranquil mood a sheet of shimmering sapphire blue. Its depths led into kettle-holes mysterious, ploughed deep by the glaciers force as they swept through. God planned that narrow land of hills and sunny slopes; between two sandy shores on old Cape Cod and inspired the mind and hand of the quiet man, who planted his gardens there, with Rhododendrons of many shades of color, hybrids all named, and believe it or not, some fragrant, of rare and exotic charm—Azaleas, too, in great profusion of color and enchanting grace, a wealth of wonderful achievement when in bloom, during the heavenly month of June. And up and down around the green grass hollow, across the lawn in sunlight and shade, the mountain laurel grew, lending its beauty in massive clusters of deep rose pink, bringing the admiration of all who paused. The old homestead, shelter of generations long since passed away, had been restored inside and out, offering welcome to all who called, and there were many. What joy in treasured memories to one alone, forlorn.

In the two years she remained there, she sold some plants and seedlings, but took no interest in continuing the breeding work. In 1945, Shawme Farm was sold, and Mrs. Alice Dexter spent her remaining years at Hartford, Connecticut, with her daughter Mary.

The reputation of Charles Dexter as a breeder had suffered because he did not wait to see all his seedlings bloom or to judge their merits before allowing them to go out. If he had stopped to consider, he might have burned inferior seedlings and would not have sent out any lacking in distinction. The poorer

varieties gave many rhododendron growers the impression that this work had not been important. That general feeling is beginning only now to be changed by the relatively few varieties (though numerically over a hundred) that have been named by those who had received plants from the Dexter estate. Most of these are commercially available on a moderate scale. (see Appendix H)

After her husband's death, Mrs. Dexter sold many more plants. Shawme Farm changed hands several times and many large specimens were taken out by contractors and sold, mostly within quick trucking distances but sometimes as far away as New York. About that time, the late Dr. Clement G. Bowers, America's first great student of the genus *Rhododendron,* was beginning to realize how much this might do to destroy Mr. Dexter's reputation entirely. Disturbed by this thought, Dr. Bowers formed an informal group to select, rescue, propagate, and distribute the finer Dexter rhododendrons which might otherwise have been lost.

1945
The First Swarthmore Dexter Hybrids

In the early autumn of 1945, the Arthur Hoyt Scott Horticultural Foundation of Swarthmore College, Swarthmore, Pennsylvania, received as a gift from Mrs. Arthur Hoyt Scott over one hundred plants. They represented eight different hybrid groups of over a hundred unbloomed Dexter seedlings.[4] This group comprises the *first* and *only* shipment of plants from Charles Dexter, or from his estate, about which we have details on the *number* of plants, their *parentage,* their *behavior,* and

---

[4]The shipment also contained a few dozen extra plants which Mr. Wood had been commissioned to purchase for others. See Appendix. D.

the *proportion* of seemingly important individual varieties which were later to be selected from them.

Although it was known that untold numbers of seedlings were sent by Charles Dexter to many places, the Bowers committee was never able to ascertain the exact numbers, parentages, or claimed parentages. However, the committee did ascertain where many seedlings were located.

Mrs. Scott purchased the plants from the Dexter estate through the help of Mrs. Dexter who, with the help of Antonio Consolini (Mr. Dexter's former head gardener), and Harry Wood (grounds foreman of Swarthmore College), personally selected the plants which later were sent to Swarthmore by truck. The plants were placed in cold frames over the first winter then transplanted to open sections of the college woods below the Scott Memorial Outdoor Auditorium.

Four of Mrs. Dexter's eight groups were claimed to be of complicated hybrid parentages involving the species *discolor, fortunei, griersonianum,* and *haematodes* with the varieties Britannia, Earl of Athlone, and Pygmalion. It was soon evident that these were too delicate or otherwise unsuited to the climate of southeast Pennsylvania. After several years, they produced a few very charming flowers immediately used for further crossing, but the plants grew poorly. They did not survive one or two unusually severe winters. The plants of the other four groups grew well, however, and attracted attention for their unusual colors and times of bloom—from very early in the season to very late.

Two of these groups had been labeled simply as *fortunei* hybrids. The plants of the first group, which Tony Consolini considered the most important, closely resembled their *fortunei* parent.[5] They grew rapidly, sometimes unevenly, reaching a height of eight to ten feet or more in ten years, broadening out

only later. They began to bloom freely at an earlier age than most rhododendrons. The flowers, which open by May 15 in the Philadelphia area, had a rather limited color range of pale pink and washy pink fading to white, yet they seemed to vary greatly because of different amounts of yellow in the throat or in the pollen on the anthers. All were deliciously fragrant.

The plants of the second group—which Mrs. Dexter preferred[6]—were distinctly different and did *not* resemble the *fortunei* parent.[7] Much slower growing, in ten years, they made compact plants only, three to four feet high and across. The foliage was unusually attractive, but there was not a great deal of bloom until the plants were eight or ten years old. In the Philadelphia area, the flowers came late, May 18 or 20. Most were delightful rose pinks, not washy pink and not fading. None was fragrant.

Many plants having the characteristics of these two groups have turned up in all other known collections of Dexter seedlings. These come to the minds of rhododendron fanciers whenever the name "Dexter Hybrid" is mentioned. Dozens have been named and introduced in the nursery trade. The plants of the other two groups at Swarthmore, on the other hand, are hardly known elsewhere (except where they have come from the original Swarthmore shipment).

The plants of the first of these two groups were labeled *Pygmalion* x *haematodes* x Dexter #8 *(fortunei)*.[8] They bloom very early—sometimes even May 8, 9, or 10. Most of the flowers are fine clear reds and much alike. Many—too many—have been named both at Swarthmore[9], and in other places

---

[5]Given Swarthmore Acquisition Number 12499. No selections from this group have as yet been named.

[6]Swarthmore Acquisition Number 12500. The only one as yet named is 12500-2 Madison Hill.
[7]It is now assumed they were hybrids of *catawbiense* Ironclads x *fortunei.*
[8]Swarthmore Acquisition Number 12507.
[9]At Swarthmore, names have been given as follows: 12507-1 Accomac; -3 Aronimink; -6 Avondale; -9 Adelphia (distinctly bicolor); -12 Acclaim; and -14 Accomplishment. (Further testing is needed to determine which are the hardiest.)

where plants were received from Swarth-more.[10]

'The plants of the last group[11] were labeled Lady Eleanor Cathcart[12] x *decorum*. They grew slowly and were a long time, about 12 years, coming into bloom. These are now tall and mostly pyramidal rather than wide and spreading. Nearly all have beautiful large, rather leathery foliage. The best would be worth growing as specimen plants for their foliage alone.

All are late blooming, opening about June 15 to 20.[13] The flowers are various shades of pink, from the true rose pinks to washy pinks fading out almost to white. We consider the late blooming very important, and have already selected and named five of the twenty plants received from the Dexter Estate.[14] It must be remembered, however, that most rhododendron growers want flowers from mid-May to early June, and are not interested in late blooms. Strangely enough, no plants resembling these have turned up in Sandwich or in any of the other known collections of Dexter hybrids.[15]

---

[10]Elsewhere, names have been given as follows: at Ardmore, Pa. by Richard Schwoebel, Dorothy Russell; at Media by Mrs. Arthur H. Scott, Todmorden; at Chestnut Hill, Pa. by Morris Arboretum, Wissahickon. In addition, note that the names Harlequin given to Sw 12507-5 in Westbury, N. Y., by Vossberg, and Red Velvet given to 12507-2 in Pine Lakes, N. J., by Knippenberg, are name conflicts and therefore unacceptable by the Registry of the American Rhododendron Society.

[11]Swarthmore Acquisition Number 12506. See Appendix D.

[12]Lady Eleanor Cathcart was a hybrid between *maximum* and *arboreum* raised by the British firm of J. Waterer before 1850.

[13]These dates are in great contrast with the three groups already noted, and with the Ironclads which, under Swarthmore conditions, bloom towards the end of May and are over by June 3 or 4. Note also that *maximum* here usually begins after June 20 and continues into the first few days of July, that *discolor* begins in the first days of July, and that auriculatum (when it blooms at all) begins between July 5-10.

[14]The following names have been given: 12506-1, Lady Decora; -3 Lady of Belfield; -5 (12) Lady of June; -7 Lady of Vernon; -9 (10) Lady of Wakefield.

[15]See Appendixes D and F.

1945-53
The Dexter Study Committee

As mentioned previously, the threatened injury to Charles Dexter's reputation as a breeder, arising from the unwise and too hurried distribution of untested seedlings, led Dr. Clement G. Bowers to bring together an informal group or committee to look into the situation and to see what promising Dexter varieties were still to be found on the former Sandwich estate, and in places to which he had sent plants.

The original group members were:

Henry T. Skinner, then Horticulturist of the Morris Arboretum, Chestnut Hill, Philadelphia, Pa.
Paul Vossberg, then Propagator at Westbury Rose Co., Westbury, Long Island, N. Y.
John C. Wister, then Director of the Arthur Hoyt Scott Horticultural Foundation, Swarthmore College, Swarthmore, Pa. and of the John J. Tyler Arboretum, Lima, Pa.
Donald Wyman, then Horticulturist, Arnold Arboretum, Harvard University, Jamaica Plain, Mass.

They were later joined by Edmond Amateis, then a rhododendron breeder of Brewster, New York, David G. Leach, then of Brookville, Pennsylvania, and occasionally by others.

John C. Wister's Report

I felt pleased (and flattered) to be invited to become a member of this group. Unfortunately, I had not been to Sandwich for over fifteen years, and knew nothing about Mr. Dexter's later work introducing new seedlings. I had, however, known the Dexter place almost from its beginning because I was a classmate and close friend of Paul Frost. He had taken me there when the plants were only two or three feet high. On later visits, I had seen how wonderfully they had grown and bloomed; and I had met Mr. Dexter. I had also, in the previous four years, watched and, indeed, studied carefully the growth and early bloom of over a hundred Dexter seedlings at the Scott Foundation.

It was a remarkable group of men. Dr. Bowers, who had received an M.A. at Cornell and a Ph.D. at Columbia University (for work at the New York Botanic Garden under Dr. A. B. Stout) was the author of *Rhododendrons and Azaleas,* the first comprehensive American book about these plants. He was regarded in the East, at least, as the leading American authority on the subject. A regular visitor to Shawme Farm, he was familiar with Dexter's work, as well as that of other eastern pioneer breeders such as Joseph Gable, Guy Nearing, and B. Y. Morrison. He had also visited the main rhododendron growers and their collections on the West coast and those in England, Scotland, Ireland, and the European continent.

Henry Skinner was a graduate of Wisley. On coming to this country, he had worked first at the Arnold Arboretum, and then at Cornell where he had received his M.A. At that time, he was becoming known as the raiser and selector of the variety Cornell Pink, the first really pink form of *Rhododendron mucronulatum.* He was soon to become better known for his travels in the southern United States to collect the finest forms of native azaleas. He received a Ph.D. from the University of Pennsylvania while working at the Morris Arboretum. In the early 1950s, he became Director of the U.S. National Arboretum in Washington.

Paul Vossberg was one of the first to experiment widely in methods of growing rhododendrons (other than the variety Roseum Elegans) from cuttings and was now doing this on a commercial scale. He also had sufficient knowledge of the commercial Ironclads of the day to be able to identify many by their foliage when the plants were not in bloom. He knew the Dexter seedlings, first in the collection of Samuel A. Everitt in nearby Huntington and in other Long Island gardens, and then from visits, with Henry Hicks, to the Dexter garden.

Donald Wyman, a Penn State graduate in Horticulture, had a Ph.D. from Cornell. Horticulturist at the Arnold Arboretum for over ten years, he was naturally familiar with its collection of Ironclads, then the largest in this country, and had written extensively on many horticultural subjects. A regular visitor to Shawme Farm, he had known Charles Dexter and was familiar with his work.

Edmond Amateis, the Brewster, New York, sculptor, had been breeding rhododendrons for some years and was to become well known, if not famous, for them two decades later.

David G. Leach, at the time, was a little-known amateur rhododendron grower in Brookville, Pennsylvania, the so-called "ice box" of Pennsylvania. He was hoping to, and later did, produce seedlings hardy at −30°F. He was even then gathering material for his *Rhododendrons of the World,* which was published in 1961.

These were the men that Dr. Bowers assembled about him to visit gardens where Dexter varieties were known to be in existence. I appreciated the opportunity to go with them and to study the Dexter seedlings which I had seen before only on a few hurried visits to Sandwich. Fortunately, visits to Mr. Everitt, as well as the collection brought to Swarthmore College in 1945, had been less rushed.

The Search Begins

At the time the group first met, the members knew of over half a dozen places to which Mr. Dexter had sent plants. As they visited these, they quickly learned of still other collections. At each of the following places, the members selected particularly fine, distinctive seedlings. These were given code numbers. Later, we were kindly allowed to take cuttings for propagation, further evaluation, and eventual distribution through the nursery trade.

Dexter Estate, Sandwich, Mass. (then owned by Col. Roy Brown)

Mrs. F. M. Moseley, Newburyport, Mass.

H. W. Fowle Nursery, Newburyport, Mass.

Ben. P. P. Moseley, Ipswich, Mass.

E. J. Beinecke, Greenwich, Conn. (Alfred Woodger, Head Gardener)

New York Botanical Garden, Bronx Park, N. Y.

Planting Fields Arboretum, Oyster Bay, N. Y.

Edmond Amateis, Brewster, N. Y.

S. A. Everitt, Halesite, Huntington, N. Y.

Howard Phipps, Old Westbury, N. Y.

John S. Phipps, Old Westbury, N. Y.

Mrs. Henry Ross, Brewster, N. Y.

Westbury Rose Co., Westbury, N. Y.

Morris Arboretum of the University of Pennsylvania, Chestnut Hill, Philadelphia, Pa.

Scott Horticultural Foundation, Swarthmore College, Swarthmore, Pa.

John J. Tyler Arboretum, Lima, Pa.

Mrs. Arthur H. Scott, Media, Pa.

Although visited, cuttings were not taken from the following:

Arnold Arboretum, Jamaica Plain, Mass.

Dr. George Clark, Newburyport, Mass.

John Parker, Huntington, N.Y.

Howard Young, Chadds Ford, Pa.

Koster Nursery, Bridgeton, N.J.

Rhodo Lake Nursery (Roland de Wilde), Bridgeton, N.J.

James Wells Nursery, Red Bank, N.J.

Henry F. duPont, Winterthur, Delaware

National Arboretum, Washington, D.C.

Biltmore Gardens, Biltmore, N.C.

Charles Dexter Owen (Mr. Dexter's Nephew) Biltmore, N.C.

Paul Bosley Nursery, Mentor, Ohio

The first of these cuttings, from Col. Brown at the Dexter Estate, were made by Richard Fillmore, then propagator at the Arnold Arboretum. The Scott Foundation arranged to have all the rest of the cuttings sent to the Westbury Rose Company to be rooted. The Scott Foundation also arranged to have clones sent from the University of Washington Arboretum in Seattle, Washington to be grafted at Koster's Nursery, Bridgeton, New Jersey. The several generous Dexter gifts to the University of Washington Arboretum were glowingly described in a newspaper clipping dated August 21, 1938. The first was a "carload of choice azaleas and rhododendrons," while the next was "scions of eighty of his choicest hybrid rhododendrons." The article noted that "contrary to usual American practice, Dexter has discarded the North American Rhododendrons in making his crosses and has used in their place the hardy Asiatics." The article concluded that the Arboretum owed a great debt to Charles Dexter for the thought, consideration, and generosity. The young plants grown from these cuttings and clones were then brought to Swarthmore to be grown on. Often, duplicate sets were taken to the Tyler Arboretum so that visiting members of The Bowers Committee, and others, could study and evaluate them in each place. Extra plants were sent to the National Arboretum, the Arnold Arboretum, and other places for further evaluation.

The above account merely records where we went and where we were kindly allowed to take cuttings. However, the editors of this book have asked for details of the places and people concerned to give some of the background of the Dexter varieties now named and reassembled at the Heritage Plantation in Sandwich by its present horticulturist, Heman A. Howard.

A Visit to Sandwich

These experiences were so long, long ago that my memories of them are pretty vague. I am not even sure whether I first went to Sandwich in 1925 or 1926. It was the year I first owned an automobile, a very second or thirdhand Chandler roadster of 1920 or earlier vintage. It was on its last legs and broke down frequently, but, even so, I had been able to get to Cape Cod at the invitation of my college classmate friend, Paul Frost. A year or so earlier, he had mentioned a big landscape job in Sandwich, and had urged me to go with him to see it. We met at the Sandwich railroad station, and drove the half mile or so to the Dexter place. Mr. Dexter, unfortunately, was not there (and I didn't meet him for another five years or so). I was charmed with the natural New England landscape and its typical Cape Cod beauty. I was at once fascinated by the rhododendrons that Paul had brought from the Farquhar Nursery in nearby Barnstable, which were planted fairly near Mr. Dexter's house. I had heard about them, of course, and was particularly interested in them because they had come from the Robert Veitch Nursery in Exeter, England. It was the most important nursery I had visited when I had been in England in 1907, nearly twenty years before.

What impressed me even more than the plants near the house were the thousands upon thousands of seedlings in the open meadows and along the trails through the woodlands. They were already 18″ to 24″ high. I was told that this fast growth had been made possible by heavy fertilizing with nitrate of potash (not of soda!). I had never heard of fertilizing rhododendrons before. I wondered if it would encourage too fast, the soft young autumn growth that would be damaged in winter. Paul assured me that this would not happen, and, as we know now, it never did. I still would not want to try it in Pennsylvania.

My next trip to Sandwich was in May, 1929 or 1930 when I saw these same seedlings, now grown to blooming size, producing the clear colors that we still do not have in Ironclads. At the time, I wished that I could get young plants to try in Pennsylvania; but, of course, even if I had had the temerity to ask then or the money to pay for them, no young propagations would have been available. I was also still skeptical as to whether they would survive without the benefit of mild Cape Cod's frequent fogs. So, for far too long, I put them out of my mind.

It was Leonard Barron who first suggested that I go to Huntington, Long Island, to visit Samuel Everitt and see his rhododendrons. I hesitated a long time before venturing to barge in on an utter stranger demanding to see his garden. But he was so cordial that after that I went several times a year during his lifetime; I will never forget his kindness. The woodland hillside planting of Dexter seedlings, azaleas, mountain laurel, and many other shrubs and flowering trees was an inspiration to great numbers of visitors. It influenced my planting work at Swarthmore College and the Tyler Arboretum, as well as, finally, on my own hillside garden overlooking Crum Creek.

The Committee Strikes Gold

The first visit of the group assembled by Dr. Bowers was in late May, 1949, to the New York Botanical Garden where a hundred or more Dexter seedlings had been planted six or more years previously. We all knew Dr. Robbins, the director. He was, as always, most cordial and pleased to have us see the plants under the guidance of Louis Politi, then the head gardener. When we reached the collection along the drive just north of the museum building, we really didn't need any guide! None of us had ever seen a more beautiful pink rhododendron. We checked the label, which read #67 (the New York Botanical Garden number), and promptly labeled it our New York #1. Dr. Robbins, when asked if we could take cuttings later, answered just as we had expected, "Certainly, and any other cuttings you want!"

We had intended to mark what we thought

were the best dozen varieties, but ended up by labeling sixteen in all. Among them were the numbers later to be named Betty Hume, Champagne, Dexter Purple, Fordham, and Tom Everitt. All of these were propagated, grown, and named by Paul Vossberg, and introduced by the Westbury Rose Company. They are widely admired and grown today, in the 1970s.

Paul Vossberg named our New York #1 Scintillation. It is almost certainly the finest and the best known of all Dexter varieties. This variety would no longer be in existence had it not been for The Bowers Committee which recognized its unique quality that day in 1949 and proceeded to obtain cuttings. Shortly after these cuttings were growing in Westbury, a flash flood washed out the original plant of our #1 (and many other plants). Today, Scintillation is widely grown and enjoyed because The Bowers Committee spotted it and had it propagated. That fact alone has justified Dr. Bower's effort in starting the group to track down Dexter hybrids.

The details of other particularly remembered trips the group took fade beside this important fact, but the editors have urged me to give further details.*

After our visit to the New York Botanical Garden, we went to Mr. Everitt's that same day and labeled some twenty plants, a few of which have since been named. We also numbered a few at the neighboring garden of John Parker. Then we visited the Howard Phipps estate and labeled nearly a dozen beautiful plants, among them the one later named Wheatley (which actually was not a Dexter seedling but a cross made by Mr. Phipps between the Dexter seedling later named Westbury and the Vossberg hybrid Meadowbrook). At the nearby estate of J. S. Phipps (which has since been given by his family to the public as Old Westbury Garden) only three were labelled, and as of the mid-1970s,

these have not yet been named or distributed. That was a long, busy, and very exciting day.

Shawme Revisited

A later, longer trip took us to the Dexter estate itself, then owned by Colonel Roy Brown. Whole hillsides were in bloom—a sight never to be forgotten. We did hold ourselves down to fourteen, although it was difficult to keep from marking more. Colonel Brown agreed that we should take as many as a hundred cuttings of each, and Dr. Wyman agreed to send the Arnold Arboretum propagator, Richard Fillmore, to pick them up in the autumn. Such a number would have made possible a wide distribution of these fine varieties within a few years.

It is a great pity that this ambitious project was not carried out. Mr. Fillmore did take cuttings but only a few of each number. As far as I know, only four—later given the nearby place names of Barnstable, Bass River, Brewster, and Bryantville—were rooted and distributed.

Some days later, two members of the group visited a smaller collection of Dexter seedlings and ran into the only garden owner unwilling to allow cuttings to be taken for distribution (which only serves to emphasize how cooperative and generous all other owners of Dexter seedlings were). The plants in question were two magnificent ten-foot specimens labeled *smirnowii* x *fortunei* and were, I believe, the only hybrids of that particular cross that the group ever found. Five or ten years later, when one of the group learned that the place had been sold, he asked the new owner if he might take cuttings of these plants. He received permission, but on arrival at the garden found only two holes where the plants had been.

After an article I had written for the *Journal of the New York Botanical Garden* about the Dexter seedlings in the gardens visited in 1949 was published, I received a

---

*Persistent devils, those Editors!

letter from Frederick Moseley, Jr. (later vice president of the New York Botanical Garden). He asked if the group had visited his mother's place in Newburyport, Massachusetts. Learning we had not known of the Dexter seedlings there, he invited me to come and see them.

Hospitality of Moseleys

I was in New England the next October and stopped at the Moseley place early one Sunday afternoon. Frederick Moseley took me along the woodland trails of the great estate to see the many thousands of rhododendrons eight or ten feet high and as much across. I planned to leave after an hour or so since I wanted to visit either Springfield or Hartford on my way home. But I was urged to stop in at the house to meet Frederick Moseley's mother and other members of the family. Mrs. Moseley, who turned out to be one of the loveliest persons I ever met, promptly asked me to stay to tea, and I rather reluctantly accepted.

That over, when I prepared—again—to leave, Mrs. Moseley said "Don't go until you tell us more about Dr. Bowers and his group." That took another hour or so, and when I started to take my leave, Mrs. Moseley then said "Don't go. Stay to supper; it's nearly ready." Then, after a large and delicious meal, came the remark, "It's very late to start out on a long drive; why don't you stay overnight?"!

I was embarrassed at such hospitality from utter strangers, but I stayed and enjoyed every minute. Mrs. Moseley's son-in-law, a British army major on leave, told us long and interesting stories of the British Army in the wartime. I remember being dumbfounded on coming down to 7:30 breakfast Monday morning to see the major coming up the hill in a wet bathing suit. He had taken a swim in the Merrimac River on that cold October morning! The thermometer hovered at 40°F., and the water could hardly have been much warmer!

Mr. Moseley told me that his older brother, Benjamin Moseley, also had very fine Dexter seedlings in his garden in Ipswich. When I wrote to him, the Bowers Committee was invited there in the flowering season. We went there early in June, 1950. The garden consisted of several acres through which winding paths were bordered on each side with Dexter rhododendrons eight or ten feet high with the deepest of deep green foliage (due, we learned later, to heavy feeding and watering) and the most magnificent flowers we had ever seen.

Benjamin Moseley was inordinately proud of his plants and of his gardening skill in bringing them to such perfection. He had every right to be. He explained their whole history at great length. He had known Mr. Dexter and had persuaded him to allow a Mr. Borowski (a well-known Massachusetts nurseryman who had worked with Paul Frost on the original planting in Sandwich) to select varieties of special merit and make layers of them. Later, when they were well rooted, Mr. Borowski brought the plants to Ipswich, prepared the soil, and planted them. Here they were after almost twenty years in northern New England with its cold winters (but fortunately within a mile or so of the ocean which must have somewhat tempered some of the coldest days).

The Bowers Committee were all enchanted by the flowers. They at once numbered ten, and the next year numbered over ten more. While we were in the garden, I was called to the house to the telephone. It was Mrs. F. M. Moseley in Newburyport. She had heard I was going to Ipswich and had called to invite me to lunch. I thanked her and said I would love to accept but that I could not because I was with friends.

She said, "Well, bring them along." I said, "But Mrs. Moseley, I couldn't. There are seven of us." She replied, "That's all right, bring them all along."

So a little after noon we drove the ten or

fifteen miles to Newburyport and sat down to a great round luncheon table: our seven of The Bowers Committee, Mrs. Moseley, her son Frederick, her daughter Miss Helen Moseley (later a Trustee of the Massachusetts Horticultural Society), and a family friend—whose name I never learned. That made eleven and Mrs. Moseley said, "Send for Charley to make twelve!" Charley, whose last name I have unfortunately forgotten, was the English head gardener who had been there almost a lifetime. He was accepted as a family member and called the younger Moseleys by their first names.

As with the Sunday dinner I had attended the autumn before, this was a wonderful family event and everyone ended up fast friends. Then we wandered through the acres and acres of the rhododendrons I had seen when not in bloom. They are very different from the ones at Ipswich. Not perfect specimens, superbly grown and cared for, but looser, more open, even straggly woodland plants surviving on their own without any care beyond the first planting. They were not selected varieties but run-of-the-mill seedlings taken directly from flats. We had numbered ten at Ipswich and so we began with number eleven and went to seventeen. I can report that in the Swarthmore plantings over the years they proved fully equal and, in my own opinion, superior to the Ipswich varieties which, through special care, had seemed so overwhelmingly better. I think the only one so far named is #13, Powder Puff.

The English gardener told us that one of his former workers, H. W. Fowle, had a few years before started a small nursery nearby and was growing Dexter rhododendrons. So we stopped in to see them and liked them enough to number them 18, 19, and 20. Number 18 was later named Newburyport Beauty.

The Bowers group, unfortunately, kept no official minutes of its meetings or of its travels so that the reports given here are merely the memories of what transpired plus the lists of gardens visited by the full group or sometimes

Dexter amidst his rhododendrons in 1941, two years before his death. Photo courtesy of W.I.P. Campbell.

by two or three of its members, together with lists of the cuttings taken for propagation.

The Heritage Plantation

After Mr. Dexter's death in 1943, Shawme Farm was sold four times prior to 1967. During this period, many fine plants were removed and either sold or given away. Fortunately, in 1967 the property was purchased by Josiah K. Lilly, III, for the purpose of creating an educational nonprofit museum of early Americana to be dedicated to the memory of his father Josiah Kirby Lilly, Jr. It became The Heritage Plantation of Sandwich.

The greenhouse at Shawme Farm in the 1950's. Photo courtesy of Colonel H.T. Smith.

The several buildings now house the many collections of early Americana gathered by the present owner, as well as those collected by his father, an eminent collector of his day. These fine collections, so beautifully exhibited in surroundings of horticultural beauty, provide the visitors hours of pleasure.

In the fall of 1970, efforts were begun to locate all 79 named Dexter cultivars then known to be in cultivation. Of these, only 18 were then represented in the collection at Heritage Plantation. By the spring of 1972, either plants or cuttings of 74 cultivars had been returned to the place of their origin.

During the summer and fall of 1972, it was decided to name some of the many true Dexters growing under numbers for several years at Swarthmore College. This was done by Heman Howard, Horticulturist of the Heritage Plantation, and John C. Wister. Through the Scott Foundation and the Tyler Arboretum, Heritage Plantation obtained additional cuttings, bringing their total to 120.

It is agreed that this is far too many; but it is the goal of Heritage Plantation to have every Dexter cultivar which has been named represented in its collection, there to be seen and judged by interested visitors.

The Dexter Plants Come Home

During September, 1972, 80 plants representing 34 cultivars were set out in the new Dexter Memorial Display Garden. An ideal location was selected with plenty of room for expansion of this valuable collection.

As far as possible, all presently available information about Mr. Dexter and his rhododendrons has, with the help of many persons (too many to mention by name) been assembled and has been presented in these pages. As more people become aware of the research, it is possible that some of the missing links of the story may come to light.

The thirty some years that have passed since Mr. Dexter's death have demonstrated how important his work has been. He was the first (with Joseph Gable and Guy Nearing, one of the first three) to draw to the attention of gardeners on the East Coast the need for producing really hardy rhododendrons more suited to our colder climate than the magnificent twentieth-century varieties that are such horticultural sensations in the British Isles and in the Pacific Northwest. Like Gable and

Nearing, he did produce the needed hardier plants with wonderful flowers. He produced them in far greater quantities than the others. The myth that he produced only plants that were like *Rhododendron fortunei* has been exploded only recently as more varieties of other types have come to light.

Detailed lists of all varieties now known to have originated with him are given in the Appendix and, with what has been told in these pages, show the greatness of his accomplishments in plant breeding.

The gardeners in the climates along the Atlantic Coast from New England to Virginia and inland to the Great Lakes owe to him, and will continue to owe to him, thanks for all that he did to give them the added pleasure of the beauty of his rhododendrons.

APPENDIX A

Dexter Seedlings Selected by John C. Wister, January, 1975

First Choice: Flowers Pink or Pinkish

Josephine Everitt. Original plant was one of hundreds of unbloomed seedlings sent by Charles Dexter to S. A. Everitt, Halesite, Huntington, Long Island, about 1940.* It bloomed the clearest pink; he selected it and named it for his wife. By 1950 Everitt began to give cuttings to a few rhododendron friends of whom, fortunately, I was one. These were rooted by Paul Vossberg in the Westbury Rose Company greenhouse. They have now bloomed freely at the Tyler Arboretum for nearly twenty years and in my own garden at Swarthmore for over ten years. These

*Note that all selections have proved plant hardy and bud hardy for many years in Swarthmore and Lima except after the unusually severe winter of 1961 when only a few Ironclads bloomed.

plants have not grown very rapidly and are still not very large, but they are vigorous, healthy, and shapely specimens.

Madison Hill. Original plant was one of twenty unbloomed seedlings labeled "hybrids of R. Fortunei" and sent by Mrs. Dexter to Swarthmore College in 1945 and there grown as #12500-4. It has proved to be a good, strong grower, the best of the twenty, and quite a number of cuttings have been distributed.

Sagamore Bridge. The original plant is still at Sandwich. In 1950 or before, cuttings were distributed under the number Dexter #180. It was named at Swarthmore where it has flowered for some twenty years, and fine specimens are growing there as well as here. It was named for the bridge over the Cape Cod Canal near Sandwich.

Scintillation. The original plant was sent by Charles Dexter to the New York Botanical Garden about 1940, and there grown as NYBG #67. The first choice of the Bowers Committee in 1949 on its initial visit to select superior Dexter hybrids, it was labeled NY #1. Cuttings were rooted by Paul Vossberg, who named it and introduced it in 1957. It is the most widely distributed of all Dexter hybrids and has been pronounced as best of them all by many expert rhododendron growers. It is fortunate that cuttings of this were taken for shortly afterwards the original plant was washed away in a flash flood.

Skerryvore Monarch. The original plant was sold about 1951, by the subsequent owners of the Dexter estate, to a New York contractor who sold it to Mr. Edwin Beinecke of Skerryvore, Greenwich, Connecticut. There it was labeled #59-49 and still later named for the Skerryvore estate by Howard Young of Chadds Ford, Pennsylvania, a nephew of Mr. Beinecke's head gardener, who classified many of the hundreds of plants grown by Mr. Beinecke. It was outstanding in bloom and often referred to as a "rich watermelon pink." My selection was made at Greenwich long before it was named. Propagations from it have been growing for over fifteen years at Swarthmore and at Tyler Arboretum.

Westbury. The original plant was sent about 1940 by Charles Dexter to Mr. Howard Phipps of Westbury, New York. In 1949 the Bowers Committee designated it Phipps #3, and Mr. Phipps allowed Paul Vossberg to take cuttings and to name and introduce it (about 1957). Mr. Phipps hybridized it with Meadowbrook to produce the variety Wheatley, which some experts considered to be equal to or even superior to Scintillation.

Willard. The original plant was sent, perhaps in the 1940's, by Mr. Dexter to Rathbun Willard, North Scituate, Rhode Island. Mr. Willard later gave cuttings to James Wells of Red Bank, who then gave plants numbered Willard #1-#8 to the Tyler Arboretum. In a test of nearly ten years, #2 was selected as the best of these and accordingly named for Rathbun Willard.

Flowers Red or Reddish.

The two hybrids Acclaim and Accomac were selected from twenty unbloomed seedlings which Mrs. Arthur H. Scott of Media, Pennsylvania, purchased in 1943 from Mrs. Dexter for the Scott Foundation of Swarthmore College.

They bore the Dexter label Pygmalion x haematodes x Dexter #8. Dexter #8 was a plant Charles Dexter believed to be *Rhododendron fortunei*. He had purchased it around 1925 from the R. J. Farquhar Nursery of nearby Barnstable. The plant had been imported from the Robert Veitch Nursery of Exeter, England, as *fortunei*. Dr. Clement G. Bowers insisted that it was *not* a pure form or even a typical example of this species, although undoubtedly closely related to it, and that it was probably a hybrid with *R. decorum*.

The plants were grown in the Swarthmore College woods under the Scott Foundation Acquisition Number 12507 and have bloomed there consistently since about 1948.

Acclaim (Sw 12507-12). This is decidedly the outstanding red at the Tyler Arboretum in Lima and was so named there because of the overwhelming acclaim given to it by Rhododendron Society visitors. The specimens were planted in 1965 when 2—3 feet high. They had been grown in the arboretum nursery from Swarthmore cuttings rooted by Paul Vossberg at Westbury.

Accomac (Sw 12507-1). A very clear red, slightly different from Acclaim and the earliest of the set to bloom, often about May 8 or 9 at Swarthmore, usually four or five days before Acclaim. It is not as vigorous, as tall, or as shapely a grower as Acclaim. It may be a touch less hardy. Paul Vossberg reported it bud-tender in his windswept nursery and not as hardy as our clones Aronimink and Avondale (Sw 12507-3 and 12507-5); but no such difference in hardiness has been noted at Swarthmore and Lima.

Todmorden (Scott #1). This, like Acclaim and Accomac, came from Mrs. Dexter but without identifying parentages and was first grown by Mrs. Arthur H. Scott at Todmorden Farm, Media (for which it was named). It was recognized as an outstanding early red from the time it first began to bloom, although it does seem to fade rather quickly. It has been more widely distributed than Acclaim and Accomac and, while its parentage is not known, it resembles them and the other Sw 12507 seedlings closely enough to make it probably of the same parentage.

The parentage of the next two varieties is not known, but they, like Todmorden, resembled so closely the 12507 group of seedlings as to make it highly probable they also are of the same parentage.

These varieties were among a group of nearly a hundred unlabeled 3—4 foot specimen plants sold about 1950 or 1951 by the owners of the Dexter estate to a New York landscape contractor who dug them and resold them to Dr. and Mrs. Henry Ross of Brewster, New York. When they bloomed, they attracted great local attention. William Efinger, a Brewster, New York nurseryman who had planted and cared for the Ross property, brought Edmond Amateis, the Brewster sculptor, who was interested in breeding rhododendrons, to see them. Together they tagged the finest ones with capital letters, running through the entire alphabet and then a second alphabet with double letters. In 1958, Mr. Amateis and Mr. Efinger took me to see the plants in bloom and at my request asked Dr. and Mrs. Ross for permission to take cuttings for the Tyler Arboretum. So, through their kindness, Mr. Efinger took cuttings of several dozen we all had chosen and, in 1959, brought us rooted cuttings of the plants we had enjoyed so much there.

Two of the varieties certainly belong in any list of the best reds and may, after further wide testing, prove to be superior to Acclaim, Accomac, and Todmorden.

Gi-Gi (Ross GG) (Named by Sidney Burns). This variety made a fine specimen very quickly both in Lima and in our garden in Swarthmore, and created such a fine display that many requests for cuttings were received. These cuttings probably have been more rapidly propagated and distributed than any other red hybrid of Mr. Dexter. It has been a consistently good bloomer, and the flowers are of good size. A difference of opinion exists as to its exact shade or tone of red, but the color has been universally popular. When the original plant was still quite small, a cut truss won a blue ribbon at the Princeton Chapter Rhododendron Show.

Glenda Farrell (Ross RR). This extra early blooming, very clear red has over the years proved to be the finest of the collection at Brewster and at Lima. When it became well enough known to warrant giving it a name, permission was given by Dr. Ross to name it for his late wife, who was well known under the stage name of Glenda Farrell.

It apparently has not been distributed elsewhere, but it is hoped that it may soon be propagated in sufficient quantity to have it widely grown and tested.

Further Notes on Selection of Varieties

I have picked the seven pink varieties: Josephine Everitt, Madison Hill, Sagamore Bridge, Scintillation, Skerryvore Monarch, Westbury, and Willard, and the fine red varieties, Acclaim, Accomac, Todmorden, Gi-Gi, and Glenda Farrell as my first choices because they are the ones I have known longest and best. Personal tastes of course enter into any selection, and probably no two persons would even pick the same ones. Indeed, it is highly probable I would not pick the same seven another year when I again see them all in bloom.

At present there seems to be a somewhat general agreement that Scintillation belongs way up at the top. I have no idea how many knowledgeable rhododendron growers know the others well enough or like them well enough to put them in a preferred group. I do, however, hope that they, and other varieties I have not included, may become widely known in our eastern rhododendron areas within the next ten years. It then would be possible for the American Rhododendron Society to make some important and authentic recommendations to those who are beginning to feel their way among the bewildering numbers of varieties that may be seen in good collections, or even among the relatively smaller numbers that will be available in nurseries. It is to be hoped, also, that such recommendations will encourage nurserymen to grow more of the many fine varieties that are now so little known. In this way, amateur gardeners, in general, will find it easier to plant more really fine varieties in their gardens.

Notes on Pink and Pinkish Varieties

Two widely different strains were distributed by Charles Dexter. The first of these resembled *Rhododendron fortunei* quite closely. The plants were (1) fast growing, that quickly grow tall and often rather straggly; (2) come into bloom when relatively young—3 or 4 years; (3) bloom early (in Swarthmore May 8) around May 12 or 14; (4) bear rather pale flowers, palish pink to even cream or apricot; (5) are fragrant to extremely fragrant.

Typical of this strain were plants selected at Sandwich in 1945 as *fortunei* hybrids by Mrs. Dexter's former head gardener, Tony Consolini, which were grown at Swarthmore under the acquisition number 12499. Twenty of these plants have been much enjoyed but did not seem to be distinctive enough from each other or from any general run of seedlings of *Rhododendron fortunei* to warrant giving clone names.

The second strains were called *R. fortunei* hybrids by Mrs. Dexter, and it has been suggested and widely believed that the other parents were varieties of the so-called Ironclad varieties like **Album Elegans** and **Roseum Elegans**. They are not as rapid growing as the Consolini plants, nor as tall, were more shapely, usually did not bloom until five or more years old, were all rose pink, not pale or washed out, and were not fragrant or at least not markedly so. It would seem that Scintillation and many, many other pink varieties must have come from this same general source. Neither of these strains had Mr. Dexter's labels with parentages.

Notes on Red and Reddish Varieties

In contrast, the twenty red varieties—some of which I have discussed under Swarthmore #12507—did have Mr. Dexter's label giving their parentages. Apparently no other plants of this parentage were distributed from Sandwich by either Mr. or Mrs. Dexter. I have called attention to the fact that the unlabeled seedling later named Todmorden evidently is from this same parentage or very closely related. This may also be true of another unlabeled seedling which at the same time was sent to the Richard Schwoebel Nursery in Ardmore, Pennsylvania, and which later Mr. Schwoebel named Dorothy Russell (his wife's maiden name), propagated, and distributed. I have not seen this in flower.

The twenty seedlings grouped under the number Sw 12507 resembled each other a good deal, and I did not consider any except Accomac and Acclaim important enough to be named. However, so many of my friends liked some of the others that I reluctantly named numbers 3, 6, 9, 14, and 17 Aronimink, Avondale, Adelphia, Accomplishment, and Agatha respectively. It is interesting to note that such a good judge as Paul Vossberg considered Avondale the hardiest and finest of the lot and Aronimink a close second, and that he propagated also #2 and #5 which were later named by him (or by Mrs. John Knippenberg) Red Velvet and 'Arlequin. I am informed that both these names are unacceptable for registration. In addition, Charles Herbert, another well-known judge of varieties, likes #11 particularly and has named it Kelley.

We have at Swarthmore a set of twenty Dexter hybrids that are entirely different from any Dexter seedlings and apparently are not known to exist in any other place. These were purchased from Mrs. Dexter in 1945 and came labeled Lady Eleanor Cathcart* x *decorum*. They form tall, rather pyramidal plants and bloom about June 15 or 18 for ten day or more. They have magnificent heavy leathery foliage. The flowers are various shades of pink, always with a heavy, dark blotch. Coming into bloom so late, they are valuable in extending the blooming season beyond that of the well-known Ironclad catawbiense hybrids until our native *Rhododendron maximum* comes into bloom. They bear the Swarthmore number 12506. The best clone had been labeled #5 and in different years also #12. It has been named Lady of June, and is worth growing in any garden that has space for a plant of some fifteen feet. Cuttings have been given to a number of friends who have reported it is difficult to root. I fear that this, as well as its late blooming date, will prevent its being widely grown.

Dexter Strain F₂ Hybrids

These did not originate in Sandwich, and, therefore, are not properly Dexter hybrids but can be regarded as F₂ seedlings of Dexter hybrids.

They are seedlings—nearly all open pollinated—of

---

*Lady Eleanor Cathcart is a hybrid between *R. maximum* and *R. decorum* raised by J. Waterer in England before 1850.

plants distributed by Mr. Dexter and at present being grown in other gardens. I will discuss them in the order in which I came to know them.

The Everitt F₂ Dexter Seedlings

About 1947 Mr. Everitt told me that George Gillies, head gardener and superintendent of the nearby Marshall Field estate, had come to look over his Dexter seedlings a year or two before and marked with ribbons the flowers he thought the finest. He had returned in the autumn to gather the open pollinated seeds, and he had told Mr. Everitt he would like to give some of the seedlings to me. So, when I arrived, Mr. Everitt phoned Mr. Gillies who soon appeared with several flats of seedlings a few inches high. These were grown in the college cold frames and in 1949, after my house had been built, some hundreds of young plants were planted on a south facing hillside, where I could see them from the house. For a year or two they looked like funny ink spots from the distance, and then began to fill in to cover the ground. It was nearly two years before they began to bloom enough to make a spectacle, but from then on have been an utter joy every year, except 1961 when all rhododendron flower buds were killed except the very hardiest Ironclads.

When they became big enough to be judged fairly (and to require thinning), any plants with defective flowers buds (bud-tender) were eliminated. In 1960, the first selections were numbered as 60 R—clone 1 and up to clone 20. When re-selections were made in subsequent years, some of these were eliminated. we now consider the very finest to be:

60 R 1—May Moonlight. Very pale cream. The earliest to bloom after May 8 or 9 and probably the most fragrant. In a wind storm in the 1970's, a heavy branch fell on this and split it in half. We did not think it could recover, but it is now, once more, a shapely specimen.

60 R 3—Moonlight Bay. The nearest to yellowish and, like most varieties of that coloring, with rather yellowish foliage if grown in too sunny a position.

60 R 4—Edgemont. A fairly rosy pink. The original plant has formed the most magnificent specimen, now after twenty five years, 11 feet high and over 10 feet across. This is the plant most exclaimed about by visitors.

60 R 9—Glenolden. Pink bud with yellow and apricot tones. When James Wells, of Red Bank, New Jersey, saw this, it was his first choice. It is a good grower, though not quite as large as Edgemont.

60 R 16—Clearbrook. Not a real white, but the closest to white we have.

The Swarthmore F₂ Dexter Seedlings

In 1948, we harvested our first seed crop from the Dexter *fortunei* hybrids growing at Swarthmore under numbers 12499 to 12507. In 1960 and subsequent years, we began making selections from these. The following seemed worthy of being named:

60 R 24—Cutalosa. This is another very pale flower but again not really white.

60 R 26—Kingswood. Very free blooming pink.

69 R 1—Lahaska. A pink much later blooming than those already listed.

70 R 1—Tinicum. A pink, probably the latest of all.

Besides the original plants from these two lots of seed, we have some propagations old enough to form good specimen plants at the Tyler Arboretum, but as far as I know none have been sent elsewhere. It is to be hoped that enough cuttings can be distributed for some consensus concerning the quality of these clones. Certainly some of them must be good enough to deserve a permanent place in eastern gardens.

Of course, as all these were open-pollinated, we cannot be positive that some have not been fertilized by foreign pollen brought from a distance by bees. However, both in Long Island and in Swarthmore, all the plants from Charles Dexter were grouped together and quite isolated from other rhododendrons and certainly from any that bloomed at the same general season. So it seems highly probable that they are pure F₂ descendants of Mr. Dexter's plants.

This is true also of the other open-pollinated seedlings I have procured from the H. W. Fowle Nursery of Newburyport, Massachusetts. Of these, Fowle #18, Newburyport Beauty, certainly deserves a high place in any collection.

I do not know of any other open-pollinated seedlings distributed from any collection of Dexter hybrids, though it seems likely that some may turn up in the future. I do, however, know of one hybrid of known parentage. This is Wheatley, the result of a cross between Westbury (Phipps #3) and Meadowbrook. This cross was made by Howard Phipps, propagated by Paul Vossberg (with permission), and introduced by the Westbury Rose Co. It must be quite widely grown, for a number of rhododendron enthusiasts have told me they consider it superior even to the famous Scintillation.

Heman Howard, horticulturist of Heritage Plantation (formerly the Dexter Estate) may yet find superior Dexter seedlings among the old specimen plants for there are so many that no one can possibly have studied them all carefully. Of course, so many already have been selected, named, and distributed that there can hardly be many outstanding plants left. Mr. Howard is more interested in bringing back to Sandwich all those that have been recognized as the highest quality. By the mid-1970s, he has been able to secure over one hundred and thirty of these, and he is on the trail of the remaining thirteen.

Other F₂ Dexters

The following cultivars were at one time classed by some rhododendron growers as Dexters but this was later proven incorrect or doubtful. No doubt many others not indicated here could be placed in this same category.

Brookville (H. Phipps#1)	(Meadowbrook x Westbury)	Vossberg	Westbury 1959
Helen Everitt	(Everitt-Fuller)	Everitt-Fuller	Westbury
Wheatley (H. Phipps #2)	(Meadowbrook x Westbury)	Vossberg	Westbury 1958

APPENDIX B ——————

Additional Species

PLANTS

The Seattle Arboretum of the University of Washington reports that in 1938 and 1939 it received plants of the following from Charles Dexter:

auriculatum	*hippophaeoides*	*racemosum*
brachycarpum	*houlstoni*	*ravum*
calophytum	*metternichii*	*smirnowii*
carolinianum	*moupinense*	*sutchuenense*
fargesi	*praevernum*	*vernicosum*

While it may be presumed that Mr. Dexter had tried to use these species in his hybridizing, there is no indication whatever that hybrids of any of these were really produced.

SEEDS · A record found at Sandwich states: "These seeds were all collected by Prof. (Sir) William Wright Smith (Director of Edinburgh Botanic Garden) for the University of California in 1933 through the Rhododendron Association of England—seeds given to Mr. C. O. Dexter and seedlings from them to Mrs. F. Moseley, Newburyport, Massachusetts, in the spring of 1934."

No trace of the following has been found in either place (which is not surprising since most are known to be tender):

achroanthum	*drumonium*	*muliense*
aechmophyllum	*fastigiatum*	*niphargum*
aganniphum	*fictolacteum*	*pleistanthum*
agglutinatum	*fulvoides*	*poecilodermum*
balfourianum var.	*fulvum*	*prostratum*
aganniphoides	*heliolepis*	*przewalskii*
beesianum	*hemitrichotum*	*racemosum pink*
cantabile	*hippophaeoides*	*rubriginosum*
carolinianum x moupinense	*hypolepidotum*	*timeteum*
cephalanthum	*levistratum*	*traillianum*
chryseum	*litiense*	*wardii*
crinigerum	*mekongense*	*yunnanense*

APPENDIX C

Original Dexter Numbers 1938-72

Mr. Dexter numbered his plants either as they were received or as they were selected among his seedlings. It is believed that these numbers were consecutive from #1 to #228 or higher. At the present time, only the following 19 varieties bearing original Dexter numbers have been definitely identified, described, named, and made available for the new Dexter Display Garden at Sandwich:

8 Wellfleet	105 Burgundy Cherry	173 Marshfield
9 Skyglow	108 Harwich	180 Sagamore Bridge
16 Sagamore Bayside	109 Great Eastern	187 Megansett
23 Chatham	121 Hatchville	201 John Wister
42 Eastham	123 Dexter's Favorite	(now a synonym
44 Fairhaven	128 Forestdale	for Janet Blair)
62 Merley Cream		213 Shawme Lake
		218 Teaticket

In addition, the University of Washington Arboretum in Seattle, which received some 60 plants from Charles Dexter in 1938 and 1939, reports surviving plants under the numbers: 5, 14, 18, 35, 36, 85, 104, 110, 127, 152, and 226 but no identifying descriptions are available.

The following additional numbers were apparently known in 1963 and reported but no further information about them has been received and all efforts to locate them have been in vain: 3, 11, 13, 17, 76, 94, 127, 129, 132, 155, 165, 172, 176, 186, 217, 221.

APPENDIX D ———————————————————

First Swarthmore Planting   1945

Swarthmore Code	Number of Plants	Reputed Parentage (on Label)
12499	20	*fortunei*
12500	21	*fortunei*
12501	6	*Britannia* x Dexter 200
12502	6	*discolor* x Earl of Athlone
12503	14	*discolor* x *haematodes* x Dexter #8
12505	21	(Dexter 26 x *griersonianum*) x discolor
12506	11	Lady Eleanor Cathcart x *decorum*
12507	23	Pygmalion x *haematodes* x Dexter #8

Of the above, the following have been named:

12500-2	Madison Hill		12507-1	Accomac
12506-1	Lady Decora		2	Red Velvet
	3	Lady of Belfield		3	Aronimink
	5 (12)	Lady of June		5	'Arlequin
	7	Lady of Vernon		6	Avondale
	9 (10)	Lady of Wakefield		9	Adelphia
				11	Kelley
				12	Acclaim
				14	Accomplishment
				17	Agatha

APPENDIX E ———————————————————

Cuttings Given (1949-53) to The Dexter Study Committee

Given by	Number of Clones
Dexter Estate (through Col. Roy Brown)	14
(through Arnold Arboretum)	9
E. J. Beinecke and Howard Young	35
Paul Bosley	6
S. A. Everitt	21
H. W. Fowle	3
George Gillies (mixture—not labeled)	40
Morris Arboretum	8
Ben P. P. Moseley	19
Mrs. F. M. Moseley	13
New York Botanical Garden	16

Given by	Numbers of Clones
Howard Phipps	14
J. S. Phipps	5
Planting Fields Arboretum (of John Parker Selections)	14
Mrs. Henry Ross (through Wm. Efinger)	10
Mrs. Arthur H. Scott	5
Rathburn Willard (through James Wells)	5
(About 50 of these may have been named later.)	

APPENDIX F

Named Dexter Clones
Compiled 1972 and revised by Heman Howard, 1977

Column A Variety (Cultivar)	Column B Code Number or Other Original Identity	Column C Named By or At	Column D Color	Column E Introduced By
Acclaim	(Sw 12507-12)	Sw-Ty	R	
Accomac	(Sw 12507-1)	Sw	R	Indian Run
Accomplishment	(Sw 12507-14)	Sw-Ty	R	
Adelphia	(Sw 12507-9)	Sw-Ty	R	
Agatha	(Sw 12507-17)	Sw-Ty	R	
Alice in Wonderland	(Ross AAA)	Ty	Pale	
Alice Poore	(Longwood 62612)	(Probably selection of BBPM)		
Amethyst—N.C.	(H. Phipps #8)	Vossberg		Westbury 1958
Andorra				
Apple Blossom—N.C.	(Everitt #3)	Everitt	P	Eastover
'Arlequin N.C.	(Sw 12507-5)	Vossberg	R	Vossberg
Aronimink	(Sw 12507-3)	Sw	R	Westbury
Ashes of Roses—Reg.	(Sel. at Winterthur)	H.F. duPont	R	Gladsgay Gard.
Avondale	(Sw 12507-6)	Sw	R	Wells 1961
Barnstable	(Brown #1)	Sw-HP	Salmon	
Bass River	(Brown #14)	Sw-HP	Pink	
Beauty of Halesite	(H.5.#1)	Schlaikjer	C	Schlaikjer
Ben Moseley	(B.P.P. Moseley #51-6 & 52-8)	B. Moseley	P	Westbury
Betty Arrington — (Reg. 1970)	(Had been sent out originally and mistakenly as C.O.D.)	Arrington	P	Tranquility
Betty Hume—Reg.	(NY #11, NYBG #165)	Amateis	P	Baldsiefen
Black Cherry— See Burgundy Cherry				
Brewster	(Brown #6)	Sw-HP	Lav.	
Brown Eyes—Reg.	(Bosley 1046A or 1052A)	Bosley		Bosley

Note: N.C. = Name Conflict; unacceptable to American Rhododendron Society Registry.
         Reg. = Registered by American Rhododendron Society.

Column A Variety (Cultivar)	Column B Code Number or Other Original Identity	Column C Named By or At	Column D Color	Colume E Introduced By
Bryantville	(Brown #70)	Sw-HP	P	
Burgundy Cherry	(Dexter #105)	Knippenberg		Knippenberg
Champagne—N.C.	(NY #2, NYBG #A)	Vossberg		Westbury 1958
Charlestown	(Everitt #7?)	Herbert	P	
Chatham	(Dexter 23)	Sw-HP	P	
Cherry Red	(Sel. at Winterthur #11)	H.F. duPont	R	Gladsgay Gard.
Clover Coe	(Planting Fields #99)	Plntg. Flds.		
C.O.D.	(Everitt #4)	Everitt	Creamy	
Count Vitetti	(Parker #1)	Plntg. Flds.		
Delicate Splendor	(Ross DD)	Ty	W	
Dexter's Appleblossom	(DE #631)	Dex. Est.—Cowles	P	Dexter Estate
Dexter's Apricot	(DE 225)	Dex. Est.—Cowles	Apricot	Dexter Estate
Dexter's Brandy Green	(DE 491)	Dex. Est.—Cowles	Cream	Dexter Estate
Dexter's Brick Red	(DE #427)	Dex. Est.—Cowles	R	Dexter Estate
Dexter's Cream	(DE #437)	Dex. Est.—Cowles	Cream	Dexter Estate
Dexter's Crown Pink	(DE #600)	Dex. Est.—Cowles	P	Dexter Estate
Dexter's Favorite—Reg.	(Dexter #123)	Rep. by Amateis	P	Gladsgay?
Dexter's Giant Red	(DE #431)	Dex. Est.—Cowles	R	Dexter Estate
Dexter's Glow	(DE #317)	Dex. Est.—Cowles	P	Dexter Estate
Dexter's Horizon	(DE #480)	Dex. Est.—Cowles	P	Dexter Estate
Dexter's Orange	(DE #296)	Dex. Est.—Cowles	Orange-Red	Dexter Estate
Dexter's Orchid	(Everitt #1A)	Vossberg	Lavender	Westbury 1959
Dexter's Peppermint	(DE #215)	Dex. Est.—Cowles	Pale P	Dexter Estate
Dexter's Pink—Reg.	(Everitt #12)	Vossberg		Westbury 1959
Dexter's Pink Glory	(DE #219)	Dex. Est.—Cowles	P	Dexter Estate
Dexter's Purple	(NY #16, NYBG #203)	Vossberg	Purple	Westbury 1959
Dexter's Red	(Morris #2)	Vossberg	R	Westbury 1959
Dexter's Salmon	(DE #62)	Dex. Est.—Cowles	Salmon	Dexter Estate
Dexter's Spice	(DE #968)	Dex. Est.—Cowles	W	Dexter Estate
Dexter's Springtime	(DE #314)	Dex. Est.—Cowles	P	Dexter Estate
Dexter's Vanilla	(DE #997)	Dex. Est.—Cowles	Cream	Dexter Estate
Dexter's Victoria	(DE #441)	Dex. Est.—Cowles	Lavender	Dexter Estate
Dorothy Russell	(Sel. by Schwoebel)	Schwoebel	R	
Dot's Cherry Jubilee	(H.S. #9)	Schlaikjer	P	Schlaikjer
Eastham	(Dexter 42)	Sw & HP	Pale P	
Edwin Beinecke—Reg.	(Sel. at Beinecke Est.)	Young		
Elizabeth Poore	(B.P.P. Moseley 52-1)	B.P.P. Moseley		
Emissary	(Ross EE)	Ty	P	
Everitt Miller	(US Natl. Arb. #19364)	Plntg. Flds.		
Fairhaven	(Dexter 44)	Sw & HP		
Festive Feast	(Ross FF)	Ty	P	
Flaming Snow	(BPPM 53-16)	Ty	W	
Fordham	(NY #13, NYBG #201)	Vossberg	P	Westbury
Forestdale	(Dexter 128)	Sw & HP	R	
Gi-Gi—Reg. 1973	(Ross GG)	Burns	P	
Glenda Farrell	(Ross RR)	Ty	R	
Gloxineum—Reg.	(deWilde rec. fr. Dexter about 1940)	deWilde	P (Late)	Rhodo Lake 1955
Great Eastern	(Dexter 109)	Knippenberg	P Ruffled	
Halesite	(Parker 4)	Vossberg	P	Westbury
Halesite Maiden	(H.S. #4)	Schlaikjer	R	Schlaikjer

Column A Variety (Cultivar)	Column B Code Number or Other Original Identity	Column C Named By or At	Column D Color	Column E Introduced By
Harlequin — see 'Arlequin				
Harwich	(Dexter 108)	Sw & HP	P	
Hatchville	(Dexter 121)	Sw & HP		
Helena	Herbert	Herbert	P	
Henry Coe	(Parker #2)	Plntg. Flds.		
Honeydew—N.C.	(Everitt #21)	Vossberg	Apricot	Westbury
Hunting Hill	(Ross HH)	Ty	P	
Huntington	(Parker #5)	Vossberg	P	Westbury
Josephine Everitt—Reg.	(Everitt #5)	Everitt	P	Eastover?
Katherine Slater	(Sel. by F. Brown)	F. Brown	P	Weston 1970
Kelley	(Sw 12507-11)	Herbert	R	
Koster's Choice—Reg.	(Everitt #6)	Everitt	P	

(Selected by Peter Koster of Triangle Nursery, Hunting, N.Y. Originally named Peter Koster, an unacceptable name.)

Lady Decora	(Sw 12506-1)	Sw	P	
Lady of Belfield	(Sw 12506-3)	Sw	P	
Lady of June	(Sw 12506-5 (12))	Sw	P	
Lady of Vernon	(Sw 12506-7)	Sw	W	
Lady of Wakefield	(Sw 12506-9 (10))	Sw	P	
Lavender Princess—Reg.	(Bosley #1021)	Bosley		Bosley ab. 1965
Louisa P. Delano		US Natl. Arboretum?		
Madison Hill	(Sw 12500-2)	Sw	P	
Marshfield	(Dexter 173)	Sw & HP	P	
Megansett	(Dexter 187)	Sw & HP	Mauve	
Merley Cream	(Dexter #62)	Mulligan or Wells		Wells 1961
Mr. W. R. Coe	(Parker #10)		P	
Mrs. H. B. Gardner	(Everitt #8)	Dexter (Cannot be certain)		
Mrs. W. R. Coe—Reg.	(Parker #3)	Coe—Planting Fields		Westbury 1958
Nathan Hale—Reg. 1973	(Schlaikjer—H.S. #10)	Schlaikjer	P	Schlaikjer
Newburyport Beauty	(Fowle 18)	Sw	P	
Newburyport Belle	(Fowle 19)	Sw	P	
Newburyport Charm	(Fowle 20)	Sw	W	
Oh Joy	(Ross -00-)			
Parker's Pink—Reg. 1973	(Parker #1 PP)	Vossberg	P	Oliver or Eastover before 1970
Peg Coe	(Parker #7)	Planting Fields		
Peter Koster	See 'Koster's Choice'			
Pink Satin	Knippenberg	Knippenberg	P	Baldsiefen
Pink Sparkler	Vermuelen			
Powder Puff	(FMM 51-13)	Knippenberg		Knippenberg
Quiet Quality	(Ross QQ)	Sw		
Ramona—N.C.		Named or Introduced in California?		
Red House	(Gr. by R. Schwoebel)	deWilde		
Red Velvet—N.C.	(Sw. #12507-2)	Knippenberg	R	
Red Yard	(Gr. by R. Schwoebel)	deWilde		Rhodo Lake
Robert Coe	(Parker)	Planting Fields		
Rona Pink	Koenig Sel.	T. Koenig	P	T. Koenig
Sagamore Bayside	(Dexter 16)	Sw & HP	P	
Sagamore Bridge	(Dexter 180)	Sw & HP	P	
Scintillation—Reg. 1973	(NY #1, NYBG #67)	Vossberg	P	Westbury 1958
Shawme Lake	(Dexter 213)	Sw & HP	P	

Column A Variety (Cultivar)	Column B Code Number or Other Original Identity	Column C Named By or At	Column D Color	Column E Introduced By
Skerryvore Monarch	(Beinecke-Goury 59-49)	Young	P	
Skyglow	(Dexter #9)	Baldsiefen	P	Baldsiefen 1960
Tan—Reg.	(Sel. at Winterthur)	duPont	Apricot	Gladsgay Gard.
Teaticket	(Dexter 218)	Sw-HP	Pale P	
Todmorden	(Scott #1)	Sw	R	Ind. Run ab. 1966
Tom Everitt	(NY #4, NYBG #205)	Politi	P	Wells 1961
Tripoli	(Ross—EEE)			
True Treasure	(Ross TT)	Sw	P	
Up Front	(Ross UU)	Ty	P	
Wareham	(Willard 1)	Sw	P	
Warwick	(Ross BB?)	Baldsiefen	P	Baldsiefen
Wellfleet	(Dexter 8)	Sw & HP		
Westbury	(H. Phipps #3)	Vossberg	P	Westbury 1958
Weston	(Sel. at Weston Nurs.)	Mezitt	P	Weston 1970
Whittenton	(Willard #5)	Sw	Cream	
Wianno	(Willard #7)	Sw	Lavender	
Willard	(Willard #2)	Sw	P	
William Rogers Coe—Reg.	(Parker #18)	Planting Fields		
Winneconnet	(Willard 8)	Sw	Pale P	
Winning Ways	(Ross WW)	Ty	R	
Wissahickon	(Morris #3)	Morris Arb.	R	Wells 1961
Wyandanch Pink		Wyandanch Nurs.	P	Wyandanch
Xerox	(Ross XX)			
Zanzibar	(Ross Z)			
Zest	(Ross ZZ)			

APPENDIX G

Organizations, Places, and Abbreviations.

RHODODENDRON SPECIES

carol. = carolinianum; cataw. = catawbiense; dec. = decorum; disc. = discolor; fort. = fortunei; grier. = griersonianum; haem. = haematodes; max. = maximum.

BREEDERS, GROWERS, ORGANIZATIONS, PLACES

Amateis, Edmond, Brewster, N.Y., Breeder. Later (1960?) moved to Florida (Member of Bowers's Group)

Arnold Arboretum, Harvard University, Jamaica Plain, Mass., Donald Wyman, Horticulturist 1935-1970.

Arrington, GA., Tranquility Nursery, Huntington Valley, Pa.

BPPM—See Moseley, Ben P. P.

Baldsiefen, Warren, Nursery, Bellvale, N.Y.

Bein, E. J. Beinecke, Greenwich, Conn. Died about 1965.

Berns, Robert & Stanley, Boston, Mass. Owned Dexter property in the 1960s.

Biltmore Estate Gardens, Biltmore, N.C. 1940-65? (Frederick J. Nisbet)

Bosley Nurs. Co., Mentor, Ohio (Paul Bosley) Planted Dexters in 1930s or early 1940s.

Bowers, Dr. Clement G., Maine, N.Y. Author of first American book on rhododendrons (1893-1972)

Brown, Col. Roy, Sandwich, Mass. Owned Dexter property 1946-1951.

Burns, Sidney V., Syosset, N.Y.

Coe, William R., Oyster Bay, N.Y., son of donor of Planting Fields Arboretum. Died about 1972.

Con.—Consolini, Antonio, Sandwich, Mass. (Head Gardener to Mr. Dexter), died 1971.

Cowles, John, Supt. Dexter Estate from 1959 through 1967.

Charles O. Dexter, 1862-1943, Shawme Farm, Sandwich, Mass. (Dexter Estate, 1943-1967).

deWilde, Roland, Rhodo-Lake Nurs., See Rhodo-Lake Nurs. Received Dexters from Mr. Dexter in 1930s.

Dexter Estate After 1969—See Heritage Plantation.

duPont, Henry F., 1881-1969, Winterthur, Delaware.

Eastover Nursery, East Northport, N.Y.

Efinger, William; Nursery, Brewster, N.Y. Planted Dexters at Ross estate in 1940s.

Everitt, Samuel A. (SAE) Halesite, Huntington, N.Y. One of first to receive Dexters from Mr. Dexter. Died about 1960.

FMM—See Moseley, Mrs. F. M.

Farquhar, R. J. Nursery, Barnstable, Mass. (in the 1920s).

Fowle, H. W. Nursery, Newburyport, Mass.

Frost, Paul, Cambridge, Mass. (Landscape architect of the Dexter estate in the 1920s.)

Gable, Joseph B., 1886-1972, Stewartstown, Pa. (Miss Caroline Gable)

Gillies, George, Supt. Marshall Field Estate, Oyster Bay, N.Y.

Herbert, Charles, Phoenixville, Pa.

Heritage Plantation (Dexter estate) Abbreviated HP, Sandwich, Mass. (established 1969).

Howard, Heman A., Horticulturist, Heritage Plantation, Sandwich, Mass. 1969-77 (Formerly of Arnold Arboretum)

HP—See Heritage Plantation (Dexter Estate) Established 1969.

John J. Tyler Arboretum, See Tyler Arboretum.

Jones, Gordon, Director, Planting Fields Arboretum, Oyster Bay, N.Y.

Knippenberg, Mr. & Mrs. John Knippenberg, Pines Lake, Wayne, N.J.

Koenig, Thomas W., Interlaken, N.J.

Koster Nursery, Bridgeton, N.J.

Leach, David G., North Madison, Ohio.

Longwood Gardens, Kennett Sq., Pa. (Dr. Russell Seibert, Director).

Luenenschloss, Carl, Fairhaven, N.J., Died in 1960s.

Mezitt, Edmund Mezitt, Weston Nurseries, Hopkington, Mass.

Miller, Everitt, Longwood Gardens, Kennett Square, Pa. (former Supt. Planting Fields)

Morris Arboretum, Chestnut Hill, Philadelphia, Pa.

Moseley, Ben P. P., Ipswich, Mass. (BPPM) (Died in 1960s).

Moseley, Mrs. Frederick M., Newburyport, Mass. (FMM) (Died in 1950s).

Mulligan, Brian O., Director, Univ. of Washington Arboretum, Seattle, Wash. Received numbered Dexters in 1940s.

National Arboretum—See U.S. National Arboretum.

N. Nea.—Nearing, G. Guy, Ramsey, N.J.

New York Botanical Garden, Bronx Park, N.Y., N.Y. (Louis Politi, Dennis Brown).

Owen, Charles Dexter, Nephew of Charles O. Dexter, Biltmore, N.C.

Parker, John, Halesite, Huntington, Long Island, N.Y. Received Dexter seedlings in early 1940s.

Phipps, Howard, Old Westbury, Long Island, N.Y.

Phipps, J. S., Old Westbury, Long Island, N.Y.

Planting Fields Arboretum, Oyster Bay, Long Island, N.Y. (Gordon Jones, Director).

Politi, Louis Politi, Head Gardener, N.Y. Bot. Garden, 1940-60.

Reid, Ray B. Nursery, Osterville, Mass. Planted Dexters in 1930s.

Rhodo-Lake Nurseries (deWilde) Bridgeton, N.J. Planted Dexters in 1930s.

Ross—Ross, Mrs. Henry (Glenda Farrell) Brewster, N.Y. Planted Dexters in 1940s; died about 1958.

Schlaikjer, Mrs. Hugo, Halesite, N.Y.

Schwoebel, Richard, Nursery, Ardmore, Pa.

Scott, Mrs. Arthur H., 1875-1960, Media, Pa.

Scott F—Arthur H. Scott Horticultural Foundation, Swarthmore College, Swarthmore, Pa., 1930-

Sw—Swarthmore College (Arthur Hoyt Scott Hort. Foundation) 1930-   Joseph W. Oppe, Director, Swarthmore, Pa.

Ty—John J. Tyler Arboretum, Lima, Pa. 1946—Planted Dexters 1954-65.

U.S. National Arboretum, Washington, D.C. (Henry Skinner, Dir., Member of Bowers's Group) Planted Dexters in 1950s.

Van Veen Nursery, Portland, Oregon (Ted Van Veen)

Vermeulen & Sons Nursery, Neshanic Station, N.J.

Vossberg, Paul, Westbury Rose Co., Westbury, N.Y.; Propagated Dexters 1949-65. (Member of Bowers's Group).

Washington Arboretum, Univ. of Seattle, Wash., B. O. Mulligan and Joseph Witt. Planted Dexters in 1940s.

Wells, James, Nursery, Red Bank, N.J. (formerly at Koster Nursery) Planted Willard Dexters about 1955.

Westbury, Westbury Rose Co. (Nursery) Westbury, N.Y. (Paul Vossberg, propagator).

Weston Nurseries, Hopkinton, Mass. (Edmund Mezitt).

Wheeldon, Dr. Thomas, Gladsgay Nursery, Richmond, Va.

Willard, Rathbun, North Scituate, Rhode Island. Planted Dexters about 1940.

Wister, John C., Swarthmore, Pa. (Former Director, Scott Foundation and Tyler Arboretum) (Member of Bowers's Group).

Wood, Harry, Head Gardener, Swarthmore College, Swarthmore, Pa. Died about 1970.

Woodger, Alfred, Head Gardener, Beinecke Estate, Greenwich, Conn. Died in 1960s.

Wyandanch Nursery, Wyandanch, N.Y.

Wyman, Donald, Weston, Mass., Horticulturist, Arnold Arboretum, 1935-70, Jamaica Plain, Mass. (Member of Bowers's Group).

Young, Howard S., Chadds Ford, Pa. (nephew of Alfred Woodger) Selected and named Dexter clones at Beinecke estate.

APPENDIX H ───────

Source List for Dexter Rhododendron Cultivars

(Compiled May 1, 1976)

Asterisk at left of name indicates cultivars being grown at this time by arboretums as well as in private gardens. To the best of our knowledge these cultivars so indicated are not available commercially.

Acclaim 12
Accomac 4, 22
Accomplishment 31
*Adelphia
*Agatha
Alice in Wonderland 7
*Alice Poore
Amethyst 3, 8, 12, 19, 33
*Andorra
Apple Blossom 12
*Arlequin 4, 19, 20, 21, 28
Aronimink 20
Ashes of Roses 21
Avondale 4, 6, 20, 22

Barnstable 28
Bass River 28
*Beauty of Halesite
Ben Moseley 4, 5, 7, 8, 12, 19, 20, 22, 27
Betty Arrington 6, 8, 9, 17, 19, 27, 28, 34
Betty Hume 3, 5, 7, 21, 26, 27, 32
Black Cherry =
    Burgundy Cherry

*Brewster
Brown Eyes 2, 4, 5, 7, 8, 19, 20, 27, 28
*Bryantville
*Burgundy Cherry

Champagne 2, 3, 4, 5, 12, 19, 27, 28, 32
*Charlestown
*Chatham
Cherry Red 16, 19, 21
*Clover Coe
C . O. D. 9, 12, 14
*Count Vitetti

*Delicate Splendor
Dexter's Appleblossom 12, 19, 27
Dexter's Apricot 3
Dexter's Brandy-Green 2, 12, 19, 27
Dexter's Brick Red 19
*Dexter's Cream
Dexter's Crown Pink 19
*Dexter's Favorite
Dexter's Giant Red 19, 27
*Dexter's Glow
Dexter's Horizon 19
Dexter's Orange 3, 19
Dexter's Orchid 4, 7, 28
Dexter's Peppermint 12
Dexter's Pink 19
Dexter's Pink Glory 27
Dexter's Purple 4, 19, 28
*Dexter's Red
Dexter's Salmon. No Source Known, Original
    plant is dead.
*Dexter's Spice
Dexter's Springtime 19, 27
Dexter's Vanilla 27
*Dexter's Victoria
Dorothy Russell 5, 8, 12, 13, 31
Dot's Cherry Jubilee 4

*Eastham
Edwin Beinecke. No Source Known
Elizabeth Poore 19
Emissary. No Source Known
*Everitt Miller

Fairhaven 28
*Festive Feast
Flaming Snow 20
Fordham 4
*Forestdale

GiGi 4, 7, 19, 20, 27
Glenda Farrell 20
Gloxineum 3, 8, 12, 13, 16, 20, 26, 32, 33
Great Eastern 2, 4, 12, 19, 20, 27

Halesite 4, 5
*Halesite Maiden
*Harwich
*Hatchville
Helen Everitt 12, 19, 28
*Helena
*Henry Coe
Honeydew 12, 14
Hunting Hill 7
*Huntington

John Wister=Janet Blair (Not a Dexter)
Josephine Everitt 12

Katherine Slater 28, 33
Kelley 32
*Koster's Choice

*Lady Decora
*Lady of Belfield
*Lady of June
*Lady of Vernon
*Lady of Wakefield
*Lavender Princess
*Louisa P. Delano

*Madison Hill
*Marshfield
*Megansett
Merley Cream 3, 8, 12, 19
*Mr. W. R. Coe
Mrs. H. B. Gardner. No Source Known
Mrs. W. R. Coe 3, 4, 5, 7, 8, 9, 12, 13, 14, 18, 19, 21, 22, 28, 32, 33

*Nathan Hale
*Newburyport Beauty
*Newburyport Belle
*Newburyport Charm

*Oh Joy

Parker's Pink
4, 5, 7, 8, 12, 19, 25, 27, 28
Peg Coe. No Source Known Original Plant is dead
Peter Koster= Koster's Choice
Pink Satin 4
*Pink Sparkler
Powder Puff 4, 8, 19, 22

*Quiet Quality

Ramona 12, 19, 32
Red House 4, 7
Red Velvet 4, 12, 19

*Red Yard
*Robert Coe
*Rona Pink

Sagamore Bayside 31
*Sagamore Bridge
Scintillation 1, 2, 3, 4, 5, 6, 8, 9, 10, 11, 12, 13, 14, 15, 16, 17, 18, 19, 20, 21, 22, 23, 25, 26, 27, 28, 29, 30, 32, 33
*Shawme Lake
*Skerryvore Monarch
Skyglow 1, 3, 4, 5, 12, 19, 27, 28, 32, 33

Tan 21, 22
*Teaticket
Todmorden 2, 4, 5, 8, 12, 16, 19, 20, 21, 22, 27, 28, 32
Tom Everett 2, 4, 5, 8, 12, 19, 20, 22, 26, 28
Tripoli 4, 7
*True Treasure

*Up Front

Wareham 4
Warwick 1, 3, 4, 5, 8, 12, 19, 26, 28
Wellfleet 21, 28
Westbury 2, 3, 4, 5, 8, 13, 19, 22, 26, 27
Weston 32
*Whittenton
*Wianno
*Willard
*William R. Coe
*Winneconnet
*Winning Ways
Wissahickon 2, 3, 4, 5, 6, 8, 12, 13, 15, 16, 17, 18, 19, 20, 21, 22, 24, 27, 32
Wyandanch Pink 3, 4, 5, 8, 12, 19, 20, 27, 33

*Xerox

*Zanzibar
*Zest

ADDRESSES OF SOURCES FOR CULTIVARS LISTED ABOVE

1. Baldsiefen Nursery
   Box 88
   Bellvale, N.Y. 10912
2. Basket Neck Nursery
   Basket Neck Lane
   Remsenberg, N.Y. 11960
3. Bear Swamp Gardens
   Ashfield, Mass. 01330

4. Beaver Dam Creek Nursery
43 Davos Street
Bricktown, N.J. 08723

5. Beeson, Mr. Hansel C. (Do Not Ship)
Friendly Hobby Nursery
3010 Alamance Rd.
Greensboro, N.C. 27407

6. Briggs Nursery (Wholesale Only)
4407 Henderson Blvd.
Olympia, Wash. 98501

7. Burns Garden Supply Co.
P.O. Box 280
East Northport, N.Y. 11731

8. Carlson's Gardens
Box 305
So. Salem, N.Y. 10590

9. Clarke, Mr. George W. (Do Not Ship)
11740 N.E. Marine Dr.
Portland, Ore. 97220

10. Corliss Bros. Inc.
31 Essex Road
Ipswich, Mass. 01938

11. Curtis, Mr. W. J.
Wil-Chris Acres
Sherwood, Ore. 97140

12. Eastover Nursery
Mr. Carmine Ragonese
44 Eastover Drive
East Northport, N.Y. 11731

13. Edwards Rhododendron Garden
6524 Elmdale Road
Alexandria, Va. 22312

14. Farwell's Rhododendron Nursery
13040 Skyline Blvd.
Woodside, Calif. 94062

15. Garden Valley Nursery Inc.
12960 N.E. 181st St.
Bothell, Wash. 98011

16. Gladsgay Gardens
(Wholesale Only)
6311 Three Chopt Road
Richmond, Va. 23226

17. Greer Gardens
1280 Goodpasture Is. Rd.
Eugene, Ore. 97401

18. Hart's Nursery Inc.
1578 Best Road
Mount Vernon, Wash. 98273

19. Hillcrest Gardens Nursery
39 Pease Road
Woodbridge, Conn. 06525

20. Hillside Rhododendron Gardens
P.O. Box 353
Manasquan, N.J. 08736

21. Hi-Meadows Gardens
Rt. 2
Mt. Solon, Va. 22843

22. Indian Run Nursery
Allentown Road
Robbinsville, N.J. 08691

23. LaBars' Rhododendron Nursery
P.O. Box 111
Stroudsburg, Pa. 18360

24. Le Mac Nurseries Inc.
(Wholesale Only)
P. O. Box 268
Hampton, Va. 23369

25. Nearing, Mr. G. Guy
267 Grove Street
Ramsey, N.J. 07446

26. Oliver Nurseries Inc.
1159 Bronson Road
Fairfield, Conn. 06430

27. Redbarn Nursery
Box 215
Pennsburg, Pa. 18073

28. Ridgecrest Rhododendron Nursery
48 Ridgecrest Drive
Ridgefield, Conn. 06877

29. Rhododendron Farm
Box 242
Mountain Home, N.C. 28758

30. Ten Oaks Nursery & Gardens, Inc.
Ten Oaks Road
Clarksville, Md. 21029

31. Vermeulen & Sons Nursery, Neshanic Station, N.J.

32. Van Veen Nursery
4201 S.E. Franklin St.
Portland, Ore. 97206

33. Weston Nurseries
Hopkinton, Mass. 01748

34. Whitney Gardens
P.O. Box F
Brinnon, Wash. 98320

Two views of Heritage Plantation of Sandwich. Located on Cape Cod, Massachusetts, this property was the home of C. O. Dexter during the years when he created the series of hybrid rhododendrons now being "brought home" by the present owners. Top, the Dexter home (1); below, a path lined with *Rhododendron carolinianum* (2).

Heritage Plantation   West

Rhododendron carolinianum [at Shawme Farm]   Howard

3   *Parker's Pink*   Knapp

Three superb pinks in the Dexter series: top and insert, Parker's Pink (3 and 4); below left, Skerryvore Monarch (5); right, Newburyport Beauty (6).

4   *Parker's Pink*   Howard

5   *Skerryvore Monarch*   Suggs   6   *Newburyport Beauty*   Howard

7   *Dexter's Pink*   Howard

Scintillation, shown at bottom and in insert, is the most widely distributed of the Dexter hybrids (8 and 9) as well as the most popular modern rhododendron in the East, according to our survey. Dexter's Pink (7) is at top of page.

8   *Scintillation*   Henning

9   *Scintillation*   Suggs

10   *Todmorden*   West

Dexter hybrids in bicolor, red and purple shades. Top, Todmorden (10); center, Accomac (11); bottom left, Dexter's Purple (12); right, Ben Moseley (13).

11   *Accomac*   Suggs

12   *Dexter's Purple*   West

13   *Ben Moseley*   West

14 *Accomplishment* Howard

15 *Lady of June* West

Top, Accomplishment, one of the beautiful 12507 hybrid series (14); center, Lady of June (15); bottom, a corner of the garden of John C. Wister (16), Swarthmore, Pennsylvania. Dr. Wister was a member of the original Dexter Committee.

16 *Wister Garden at Swarthmore* Suggs

17   *Gigi*   West

18   *Skyglow*   We

The wide range of color in the Dexter hybrids is revealed in this selection: top, left, GiGi (17); right, Skyglow (18); bottom left, Josephine Everitt (19); right, Dexter's Spice (20), a superb rhododendron among the scarce white Dexter hybrids.

19   *Josephine Everitt*   Suggs   20   *Dexter's Spice*   Howa

Merley Cream   Livingston

22   *Champagne*   Suggs

Brown Eyes   Howard

Five outstanding Dexter hybrids: top left, Merley Cream (21); right, Champagne (22); center, Brown Eyes (23); bottom left, Wyandanch Pink (24); right, Wissahickon (25).

Wyandanch Pink   Suggs

25   *Wissahickon*   Howard

26   *Louise Gable*   West

27   *Polaris*   Wes

28   *Joseph B. Gable*   West

Joseph B. Gable, center (28), and two of his choice azalea hybrids: Louise Gable, left (26), and Polaris (27), right. Below is a view of the Gable home, with a foreground of *R. mucronulatum*, pink selection (29).

29   *Gable home and Pink Mucronulatum*   West

CHAPTER II

Joseph Benson Gable
1886—1972

The first quarter-century of rhododendron hybridizing in eastern North America passed virtually unnoticed by the average gardener and by the nurserymen who supplied rhododendron and azalea plants to the gardens of the Middle Atlantic States and Eastern Canada.

The pioneer breeders, however, were well aware of the opportunities—and the problems. One of these men, Joseph B. Gable, wrote of "Twenty-five Years of Rhododendron Trials" in *The Rhododendron Yearbook* for 1948:

Climate to be sure, in which the intense heat and dry atmosphere of summer is not far behind the sub-zero temperature of our winters in its adverse effects, is by far the most serious of the factors that tend to inhibit our growing the rhododendrons from those parts of the world where the finer species grow and also the great multitude of lovely hybrid sorts now available from across the Atlantic and latterly from our own Pacific Northwest.

In fact there is no other inhibiting factor that can not be easily met and I consider the successful culture of *hardy* rhododendrons much less of a problem than that of the modern rose. The difficulty lies in the paucity of species and varieties that we can truly call hardy in these parts.[1]

Six years later, in its issue of March 20, 1954, the *Saturday Evening Post* awakened the general public. In an article entitled "The Flowering Forest of Joe Gable" a blaze of color dramatized the work of the Pennsylvania nurseryman.

The reason for the dramatic impact of the article was not that Joseph B. Gable was the *only* hybridizer in the East (the work of Dexter and others had been going on for some thirty years) but that rhododendrons and azaleas were both coming forth with finer flowers and tougher plants from a dedicated man in Stewartstown, Pennsylvania—in the very center of America's great Atlantic seaboard garden area.

An important by-product of the Gable story was an awakened interest in the work of other eastern hybridizers, and encouragement for patient amateur gardeners to enter the ranks of hybridizers.[2] C. O. Dexter had already completed his work and the Bowers Committee was hard at work identifying and evaluating the great series of rhododendrons then

known as the Dexter Hybrids. Morrison's great series—the Glenn Dale azaleas—was becoming available to gardeners. Many of the Shammarello rhododendrons and azaleas (bred for toughness in the climate of the Great Lakes) were finding their way into eastern gardens. The story of "The Flowering Forest" was the turning point. Eastern gardens were to be transformed.

As his biographer expresses it, "Joe Gable was the one who made the growing and hybridizing of rhododendrons look deceptively simple, thereby encouraging a school of novices whose graduates can be found today busily planting, crossing, and seeding up and down the eastern seaboard."

Over a span of more than 40 years in which his enthusiasm for the genus never gave out, Gable abetted the aspirations of hundreds of correspondents and visitors to his little nursery at Stewartstown in central Pennsylvania's York County on the Maryland border. They came to take heart from the obvious, that an amateur without much money could aspire to enter the exotic world of rhododendrons.

There was the simplest of do-it-yourself setups, long before that phrase had come into fashion. The visitors looked over the tiny leanto greenhouse, the homemade beds and shade houses, the propagation flats set out under the trees, the woods plantings lined out in clearings without benefit of irrigation or feeding, and concluded that they would do as well, or better, to Gable's great pride and pleasure.

There was the man himself, built small and spare for a lifetime of hard physical work, in the farmer's uniform of bib overalls, battered felt hat switched to a 50-cent straw in summer, wide blue eyes forever bemused by the wonders of the world of nature. That same wide-eyed wonder was on his face as a husky blonde baby taking in the view from his mother's lap. Contrary to the assumption that horticulture aptitude was to spring full grown from a York County cornfield, the baby al-

---

[1]Joseph B. Gable, "Twenty-Five Years of Rhododendron Trials," *The Rhododendron Yearbook for 1948,* ed. Robert Moulton Gatke, (Portland, Oregon: Binfords Mort, 1948).

[2]See Chapter VI—"Contemporary Hybridizers"

Joseph Benson Gable

ready had two solid generations of addicted amateur horticulturists behind him.

The Gable Family

According to family tradition, the Gable clan's arrival in the New World coincided with the Revolution. From a Daughters of the American Revolution point of view, it was not a fashionable beginning.

The first Gable in America is said to have been a Hessian mercenary, who got to Pennsylvania by having been sent to a frontier prisoner of war camp. Imprisoned at Camp Security, near York, he was either released on parole after the war or walked away, as many did, to help settle the new country. He presumably squatted on his piece of America,

in the Muddy Creek hills a few miles south of the camp. A fifth generation Gable operates a potato farm there today.

Joe Gable preferred to dwell on this inauspicious arrival over more orthodox ancestors and delighted to tell that his grandfather Israel Gable was illiterate until his marriage to a Hopewell Township school teacher, Catherine Anstine. It was a family saying that once "Pap" started reading, nobody was ever able to stop him. His legacy to his only Gable grandson was a well-used library containing Latin classics in translation.

Israel prospered from farming and assorted experimental enterprises carried out in the same Leib's Creek hollow which the grandson eventually was to put to the queer crop of rhododendrons. He had a neighborhood reputation for eccentricity, having paid to have his barn raised because he would not supply whiskey for the usual free help, and because, after having made and donated the bricks for the new Methodist Church, he forever refused to enter because there had been a Masonic cornerstone laying.

His children carried on in the same vein. Seventy years later, a local woman remembered the odd household at "Gable End," Israel's good brick house built in 1854 south of Stewartstown, where the daughters read, painted, wrote poetry and "recited," but did not do housework. "Gable End" produced six teachers who later branched into the hardware business, law and the Chautauqua circuit as elocutionist and musician. Daughter Elizabeth was graduated from Women's Medical College in Philadelphia and practiced at her home. Annie, the youngest, went off to join a vegetarian colony about 1905 and made her living as an artist and teacher of art.

Benson, father of Joe Gable, taught school into his mid-30's, ranging as far away as a sod schoolhouse in Nebraska. He was a grave and scholarly man, accurately summed up in his obituary in the town newspaper in 1927, "He had a keen mind, absorbed a good education and kept on learning all his life." His interests were chiefly in the natural world. He was an amateur astronomer, a birder and always ready to try new varieties in his young fruit orchards. He was said to have been first in the locality to raise strawberries commercially and promoted an apple variety called Gable's Seedling, no longer in existence.

Benson Gable had taught children of the James Henry Amos family at Youth's Benefit School near their home at Upper Cross Roads, Harford County, Md. The Amoses were 17th century settlers. One ancestor, after a tour of French and Indian fighting, had renounced war and founded the Fallston Friends Meeting. Another was Washington's Maryland quartermaster. Their former teacher had kept up a bantering correspondence with James and Mary West Amos' four little girls and came home to find young Caroline grown to a lively teen-ager at the Baltimore boarding school which was later Goucher College. The correspondence turned flirtatious and then to love letters. They were married in 1885. The bride tried to back out at the last minute but was dissuaded. Benson was 35 and Caroline was 18.

The Gable farm was divided with Benson acquiring less than a hundred acres at the north end. Located on the ridge between the Deer Creek and Muddy Creek watersheds, it was steep and rocky with acid soil and excellent drainage. Not prize farmland by local standards, but there was no better land in the area for growing rhododendrons.

The young bride felt alienated in the old Gables' house and went home to await the completion of her "cottage" in a grove of chestnuts and oaks on the road to town. By the etiquette of the time, their daily letters did not mention the coming baby. They do make plain that the April-August marriage had turned into a great love match. The first of their two children, Joseph Benson Gable, Jr., was born in the house of his Maryland grandparents on October 22, 1886, and carried into his parents' new home Christmas Day. There, except for intervals at boarding

schools and in the Army in World War I, he lived for the rest of his 85 years.

Childhood and Youth

The happiest childhood years for the little boy and his sister, Mary Elizabeth, were brief, for Caroline died of blood poisoning when Joe was five. His clearest memory was of his reading the newspaper aloud to her while she worked in the kitchen. A young German housekeeper came to mother the children of the grieved household until the father married Emma Smith, also a former student, several years later.

In the one-room rural school behind the Gable woods, precocious Joe was put immediately into the third reader. His first teacher remembered him as her most mischievous pupil, also her brightest. His first letter of record was to his Grandmother Amos. "I saw a red bird," he wrote. "The seed catalogue came today." The children were often at the Maryland relatives', and Joe observed that his grandmother always left the household work to the old woman who came up from the former slave quarters, while she worked in her garden.

The pattern of roaming the woods was to be lifelong. In those boyhood rambles he sniffed the spicy native *nudiflorum* azalea, which was called honeysuckle, tramped up banks of *Kalmia,* and when his hunting and fishing took him as far as the lower Susquehanna River, saw magnificent growths of *maximum,* "bull laurel" to the hunters. At home, he transgressed by carrying a seedling white pine from the woods in his Sunday handkerchief. The tree, much the worse for ice storms, still stands at "Little Woods." He robbed nests for his bird egg collection and shot songbirds until the day he looked closely at the intricate pattern on the fox sparrow he had just killed and renounced this boyish degradation on the spot.

His strong and hard-working father set the

pattern of long days in the fields and orchards. There was still time for baseball, the Sunday games carefully concealed, and for winter sports. The father aspired to the best education he could afford for his bright children. So country school, which was the norm for country youngsters of that time and place, was followed by terms at the private Stewartstown Academy, forerunner of the high school, and at York Collegiate Institute where a good teacher impressed on Joe the scientific approach. The sports-minded scholar's clearest school memory, however, was of being lifted with the football into the end zone to score against arch rival York High School. That night young vandals of the YCI, Joe among them, crept with paint buckets into York's Continental Square and painted the winning score on the street.

A summer's work with a surveyor gave Joe the idea he wanted to do that work. Instead, he was steered toward the family profession, teaching, which he detested, and was sent to Millersville Normal School (now a state college). In the spring of his first year, his conscience wrestled briefly between a mathematics examination and baseball practice. He did seven of the ten test questions for a just-passing grade ("I knew they were right," he explained long afterward) and went out to play. The offended professor tore up the paper. Afraid to face his father with a failing grade, Gable disappeared.

The Millersville lake was dragged before the runaway crept home after several weeks of working on upstate farms and sleeping in barns to settle into the farmer's life he had been educated to rise above. His classical education had, however, laid firm foundations in Latin and German, useful tools to the future self-taught botanist.

In the next decade Gable showed little promise of that future. He read up on the new game of basketball and trained a local team without ever having seen a game. He played pool in the local hall, took up cigarettes and renounced them one day while plowing. He

perfected his hunting skills and began a lifelong autumn custom of spending weeks in the central Pennsylvania mountains. Fellow gun club members called him Daniel Boone in tribute to his woodsmanship. He considered going with a friend to Arizona but was dissuaded by his father.

Music was another growing interest of those years. While playing with the Stewartstown Cornet Band at a summer picnic he met his lifelong love. Mary Belle Dalton was a handsome outgoing brunette; a farmer's daughter from nearby Baltimore County, Md. She had serious obligations at home to an invalid mother but by the time Gable went off to war in 1918—a draftee of nearly 30 who didn't ask for a farm worker's exemption— their engagement was sealed with a very small solitaire diamond.

Courting was with horse and buggy (not a very fashionable turnout in the eyes of Mary and her brothers). On one of the trips, the future naturalist almost drowned. He was accustomed to sleeping on the way home, with the reins wrapped around the whip socket and the old horse finding the familiar route, then waking the sleeper as they clattered onto the Gable barn floor. One rainy night, Gable awoke on the Deer Creek bridge with water over the buggy floor. The horse made it across, just before the bridge went out.

Gable went overseas in 1918 as a bass horn player in the 319th Field Artillery Band, 87th Division, and passed safely through the big battles of the war, doubling as orderly, aid man and attendant to cavalry horses. After the Armistice, the band had some pleasant months playing engagements on the French Riviera, during which Joe and another soldier went briefly AWOL to hike a Pyrenees pass into Spain and dance with some smugglers' daughters.

Long afterward, Joe remembered the rhododendrons he glimpsed blooming behind the gates of estates he saw from a troop train crossing England and dated his serious interest from that day. The family regarded the memory as somewhat romanticized.

He was home again in May 1919, met and serenaded by his band friends at the Stewartstown Railroad station. The Benson Gable farm was turned over to the new Mr. and Mrs. Joseph B. Gable shortly after their marriage August 28, 1919 in the West Liberty, Md., Methodist Church. They went off on their honeymoon to Virginia Beach in the only new car they were ever to own, a model T Ford, bought with Gable's Army pay.

Family and Farm

The next decade, hectic in retrospect, was the time of Gable's real commitment to ornamental horticulture. Snapshots of those years show him looking thin, sunburned, fit and very happy.

The farm he stood to inherit was planted mainly in apple trees, with the locality's standard sidelines of grain and hay for livestock and potatoes for a cash crop. The stock always included a pair of big mules named Bob and Beck, the names perpetuated as they were replaced, and a couple of horses, never the riding steeds the young daughters yearned for.

A tremendous amount of hard work kept a farm afloat in those days. The serious working year began with hand pruning of the fruit orchards and passed through plowing and harrowing with the mule team and spraying the orchards with hand-held sprayers in clouds of evil sulphur smelling chemicals. Summers brought the hot days of grain harvest, the threshing days traded with the neighbors, and haying, the high wagon loads lifted by an overhead fork into the mows and then hand forked, night after night, through trapdoors to the mangers below. The cows were driven back and forth on the hill to pasture and hand milked, while hungry cats waited in the shadows for their warm bowls full. Chickens and ducks ran free, which made

for precarious footing and much searching in the mows to find the nests before the hens went broody and spoiled the eggs.

Fall was a race against the first freeze with the apple pickers working, for 10 cents a bushel, high on wooden ladders set in the tall trees. After the hauling, sorting, and selling came the winter work; wood cutting for the kitchen range and parlor stove, the continuous stirring and banking of the fires, even ice cutting from the pond. The blocks were stored deep in sawdust and lasted to chill the next summer's first pitcher of lemonade, faintly flavored by sawdust.

The plumbing and wiring were do-it-yourself jobs. The water system was homemade and temperamental, requiring frequent trips to the ram pits near the old Indian springs in the hollow (called so because of the many Indian artifacts turned up there).

The Gable house filled rapidly with babies in the Twenties. Death of the first daughter, Anna Caroline, when she was three months old was the new family's first great grief. Mary Caroline, Elizabeth, Louise and Isabel followed at yearly intervals, then the eagerly awaited little brother, James Benson, was born in 1927. The death of Isabel at age three was another lifelong sadness.

Beginnings of the Nursery

In the middle of these busy and hard-working years, Gable decided to become a nurseryman. Characteristically, he seems to have begun by reading and writing wherever he thought he could get more information. By good luck, he made contact with the prestigious Arnold Arboretum in Massachusetts and came to the attention of its famous director, Dr. Charles S. Sargent. Soon, Gable dared to send to the Arnold bundles of native azaleas which looked to him to be several species. Back came the Arnold's notes, repeating patiently that everything in the last bundle was again *nudiflorum*. Sargent and the arboretum did not give up on the eager novice and books, other publications, seed and plants flowed to Stewartstown. Gable's curious mind was off in new directions. There was no doubt that in a world of the intellect far removed from cows and frozen apple blossoms, Gable was off on trails of exploration with Bartram, Wilson and other new found heroes.

The children sensed their father found compensations of the spirit for the confining life of a small-time farmer in the adventures of the plant explorers he read about. With their father, a delightful story teller, they tramped through Georgia to discover the *Franklinia,* or crossed the Asian mountain passes with Wilson packing his precious *davidii* seed. When this Wilson story reached its climax and the seed packet pitched into the river, the small audience around the parlor chunk stove felt the loss keenly.

In the expanding home library the Wilson books were thumbed favorites. Bailey's *Standard Cyclopedia of Horticulture* was another well worn reference. Throughout his lifetime, Gable was hopelessly addicted to literature of the natural world. He would rush into the house from outdoor work, look up whatever plant or bird was on his mind, and go back to work, turning over the new information. Often he brought some small wildling to show—a sprig of arbutus, a hummingbird folded in his straw hat, a baby rabbit held gently in closed hands. Bumblebees buzzed around him constantly in the nursery with never a sting. He did not like snakes but would not kill them. A deer sighting, the first oriole song of the season, the arrival of the house wrens were big events.

The first price list extant from Gable's nursery is dated 1926 in his handwriting. It was the single sheet, folded in thirds for a letter envelope, which was to be his sole annual promotion for the next 30 years. Botanical names were carefully included for an assortment of material ranging from Iris

Kaempferi to Cedar of Lebanon, a foot high, 35 cents apiece, a dozen for $3.50.

Among the evergreens was a modest selection of rhododendrons—*carolinianum* and *catawbiense* at 25 cents for foot-high plants, transplanted *maximum* for 40 cents. "Perhaps the loveliest of our flowering shrubs" was the slightly editorialized description.

The list of deciduous trees and shrubs included the native azalea species *arborescens, calendulaceum, canescens* and *vaseyi.* There was no reference to evergreen azaleas except perhaps in the notation "Many other plants not listed. If you ask for what you want perhaps I have it." Once again, a practice familiar to customers of later years was being established.

The correspondence was starting to flow; mail time was becoming the high point of the day. Letters from George Fraser and James Barto on the West Coast were among the first important contacts. E. J. P. Magor in Cornwall probably was Gable's first British contact. Seed and pollen came with the letters, along with the exchange of information Gable hungered for.

It is hard for the rhododendron enthusiast of today to appreciate the value of such an exchange. There was no American Rhododendron Society, no literature or experience which even remotely applied to the climatic conditions in which Gable would have to work. The correspondents owned and grew the plants for which he yearned, those exotics which had so far lived for him only in books. He would have to find out, by simple trial and error, which ones would live at Stewartstown, Pennsylvania.

By the 1929 catalogue, he had plunged into the trials with enthusiasm. The list was now four folded pages with several evergreen azaleas included. A two-foot Ledifolia Alba, its hardiness untried, was available for $2. No hybrid seedlings were listed but the range of species seedlings was remarkable, thanks to the Arnold, (and in the light of his later knowledge, downright comical.) Several were to be the Asiatic foundations of Gable's hybridizing, like *brachycarpum, decorum, discolor, fortunei, metternichii* and *smirnowii*. A greater number of the trial babies were to sink without a trace from the Gable nursery beds. In this category were such far-outs as *baileyii, eriogynum* and *polylepis*. Azalea names were mixed with the others. They were priced at 50 cents apiece, a collection of 20 for $7.50. Five Ironclad rhododendrons were offered at $5.00 each, the most expensive item on the list, reflecting what he had paid for grafted plants.

A handwritten note on a copy of the 1929 catalogue emphasizes that the Chinese rhodos were very small. "Next year," Gable wrote, "I hope for 500 or more seedlings to show their first flowers. A very few of these will flower this year."

The nursery expansion was going ahead through years of change in the Gable family. Benson Gable, august and revered, died in 1927 at his retirement home across the highway without recorded reaction to the new uses to which his land was being put. After a partition for the sister and lots for the six grandchildren, the farm was Joseph Gable's. The deaths at "Little Woods" during this time of little Isabel and of James and Hannah Dalton, parents of Mary Gable, were times of grief. Around the corner lurked the Depression and its body blows to the rural economy.

The single most important contact Gable was to make toward his expanding collection and knowledge also came in the late Twenties. Tentative letters from Guyencourt, Delaware, were soon followed by the first visit of Guy Nearing and a fruitful friendship and collaboration chronicled in the Nearing letters which spanned about 20 years. (Gable's letters to Nearing have not been located.)

The Nearing Friendship

G. Guy Nearing, the more sophisticated plantsman, was already committed to his lifetime of work with rhododendrons. His respect for Gable's enthusiasm and native talents were evident. The ideas flew back and forth over the next decade along with pollen, seed and plants, exchanged so frequently it is sometimes difficult to separate the accomplishments of this fruitful period of their work.

Both were enchanted with the lepidotes. Their first named selections were such familiar ones as Gable's Conewago (one of several Indian stream names he used) and Nearing's Windbeam, which nearly a half century later are confirming the hybridizers' judgement with faithful annual performances in thousands of gardens where showier hybrids have come and gone.

A shared ambition was the creation of the great all-American red rhododendron. Much as today's hybridizers aspire to achieve a hardy bright yellow, Gable and Nearing made every available mix toward this goal. The aspiration accounts for the prominence of tender *haemotodes* and *griersonianum* in the early crosses, transmitting their virtues and shortcoming to succeeding generations of hybrids. The old Waterer *catawbiense* hybrid, Atrosanguineum, figured large in their planning as the potential hardy parent, its magenta tints and truss deficiencies hopefully to be overcome in combinations with more elegant mates. The reasoning, at least at the Gable end of the experiments, was naive by today's standards. It was simply that a tender exotic combined with something hardy, if utilitarian, would bring about hybrids both exotic and hardy. Sometimes it did. Mary Belle, a ruffled beauty of peach, coral and yellow blend came from one of these tries at hardy reds, the crossing of Dechaem (*decorum* x *haemotodes*) with Atrier (*Atrosanguineum* x *griersonianum*). There wasn't a red in the seedling lot but there was Mary Belle and Flamingo, a rich coral.

It should be remembered, too, that the dry pollen from the West and abroad was used immediately on whatever seed parent was in bloom. So when Lionel de Rothschild's *wardii* pollen came from England, it was only good luck that a Catalgla was opening.

Sometimes it was just proximity that brought about crosses. There might be a Rock 18139 seedling in bloom beside *houlstonii.* The spur-of-the-moment cross would be made. Next spring, remembering that both parents were somewhat bud tender, Gable may have considered dumping the pot of seedlings to make room for something hardier. Optimism prevailed and Dr. Rock, a peach-tone with good restrained growth, was the outcome of the casual mating.

The Nearing correspondence tells of continuing tribulations, mostly caused by weather. Extreme cold and flooding rains were followed by prolonged droughts. Hungry grasshoppers and mysterious diseases were worrisome. All such trials, combined with the unsuitability for his growing conditions of many of the species, gave Gable his lifelong respect for hardiness as a first criterion and primary objective.

Four Decades of Nursery Observations and Research

His compiled notes, with the earliest entries made in the late 1920's, are his observations of four decades as a grower of rhododendrons. One's first reaction is likely to be wonderment at the overwhelming proportion of failures to successes. Put out to sink or swim, these foreigners often lived only briefly, or gave up after a few indifferent years.

"Following the name is the date of its first cultivation here. The second date, if any, is that of its loss," the prefacing note states. The comments are often humorous. After some (*arboreum* x *calophytum*) crosses, acquired early in the game from Magor, Gable commented: "All of the above surrendered to the elements with only token resistance." The hybrid, Alice, tried twice over a 10-year period, finally was written off with "Alice,

where art Thou? Requiescat!" After the demise of Rex a wistful note, "How I wish I could grow it, long enough to see it flower."

He recorded that his plants had experienced a minus 29°F temperature, and family memories are that the Thirties winters were rigorous. Around these conditions and his limited facilities evolved the procedure by which Gable sprouted seeds—the seed dried in fall on the kitchen shelf, sown in mid-winter in a spaghnum and peat mixture in the basement of the apple shed in six-inch clay pots, pricked out in pots of the same size whenever the spring work permitted, transplanted in two-inch pots the next year, then to larger sized pots as their progress required. The pots were bedded in peat in homemade frames which were manufactured in the barn in bad weather along with frames at first covered with burlap.

Finally, the plants were graduated to cleared patches in the hardwood acres downstream from the farm springs, set in numbered rows for inventory purposes. Perhaps there was time to soak them before the planting, but from then on, they were strictly on their own. Often, the planting had to be done off season. The little rhododendrons, innocent of spraying, pruning, watering and feeding, made it strictly on their own, or failed if temperatures and rainfall could not sustain them.

In the early Thirties, rhododendrons were still pretty much Gable's hidden vice. Publicly, he had progressed from novice plantsman to a respected small-scale nurseryman with an above-average selection of shrubs, conifers and deciduous trees. He had the strong back he saw was the nurseryman's best asset, and his prices were modest. Landscaping work took him as far as Baltimore and the Philadelphia suburbs. Old plantings of his in York and Stewartstown can still be identified by the hemlocks and Concolor firs he liked, and by big old azaleas with which he was achieving his first modest fame as a hybridizer.

The basic cross was (*kaempferi* x *poukhanense*.) By his own record, "This cross is the foundation of the Gable hybrids now known on the market to some extent, though practically all of them are the result of future matings. The first generation was some 95% lavender or mauve, just a few with shades of pink or rose. All are vigorous things of great hardiness," adding, "They should be very hardy sorts for northern sections."

Successive generations of these azalea seedlings were lined out along the upper edge of the orchards below the farm buildings, where a few tough originals like Kathleen and Mildred Mae can still be seen, and along the highway in a nut orchard toward town, where the James Gable house is now located. The plantings were worked by mule-drawn garden tractor, like the plots of other nursery stock at the foot of the hill and across the highway, where Dr. Morton Krechmer's house and veterinary hospital now stand.

As selections were made for numbering and evaluation, the rest of the lot would be taken off, singly to retail customers or by the truckload to other nurseries and gardens. The standard price was a dollar per husky, field grown plant. Gable sold seedlings, partly because he had to to keep his small enterprise afloat, partly to make room for more seedlings and partly because of his sneaking belief that they all deserved a chance. In this way, some inferior plants were dispensed but there was always a customer to claim he had the best of the seed lot.

A truckload sale loomed large those years in the shaky economy of the "Little Woods" operation, where the Depression arrived promptly and lingered for a decade. Innocent of any instinct at money-making, Gable deposited his intake in his overall pocket or his checking account, about which the local bank called periodically to report an overdraft. Stacks of cancelled short-term notes explain how these crises were met.

Afterwards, the children would remember no real privations. Nursery expansion had not yet squeezed out farm operations, so there was still milk from the barn, fruit from the orchards, vegetables from the garden and potatoes from the fields. Wild strawberries and asparagus were abundant in the orchards, berries in the meadows. Mary Gable was an expert at conservation of these resources. She stored root vegetables, plucked chickens, salted fish, canned, jellied and pickled all summer and fall, served apples a dozen different ways and filled lunch boxes, when there was no meat on hand, with nut and fruit fillings of her own creation. Clothes were turned and altered as they were handed down through the family. Socks were darned heel and toe, household linens patched so many times there was sometimes more patch than original cloth. It was Mrs. Gable, too, who bartered rhododendrons for a good living room suite and apples for an antique walnut secretary.

The children, thus prepared to appreciate today's make-do generation, went to school with children of other farm families in similar circumstances and with poorer youngsters whose parents had migrated from Appalachia. They absorbed the concept that "getting along" was character building, even heroic.

Through these hard and productive years, Mary Gable gave her husband unstinting support. Her children early absorbed her understanding that the father's work was special and came first when family priorities were being decided.

A great testing came in January, 1933. Gable worked at farm chores while ill with a fever, went shivering to bed and woke with bronchial pneumonia which kept him confined for eleven weeks. The crisis days were followed by weeks of coughing. Mary stoked the fires, stretched the winter food stores and gathered her children and the nurses for nightly prayer meetings. Judged too ill to be moved to a hospital, Gable was cared for by anxious friends including the second-generation family doctor, Evans Free, and by a good plantsman, Dr. George Zimmerman of Harrisburg, with whom Gable had been tinkering with the idea of vaccines to combat the

American chestnut blight. Zimmerman administered one of his custom-made vaccines and an anxious daughter climbed Gable's white pine, now grown tall, to see into the sickroom and watch the inoculation. Something in the treatment worked and eventually Gable, weighing less than a hundred pounds instead of his standard 150, walked shakily out into the spring sunshine. Looking back, it seemed a turning point.

The livestock had been reduced to a milk cow and a few chickens. The temperamental water system was replaced with a strong artesian well, the stoves with a hot air furnace. The apple market at least could get no worse and the steady, if modest demand for his nursery stock was building. Consciously or not, Gable began to reduce the general farming and fruit growing. He admitted long afterward he had never cared much for being nursemaid to a cow.

The first broad-leaf hybrids were setting buds. Caroline, a strong growing and shapely plant with big mauve-edged fragrant trusses, either bloomed for the first time that spring or came to the sharpened attention of its grower. Believed to be a *decorum* hybrid, this seedling prompted Gable to make a note to himself on the importance of keeping better records. (By nature methodical, he never had time to do this as fully as he would have liked.) Caroline was named for his young mother and continued to please him through the years he watched it grow to tree stature with a 31-inch trunk.

Many of the Gable creations which have made it into the trade bloomed first in the next decade. May became the farm's real month of harvest, as seedling groups came into exciting flower or proved a disappointment. The woods plantings were extended uphill from the stream borders as the number of seedlings "for watching" grew into the thousands.

The end of short-term financing at the bank was still some years off. The three daughters were coming to college age. It was assumed by all concerned that they would go to college, whether or not the money was in sight, and they did. An orchard was sold off, a campus landscaped and an ancient Buick seven-passenger kept going far beyond its rightful years. Caroline went on to a newspaper job, Elizabeth to be a home economist, Louise a music teacher. The GI Bill was to see son James through Penn State University, eventually to become an administrator in a vocational-technical school.

The circle of friends and collaborators widened yearly. Ernest Wilson had written of Sargent's death. First with the Zimmermans, and later on a grand family fling, financed by his Army bonus, Gable went to New England and explored Mt. Washington for *lapponicum*. (It did not survive the transplant.) There was finally a trip to the Arnold Arboretum. Visits to Swarthmore solidified friendships there. Mrs. Mary Henry, the Philadelphia plantswoman, was an old friend now. Trips to the Northwest and England were only to dream about.

Growing Conditions·

Stewartstown is in York County in the southeastern part of Pennsylvania, about 50 miles north of Baltimore, Maryland and at an elevation of 870 feet. The major soil types at "Little Woods," Joseph Gable's home, are the Chester-Elioak-Glenelg soil associations as identified by the U.S. Department of Agriculture. These silty soils are deep to moderately deep, derived from underlying schist or phyllite crystalline rocks. They are classed as "well drained," having a percolation rate of from 2 to 6 inches per hour. Their soil profile is poorly developed, that is, the subsoil is generally as well drained as the surface layer. Depth to bed rock ranges from 4 to 6 feet. Quartz fragments are numerous in some areas, and especially at "Little Woods" in the areas where Mr. Gable planted out his rhododendrons. The pH ranges from 5.2 to 6.7, being more acidic with depth. Mineral nutrient content is medium to high and the soils are well suited to fruit growing and general farming. The soil associations of Chester-Elioak-Glenelg are more productive than some other types of soils found in York County. Moisture capacity, or the ability of the soils to hold moisture above and beyond that amount which results in plant wilting, is moderately high.

Stewartstown's climate may be described as "humid continental," with an average annual rainfall of over 40 inches. The driest year of record (up to 1959) is 22.9 inches and the wettest year is 55.9 inches. (This may have been exceeded in 1973-74-75 which were very wet years.) One of the more severe dry periods was during September and October, 1947 when 38 days passed without measurable rain. An even drier period occurred during the summer of 1966 when less than 1 inch of rain was recorded between late June and mid-September while the general ground water was very low after several previous dry years. Thousands of mature rhododendrons and azaleas perished at "Little Woods" and were eventually burned in gigantic bonfires.

The maximum recorded temperature (at York) is 107°F while the minimum is -21°F.

After growing seedlings for several years in clay pots, Mr. Gable planted his azaleas in full exposure, while the rhododendrons were lined out under the high shade of tall oaks. Little soil preparation was needed.

"Little Woods" is on a north and east facing slope, with Leibs Creek, normally a pleasant brook, at the bottom of the slope. The northeast exposure, many tall oaks, and the small brook help to cool the rhododendrons during the hottest weather. The extensive plantings, many over 40 years old, protect individual plants during occasional high winds.

Recognition Comes

In 1938 Gable received the Jackson Dawson Medal of the Massachusetts Horticultural Society for his work as a hybridizer. It was encouraging recognition for the man who had taken off on a rather lonely course so few years before.

Formation of the American Rhododendron Society in 1944 supported his conviction that rhododendrons had an important future in American horticulture. Gable and Nearing earlier had exchanged ideas for such an organization and had drawn up a modest list of prospective members. The Quarterly Bulletins, although at that time written from a northwestern United States perspective, were eagerly read in place of the often extraneous information to be gotten from Royal Horticulture Society publications.

World War II further shaped events at "Little Woods." The good cheap local help of the Depression years was gone. With it went the landscaping and then fruit growing, a decision hurried along by the first hungry invasion of the Japanese beetle. Gable continued to ship plants for a few years more, his wondrously constructed packages of wood, burlap and binder twine leaving on the shortline Stewartstown Railroad for eastern seaboard designations.

When the orchard service was cut out, more time was available for expanding the woods and seeing the visitors who came to expect long tours, leisurely conversations and Mary's pie. The nursery line gradually contracted to rhododendrons and azaleas, with a few companion plants. It was this stock, more and more of his own origination, which his little business offered for the more than 20 years he was to be active as propagator, salesman and principal digger.

Azalea hybridization had ceased to be a major interest. Gable was convinced that far too many clones had been named by too many, including himself. Some nurseries were labeling incorrectly and that bothered him. So he tended to put azaleas out of mind, even as they became the major commercial success of his life's work.

About this time a number of growers, most

of them with kind intentions, undertook to make Gable richer by helping with propagation and promotion. If he sensed a genuine love for the plants behind their efforts, he enjoyed the attention, was generous with cuttings and grateful for the small profits the nursery was starting to turn. In the end, though, his basic disinterest in making money won out. The concept of mass production bored him and besides, there would not have been time for his real work of planning and crossing.

A more complex man than he appeared, Gable could be fiercely scornful of dishonesty. There was the occasion when a large scale wholesale grower called him to a conference. Just give him a new azalea or rhododendron—any one, regardless of its merit—for patenting and promotion and he could guarantee that both of them would make money. Gable quickly ended the conversation and the daughter who was present still remembers his snort as they drove away.

A fine new crop in the enthusiastic generation of younger people was entering the field. They were as eager to learn as Gable was to share his experience. His interest and pleasure in the more sophisticated body of knowledge which rapidly developed was keen and appreciative. He was proud of David Leach's accomplishment with *Rhododendrons of the World*. His well-worn copy is inscribed by Leach "To Joe Gable, who is to blame for starting it all."

The first of the nine Gable grandchildren were another new crop which began arriving in 1950. Soon small helpers were digging in the nursery sandpile, begging for rides to the woods in the old pickup and having his or her own rhododendron or azalea named. The children are Mary Ann, Judith, Robert and James, who belong to daughter Louise Allison; Margaret, Kathleen and Mackenzie Kantruss, daughter Elizabeth's children, and David and Lisa, offspring of son James.

The year 1954 brought another health crisis. Gable fractured three vertebrae, the result of a fall from a ladder. A worse result, as time was to prove, was an eye hemorrhage which left permanent vision impairment and was to be the first of a series of these difficulties. Washington nurseryman Milo Coplen, in his kind plotting to make his friend famous, instigated a feature about Gable in the Saturday Evening Post. The piece came out that May, while Gable was still in the hospital. There was no digging that spring or fall. Gable was back at heavy work the next spring but there were premonitions of mortality. Once again, a lucky friendship grew with Henry Yates of Frostburg, Md., whose enthusiasm, energy and ingenuity were to help prolong the productive years.

Yates told how he came to Stewartstown with a request for rhododendron seed, any seed, "to fool with." Gable replied that it might as well be good seed and a fruitful collaboration was begun. Yates quickly specialized in seeding techniques and for the rest of Gable's working life annually delivered flats of husky plants grown from Gable's and his own crosses to restock the beds and insure a new generation of hybrids. Many are still under evaluation and there are some still to bloom.

Gable enjoyed the role of senior oracle and was pleased with the various awards and citations which were accumulating around his "Office," a converted reed organ case with a battered portable typewriter on which he pounded with two fingers. Once received, though, he did not seem to think of the honors again. The stream of visitors and correspondence was often a heavy burden, so much so that he annually threatened about late May to put up a "Nursery Closed" sign and get on with what he wanted to do. He never did this.

There were several happy trips to the Asheville, North Carolina, area to see the glorious natives, in the mountains and in friends' collections. Another good time was a trip to the 1961 Portland convention, where seeing Halfdan Lem and his garden was a special joy. The two had been in touch since Lem's Alaskan days.

At home, unwinding was usually a tramp through the woods with one of a succession of fox terriers, named Billy, Butch and Buster; with Caroline's sable collie Bonnie, who was to have a matching rhododendron named for her, or with the spaniel Huck Finn. Sometimes he would escape to music. There was choir practice at the Methodist church where he taught Sunday School for 30 years and had been lay reader. When he retired from band and choir on account of advancing deafness, he unwound evenings in target shooting or with his old baritone horn, sitting in the dark blowing the airs for Wagner's "Pilgrim's Chorus" or "Evening Star." When the tune changed to "Going Home" or "Taps" it meant to the family that dad was a bit tired and depressed that evening. It was time then for someone to lure him to the piano with a good thumping Methodist hymn that would send him humming off to bed.

In 1964 the garden and woods had a great burst of bloom. The number of seedlings tagged that beautiful spring surpassed fifty. With his dimming sight, Gable went about the woods happily applying the white plastic tags and the four x's he gave for a superlative. Sometimes he used the pseudonym "Mr. Selby," although a lot of people knew it was just an attempt to save the plant from a persuasive customer.

Such occasions balanced the bad times, like the summer of 1966 when almost no rain fell from late June to mid-September. The unwatered woods plantings wilted severely and looked to be dead or dying. Gable was more philosophic than most visitors, who were distressed by the sight. Many plants had to be cut away afterwards but the revival process continued into the next spring and many revived, or sprouted from the roots. Thanks to the industry of Henry and Maletta Yates, there were plenty of seedlings ready for transplanting in the empty spaces.

Gable was then in his 81st spring and working almost as hard as ever. However, he was increasingly isolated by his deafness and deteriorating vision. The pickup truck's fenders were dented from encounters with the barn door and trees. Most often, it was Henry Yates' hand which did the crosses the two plotted in their winter letters.

On his last walk alone, he walked blindly into a brush pile and got his feet hopelessly entangled. The old collie, also growing blind, stood by barking anxiously until rescue came. She thus repaid the time the previous winter when Gable had waded waist deep into the pond to pull her out as she floundered in broken ice.

The last three years passed in darkness and advancing arteriosclerosis, with his faithful Mary always close by. Gable died July 21, 1972, three months before his 86th birthday. Mrs. Gable's tired heart soon gave out and she died a year later, on the anniversary of his funeral.

In the final years Gable was often asked to reflect on his life's work. He spoke regretfully of not having done more with the lepidotes and the natives, particularly deciduous azaleas. He wished for more time for backcrossing.

The perfect red-flowered rhododendron which he and Guy Nearing had schemed for in their crosses 40 years before was still to be achieved, as was the true hardy yellow to which he aspired in the last years. Hardiness was still an elusive and puzzling factor. The eastern nursery trade still peddled mostly Roseum and a few Ironclads. In short, there was still much to be done, a lot more information to work with and he only wished he could hang around to see the outcome.

Joe Gable's legacy continues. Several of his friends have been at work tirelessly in a Gable Study Group, formed by the Potomac Valley Chapter of the A. R. S. and dedicated to locating the rhododendrons and azaleas originating with Gable, and correlating the records so that those who carry on will have the benefit of his experience. One can almost hear him chuckle as he adds "and his mistakes."

Gable in his 80's under the original Cadis

The Gable Journals

Editors' Note

Joseph Gable kept extensive records of his many crosses, and of the plants resulting—success and failure alike. He also recorded carefully the trials of many species and of individual seed collections within a species. These records bear witness to Gable's keen observation, broad knowledge and infinite patience.

The quality of the writing, the wide spectrum of his trials, and the value of his observations tempts an editor to say "let's include it all." Space limitations, however, have dictated extensive cutting. To give the reader an appreciation of the scope of this work, the titles of many of his hybridization attempts are included in Appendix B of the Gable Study Committee report that follows.

Joe was always willing to share his hard-earned knowledge. He tried to answer all questions put to him concerning the origin of his plants, his successes, and failures.

In contrast to the generally advanced premise that primary crosses often result in hybrid vigor in the first generation, the many crosses by Joe exhibited a wide, well-distributed range of genetic compatibility. A surprisingly large number of crosses resulted in what Joe called "hybrid senility" to distinguish this characteristic from "hybrid vigor." The only way to know which will occur is to make the cross and grow seedlings on.

In crosses where a tender parent was crossed with a hardy parent, the usual result for Joe Gable was for only a few seedlings (or none) to survive out of large populations (500 or more).

Seedlings were planted in woods and "forgotten" for a while—then the survivors evaluated for a number of years. The first consideration was "growability"; the second, flower quality; the third, plant habit.

Notebooks and File Cards of Joseph B. Gable

Rhododendrons

adenogynum s. taliense. s.s. adenogynum. 1930. Apparently lost 1949 . . . series grew very slowly with much dying of branches. And also in common with all its ilk it is subject to the attack of the larvae of a minute bark beetle that I have noticed in this and in the Lacteum series of rhododendron. This damage increases in severity of infestation as the plants grow older and it could easily be the limiting factor in attempts to grow these rhododendrons.

Adenogynum flowered in 1947 and 1948 on a dying plant which probably kept it far from doing its best so I must refrain from the adverse criticism I feel due, from what I have seen.

In the last summer I have observed what seems to be the same bark beetle as above in *sutchuenense* and some other old plants that are not in good condition. It remains to be discovered whether the beetle is responsible for the deterioration of these plants or whether it is an insect which feeds on the bark and wood of plants and parts of plants which are already in poor health.

adenopodum s. ponticum s.s. caucasicum. 1934. Flowered 1940 and every season since in the open with no protection. Mr. G. G. Nearing gave me three seedlings of this species. One was planted out, the other two kept in pots in frames. The outdoor plant only survives and is a happy healthy specimen all the year around. It was frozen once when in full flower but so were *carolinianum* and *Schlippenbachii*. Of the three, *adenopodum* suffered least.

The pale pink flowers are clear in color and are borne in many flowered trusses, the dark green upper surface of the long narrow leaves contrasts markedly with the heavily felted, fawn colored undersides. The habit is densely branching, all tending toward its winning the two stars of its British rating in eastern U.S. competition also.

Unique in being the only species from the Himalayan-West China section ascribed to the Ponticum series.

As I start over my notes to keep them up-to-date,

here is a plant that it will be difficult to pass without a new word of appreciation each season. It is superior to any species of the Ponticum series, unless it be Glass's white form of Catawbiense that we are growing here and, since it flowers somewhat earlier, has no direct competition from that lovely rival for the Miss Ponticum award.

My plant does not set seed alone and hence all propagation has to be from grafts—so far, no cuttings or other means have succeeded. When impregnated with other pollen it is quite fertile which gave the idea that perhaps its sterility is due to the absence of some insect to pollinate it, rather than plain self sterility. So it has been tried with its own pollen with some apparent success as it set a few seeds.

Albert Close—rhod. 1951. A hybrid of *maximum* x *californicum* which was admired by Dr. Close and named in his honor. It is a late flowering pink, heavily spotted in the throat with chocolate red and should grow into a large plant.

1955: Such grafts as I have had to offer sell well, perhaps because of its late flowering. The longer we grow this, the better we like it. It is definitely not a "showy" rhododendron—perhaps it is our regard for the fine old gentleman who selected it—not knowing it would bear his name.

1959: Grows readily and better from cuttings than from grafts and we consider it quite a desirable plant.

Albrechtii s. azalea s.s. canadense. 1926. The descriptions of this species in the various works leave much to be desired in uniformity and any personal attempts to review its taxonomy would but result in "confusion worse confounded." First let us consider the plant growing here under this stage and leave the learned discussions to the learned.

Our plant resembles *Schlippenbachii* somewhat though a little smaller in both leaf and flower and much less vigorous grower. It opens its bright crimson pink flowers a day or two ahead of that species which description agrees fairly well with the British Association's *Year Book* and would seem to merit this species a four star rating here also.

It is a much more showy plant than *Schlippenbachii* because of its color, but it will never attain the stature of that species as my plant nearly a quarter of a century old seems to be standing still as far as height is concerned. I imagine 4 to 6' will be its ultimate stature in our area. In contrast with *Schlippenbachii* it is very difficult to propagate here. Bears few or no seeds and no cuttings have rooted, only a few layers which rooted slowly.

This old plant died this summer (1950) after flowering very heavily in spring. Now all the plants of this species alive here are commercial seedlings. I am very much puzzled as to the cause of its demise after growing lustily and being in every appearance of good health until about its flowering time this spring.

Whether love or hate, the rabbits insist on destroying every shoot that extends above the snow line *every* season. There will have to be some postseason rabbit hunting—each season—I fear.

ambiguum x mucronulatum. 1940—1952. This is the reverse mating of the successful "Mucram" (*mucronulatum* x *ambiguum,* 1930), does not grow well seeming to have inherited hybrid "senility" rather than hybrid "vigor." It is doubtful from its present status if it ever flowers.

In 1952 only two very puny, killed back, plants were noted and were not listed as living.

America. Since this Catawbiense hybrid variety has most successfully withstood our 'test' winters it is regarded here as the very hardiest of that class of red hybrids. Grows leggy when young but old plants are, generally speaking, quite presentable and the color is not excelled in its class.

1956: America has been found to root easily from cuttings.

The hybrid Nova Zembla which bears a close resemblance to America is becoming better known in Eastern U.S. and seems to have some characters superior to that variety. It remains to be proven if it is as hardy, in temperatures below $-20°F.$

R. obtusum Amoena. This azalea though fairly hardy here is losing out to better colored sorts. However in about every other plant character I know of no azalea which excels it. In edging borders and the front of foundation plantings its habit is ideal and the bearing and arrangement of the flowers among the fine dense foliage is not too far from ideal. If one envisions a garden of amoena type plants in every known azalea color, its activation appears as a worthwhile challenge.

Amphion. This hybrid, commonly in commerce in this country under the above name was originally known as "F. L. Ames." The true "Amphion" was red—reputedly. I have never seen it.

However "our own American Amphion" is rather unique among the *Catawbiense* hybrid group, enough so to afford an accent of relief in group planting. In personal experience no rhododendron has produced poorer flowers among its hybrid progeny than just this sort and the best have been nearly as good as Amphion The poorer ones revert to the unspeakable.

arborescens x calendulaceum. 1930. I have yet to see a poor flowered seedling from this first generation crossing. This hybrid had been previously made at the Arnold Arboretum I believe but was made here independently. The flowers vary all the way from pale yellows to intense orange scarlet, and the plants are vigorous, growing into large specimens though they start from seeds rather slowly. 1956: From what we have seen here we recommend that American growers of native azaleas use this as a basic hybrid in their breeding in those areas where hardiness is a limiting factor. With its wonderful variety of coloring—all clear—it might not be well to preclude it from experiments in milder climes! Orange, scarlet, yellows, striped and with no trace of magenta ever, the seedlings are not intermediate in flower color but one gets anything from vivid to palest hues in the first generation. So I recommend—but have done little with it myself.

arborescens s. azalea s.s. luteum. The best native white-flowered species in our area, easily obtainable but not nearly as generally planted as its merits warrant. If but given the chance it dominates the azalea garden in late June with both beauty and fragrance.

My only experience with this species growing naturally was along a rocky mountain torrent some miles north of Uniontown, Pa. The only plants I saw were growing right along the margin of the stream and wherever an opening offered on the margin of an eddy there seemed to be always a white bank of billowy fragrance right down to the surface, and one pool was even calm enough to reflect the picture. Ever since that I have recommended the planting of this subject in like sites when the opportunity afforded. In addition to its beauty, it flowers when such cool spots are likely to be appreciated.

arborescens var. glaucum. (probably var. *Richardsonii Rehd.*). A plant here tagged as above was collected in the mountains of western N.C. Its smaller size and very glaucous foliage together with pale pink flowers suggest Rehder's variety Richardsonii which it could easily be! It is an attractive garden plant with its blue foliage accents, and differs enough in botanical characters to be truly termed a variety. On top of a mountain in the Smokies—is it Waya Bald—there are extensive thickets of *A. arborescens* which seem to be all of this variety.

arborescens x occidentale. 1926; 1947. Seedlings (F_2) of this hybrid by Mr. George Fraser of Ucluelet, B.C., Canada, first flowered in 1934. At first we thought we had captured much of the character and beauty of its western parent in a plant sufficiently hardy to endure but it suffered too much from winter cold and now is but a memory.

It is a pity that no hybrid—or at least none known to me—of our western *occidentale* is hardy in our area as there is a charm about this plant that we do not get from any other of its group. Here is hoping that a hardy hybrid of *R. occidentale* turns up yet.

arboreum s. & s.s. arboreum. Seeds of various forms of this species have been sown here from time to time. None have proven sufficiently hardy to live outdoors and flower but this species is one of the few that thrive through periods of intense summer heat—a limiting factor in the cultivation of many exotic types, and a character that it may impart in some measure to its hybrids.

The blood of this species is supposed to be the color factor in our older Catawbiense hybrids and well it may be but it most obviously remains for some plant breeder to combine the characters of hardiness of *R. catawbiense* and the color of the blood red *R. arboreum* to an extent anywhere near approaching the ultimate—and I might frankly state right here that no real plant breeder's dream is limited by so called 'ultimates.' That word does not belong in our vocabulary, as there is no limit to the potentialities of plant improvement.

(File card: all seedlings lost 1941)

arizelum s. Falconeri. This species which collectors seem to find everywhere in West China has so far eluded me. Neither the series or the area from which this species comes promise much in hardiness. (File card has date: 1930)

atlanticum s. azalea s.s. luteum. This native species found in this locality a few years ago, establishing a new northern station for it, is extremely variable. In fact every clump in a meadow will have some variation from every other clump. The better forms are potentially useful ornamentally but so far have not been much disseminated. Plants from here have been distributed to several northern stations in the hope that it is a hardier type. This species is so variable that any comprehensive effort at varietal taxonomy might only add to the confusion but a few varieties might be separated for commercial purposes at least and we have been growing one—a pink form— sparingly.

To the propagator, this species and sometimes its hybrids offer a rather unusual method. The species is stoloniferous and these underground stems or runners may be cut into 1″—2″ sections in fall or early spring and potted or planted in flats for a year. In fact it is good to keep plants intended for sale in pots until sold as this keeps these stolons from intertwining with all other plants in the bed and results in much better looking clumps to sell. Such hybrids of this species which produce these stolons, several are noted, may be increased by the same method.

(File cards) Atlantic Type A: Differing from the type in its purple foliage especially conspicuous in spring and fall. Clonally propagated. Atlantic Type B: Pure rose pink flowers of very clear shade. Varies considerably from the type in appearance but identified as that species by Dr. C. S. Sargent at the Arnold Arboretum to whom both flowers and plants were sent.

atlanticum x arborescens. 1938. Flowers regularly and almost too profusely. Though rather compact growing the single florets are ridiculously small in some seasons.

atlanticum x calendulaceum. 1925. In general these seedlings have been much like Anneliesae but the plants are smaller and more compact and they are generally quite sterile while Anneliesae bears seeds. However, since former notes were written, a single plant becomes increasingly outstanding with the years, with its coat of scarlet flowers worn in late May. This plant produces seed regularly. Results to date seem to indicate that this seed germinates very poorly, if at all.

atlanticum x japonicum. 1926. Flowered 1929. Several seedlings of this mating are fairly good and one—the outstanding one that the hybridist hopes for in each new lot of seedlings—is a gem. In coloring its flowers resemble a miniature five-petalled Regal lily, same yellow throat, same purplish stripe on the back of each petal; and different, though just as delicious fragrance. The plant now 7' high, is regularly and completely covered with flowers in early May.

And I suppose this is as opportune a place as any to note a certain form of injury to azalea flowers that I have never seen published or written of before, i.e., "bumble bee" damage. The Luteum subseries suffers generally together with a number of other species and hybrids with narrow long corolla tubes. These big bees cannot crawl down the tube for the nectar so they cut holes in the corolla tube from the outside causing the petals to wilt prematurely.... Spells of hot dry weather in the flowering season greatly accentuate this damage. Even the whitehead bumble bees (which every country kid knows cannot sting, greatly to the discomfiture of his city cousins) which are not bees at all but the mature form of a wood boring insect, know the secret and I have seen them both open new holes and visit those already opened by other bees.

The use of DDT seems to be reducing the bumble bee population which helps the problem here but this is a very useful little insect in some angles of agriculture and horticulture and his extermination is not desirable. (File card: referring to the plant like a regal lily—absolutely sterile, no further breeding experiments have been possible. The best plant finally bore a few seeds, 1937.)

Atrosanguineum x floccigerum. Atroflo 1940. This cross has been flowering now for several seasons and shows promise of becoming a worthwhile red flowering garden plant despite occasional winter damage to the buds. So far no *plant* has been hurt. The flowers are large, almost huge, with long corollas and wide spread limb, and the color in all seedlings has been good. It also has a distinctly "different" look.

Atroflo bears little seed or pollen and such hybrids as we have been able to procure from it are in very small numbers.

The name Atroflo should belong solely to a selected seedling and its progeny as a clonal name, but in practice this has become confused. We are trying to get our slate clean and I believe we have all labels correct at last. The foliage of Atroflo is of extraordinary excellence and the variety should become popular where buds are hardy. We are growing seedlings and hybrids of it hoping to come by a bud-hardy counterpart but it is stingy in both seeds and pollen production.

We are propagating a seedling that is fairly bud-hardy, but our best flowers and foliage are on a rather tender clone.

Atrosanguineum x Fortunei. 1940. Flowered 1948. Only a scattering of these have bloomed so far. One has been tagged, a very pretty pink and very early.

In spring 1950 another seedling produced a single truss good enough to make it a thing of great promise. Now it must continue to flower freely, prove sufficiently hardy and keep its good foliage and plant habit for a number of years and we will nominate it for our *Number 1* pink. Really we think it that good.

The beginning of the flowering of this hybrid revives interest in comparing it with the much smaller hybrid *decorum* x Atrosanguineum, the description of which will be found in these notes under Decatros. At present we may note these comparisons though Decatros is eight years older than our present subject.

Flowered at eight years from seed. Much variation in all characters. Some flowers good, others poor. All plants in good health.

No signs of injury from winter cold. Most plants flower sparingly so far. Best plant has superior flowers to any of the decorum hybrid, some others are worse than anything of that mating.

1954: The plant above nominated as our *Number 1* pink seems to have been elected. It is now known as Gable's Pink No. 1. The only problem is to propagate enough to introduce it. It propagates readily from both grafts and cuttings but like all new rhodos it means years of waiting even so. Now named David Gable.

Atrosanguineum x Griersonianum. Atrier 1940., Flowered 1945. Several dozen of seedlings of this first cross have flowered now (1949) and if it proves really hardy—which I much fear it can not—it should be a real acquisition. The shading varies but all are of scarlet and crimson coloring, very bright and the trusses on some plants are simply huge. I surmise however that its greatest value will be as a parent of hardier sorts.

Dozens of seedlings in the woods have been killed to the ground and some entirely. In fact some 90-95% have proven worthlessly tender. But there are—to me quite surprisingly—a few plants that have now passed five winters unscathed. Two of these out of some two hundred or more originals look fairly promising. In fact I can see no reason at all from their behavior why they should not be propagated except that I just am unable to trust such a mating to prove dependably hardy....

This cross was made only for further use in hybridization experiments. I had no slightest idea that a single seedling would prove growable in the open. Quite probably none of them will.

In spring 1951, a new seedling as yet unflowered and never injured by winter cold opened its first florets. The flowers were large, the truss wide and floppy, and the color about identical with Dresselhuys. Another, as yet unhurt, has buds for 1952 and how we hope it will be better in color. 1953: This seedling a "stinker."

1954: This is proving to be one of my outstanding hybrids and I am using it freely as was my first intention—for further crosses a few of which have started to flower. Nevertheless two of the original seedlings are being propagated. The one mentioned above (colored like Dresselhuys) is much better than that hybrid and apparently as hardy. Another with flowers almost the color of *Griersonianum* also seems hardy enough but is inclined to grow rather prostrate. It is known as Atrier#10 as a clone.

1956: Atrier#1, Atrier#10, Atrier (Hardy) & Atrier Oak are being propagated to test which may be the better one to introduce.

(Atrosanguineum x Griersonianum) x (decorum x haematodes). 1947. 1960: Out of this lot we have a peach color flower with excellent truss and very good foliage and plant habit. It may be the best thing produced here and is named Mary Belle for my wife.

Atrosanguineum x repens. 1938. One plant flowered in 1949, an unhappy, unhealthy miserable little plant, with very dark buds that failed to open fully. There yet remains an apparently very healthy plant which retains the event of its flowering as an incentive to longevity on my part!

1950: This plant bears its first flowerbud for Spring 1951. Its flowering was its nemesis. Quite worthless.

Atrosanguineum x Thomsonii. 1932. This hybrid, which flowered as long ago as 1940 for a friend on Long Island, has only so favored us during the last three seasons (46, 47, 48, 49)—*four* seasons—but the plant flowering in 1946 died before it ripened its seeds. The plant habit is good, semi-dwarf, round leaved dark green foliage is pleasing, the redness of its flowers, comparative size of corolla and truss leave little to be desired but why does it have to be so stingy with its beauty? Produces very few buds to a plant so far.

Hybrids of *Thomsonii* would be very acceptable if matings could be made with more vigor. They seem however to possess a constitutional allergy to something they find here and have to be coddled along. I am not too sure it is winter cold, but rather suspicion it is somewhat of an uncongenial parent—one that produces hybrid senility in its mating with species of other series rather than the hybrid vigor that we hope for, and which produces our more successful varieties.

One side of a 4' plant was well furnished with blood red trusses spring 1950. Very beautiful and if it only keeps this up—quite worthwhile. But there are several of these eighteen-year-old seedlings that have yet to flower.

1953: Have lost this "best" seedling and have only one graft and about 100 F$_2$ seedlings left. This was a real loss as I know of no other hardy clear deep red with such handsome flowers and foliage so early in the season. The plant apparently died of blight which is so often the limiting factor in the cultivation of the species and hybrids of its series.

1956: The clone Atsonii is lost in entirety but we still have a few seedlings.

Augustinii s. triflorum s.s. Augustinii. 1925. Several sowings of seeds from several sources have resulted in a various group of plants now growing (or formerly growing) here under the above caption. Heralded as the Blue Rhododendron, plants grown from seeds from Mr. Magor have opened striking delphinium blue florets up to 3" in diameter, a wonderful show when it flowers well. But it loses many buds in some seasons, perhaps not so much from midwinter cold as from impatience for its beloved springtime. The plant is apparently hardy enough and, with all its faults, rather indispensable. Roots quite well from cuttings.

No other of the several variations of this species has proven hardy except a single plant with nearly white flowers—something the shade of the bedsheets when the household authorities use too much bluing—and this plant got broken down last spring and may not recover. Some of the variations of this species are extremely poor so if you are in search of it be on the watch for the one and only genuine!

A number of nurseries—on the West Coast at least—are propagating "true blue" strains.

1956: Our one old plant left from Magor's seedlings grows and survives our winters well enough and succeeds in opening enough florets about one year in three to justify the four Xs it is given in Britain. At its best it is superlative.

(File card: R. Augustinii Best Blue 1932. From Magor. Flowered 1939. All buds killed 1940. And again in 1941.)

auriculatum s. auriculatum. 1926. This species can

be grown outdoors here only in well protected sites. Where protected from high wind and direct winter sunshine the plant seems satisfactorily hardy and the flower buds generally winter well. Like all plants, it is hardier when in best condition and care must be taken to keep it in good tilth. The flowers are fragrant, white, immense, and very late—sometimes in August. If the weather is very hot, as it is more often than not, the flowers are quickly spoiled by the heat and sometimes brown before fully opening. It cannot be recommended as an addition to the beauty of an outdoor garden in our area but can be grown and flowered with reasonable care.

(File card: This species can be said to be only fairly hardy here. Can withstand −20°F. in protected situations. Flowered July 1940 from partially frost-killed buds in lath house. Immense fragrant flowers but too late. Good 1941 & '42 & '43.

auriculatum x discolor. 1944. A fast growing lot but seem more tender than *discolor* to winter cold.

Flowered spring 1950 with white late flowers scarecely as good as either parent. However there are more seedlings to bloom. The plants are vigorous and well branched, which last named character is none too pronounced in either parent of our subject.

1954 (or 3?): Among a number of others opening flowers for the first this spring, two had flowers over 5″ across. However neither plant looks like an acceptable garden subject for the smaller planting or the average commercial grower, but might be of value in further breeding.

1959: In due process of the "survival of the fittest" a seedling about 8′ wide and high is definitely the winner. If its flowering coincides with weather somewhere under the 80s it makes quite a show—when most others are gone. This plant resembles the seed parent in foliage but is more compact, branching type and some two weeks to a month earlier (can this be correct? J.G.) to flower than discolor. A very hardy and thrifty plant but loses some buds in severe seasons.

austrinum. 1928; 1946. This southern species surprisingly proved entirely hardy though it is now lost from neglect. The little flowers are fragrant and pretty though not showy. The purple stripes on the corolla ridges are prominent. I would like to have it back.

austrinum x luteum. 1936. This is proving to be one of the finer things of its season here. Light shades predominately pure yellow, fine fragrance, foliage of prominent glaucous tinge on large tall growing plants make one wish to increase the measly three specimens to dozens or hundreds.

Bearing seeds plenteously we have relied altogether on this means of propagating this, thinking that the normal color variation in the F_2 seedlings would be welcome. But we are able to grow very few plants. The seeds do not germinate well and the seedlings seem weak growers. Layering may be the only successful method of increase.

1956: We now have 70 seedlings of this hybrid coming along. They represent about a quart of seeds sown. We ought to get some fine things of these good parents and also a few that bear more fertile seeds. We have had a few seedlings to flower, all in very acceptable shades of cream to a deeper clear yellow.

Bakeri. 1956. We have had this several years without getting it into our notes, but it has yet to flower so little can be said except that the plant appears hardy enough.

1959: This species has flowered here and I have had the privilege of seeing it in quantity in its native haunts but I will leave the description to the learned, except to state that it is one of our most beautiful and striking species. A seedling of the form known as Camp's Red is the most intense scarlet I have seen in the genus—even though it has been moved to a lower altitude. But let me state that I do not believe thoroughly in the theory that colors are inclined to thin out when plants are removed to considerably lower sites, though soils and drainage differences may exist that will also produce marked variations in this respect.

(Boule de Neige x Fortunei). 1932. This clone, the only seedling selected, has white flowers, fine lustrous foliage, and excellent plant habit, much superior to its parent Boule de Neige which it may well replace.

It is being propagated with a view to introducing it in the trade and I see no reason why it should not find a welcome as a superior early white. Because of the tendency of the Boule de Neige hybrids to give so many worthless seedlings and so very, very few of any worth, Beaufort has been little used in further hybridization experiments. This may be poor judgment but I had much rather grow a group of seedlings all of which are so good that one has much trouble in selecting the better ones—the hybrid of *R. discolor* x Caroline for instance—than to make selection from a batch of such poor flowered things as this Boule de **Neige x *R. Fortunei*** cross where the few, if any, worthwhile plants stand out so prominently in contrast. In fact, the better ones have so little competition in such company that they may appear better than they are and it is only when they can be judged with the best of other groups that one can make a fair decision. Some superior things *may* result as our subject here is truly a 'superior early white.'

About 1925? This has resulted in the best hybrid seedling I have produced from Boule de Neige—in Beaufort (described separately). One or two other seedlings are fair but the most of them would be prettier if they made no attempt to flower.

1951: We have sparingly propagated another seedling—in addition to Beaufort—and it pleases us more each season. It has fine, medium dwarf, plant habit and large pale mauve flowers turning white. The foliage is small and somewhat twisted but the dense twiggy habit makes it a presentable plant.

Beni-kirishima. *The following crossed out:* This standard double salmon red flowered dwarf is a remarkably good seed parent—in my experience. It is not hardy in itself here and though I have flowered many excellent seedlings only one—the clone H-12-G—survives. It is much superior to Beni-Kirishima both in flower and plant but loses buds here in some winters.

"For hybridists who work where this plant is hardy, this should by all means be tried as a source of double flowered late dwarf varieties."

1956: I wish I could cancel out all of the things I have written above, I find that the Beni-kirishima I had was probably mislabeled.

Beni-kirishima x Caroline Gable (*poukhanense x Hexe) x (Kaempferi x poukhanense).* (File card: x 96G) 1941

Only the clone H-12-G remains of this mating. Some of the others winterkilled, others were discarded and a few sold, but this has been held for propagation. It has very double deep salmon red flowers, lustrous evergreen foliage, and dwarf habit. It occasionally sends up a strong growing shoot in a single season but immediately subsides into a flowering branch. It could be hardier as it loses buds to some extent. *Very* late flowering.

Blue Peter. 1954. It seems about time to record the performance of this best of all blue broadleaves. It has shown no least sign of winter injury, seems to grow naturally into a nice plant, branching well and with foliage of good color. It registers as attractive with most visitors who see it in flower and we are going to try to carry it regularly on our sales list—if we can ever build up a sufficient stock!

Blue Tit. (*impeditum x Augustinii*) 1936. This hybrid by Mr. J. C. Williams of Cornwall, England, in 1933 was obtained from Magor in 1936? At any rate it is a fairly hardy plant but loses its buds to some extent, never having lost them all or never having carried them all through any one winter. If it were a strain of indigo it would scarcely be blue enough to be outstanding, but being a rhododendron it is definitely blue. A nice thing and very lovely when it flowers well.

In 1952 I obtained 25 plants under this label from van Veen of Portland, Oregon, and find this clone quite different from that obtained from Mr. Magor, having much smaller leaves and flowers. In this short trial it seems to be more hardy—or more nearly hardy—but its flowers are not of the attractive blue coloring of Magor's plant.

1955: Blue Tit is doing well and is a good dwarf to grow on for sale.

1959: I can now state certainly that the Blue Tit from Mr. van Veen is the true variety and also that it is hardy enough to be satisfactorily grown here.

Boule de Neige. This old garden hybrid supposed to have caucasicum 'blood' has been used quite a bit in hybridizing experiments here. A few good things have resulted but most were mediocre and some are awful with an inflorescence that balls and never opens. Some plants two feet high have flowered well for years while one now 12′ has yet to bloom. Lack of hardiness even when crossed with hardy species and hybrids suggests that there may be a tender gene or two in its makeup. A few are hardy. (Filed card: 1920)

Boule de Neige x calophytum 1933. Several plants of this flowered in 1951. It is not outstanding in flower but the foliage and plant are very good. A peculiarity is that the flowers grow after opening, doubling or trebling their original size, and we know no rhododendron which holds its flowers so long in good condition.

1955: One plant of this grows on and carries on the tradition of its *R. calophytum* parent with its large handsome leaves. The flowers are more like R. *calophytum* than Boule de Neige. It is a very nice looking thing but we have done nothing about its propagation.

Boule de Neige x sutchuenense. 1933. Both Nearing and I made this same cross the same season, and now I have no way of telling "which is which." They are an extremely variable lot—as are all B. de N. hybrids. After seventeen years I still keep about a half dozen plants—just for variety's sake I guess. One plant in particular is a real success as a plant with dark green foliage, reddish petioles and good branching habit. It flowers very early, escaping frost damage entirely perhaps once in five years, at which rare intervals it is quite charming. (File card: One plant opened one lovely flower in 1942. Several are in bud 1943.)

1955: This one plant we have been propagating as it is a fine looking plant and we feel it worth taking the risk of an early frost to have it around. We call this clone "Bo-Sutch" on our inventory lists and as with some others it seems this abbreviation may become the published name.

"Bo-Sutch" 1956: The clone mentioned above. It is a fine plant and propagates nicely but flowers a little too early.

Boule de Neige x sutchuenense x haematocheilum. 1943. A very foolish hybrid to have made as both parents are much too precocious for our late frosts but these seedlings are coming along.

1955: One of those things that lives on and does nothing worth recording. Five plants remain, having attained a stature of one foot each in twelve years. An inch per annum.

1960: Two or three of these have flowered very early. Pretty.

brachycarpum s. ponticum s.s. caucasicum. 1927. Hardy compact and slow to flower, this species is outstanding among the hardy rhododendrons for its excellent foliage and plant habit. Its small pale pink or light cream colored blossoms are borne on many flowered trusses in mid-June. Compared with most other rhododendrons, it is more difficult to transplant successfully in mature sizes.

1955: It is apparently a number of years since any comment has been made on this species, in which space of time a hundred or two specimens have been allowed to grow on in the wood without pruning or care of any nature except to keep the sprouts and briars cut out every year or two.

In this time some plants are 8′ high while others are only 3′—4′. The conditions are equally good all through the planting and *R. maximum* among them is uniformly two to three times as tall. Plants that are not crowded are wider than high and the branches cover the bases well. The large dark green leaves add to their attractiveness.

But now to list the faults of this species. Of these old plants, not half have borne a flower truss. I expect 75% would be a closer estimate of the barren ones. In winter the leaves remain curled up longer and more tightly than any other rhododendron that is a living plant. And they are very sensitive to drought too—as regards this leaf curling.

Yet a few plants flower heavily each season, it is a very hardy sort. The flowers while small are prettily marked and no offensive colors. A great many of its hybrids are altogether worthless but a few are also very fine. It hybridizes naturally with the *R. maximum* growing near it. In fact one sowing of brachycarpum gave seedlings that were nearly all hybrids with *maximum*. And this hybrid in general is no good, having very poor foliage that browns and looks as if diseased, but a small percentage do have nice foliage. Its progeny is often rather stunted and lacks vigor but in this too a few plants often turn up that grow satisfactorily. The foliage seems rather resistant to disease and insects and is heavy enough to withstand wind damage.

It will certainly never become as much a part of our hardy hybrid race as our *R. catawbiense,* but I predict that it will gradually infiltrate into many fine hybrids especially of the low compact type on account of its good foliage and plant habit and that it has no purple tints to breed out in later generations.

It has been claimed that this species is the source of double-flowered hybrids. I have had a few that showed this character in part but nothing yet that is worthwhile in itself though I have a few seedlings crossed with other things that show a little petaloidy, coming on with that hope.

(File card: In flower bud spring 1936)

brachycarpum x decorum. 1940. A rather dwarf group of plants some less than 8″ high in eight years, some approaching 2′. All of them wider than high and generally bearing neat attractive foliage to the ground. A number of plants have yet to flower though several have blossomed profusely for three or four years. The flower color is basically white varying but little on the separate seedlings, florets medium to small in size and well-formed and well-filled trusses.

So far we have done nothing about this hybrid but watch it—no superlative seedlings or anything.

1954: We have now selected one of these seedlings for propagation, on account of its fine foliage and good sized trusses of flowers on a low growing plant. The trouble— it makes propagating material so slowly!

The above clone is coming along nicely and is now named Milo for my friend Mr. M. G. Coplen.

brachycarpum x Essex Scarlet. 1938. Flowered 1945, and all seedlings have now flowered. We have selected several of red color and watched them for a while but most of this crossing were poor to utterly worthless. Most have good plant habit.

The above should be slightly qualified, I think. A plant that one of those borers about as thick as one's little finger caught up with and destroyed bore fair size trusses of dark rose red and had excellent plant habit and foliage. It was being saved for possible future hybrids.

1955: Yes, several seedlings of this cross *were* fairly good and it is possible that the plant I had named the Cardinal, only to find that another hybrid had been named Cardinal previously, is of this parentage. It is known only as a Brachycarpum hybrid but everything points to this origin. The Kentucky Cardinal, as I guess I will now call it to distinguish it from a British Redcoat, is a healthy plant and keeps its vigor. All other seedlings of this cross have deteriorated and died or are nearly dead at this writing.

brachycarpum x maximum. 1945. These species seem to intercross freely when grown in proximity. In fact I am sure that brachycarpum seedlings have been sent out that will represent this natural hybrid rather than the true species. *Brachycarpum* will apparently have to be isolated from plants of *maximum* or carefully self-pollinated to have them come true from seeds. As they grow here now I get over 25% of this hybrid from open pollinated seeds of *brachycarpum*.

This hybrid bears its first flower buds for spring of 1952. Several plants of this hybrid have now flowered with about what one would expect from it. The big disappointment is in the foliage, which while fair in some seedlings, is far from what one would expect from two parents with superb character in this line.

1954: We now have a plant with superb foliage of this parentage with flowers no better than the parents but we think it should be a good parent (if it does not give too many seedlings with as poor foliage as the first cross).

1960: We call a clone of this "Bramax."

Brittania x America. 1941. Flowered 1949. This international hybrid has exhibited one truss on one of its seedlings that is equal to or perhaps superior to Brittania itself. Now if it only proves hardy through the years! Though it did not look as well in spring 1950 as its first truss it was very pretty.

1952: This plant has been rather seriously injured by winter cold in winters of only medium temperatures so it will be dropped for propagation.

In 1952 another seedling flowered with florets larger and slightly paler than Brittania. Now *if* it proves hardier than Brittania and *if* it is equal in plant habit and foliage to that variety, it *may* supersede it in our gardens in this area.

1955: It might be well to note here that Brittania hybrids in general have not done well and I have grown (or rather tried to grow) quite a few of them. I do have some that flower with red flowers and may be hardier—I think they are—but with Brittania itself in flowers one gets sort of an unpleasant sensation in the nostrils when regarding such of its progeny that I have been able to flower.

"Cadis". A selected clone of Caroline x *discolor*. Named about 1949. This is one of our very best hybrids so far and we intend to propagate it to the limit. It is a large growing type with large pink flowers but we will defer a complete description until we use a color chart and the like.

We have not yet used that color chart but this hybrid is still rising in our ratings. It is floriferous, healthy, propagates well, and those who see it in flower want plants.

calendulaceum s. azalea s.s. luteum. This hardy and eminently satisfactory native azalea is too well known for me to attempt any comprehensive description here. One may select quite a color scheme from its yellow, orange, and scarlet hued variants.

This species may be propagated in several ways but plants on their own roots are better. This can be done by conventional layering but it may be worthwhile to

mention another system that is applicable to this azalea and, though perhaps in a lesser degree, to its hybrids and some other related species. That is to dig the plant by cutting around it with the spade or shovel and lifting it with as little disturbance to the ends of the cut-off roots left in the soil as possible. The hole may be left open or partially filled with leaves, weed and trash of a loose nature to hold a little moisture. The cut root ends will send up shoots which may be taken in a year or two and lined out. From large plants we have taken from thirty to forty small plants in two years.

By this method, clonal continuity is secured in the same way as with grafts, layers, or cuttings and the stock of fine flowering specimens may be multiplied just as assuredly true to type.

Two other methods involving basically this same principle have suggested themselves but we have not yet tried them here.

It may be that if these cut-off root ends are dug and potted immediately on digging the plant and placed in a frame where proper care and water can be given, they would root well enough and the unsightly holes need not be left open.

Or if it is not desirable to move the plant the root ends may be cut off and dug from it, leaving it in place, and caring for them as in the paragraph above. In experimenting with this method I would not cut all the roots, leaving about half to ensure the health of the old plant, but would cut those taken rather close to the base of the old plants. It might be possible to succeed with sections of the roots taken if they are of sufficient size.

It is true that these methods of propagation are somewhat analogous to that given under *atlanticum,* q.v., but in that case the underground shoots used are subterraneous stems of the plant or stolons rather than true roots which are dealt with in this case.

Camp's Red—R. cumberlandense.   1938. This has been identified with *R. cumberlandense,* a new native American species first described in 1941. When this first flowered for me in 1938 from seeds generously given me by Dr. Clement G. Bowers I wrote before I knew a new species had been described: "Flowered 1942 in deep orange scarlet. Apparently deserves to be called at least a new variety if not a new species." My 1946 notes on it read, "This azalea from seeds from Dr. Bowers has flowered here the last two years. While not all the seedlings flower in the glowing scarlet color described by the discoverers there seem to be several other cultural differences between this and *R. calendulaceum* in its typical form. It flowers later, grows more slowly, has slenderer twigs, smaller flower buds, is rather more floriferous and a much larger proportion of its seedlings are scarlet (flowered) than that well known species. Whether or not there be taxonomic differences, I leave to the taxonomists."

In 1950 I might add that the taxonomists have settled the point in question, that very fine yellow shades occur among the seedlings, that it will rarely produce a seed in cultivation unless hand-crossed (suggesting that some insect pollinates it in its native habitat that is not found here). That it is proving to be a plant of rather low habit (it seems doubtful if it exceeds 4' in ultimate height), that it germinates very poorly from seeds, even when hand-pollinated, and that if it can be reproduced in sufficient quantity it will become a valuable addition to our present native species in our garden plantings.

Camp's Red is now considered to be the same as R. cumberlandense or possibly a variety of that species, by our botanists.

1959: The finest bright scarlet flowers so far borne here on any azalea are those of a seedling of Camp's Red. And they last well on the plant—two weeks. Some seedlings show a terra cotta hue which is quite unusual.

campylocarpum x Fortunei. 1947. From Hardgrove.

1952: Proving rather tender, this has yet to flower. From appearances I very much doubt if my plant is really this hybrid.

1954: Flowering for the first last season, this plant has good sized trusses of lovely pale apricot flowers and if hardy through the years will be quite an acquisition. Its flower characters would seem to prove me wrong in doubting its given parentage were true. But the foliage *does not* suggest campylocarpum.

1956: Hardly a success in itself but may be a stepping stone.

canadense s. Azalea s.s. canadense. 1925. This native species of Pennsylvania swamps and northward is of little commercial value, though it is unique and interesting. A hybrid of this species and *R. Japonicum* known as *R. Fraseri* is named for the originator George Fraser and is the only hybrid of this azalea that I know of. *Canadense x Schlippenbachii* 1935; from Frank Abbott having flowered as canadense only.

canescens s. Azalea s.s. luteum. This southern species said to resemble *R. roseum* is inferior in both color and hardiness as it grows in our part of the world and except as another species in attempts to form complete collections has no value here whatever.

(File card: This southern azalea differs from *R. roseum* which it much resembles in many characters by its longer corolla tube and seed capsules which last also split open and disperse their seeds much earlier in the season.)

Caroline. 1927. This seedling clone, which grew up in a group marked Decorum hybrids back in the beginnings of rhododendron hybridization here, when the importance of accurate records had not yet been learned, is an instance of the desirability of keeping a plant under observation long enough for it to exhibit its true character. At first flowering, other seedlings attracted more attention, but as the years passed and this seedling grew into a large most shapely specimen with healthy dark foliage covered annually with large deliciously fragrant flowers of pale orchid lavender that persist unusually long, it became more and more obvious that it was easily the outstanding seedling. Though tall growing its branches persist to the ground and it flowers on the lower limbs as well as on the upper. It also bears many trusses on the inside of the plant where the shade is dense.

This is the first of our original hybrids that we tried to propagate extensively and it was found quite difficult, slow to layer, almost impossible from stem or leaf cuttings and grafted on ponticum understocks such a failure that the propagator we had then lost all interest. Then Mr. M. G. Coplen of Rock Creek Nurseries, Rockville, Maryland, tried it and since then it has been going strong. It would be quite unethical for me to explain what I know of his methods here—or anywhere for that matter—but he grafts them.

1956: I must record here that Mr. Warren Baldsiefen has been rooting this variety well from cuttings and that, from his instructions, I have been able to root a few myself. They grow much better on their own roots.

Caroline x discolor. 1938. This, the source of the superlative Cadis, is notable mainly for that one seedling although I am not too sure that Gable's Pink #2 is not properly included here, though it may belong to the reverse cross which is very similar—as it probably should be.

Caroline x (discolor x Caroline) = "Disca". 1948. Caroline crossed back on the best hybrid it has so far produced.

carolinianum s. carolinianum. A native species easily grown and an excellent ornamental if its special requirements are met, it being unusually particular in its need for perfect drainage. It also grows rather thin in too much shade, preferring somewhat sunny sites. Even more essential for the enjoyment of its maximum beauty is the removal of the faded flower clusters—a task approaching the infinite on large plants.

(File card: easily hurt by seed production)

carolinianum x racemosum. F.P.I. 56363 1928-1958. This mating with a rather tender form of *racemosum* produced plants that seem quite hardy and which flower very prettily when they escape late spring frosts. The color is a mayflower pink and they may open even in advance of *R. mucronulatum*. In contrast with the very fertile hybrid of *carolinianum* with *racemosum* F.P.I. 59717, (Conestoga), this is a mule, absolutely sterile.

1952: Now lost.

(File card: This form of *racemosum* is both too early and too tender to grow here but hybrid seedlings seem hardy but more susceptible to spring frosts than Conestoga.)

carolinianum x spinuliferum. 1933. A Nearing hybrid. The flowers are pretty and the plant surprisingly hardy, but it does not grow well and out of flower is rather unattractive. Sterile.

1956: I am unable to add or detract from what I had written above. The few florets it bears are pretty, unusually so, but there is no worse looking *live* plant on the place.

Carolinianum Album. If this native variety were found somewhere in west China or other exotic site it would be determined at once a distinct species but American forms are not so strictly classified. It differs from the type in characters other than its coloring alone and also flowers later. When well grown it is a very good ornamental.

(File card: also hybrids of white and pink *carolinianum* with other species produce quite different results.)

1959: The principal fault of this variety seems to be its tall open habit. We now have a seedling that is dense in foliage and free branching with short annual growth.

Carolinianum Album Compactum. (Gable) 1956. We are having fair success with this and it seems to be really worthwhile. Roots fairly well if taken very early.

Carolinianum Aureum. 1934. Name given here (has no taxonomic standing) to a form with yellow buds opening to cream colored flowers. A collected plant.

Catalode. 1959. Catalode is a hybrid of Catawbiense Album (a standard hybrid) and Loderi. It is one of our best whites (if not *the best* white) we have originated with heavy dark green foliage and white flowers but no trace of lavender in bud or flower. It is easy to propagate, a rampant grower and flowers profusely from two year cuttings on.

catawbiense x discolor. 1938. Have now flowered about 50 seedlings of this hybrid and find that they vary more in flower than most primary hybrids. In this particular, as was to be expected, they are superior to *catawbiense* but on the whole quite inferior to *discolor*. A few plants have opened rather nice flowers but only one is saved for possible propagation. The plants, foliage and habit are as much alike as "two peas." (Perhaps 200 peas.)

As a plant it is the happiest, healthiest, growin'est rhododendron on the place.

1952: Three plants have now been noted with flowers quite superior to the 'run of the mine' seedlings. In fact we think them fine enough to propagate and they are as alike as *three peas*. No doubt some variation will show up later and on more meticulous inspection.

catawbiense x Fortunei x Campylocarpum. 1943. In the light of later and perhaps better things the first flowering of this number has lost much of its original glamour and my former notes are obsolescent to some extent. It may still be stated, however, that all things considered this is a happy healthy lot, very hardy and attractive the year around, and that the first good selection known as "C-11" is yet the most attractive of the lot, still bearing flowers of bright pink in trusses superior to any of the named pink hybrids in the trade in our part of the country. It has proven difficult to propagate.

The fault of this group as a whole is the indifferent coloring of the flowers and in many seedlings, their scarcity.

The clone of this known as "C-11" is one of our best hybrids, with dark green foliage and good habit in an upright form.

(Picture with File card: *R. catawbiense* hybrid F. L. Ames x *R. Fortunei*. Flowers pale pink.)

(File card: first flowered 1933 (referring to title of cross, not picture). . . . The McFarland selection, a lovely pink is being propagated.)

(File cards only: *cat.* x *Fortunei* 1938, cross
      catawbiense x *Fortunei*, selfed, 1938
      cat. x *Fort.* F$_2$ 1938
      cat. x *Fort.* selfed, 1937.)

catawbiense x Fortunei x Campylocarpum. 1943. Seedlings have dwindled to one which has yet to flower.

1954: This one plant has flowered and is nice but scarcely good enough to propagate.

1954: Another seedling of this turned up when it flowered and looks very, very good but it was broken back to one little side twig.

1960: A beautiful apricot-colored seedling flowered in 1955 and was found to have the above parentage on the label. We like it and it roots well from cuttings.

catawbiense x Fortunei (C-11) x Caroline. 1940. A few of these have borne a truss or two lovely enough to make one impatient to see the remainder.

A 1951 clonal selection of the above is Gable's Pink #2—temporarily. It has fine large flowers, and good foliage but the habit is open. Since it is a strong grower and will probably attain considerable size, it should fill out better when more mature.

1955: Gable's Pink #2 is proving to be one of the best things we have originated.

Cathaem (Catawbiense Red x haematodes A. A.) (q.v.) 1933. While there is little to be said for the potential commercial value of this lot of plants, perhaps I have found more of personal interest in watching the various seedlings of this mating mature and come into flowering, than any other one cross made here.

The plants are much alike. Good foliage, slow growing medium dwarf in stature and tending to grow to one side with limbs touching the earth and rooting from the stems. The flowers however vary considerably. In color through fairly good red and pink to pale pink with heavy red spotting that shows through on the outside of the corolla in some while others are quite spotless. In form they vary from normal single florets to one which has a corolloid calyx (hose-in-hose) equalling the corolla in size.

In another the corolloid calyx is reflexed as in a cyclamen. The trusses are about the shape and size of Boule de Neige or better.

Though these might be of much interest to the hybridist and azalea fancier, they grow so slowly that even though they make very lovely garden subjects, the commercial propagator will be discouraged from the outset.

Cathaem #1. The clone with the corolloid calyx reflexed.

Cathaem #4. Cathaem #4 is the clone with a corrolloid calyx which seems hardier, in fact we have nothing to record against its being altogether hardy.

1954: We have now been trying to propagate this number for possible introduction and find that it roots well from cutting.

Cathaem #7. This clone has single flowers (no corolloid calyx) of good size and color quite early in the season. Slow growing but seems to be very easily rooted from cutting.

catawbiense x Michael Waterer. 1931. Hybrid by George Fraser. It seems likely that Mr. Fraser used the variety of *catawbiense* known as *compactum* here as the plants have been rather dwarf and dense in habit. Several of these flowered from deep purplish red to purple and one of the reds that flowers very profusely is being propagated under the tentative name "Camich." q.v.

Catawbiense Album. I do not agree with the classifications that regard this as a clone of the species *catawbiense*. The leaf shape and flower form differ from the typical species and the finer, much less noticeable pubescence on the new growth tend to separate it as a hybrid clone, perhaps the best of the old white Catawbiense hybrids for our area.

Catawbiense Album x Loderi. (Catalode) 1932. A rather straggly lot of plants whose best plant, though it also "straggles," bears large flowers of purest white with no trace of purple or pink blush even in the bud stage. A most unusual character in white flowered rhododendrons. The leaves are very large and lustrous but inevitably injured by bugs and worms—which character is also unusual—in Fortunei hybrids.

1946: That "best plant" is now a selected clone, Catalode. Catalode has given no trouble from winterkilling and may be worth propagating, as its large lustrous leaves attract attention at all seasons. We have been unable to obtain seeds in several attempts to breed hybrids from it.

1955: This is proving a good rhodo and is growing well from both cuttings and grafts which flower freely at an early stage. Customers and visitors admire it and try to buy it. (County of York)

Catawbiense Album. (Glass) 1939. Flowered 1943. Seedlings of a natural white form of the species discovered by the late Powell Glass of Lynchburg, Virginia, all of which have flowered white. Aside from the obvious value of this discovery to the hybridist, this plant has definite value in itself, being a beautiful white in its own right. It should soon be available commercially as it comes true from seed—and seeds have been sown by the thousands. I think this fine variety of *catawbiense* should be botanically named for Mr. Glass by some taxonomist.

Although its affinity to *R. catawbiense* is undoubtedly very close, it possesses longer petioles, leaves approaching oblong in shape, twigs and branches somewhat more slender and the foliage is a lighter shade of green. Beds of small seedlings are easily separable from the type by these differences in appearance. Also coming true from seed—at least when isolated from pollen of the type—it would seem to rate a distinct varietal name.

While coming true from seeds this variety is less vigorous and more difficult to grow by this method than typical *R. catawbiense*.

1955: We have run into trouble with our seedling of this. A number of them flowered purple or lavender this spring and we are at a loss to explain it. These seedlings were started by a nurseryman friend for us whom we do not blame for anything intentional but somewhere along the line they must have gotten mixed with the typical *catawbiense* as all seedlings in this lot seem to be typical species with no white ones whatever. We have withdrawn this item from our list until we get things going right again.

Mrs. Powell Glass. 1952. This hybrid of *decorum* &

Catawbiense Album (Glass) has been named for the widow of the discoverer of this white variety of *catawbiense* used in this mating.
(now "Anne Glass"—Ed.)

Catalgla x Wardii.   1948. 1954: These seedlings—of which there are now 40—6"-18" high, are of almost ideal foliage and plant habit and very attractive. (In ink.) We have no "butter yellow" flowers to boast about from this mating but we do have some very nice plants with lovely dark foliage. The flowers are mostly of a biscuit white with dark throat but one is apple blossom pink. Further matings would seem worthwhile.

Catawbiense Compactum. This variety is indeed distinct and should be very useful in breeding for though it seems to be a form dwarfed by ecological conditions, seedlings grown from collected plants are more compact than the type. The variation in form of these seedlings is interesting as some very dwarf plants with small leaves are obtained while others vary toward the species type. However all the flowers I have seen on Catawbiense compactum are dull purplish color with very slight variation.

1955: Certain clones that I have separated from this variety for their dwarf stature have proven too lacking in vitality. One plant never reached a foot in height, bloomed heavily for a number of years, never produced a viable seed whether open or handcrossed and died for all the world as if it were prematurely aged.

caucasicum s. ponticum s.s. caucasicum. 1926. And several later sowings. Caucasicum does not choose to succeed in our part of the world. Supposedly hardy, it has failed to produce a flower in 24 years of existence—and it barely "exists."

Such hybrids as Boule de Neige and the plant that succeeds in our gardens as Cunninghams White (quite controversially), also our *Jacksonii* are reputed to be hardy with us because of their *caucasicum* genes. But I have never been able here to breed any *hardiness* into any hybrid by their use. True I have a number of crosses of these hybrids that succeed but only when they are mated with something that will in itself succeed also.

As examples, Boule de Neige x *Fortunei* produced a group of seedlings most of which were more tender than either parent and a few "hardy" ones show indications of being on the border line. Boule de Neige x *sutchuenense* seedlings have resulted in only a half dozen hardy plants surviving the test from the 118 planted out in 1942 by my records. And the survivors are scarcely as hardy as the parents.

Jacksonii crossed with Catawbiense hybrids gave us very hardy plants and we find our one plant of Jacksonii entirely satisfactory. So, since Jacksonii is a hybrid of *caucasicum* and *arboreum,* it would seem there must be something of hardiness in our subject somewhere.

Altogether this is a puzzling species and though it and its hybrids would seem to be of much potential value to the hybridist, it has been quite disappointing on the whole. Better luck to the next guy!

Caucasicum apparently succeeds in Britain and hence should grow in the Pacific Northwest, but I never heard of anyone flowering it in the U.S. The late E. H. Wilson wrote me that it "exists here (in the Arnold Arboretum) as a miserable plant but never flowers."

In addition to a reprehensible habit of imparting tenderness to winter cold into its progeny, this species even throws a large percentage of seedlings that possess only stamens and pistil, or if calyx and corolla are present they are but rudimentary. In some crosses as many as 90% of the seedlings that survived to flower have been eliminated from consideration on account of too great an incidence of this mutation.

Such a condition will occur perhaps in any hybrid occasionally, though the only ones we have encountered are in hybrids of our present species *R. brachycarpum* and hybrid we know in America as "Amphion," though it may be properly known as "F. L. Ames." And in every one of these the loss of otherwise fine, shapely plants with one's ideal of foliage and plant habit showing most promisingly, is so disheartening as to approach the maddening.

1954: Finally flowers on *caucasicum* and on the one old, 1926 seedling extant. Three trusses, none of them filled, and hidden down in the very dense foliage of this species they certainly made no show at all.

In 1955 this largest old plant flowered freely all over and since the plant is a fine well-shaped thing with dark green, very rugose rugged foliage it was a pretty subject—once in all these years! For which I am duly grateful.

Chapmanii s. carolinianum. 1948. From the Morris Arboretum. In bud for 1950. Flowered spring 1950. From its first flowering I could call it the prettiest species of the series. Flowers clear rose and the truss containing more florets than the other species I have seen. One plant has endured two winters (two mild winters) in the open but as yet it has had no real test of what it may endure, in the matter of winter cold.

1951: This plant has survived the 1950-51 winter which has been colder than its first two and has damaged many plants.

Obviously I have expressed too good an opinion of the flowers of this species from the first truss I saw on a forced plant. Out in the open they are small and washy in color in my two plants.

Chapmanii x mucronulatum (& Conemaugh?). 1951. A fast growing lot. A few seedlings are in bud for 1954.

1954: The few that have flowered are scarcely worth the trouble of description. At least they can wait.

1956: Flowers later than mucronulatum and with larger paler flowers more nearly pink in color. A rampant grower.

Charles Dickens. Hardiest of the "Old Guard" hybrids and one of their better "reds."

chrysanthum s. ponticum s.s. caucasicum brachycarpum, (niko-montanum). 1932. Hardy, slow-growing and even slower to bloom, we probably have the upright form, niko-montanum, rather than the type. In 17 years, the 100 or more seedlings here have only produced about a half dozen trusses. They are better described cream than yellow in color and both trusses and flowers are small. The tallest of these plants is now about 18″.

At one time I regarded this as possessing potentialities for hybridizing experiments to obtain yellow coloring in a hardy plant. I find the color character almost neutral, little if any better than other cream-colored brachycarpums, the flower size even smaller than that species, the indisposition to bear flowers even more chronic and poorer foliage. It is undeniably dwarf and slow growing and *should* possess a considerably greater margin of hardiness.

1955: This note I should have added several years ago. This item is certainly not typical *R. chrysanthum* ... I am guilty of selling hundreds of these as *R. chrysanthum* before I knew the difference. I only hope my customers like them well enough to forgive me.

1956: I have decided, with much help from Mr. David Leach, that my *chrysanthum* is really the variety of *R. brachycarpum* known as niko-montanum. (File card: one plant flowered, 1940.)

They are variable in habit, some plants being nearly 4′ in height and some not yet 1′ in 23 years. Incredibly slow to flower, about 10% of them have produced a few flowers. The trusses resemble a small brachycarpum and the florets are much like that species but not nearly so many in a truss. The leaves dark green and lustrous, somewhat convex with a heavier indumentum nearly white when young turning to cream or pale buff. The leaves are smaller but the foliage is even more attractive. I have very few hybrids of it from many trials and only that with *R. Fortunei* looks like it will live on.

Conemaugh (racemosum x mucronulatum). 1927. Flowered 1929. Rather small shrub, upright in habit with pink flower blooms with mucronulatum. The leaves are lustrous and remain well on the plants until late winter, when they begin to fall. Very hardy and easy of propagation. Also forces readily almost any time during the winter.

Conemaugh is the name of a clonally propagated variety and seedlings should be sold only as "seedlings of Conemaugh" and not simply under the varietal name. Any other seedling except the original Conemaugh selected for propagation clonally should be given another name.

We have been watching another seedling—second generation—of this hybrid for some time and it seems to be definitely superior to the original selection. As yet it is unnamed but it will *not* be called Conemaugh.

(File card: Grows rather tall for its age and extremely floriferous when its precocious buds escape late frosts. It will flower in January if there are a few days of warm weather ... roots readily from July cuttings.)

Conestoga (carolinianum x racemosum F.P.I. 59717). 1929. Very free flowering small shrubs. Selected seedling named as above. Have better luck propagating it in late years. It may become a commercial variety when better known as it is quite attractive. The coloring is pink, a little better than the average *carolinianum,* and it seeds heavily.

Second-generation seedlings have flowered and most are pretty but nothing to quite take the place of the clone Conestoga, though there is one low spreading one that we are watching and perhaps will propagate. It has borne the tag Mayflower for several years but no cuttings have rooted—1950.

1954-(?) Conestoga sdlg. #1. A chance seedling that we hope may take the place of Conestoga which apparently dies out in 5-10 years both for me and for my customers and friends who have tried it. *I do not know of a single living plant of true Conestoga now.*

Conewago (carolinianum x mucronulatum). 1930. Flowered 1932 and has not missed a season since. These seedlings were much alike but one was selected as possibly the better and given the above clonal name. It is definitely good with flowers larger than either parent and a season all its own compared with our present garden varities. It roots from cuttings with much difficulty and we have been layering with fair success but it is slow.

1950: One branch bent over and covered for two growing seasons resulted in 64 nice plants for lining out. Better, much better, than we have been able to do by any other method.

1955: We still get nowhere trying to propagate this item. It sells like hot cakes when one has them to sell.

1959: We have found that most lepidotes root rather well if taken early—very early—and we have been having reasonable success with Conewago too. [In ink] The twigs and large limbs of Conewago are broken by snow and by accident quite easily. Our old plant was 3/4 destroyed in 1957. The varieties below do not break easily.

Conewago Improved. 1959. A seedling that has better flowers and foliage and a definite improvement in these characters, but it remains to be tested more. Perhaps the best of the Conewago sdlgs.

Conewago Special. 1953. A seedling of Conewago with better colored, larger flowers and a disposition to root rather freely from cuttings. As Conewago is so difficult to reproduce clonally this may supersede it in the trade.

1959: It still remains to be seen if this is as hardy north as Conewago, which customers report hardy in almost unbelievable areas.

Conewago #2. 1930; 1956. A lighter colored flower than the type.

Conewago #3. 1950 (?). A volunteer seedling of #2 with larger and lighter colored flowers.

croceum s. Thomsonii s.s. Souliei. 1932. Have sowed several lots and collectors numbers of this species with little success and have only flowered two seedlings of Rock's No. 24495 and these have more brown and green in their make-up than yellow. All the species tried here of this affiliation are difficult generally and even when brought to the stage of bearing flower buds the buds are hard to winter, even with protection.

I do not know what species will be used to perfect the first yellow flowered rhododendron hardy in the eastern U.S. or what hybridist will mate them, but I feel sure of one thing—he will earn his laurels. (File card: Flower bud in 1939 died though protected. Same 1940. Again in bud 1941.)

Cunningham's White. The true Cunningham's White (*maximum* x *cinnamomeum*) is probably known in this country but we have a Caucasicum-Ponticum hybrid that may have had its origin in this country from imported hybrids that were grafted on it and then suckered up and outgrew the original hybrid. In fact, only a few miles away I knew a plant of that type. It had two colors of flowers—white and red when I first knew it. Now it is all white. I think it is called Cunningham's White by the late E. H. Wilson in *Aristocrats of the Garden,* but I seem to have lost my copy of that. At any rate it has some standing in Eastern nursery lists under that cognomen, and I obtained my original plant so tagged. And, for want of a correct name it has continued under this tag down to the present time.

Whatever it should properly be called it is a very good plant, dense in habit and good foliage and opens its blush fading to white, flowers in the very early spring. It is one of those rhododendrons that opens a few florets in autumn rather regularly and too much of this of course, spoils the trusses for the ensuing season.

1959: There seem to be several strains of this in the trade under the same name; they are very much alike but a very dense type from an Oregon grower is not as hardy as the two types from other sources. But all of them flower early and repeat again in July and August. These flowers come from the buds that should hold until the next spring with the result that it seldom flowers as heavily as it should.

(File card: One rooted cutting from Nearing and one layer from Dr. McFarland.)

dauricum x mucronulatum. 1929. Seem to be no different from *mucronulatum* itself. In fact I do not know which is which.

Davidii s. Davidii s.s. Fortunei. 1932; 1951. 1932: Though reputedly not in cultivation Mr. Magor sent me seeds so labelled and there is yet a plant surviving. It does not grow very well, still I have noticed no winter killing—and no flowers.

This plant was picked out by a borer, and now (fall 1950) seems to be doubtfully alive.

All the *Davidii* subseries are found in Szechuan and Hupeh where such Chinese species as are hardy in the eastern U.S. are mostly found. It might be profitable to give them all a fair trial in the Philadelphia-Baltimore-Washington area.

David Gable (Atrosanguineum x Fortunei). 1959. (Also known under the caption Pink #1.) Among the pinks of our own origination and such commercial varieties we have been able to grow here, David Gable is superlative. It is a deep pink and with its large flowers, fine foliage, and sturdy growth would perhaps be compared with Cynthia to which it will be found superior in every character except that those who require a pointed, classic type truss, might find it wanting. The truss is full and larger than that of Cynthia but the top is rounded, not flat but not with the peak which we admire in Cynthia. It is much hardier than that variety. In fact we have yet to see the slightest injury of any kind from frost—or anything else for that matter. It does not grow as tall and open as Cynthia and has a wider, more spreading habit, though quite a vigorous grower. It seems also to inherit the *Fortunei* resistance to pests and disease.

Out of flower the foliage is superb and visitors occasionally remark that they would be willing to grow it for the foliage alone if it never flowered.

Decatros (decorum x Atrosanguineum. 1932. This hybrid flowered early and many seedlings bore very good flowers. As a group they were none too bud hardy and some plants have been hurt. Several of the hardier and better flowered were saved and propagated to some extent. One a white with ruffled florets over 4″ in diameter. This whole lot seemed to develop an allergy towards growing and have aged prematurely, therefore we are doing very little with them at present. Reports from arboretums where some of these were planted report the same difficulty.

In this group of seedlings, the name Decatros (an

abbreviation of the first syllables of the two parents of the hybrid) seemed to stick to all seedlings, although it was not so intended. A few forms have been clonally propagated, as Decatros White, Decatros Pink No. 1 & No. 2, etc., but no plant of this group has been given a distinct clonal name, i.e., a name for possible commercial use. From all present indications I do not believe anything in this lot will be hardy enough to be introduced to the trade here, even though some bear beautiful flowers.

1952: There remain just a plant or two of the original seedlings that grow well and one of these has nice pink flowers. We have propagated just a few of them. In comparison to our old *catawbiense* hybrid pinks, it is superior in flower and of equally good foliage and plant habit. But we have several pinks of other types that outclass it and it may be abandoned. It is a good rhododendron.

We can think of one good use of the prematurely aged plants of this hybrid with their fine, almost huge trusses. Those who go in for plant antiques after the style of the picturesque Japanese dwarf culture should have little trouble keeping these in scale and conformity.

Decatros, best white, clone. 1957. This clone selected a few years back is being sparingly propagated for trial. It is a seedling with the premature aging complex and the plants may become dwarfs, though newly rooting cuttings seem to start off with normal rate of growth.

decorum s. & s.s. Fortunei. 1924. Flowered 1929. A tender species in most forms but some collector's numbers are more nearly hardy. However, one and all lose their flower buds on occasion. The large white or pale blush seven-lobed florets are shaded with yellow in the throat of most forms and no rhododendron species that has flowered here is more deliciously fragrant. In all, 14 seed and collector's numbers of this species have been sown here. In the trade—or at least in the seed trade—this is much confused with Fortunei and both species together with what appear to be hybrids between them have been grown under the *decorum* label here.

In spite of all this, *R. decorum* occurs in nature in that section of China where our hardier species are wont to grow and a hardy type *should* be found. If we could rule out its tender streak it would constitute a real asset.

Decorum. Forrest 30887. 1936. Of all the forms of *decorum* tried here, this has most nearly pure white flowers. It does not winter a bud in the open but, like most forms of this species, it will flower two or three years from seed. Oddly, plants of this number seem hardier than most decorums but the flower buds lose out.

Decorum (lath house.) Source and time of acquisition unknown. This decorum has attained a greater height and borne larger flowers than any other of the hundreds of this species that have been planted out and of which I doubt if a half dozen now exist. Protected by a lath house for years but now still standing unproteced in its ruins, it bears beautiful trusses of huge flat flowers in seasons when the buds escape injury but the plant is one of the most gaunt and ungainly looking rhododendrons imaginable. But the leaf, flower—and label—say *decorum*.

decorum x Griersonianum x America. 1941. Flowered 1951 with 4″ florets of pale cream shaded salmon. Plant very vigorous in growth and spreading in habit. The plant has been hardy out for 5-6 years, but we will watch the buds with bated breath.

1953: Two seedlings flowering this season are both tops. One is a white with flowers like a Madonna lily on a long upright flower stem that helps its lilylike appearance, the whole truss being about 9″ high and 7″ wide or a little more. About 15 florets in a truss. There is not a suggestion of the pink purple or red shadings even in the buds, which are greenish white with yellow shadings opening into a pure white lily-shaped floret with yellow throat. The general appearance is so much like a many flowered truss of lilium candidum that the only name we can seem to think of for it is **The Madonna.**

Donald Hardgrove of Merrick, L.I., reports also a white flowered seedling of great beauty from this same lot of seeds, but we must compare them before we write more.

diaprepes. 1952. Three small plants from Nearing.

1957: The above are growing nicely, one outdoor, the other is taken in a cool cellar during the winter. Now have five more small plants from Roland de Wilde that seem to have smaller leaves than the Nearing type.

1959: One seedling lost its buds but no damage to the plant in '58. Other seedlings are budded for 1960.

decorum x Griffithianum x Kettledrum. 1944. From Nearing. Had a very fine flowered seedling in 1951. The seedling mentioned has flowered each season and we still consider it a fine thing though its flowers have never again reached the size of its first blooming. Several others of this cross have flowered—not so good as this first one—and we still have a number to prove themselves. This seedling is now the clone named Gretchen. Flowers regularly and heavily.

dichroanthum s. neriiflorum s.s. sanguineum. 1930. Lost. Apparently very difficult in our climate.

dichroanthum x haematodes. 1932. This I probably wanted to flower as much as any thing I ever had but it refused and is now lost. (File card: From Magor. Slow but fairly hardy.)

discolor s. & s.s. Fortunei. 1924. When we finally got the true species, it proved to be a very hardy, dependable rhododendron. Three small plants from the Arnold Arboretum under the date and label proved true, but many, many plants raised from seeds from commercial and botanic sources proved untrue. Perhaps no mistake of the source personnel but rather from the facility with which plants of this genus "take" foreign pollen and produce hybrid offspring when single plants of a collection are the source of the seeds.

Experiments and experiences here to date all tend to the opinion that this species is one of high value to rhododendron breeders in our part of the world. Its color genes posses no objectionable shades, it is hardy enough in itself, though we doubt if it has any great margin of hardiness, it is late flowering and never caught by late spring freezes, a very valuable character in many sections of the eastern U.S. It crosses with almost any other broad leaf species and the resulting seedlings are generally healthy and free growing. The one possible drawback is that its seedlings are prone to be slow coming into flower, but I know of no other situation of the rhododendron hybridist where patience proves more of a virtue.

There seem to be several forms of *R. discolor*, some of which I have little experience with, others with which I have had my surfeit.

To consider the last first, the first "discolor" plants I raised were all untrue to name. I sold a lot of them quite innocently, believing them to be true—I am still hearing evil things of them.

The *discolor* from the Arnold Arboretum I regard as typical and I use it in practically all my crossing. Seedlings of this type come true and we offer this type for sale as *discolor* on our lists.

Then we have a form of *discolor* grown from seeds from the late Lionel de Rothschild. This lot varies much more than our "standard" A.A. type. One plant has flower buds as large as chicken eggs but the flowers were no larger than our typical pigeon-egg size buds. It is too early, however, to make any comprehensive appraisement, since only a small percentage have flowered so far.

Personally, I consider *discolor* and *auriculatum* very closely related. This type from Rothschild reminds one somewhat more of *auriculatum* than the Arnold Arboretum type.

discolor x Caroline. Disca (one seedling) 1938. With many unflowered seedlings still to prove themselves, several of these have produced excellent flowers. The one seedling called Disca has the largest flowers I have yet seen on an outdoor rhododendron. We have great hopes for it.

Double Flowered White. 1954. This was first noted in 1951 or '52. It is a seedling of the *catawbiense x Fortunei* (C-11 clone) and *Smirnowii x Fortunei* (clone Katherine Dalton). A fine foliaged, healthy looking plant, with large double white flowers. However, it loses so many buds in winter (or perhaps from premature growth in fall, from its *Smirnowii* parent) that only an occasional floret has survived to bloom. So far it has not produced pollen to fertilize another rhododendron (I tried it on the preceding entry) neither has it produced a viable seed from other pollen. As with this whole mating it is *not* free flowering.

Essex Scarlet. 1932. With a little care to plant it in a site protected from high winter winds, this hybrid succeeds very well indeed. It has been opening its intense scarlet flowers regularly since 1936. The plant is inclined to grow tall and sparse and needs correction. No other red flowered hybrid I have used in my hybridizing experiments has so consistently bred its red coloring into its offspring as this.

For some reason this hybrid, given one star in the English ratings, is not commonly offered. It may be difficult to propagate, which often constitutes the limiting factor when a number which is always in demand is not generally listed.

1954: The flowers of a rhododendron, no matter how desirable, last but a week or two—seldom two—and all the rest of the year we see only the plant. A well-grown plant of Essex Scarlet is hard to come by or to grow, and one should bear this in mind when planting in its permanent site. Its flowers rate so high among our proven hardy reds that it is a must—if obtainable.

1959: Essex Scarlet apparently imparts its red hues to its hybrids more readily than most sorts; even when the colors are pink or rose, there are spottings or shadings resulting in a finesse that pleases in an unusual percentage of the seedlings. We are just beginning to reap results in many of our matings. To be sure, one gets somewhat of the grapevine growing habit of Essex Scarlet, but the trusses are generally well filled and well shaped, and the natural plant habit can always be altered somewhat by proper pruning.

(File card: Rather tender but worth protection, this plant has broken at the graft union and is no more. From Ostbo: this flowered here 1936 and is the most brilliant scarlet I have yet seen. Surpassed by At-ronerum? and *floccigerum*. Flowered in lath house all unhurt in 1940 and 1941.)

Essex Scarlet x America (Three Star). 1949. An Essex Scarlet hybrid with very deep red flowers that last two to three weeks in good condition. Seems to be quite worth an attempt to propagate. Free flowering.

1953: We like this hybrid more each season. (See under three star.)

floccigerum s. & s.s. neriiflorum. 1930. About 1943. Rock No. 18469. From its reputation in the books I never figured much of value would come from this species, but it has given me a few most promising hybrids. Only wish that while it was with me I had used it more.

The only plant I protected until it flowered in 1936 had orange scarlet flowers shaped much like Campsis *radicans* and about the same size. It was a very straggly grower, when it flowered, however, it redeemed itself. Its hybrids with Atrosanguineum and *smirnowii* are both fairly hardy, with large flowers and good color in all seedlings flowered.

It seems extremely difficult to obtain hybrid or open pollinated seeds that will germinate from my hybrids of this species.

(File card: Flowered 1936—flowered until 1940. Very tender. Got killed back badly but apparently on the mend again 1942.)

Fortunei s. & s.s. Fortunei. 1926. Definitely hardy through our eastern winters, this species puts forth its new growth in time for occasional injury from late spring frosts. Planted on an open woodland slope, it is not yet injured and flowers regularly. While it enjoys plenty of water, through the spring growing season at least, it seems able to endure drought better than most exotic species. Its very pale blush to nearly white flowers are deliciously fragrant and often between 4"-5" in diameter.

1959: Both for itself and its values in hybridizing, probably the most valuable of the exotic species for our area.

Fortunei Cream x 18139 R. 1960. We now have hundreds of seedlings coming along of this mating. Three plants of the older generation have flowered in very pretty apricot shades. Present indications are that it will be a worthwhile hybrid.

Fortunei hybrid. (Sir James) 1936. From Henry Hicks. This plant given me by Henry Hicks has grown into a most lovely rhododendron and we are trying to propagate it. It is a wide spreading plant being now about 7'-8' wide and 3'-4' in height; the ends of the branches touch the ground on all sides. The leaves are large and lustrous, plenteously borne, and the flowers are pink, medium in size, in a truss more like *catawbiense* than *Fortunei,* except that both florets and truss are larger than those of Catawbiense.

Our son, James, selected this as his favorite plant as a boy and we forthwith named it Sir James.

Gable's Pink #1. 1940. A seedling of Atrosanguineum x *Fortunei,* the best one to date. Proving a superlative number.

1953: I regard this one of the finest things produced here so far. The flowers are medium large, of good color, not as deep pink as Cynthia but in large, well-shaped trusses. Its fine plant habit and foliage make it a superb evergreen at all times. We are doing our best to build up a stock of this and the following but it seems slow.

1959: Now named David Gable. We consider this as probably our best hybrid.

Gable's Pink #2. A selected seedling of Caroline x *discolor.* Lighter colored than #1. A very healthy grower and flowers last well.

1953: A tall, rather open grower of symetrical tree form habit, quite different from the #1 above but good where one wants a tree. Its 3-1/2"-4" florets are borne in large trusses and, as noted above, they last well in good condition. Easy to propagate.

Gable's Pink #3. Selected in 1952. This is a seedling of *Catawbiense* x *discolor.* It seemed there just had to be a clone of this happy, healthy lot of youngsters selected to propagate, and this is it, though it was really difficult to determine which was best in color and foliage.

Goldsworth Yellow. 1934. For sixteen years this has opened its apricot buds into paling yellow blossoms with commendable regularity, and there would seem to be no reason why it should not be recommended for general culture, but as it has been reported tender by some authorities I have been loath to press the point. However, its color is better than any other broadleaf yellow we can grow, it is rated three stars by the British Association and I would not want to be without it. In hybridization it often refuses to set seed, while in other seasons they are produced plentifully so don't give up too soon.

1950: Many nurserymen are stocking up on this variety now and it may soon be well known in our gardens.

(File card: Flowered 1935. Attempted hybridization and cuttings.)

Gretchen. 1947. A fine pink hybrid from Nearing's seed. (*decorum x Griffithianum* x Kettledrum is the hybrid of which this is a seedling).

Griersonianum s. auriculatum. 1929. Tender to be sure, but I try to keep it for the geranium scarlet flowers, for use in breeding. It is one rhododendron which seems to endure summer heat with impunity. This species is not only tender—it is d--- tender! In order to flower it, the buds must be protected from all semblance of frost. First-generation hybrids are fairly frost-resistant, hence there is hope of infusing its superlative red tints into hardy strains.

haematodes s. neriiflorum s.s. haematodes. 1930. It has always been my contention that this species will prove one of the more valuable for the breeding of dwarf, hardy reds of better color than those now generally obtainable. In itself it will never be a successful garden plant in our part of the world. Have made several later sowings than this but all fail to survive (1950). The late E. J. P. Magor wrote me that his plant of *R. haematodes* "is twelve years old, has flowered for seven years and is not yet a foot high," and most of my hybrids are from pollen of this plant.

haematodes A.A. 1929?. Two plants received from the Arnold Arboretum as *R. haematodes* have flowered here. Evidently hybrids of this species, they bore beautiful red flowers of great substance and clarity of color. On one of these plants the calyx was corolloid (this is the Conewingo of the British Assn. Year Book), which is an example of giving a name to a plant variety before it is proven as it did not prove hardy here and is now probably extinct except for a single unhealthy looking cutting. Neither plant was fully hardy though they endured a few winters outside with injury. In our records we have endeavored to use the above name with A. A. in all crosses in which it was used. (q.v.)

hemitrichotum s. scabrifolium. 1934. From Nearing. A friendly, thrifty little species that seems to love to grow and flower. In general appearance it much resembles *racemosum* but is placed in a different series by those who should know. It is not as hardy as that species and flowers later. It may now be lost as sorts that are not hardy have a way of doing.

Henrietta Sargent x discolor. 1939. Seedlings have splendid foliage but formed its first flower bud in fall 1949.

Hexe. 1926. This old greenhouse azalea has managed to exist outdoors for 24 years. It has been frozen back, perhaps oftener than not, and had its share of other mishaps, but it still hangs on and flowers more or less according to its fluctuating condition. It has proven a fertile source of hardy red hybrids.

Houlstonii. 1936. Apparently hardy to winter cold but makes its new growth far, far too early; invariably cut by frost in spring when nothing else is advanced enough to be hurt. Sorts with this failing seldom flower as no flower buds are formed on second-growth wood for the next season.

In bud 1952. This bud wintered but only by wrapping the whole limb in a huge burlap did I save one huge 5″ floret from the spring frosts. This floret produced the largest seed capsule this grower has seen on a rhododendron.

Houlstonii Fort. s. & s.s. 1956. The plants were finally all left unprotected to see if they could take care of themselves. The plant that has come through this survival of the fittest test better than the others is about 5′ high and wider than high. It produces flower buds freely; they winter but only now and then escape spring frost well enough to make any show. When it succeeds in this it is quite a lovely species. Another inhibition to its flowering is the freezing back of the new growth—sometimes twice in one spring season. It breaks out new growth well enough but this second—sometimes third—growth does not form flower buds the first season. (File card: 1936 date for seeding)

So, while growable and interesting, and lovely at times, it can scarcely be termed dependable or satisfactory for the garden.

Houlstonii x vernicosum Aff. 18139 Rock. 1955. The young seedlings produce a high percentage of plants with highly colored new growth. Some with bright bronze red leaves approach the spectacular and may be worth growing for this feature—if the flowers are not too poor, for we have yet to see one flower.

1960: Had some good apricot flowers, very good.

horaeum s. neriiflorum s.s. sanguineum. 1934; 1944. Never flowered. Just another incorrigible alpine.

impeditum s. lapponicum. 1930-1940. Like most of its *lapponicum* series, it thrives for a while then passes out. Hot summer weather seems to be the limiting factor again. One of the prettiest of the series.

Ignatius Sargent. 1954. One of the poorer of the old Catawbiense hybrid reds. But I still grow a few. One reason is for the unique raspberry jam fragrance of its flowers, I have not noticed this in any other rhodo.

indicum (Sweet). The azalea indica of Linnaeus is better known in our garden as azalea macrantha. This species and none of its varieties have proven hardy but some of its hybrids have great value in that its habit of flowering late is transmitted to them in part and they escape spring frosts more often than the earlier types.

indicum x (Kaempferi x poukhanense.) 1928. Flowered 1931. Resulted in a race of both single and double flowered sorts (truly double, not hose-in-hose) which have in some cases fifteen corolloid stamens inside the original five petals. Two selections are named Louise Gable and Maryann. (File card. There are shades of flame, rose, pink, salmon, and lavender but no true reds among this group.)

Isabel. 1926. *R. obtusum* Hexe x *R. obtusum* Pink Pearl. This has proven too tender outdoors, as are both its parents. It is being grown by the thousands in local greenhouses for forcing and so merits a name and description. The foliage is very bright green and lustrous and well retained under glass. Plant habit is good and dense and produces its clear apricot rose hose-in-hose flowers in great abundance. *Named in memory of our little Isabel.*

Jacksonii sdlgs. 1926. Grown from seeds from the late Dr. C. S. Sargent. As usual, these seedlings were given the "survival of the fittest" test for hardiness; those that did not flower nicely have been discarded. The survivor bears flowers exactly the shade of Cynthia and the markings are alike, though they are much smaller. The plant, however, grows very slowly compared with Cynthia's irrepressible vigor, and the leaves also are smaller. It should prove a good thing.

   . . . Confusion or error exists in the nomenclature here. These seeds came labelled "Venustum," with *Jacksonii* in parenthesis as a synonym.

   The *British Association Yearbook* lists *venustum* as a variety of Nobleanum, which is a name given to a group of hybrids of *caucasicum* and *arboreum* & NOT a clonal name.

   The Arnold Arboretum bulletin names *venustum (Jacksonii)* as a hybrid of caucasicum and arboreum.

   The *Yearbook* above lists *Jacksonii* as a hybrid of Nobleanum and *caucasicum*.

   In the end, there is no strain in any of the above except *arboreum* and caucasicum (both of which, I might add, have proven tender here and it is remarkable that some seedlings are hardy as any Catawbiense hybrid!).

   In all my records the name *Jacksonii* has been used, perhaps because it seems to be better known on our side of the water. I have written the above in the hope it may lessen rather than add to the confusion of names. I still so *hope.*

   Several lots of second generation seedlings have been grown from our Jacksonii, and from our experience here I would be led to recommend that the hybridist seeking plants of low stature, good-sized flowers in well-shaped trusses, with deep pink to red coloring could do well to use this strain in introducing caucasicum blood rather than such hybrids as Boule de Neige, Cunningham's White (American version), Cunningham's Sulphur, or Caucasicum Stramineum, all of which have produced nearly all tender offspring of poor color. To be sure there are a few exceptions, but the trend of further experiments here will be along the lines recommended above.

   (File card: Flowered 1939.)

Jacksonii #5. 1948. At least two weeks earlier than any of the above, flowering with or a little in advance of *R. mucronulatum.* It seldom has been caught by late frosts. A very lovely variety. We will note here something that may be purely accidental but so far

apparently just as "purely" inexplicable, i.e., the very earliest sorts to open their flowers are not so frequently frozen as these second early types that follow by two weeks or thereabouts!

Jacksonii #6. 1950. The gem of them all flowering for the first time this season with pure cherry red blossoms very close to Madame de Bruin in color, but with plant habit and foliage far superior to that variety, whose everyday dress is unbecoming. Our new seedling has lustrous rugose, almost bullate leaves, slightly convex and the low, spreading plant is abundantly furnished with them. In fact we know of no red flowered rhododendron, growable in our area with anything near as attractive a plant. The plant stood in an open bed, unprotected for some six to eight years so it is obviously fairly hardy though we know only too well that calamity may yet overtake it. It is the top red of the Gable nursery at the moment.

   1954: This selection (which I would rather propagate commercially than any other of my hybrids) is proving exceedingly difficult so far along that line. In fact, at the end of 1954 I have only one graft and the original seedling. Perhaps it needs to be layered but it just must be propagated somehow.

James B. Gable #1. 1954. This name was given to an azalea raised from seed collected in Japan during the late war by my son, James B. Gable. A large group of seedlings were started but only a few survived a plague of crickets that, unnoticed, ate off the tiny seedlings. Several were raised to flowering. We liked this one and started propagation but it has proven too tender for our climate and probably all are killed now. From the great variation among the few seedlings flowered I think they were seeds from a hybrid group.

japonicum x calendulaceum. 1928. Flowered 1934. Bright scarlet red to *white!* Imagine a *white* flowered seedling from a cross of such brightly colored species. These seedlings were in demand from customers and sold quickly down to a few that we had marked to save, a red, a white, and a yellow—all absolutely sterile.

japonicum x luteum. 1929. My cross of this resulted in seedling without cotyledons! To be sure, they never developed though they lived for months. Have long intended to make the same cross again and see if the same thing happens.

Kaempferi. 1926. So well known that a description is superfluous but I might add just a cultural note to say that this species is less hardy than *poukhanense* in bud and that hybrids showing much influence of *Kaempferi* are often as difficult to root from cuttings as the species.

   Much use has been made of this species in producing new hardy varieties but observations of some of these hybrid groups, which we are led to believe are *Kaempferi* crosses, show very little exterior evidence of its use.

Kaempferi x Maxwell. 1930. Very vigorous seedlings with large flowers of pink to red shades generally suffused with salmon. Like Maxwell they are somewhat bud-tender but generally winter fairly well. I much suspicion that the No. 45G or Iroquois is of this lineage, after some years of confusion concerning its parentage. It is excellent, with large salmon red flowers and good plant habit but loses so many flower buds that we are not presently propagating it. The original seedling, now on our lawn, flowers regularly, protected somewhat by the house and neighboring shrubs. Another seedling with smaller flowers of much the same coloring, H-2-G, has been propagated to some extent. It is much hardier than Iroquois, flowering dependably in a very exposed situation, and grows more upright than that variety.

Kaempferi x poukhanense. 1929. This cross is the foundation of most of the Gable hybrids now known on the market, though practically all of them are the result of further matings. The first generation were some 95% lavender or mauve, just a few with shades of pink and rose. All were vigorous growing things of great hardiness. Old Faithful and Big Joe are first-generation selections, and 114G and 115G, second-generation finds. All root dubiously from cuttings which much retards their general introduction. They should be very hardy sorts for northern sections.

Kaempferi x obtusum var. Yayegiri. 1929. The fine lot of first-generation seedlings and the good things that have been bred from them still make me think that some supernatural influence must have given me the happy thought. Yayegiri being hopelessly tender here and of much the same color tints as *Kaempferi* would seem to inhibit much of value resulting. Chinook and Mary Dalton are named selections but so many nearly identical seedlings had to be discarded that I often wonder if I did the best possible. After these years of observation I rather prefer Mary Dalton of these two. They are so alike that there is no use growing both. (File card: Yayegiri. Flowers 1931. Hose-in-hose flowers of intense flame color occur in some seedlings. 11G and 111G are the best two seedlings so far.)

Katherine Dalton. 1934. This named selection of the *smirnowii* x *Fortunei* hybrid was the largest flowered rhododendron I had seen at the time of its first flowering. 1939. It would still be good enough if we could find a way to propagate it profitably, and if it were a little more bud-hardy. Perhaps we will drop it, though I wish some grower in a slightly milder clime would adopt it. (File card: Flowering with R. *carolinianum*.)

Keiskei. 1932. One of the very few yellow evergreen rhododendrons we can grow, this plant becomes of increasing interest and beauty as the plants increase in size. Plants 6'-8' in height covered with their pale yellow flowers in very early spring make a real show. As with all very early sorts, one must chance their losing buds from late frost.

The Cardinal (name tentative), now **Kentucky Cardinal.** 1948. A clonal selection whose parentage is only known as Essex Scarlet on my tags. It is cardinal red in flower color, the leaves are dark green and more plenteously borne than on most of our common red hybrids. The only fault detected so far is a tendency for the edge of the corolla to wither before the rest of the flower fades, but its general appearance and brilliance of color are very striking.

I believe that The Cardinal is a seedling of the Essex Scarlet x *brachycarpum* cross.

1952: This is a good rhododendron. It holds many dark leaves over the winter on a good-looking plant and its buds have yet to lose a floret from winter cold. When propagating material is cut, it is slow to break new growth. This may retard its introduction to the trade, but it is still a good rhododendron.

1956: The name of this clone must be changed, I have named it Kentucky Cardinal in deference to an English rhododendron previously named Cardinal.

Lady Grey Edgerton. 1956. 1959: This old hybrid, given one star by the English, does not develop much character to appreciate until it has reached a considerable size. It is quite hardy, tall growing, and pretty in flower, but to us its most unusual trait is its resistance to hot weather and summer drought. When the whole planting is wilted and looking like it is on its way out, Lady Grey is as crisp and fresh as if on an April morning after an evening shower. Why?

Lady Alice Fitzwilliam. 1932. Very tender; sent all remaining plants to friends in California where I hope they prosper.

Lady Mitford x Fortunei (Ladifor). 1932. This hybrid from Nearing produced one of the loveliest rhododendrons that has flowered here. The deep pink flowers, somewhat flushed with yellow in the throat are bright and of clear color, trusses are unusually well formed and the fragrance is delightful. The plant grows well, bears dark lustrous foliage, and it easily rooted from leaf cuttings ... so my 1946 notes tell us. Flowered 1939. (File card: 3"-4" in diameter.)

Since that time the original plant was moved and in the process partly broken at the base, losing most of its root system. It had a hard time of it but is coming back nicely now. As to hardiness there is no record of any injury from cold in eighteen years.

lapponicum. The type species collected from the summit of Mt. Washington grows prostrate but plants grown from seed collected by Mrs. Norman Henry in northern British Columbia are quite upright in habit. The true species will never become popular in gardens as it is too difficult, but its hardiness may prove of value in hybridization. The eastern form has flowered here but the B.C. form is apparently slower. All this species is lost. 1950.

longuesquamatum s. barbatum ss. malculiferum. 1930. Flowering in 1940 and each season since, this is one of the few species from West China that can be grown satisfactorily in the open. In addition, it is quite attractive and worthwhile. The stems are thick and heavy, the leaves dark green and substantial, and the pink flowers are marked with a showy crimson blotch in the center producing a rich orchid effect. We thank the collector who sent us this "different" rhododendron. It rates four stars in our collection.

Longuesquamatum Hybrids. 1941. We have tried a number of crossings without much success. A plant or two of several matings exist and we just group them here until something happens—or does not happen.

Loder's White. 1949. Perished in a cold frame, winter 1953.

macrophyllum. 1955. This controversial species from the northwestern U.S. lived only one year. I do not think it was winter-killed.

1959: A plant of R. californicum, one of a lot grown from seeds, lived here for 30 years and is still alive. However, it is obviously not too happy.

macrosepalum. 1931. Often listed as R. linearfolium var. macrosepalum and scarcely hardy here but is worth a place in collections for its unique appearance with its long sepals and hairy leaves. Also its fragrance is incomparable, it resembles nothing else we know of.

Macrosepalum hybrids. 1937. Flowered 1940. Crossed with various hose-in-hose varieties of the obtusum group with the idea that the long conspicuous sepals of macrosepalum might produce rather larger hose, or corolloid calyces, than usual. This brainstorm proved correct and one number F-4-G is being propagated under the name Fuchsia on account of the heavy, partially pendant flowers. This one attempt would suggest that some azaleas of a noticeably different habit might be developed by the use of this species. It is none too hardy and has lavender flowers—two obstacles to be overcome. Carries only a mite of the wonderful fragrance of macrosepalum.

(File card: R. macrosepalum x 11G 1937. In flower bud for 1940.)

Madonna. 1953. White Madonna lily-like florets on a long rachis that prompted nearly all who saw it to exclaim, "Why, that looks like a lily," gave this its name. This is more fully described under *decorum* x *Griersonianum* x America, of which cross it is a seedling.

Makinoi. 1940. Flowered 1946. It seems to me the most growable of that group of species from Japan which center around *R. Metternichii* and, if well known, to become of value as a garden plant. It is dwarf and slow growing, with very long narrow leaves of an attractive color and contrasting indumentum. The flowers are pale pink, born in large trusses for a small plant and many flowered (as many as 30 florets in a truss). In general appearance there is some resemblance to *R. adenopodum,* i.e., the narrow leaves, their indumentum, flower shape and color, and the shape of the trusses. *Makinoi,* however, has more florets in the truss and is much more dwarf and slow growing. I have crossed the two species with no results so far but seedlings—a very interesting looking lot of "kids." *Makinoi* makes its growth late, covered with a soft white indumentum when new. *Should* be an excellent parent of low, slow growing type hybrids?

1940: We have raised many seedlings of this species in these 20 years, and find they vary extremely in growth. Also, all that have flowered have done so in May, and R. makinoi should flower in Aug.-Sept. I had sold hundreds of these before I caught up with this error. Perhaps our strain is closer to R. degronianum, but the foliage is considerably more narrow than that species. In the "dwarfer" types of seedling, the foliage is recurved and revolute to near cylindrical. In fact, this is R. makinoi in all but the time of growth and flower. We have flowered many hybrid seedlings of this without getting one that's worthwhile.

Maximum Hybrid #5. (now named George Fraser) 1931 (?). 1955: It seems time to describe this unusual and perhaps worthwhile hybrid. From the same source and probably of the same—but unknown—parentage as Maxie above. This is now the tallest rhododendron plant on the Gable acres. Obviously, the seeds from which these two hybrids were grown contained a lot of plain maximum and some 10-20% of hybrid seeds. As they came from George Fraser of Ucelelet, B.C. (on Vancouver Island) and as I had nothing to do with the crossing, care or gathering of these seeds, I will not attempt to form conjectures as to the cause of this.

But some half dozen years ago in a thicket of 10'-12' *maximum,* I noticed a fine pink truss of flowers. When I dug my way into it I found what is undoubtedly a hybrid plant, and since it resembles maximum so much that its hybridity had not been suspected previously, it is undoubtedly too much a Maximum hybrid. Since the flower was so fine I immediately cut, dug, and tore all plants and branches of *maximum* away that were touching or close to this plant, since when it has developed amazingly.

In spite of its height, it is of what is ordinarily termed the "weeping" habit. All its branches except the top leaders drop sharply downwards along the stem—so much so that all the branches from a height of several feet are prostrate on the ground, forming a circle perhaps 18' in diameter (we covered all these for layers this summer). Now it is flowering much more freely and it promises to be a nice late pink of very hardy nature. It will require *room* and will be a plant to cover up and blank out those "huge bare places." Outside of a few natural layers we have taken, there has been no propagation.

maximum x californicum. 1930. From Fraser. Flowers nicely but is scarcely good enough to carry any further. It has excellent foliage and rather small mauve flowers profusely borne but opening late. Plant habit too is very good.

maximum x discolor. 1934. From Nearing who somewhat suspicioned whether the form of discolor used was altogether true to name or possibly a hybrid. Later I made the same cross using my own plant of discolor and got a group with narrower leaves and smaller flowers but not much different. The result, speaking collectively, of all seedlings that have flowered is white flowers larger than those of *maximum,* a plant that more resembles *maximum* than *discolor*, possibly better foliage than either parent, on a large growing but well furnished plant; so far have not noted a plant sufficiently free flowering to commend it on that score.

maximum x discolor x discolor. 1941. There are now two good size plants so labelled that flower regularly and profusely. From every indication that I can find, this lot must have become mislabelled. The plants resemble a slightly glorified maximum and no more, so I much suspect that the tag should read: (*maximum x discolor*) x *maximum*?

maximum x haematodes. 1935. Flowered 1942, a few seedlings have yet to flower. An unusually variable lot of seedling for a first-generation interspecific hybrid, which would seem to indicate that R. *haematodes* must be somewhat variable in character. The pollen of *haematodes* used came from Magor and hence presumably true and not the A.A. hybrid. (See *haematodes* A.A.) Most of the seedlings have salmon pink flowers, not much larger than those of *maximum* but varying considerably in both size and shading. There is a tendency to a small fleshy calyx in some indicating *haematodes* influence. The plants grow much more slowly than *maximum,* though some grow three or four times as fast as the more dwarf ones.

The best seedling to flower so far has rather small leaves and flowers of salmon pink with red shadings; it blooms very profusely every season.

One plant with coppery red new growth that is quite distinctive has yet to flower, the seedling with the largest leaves, dark green and rugose, has its first flower buds—and lots of them—for spring of 1950, fifteen years from the sowing of the seeds: Spring 1950. The best plant of this hybrid to flower here is definitely the one last mentioned above. Flowers of good size, opening salmon red in the bud, fading to a yellowish salmon pink. We also had a graft of one of these seedlings, on *maximum* stock, that seems to be a tetraploid form with leaf and flower size treble that of the scion plant. It flowered once.

1952, the plant with copper red new growth opened *yellow* flowers!

1959: My description of this above should be edited but will just name here the clones we are propagating sparingly.

Maxhaem Yellow: Form with the striking bronze new growth and yellow flowers with pink stripes.

Maxhaem #7 (or Maxhaem Salmon): A medium growing sort with salmon pink flowers.

Maxhaem #10: Striking rugose leaves and red flowers of good size of deep red shade. A good garden type that presents a contrast to the ordinary types.

maximum x haematodes (yellow flowered). 1935. As stated in the previous entry, the seedling that had such prominent bronze red coloring in the new growth (and was set aside to be saved for that character alone) has flowered in pale yellow for 3 seasons now (1953). It is a good thing—though one could wish for larger flowers. We do not have, or know of any rhododendrons with better foliage or plant habit. We regard it as an A1 rhododendron with any color flower and since it is an addition to our scarce hardy yellows it is superlative.

maximum x minus. 1925; 1932. Of about 200 seedlings, one lived until 1932. It had attained nearly 1' in height and some half dozen leaves and represented the maximum stature of any seedling.

micranthum s. micranthum. 1927. Hardy and reliable, also attractive when well placed but difficult to sell as rhododendron. Posed as an evergreen spirea species, it might have a future. The minute white florets seem to have deterred all would-be hybridists to date.

minus. 1927. The original plant of *minus* is now perhaps the largest plant of rhododendron on the place—in spite of its name—some 12' high and 15'—18' in diameter. Not too showy but nice to have around. Still growing apace.

minus x carolinianum. Intermediate between the parents in all characters, this hybrid first made by Dr. Clement G. Bowers may be of use in very cold climate to carry the season of flowering through. Here it suffers by opening at the height of the season when too many showy sorts surpass it. It should be good to cross with the more tender lepidotes to get some variation without loss of hardiness.

Mrs. C. S. Sargent x discolor. 1938. Fine looking plants but I am getting tired looking them over for flower buds...

Mucronulatum Pink XXXX. 1952. This seedling of *mucronulatum* has deeper and perhaps clearer pink colored flowers than our Mucronulatum Rose, but the appearance of the plant leads me to sometimes doubt if it is a true *mucronulatum* seedling or if a *chance hybrid* may have occurred. The color is good, and the first dozen or so of rooted cuttings look very nice.

1955: This is growing in our esteem with every season. We are doing all we can towards its propagation. It is now named R. Pioneer, q.v.

mucronulatum s. dauricum. 1929. One of the hardiest of rhododendrons, this species loses its buds because it will try to flower whenever there are a few days of warm weather in winter. This species has been an asset in hybridizing since it seems to be able to transmit its hardy traits to its progeny regularly. It may—or may not—be worthwhile to call attention to the fact that this is a true rhododendron of the lepidote section and belongs with *carolinianum*, *minus*, *racemosum*, and the like and is not a species of the azalea section though often so listed. With those who would call the azalea section of the rhododendron genus a genus of its own I have no serious quarrel, but with the arbitrary separation of a true rhododendron into the azalea section I have little sympathy.

Mucronulatum Rose. A superior colored form of the species that is being propagated sparingly. (File card: Mar. 20, 1946, flowered. Always a few days later than the type.)

mucronulatum x ambiguum. 1930. Flowered 1933. Only succeeded in raising and flowering a single plant of this mating. It resembles Conewago very closely, the uninitiated would have trouble separating them. It roots from cuttings much better than Conewago and is sterile. It may be an even better commercial plant than Conewago as it loses no vigor in seed production. The rose color of both of these would not be too attractive in mid-season but opening with the season to themselves they are in demand. (File card: only a trace of yellow shows in the flowers. Cross made again 1939.)

Nova Zembla. 1959. We wish to add to our appreciation of this last hybrid introduced from Holland by the late Peter Koster's Nurseries, Bridgeton, N.J., and the Bagatelle Nurseries on Long Island. It is very similar to a former introduction of his, America, probably now the most popular red in the Eastern trade. But it is a better, more shapely grower. Flowers show better, leaves a darker green and more of them. When it becomes plentiful and more available, it will outsell America. It will undoubtedly get confused with America in the public mind but side by side on the roadside stand, it will outsell it.

nudiflorum. One of my first interests in plants was the collection of some of the variants of this azalea which grows abundantly in this locality. Some of these are described below. The names given here are just what I tagged them to distinguish them and may have no valid horticultural—or botanical—standing.

1949: This azalea, the most common undershrub in uncounted areas of woodland in our area, is an extremely variable species. This variation apparently has not been the result of natural hybridization, the only other species I have seen growing naturally east of the mountains (some 60 miles west of us) is R. atlanticum. I have found only one instance of this hybrid—*nudiflorum* x *atlanticum*—and it is easy to recognize, so I am sure it does not occur frequently.

nudiflorum var. album. Plant with pure snow-white flowers found near Shrewsbury, Pa., was sent to the Arnold Arboretum. I kept a natural layer, which died.

nudiflorum var. aureum. A variation of *nudiflorum* occurring naturally in this locality in which the florets have a yellow or orange blotch under the upper corolla lobe or occasionally with a yellow tint permeating the whole corolla. Best plant sent to the Arnold Arboretum. I have never heard how it prospers.

(File card: kept a rooted layer which is now flowering each season—the prettiest nudiflorum? Should be used in hybridizing.)

nudiflorum Flore Pleno. Occasional plants of this native species are to be found growing locally; a percentage of flowers have petaloid stamens. Again, the most notable of these found was sent to the Arnold Arboretum and I have no record of its behavior since. It had 5-10% double florets. Seeds from it were sown here in the hope that some seedlings might produce all or at least a larger percentage of double flowers. This has not been realized.

(File card: The seedlings have as yet not produced double flowered forms of note.)

occidentalis. 1928-19??. My experience with this lovely native of the western U.S. is that it will not live for any length of time in the east. Have heard other would-be growers express the same opinion. Tried it from three separate geographical sources.

Pennsylvanicum. 1958. A natural hybrid of *R. atlanticum and R. nudiflorum* occurring in woods $^1/_2$ mile S.E. of Stewartstown, Pa. Only known to me in an area about 50′ in diameter and probably representing a single clone that has spread by stolons, in which habit it resembles atlanticum. Flowers pale blush fading to white, fragrant and intermediate between the parent specii in time of appearance. *Discovered some time previous to 1917 when I entered the service in World War I* and the above name was suggested in correspondence with Prof. C. S. Sargent about 1926. (File card: stamens often petaloid. Discovered by me.)

ponticum s. ponticum s.s. ponticum. 1930. This species so useful in British and European rhododendron culture is a detriment rather than a help to growers in the eastern U.S. Its color is worse than catawbiense, and its tenderness combined with its susceptibility to wilt or blight have adversely affected . many of our hybrids. If we must graft, we should use another stock if possible.

poukhanense (R. yedoense var. poukhanense). 1920. Flowered 1922. This Korean azalea has most all of the characters that a breeder of hardy hybrids is looking for. Hardier than any other of its subseries, plant habit close to the ideal, flower size good, easily propagated from cutting, and a good grower in either full sun or partial shade. Its poor color is much complainted of but there are color forms in the species itself that are quite acceptable to all but the most rabid magenta haters. It has been much used here. If fact, I do not see how the "Gable" azaleas would have been possible without its ever present help in time of trouble.

This and its following hybrids will not be described at length here. Parentage of many varieties being noted under the azalea notes.

poukhanense x Kaempferi. 1924. With both parents hardy and a combination of all the primary colors in its makeup, we have found this is a good "foundation" to build on. In itself there are some beautiful pink, salmon and rose shades. A selected clone is Big Joe. F_2-Miriam. (File card: A very hardy and free-flowering race of many colors and large flowers. After several generations of hand-crossing selected seedlings, there are shades of deep lilac to light lavender, deep bright pink to blush, and salmon pink to orange scarlet. A number of seedlings are being clonally propagated under number.)

poukhanense x Hexe. 1926. Though Hexe is tender, this hybrid is seldom slightly injured and has been the source of practically all our hose-in-hose and red forms. All flowers of the first geneation are magenta purple—horrors! A selected clone is Herbert. (File card: Flowered 1928. This hybrid has produced a low growing, compact lot of plants, evergreen, with both hose-in-hose and single flowers from pale to very deep reddish magenta.)

(File card only: Poukamalum = *poukhanense x obtusum*
"Hexe" *x Kaempferi x Phoeniceum* "Malvatica"

1930: In this crossing some very choice varieties have been obtained and are being clonally propagated under number. Deep true red colors much purer than Hinodegiri have been evolved and these have been used in making further experiments in hybridization.)

poukhanense x mucronatum. 1928. Flowered 1930. Fine, large bluish lavender flowers with crimson spotting. Very vigorous grower with fine plant behavior. Selected clone Mildred Mae.

(File card: the flowers are not long retained. Stamens 10. No azalea hybrid I know possesses a better vigor and plant habit. F2 seedlings are yet to flower.)

prunifolium Azalea s. luteum s.s. 1956. A single plant flowered. Its late orange scarlet looks worthwhile.

1960: This plant does very well.

Pygmalion x haematodes. 1954. A Dexter hybrid that we like *very much* and it should have a name, but if so we do not know it. A rather dwarf compact grower with tight trusses of crimson flowers that *last unusually long.* (Dorothy Russell, prob. Ed.)

pubescens x racemosum. 1937. One of those subdued bits of loveliness that one realizes will never become a sensation or even a popular garden plant with a gardening public so thoroughly sold on the sensational, such as our American, but which nevertheless wins a place in one's affection and must have a bit of room assigned as its very own. It shows signs of grief in too much exposure.

pyncocladum s. lapponicum. 1934; 1938. No *R. diacritum* is the correct appellation—we are told!

racemosum s. virgatum. 1922. The typical form of *R. racemosum* from commercial seed (English) is a taller, more vigorous shrub than the following varieties. Also it seems to be more tender. However it has lived outdoors without protection for 28 years. Though often killed back partially, it generally has at least a few flowers. Indeed, with all forms of this species growing here, some sort of occasional killing back or pruning off the older stems seems almost essential to the well being of the plant. Far too many flowers and seeds are borne on this older wood, and so much vitality is consumed in their production that the plant does not renew itself well unless severe measures are taken.

racemosum Pink. 1950? A pink form of this species that is unusually attractive and seems somewhat hardier than the type. The leaves are *not* glaucous below in this variety.

racemosum 19404 Forr. 1924. This, regarded as "possibly the best form" in England, is also quite good here. Like all alpines in this group, summer drought is more apt to be injurious than winter cold. This condition must be corrected by the use of the hose and not with retentive solid mixtures, as the drainage must be excellent, whatever the surface slope. Rather early to flower, late frosts are a problem, but otherwise this plant manages to be a success with us. It is an effective and beautiful ground cover planted en masse at the base of large boulders or on a well-watered bank, preferably a north slope. (File card: low, compact)

racemosum 59717 F. P. I. (Rock Coll. No.). 1924. Everything in the above varietal description applies here also, except that this is a slightly more vigorous grower with leaves and flowers a shade smaller, and, through the years, it has been noticeably hardier. Our stock grown from seeds of old plants growing side by side is undoubtedly hybridized and represents a cross of the above two varieties now. (File card: Flowered 1926.)

racemosum x carolinianum (Conestoga in reverse.) 1927. Flowered 1930. This reverse cross of Conestoga seems not to have produced any seedling as good as that variety. A little plant with very dense habit that seldom flowers is a success as an evergreen.

racemosum x Keiskei. 1934. Growing all over the place like a weed, this most precocious little rhododendron often has its flower buds killed in the opening stage. The color varies from pale pink to white seldom with much of *Keiskei's* yellow except in the bud stage of some seedlings. From Mr. Magor, who supposedly used typical *racemosum* as a parent. If the cross were remade using one of the dwarf hardier varieties of *racemosum,* it might be an improvement. This is good.

Rachel Biggs. 1935. Hybrid of *carolinianum and Kaempferi* from Nearing. As would be expected, it is a most unusual plant perhaps best described as intermediate between its parent specii in all respects. Growing vigorously at times and rooting well from cuttings it should have been continued but, like other wide crosses, plants often died lock, stock, and barrel with no obvious excuse. Probably lost about 1945. Fairly pretty but botanical interest was its best trump.

reticulatum. 1930. When in full flower presents the same color effect from a distance as *mucronulatum* and is often better clothed with bloom. It is not as bud hardy as that species, though seedlings and varieties (?) vary much in this respect, some plants never showing injury. In our experience i does better as a woodland plant than in sunny sites. Under the name *rhombicum,* now said to be a synonym for reticulatum, a plant is growing here with definitely superior flowers as much as 4 ½" across and prettily marked. Unfortunately this is one of those with the buds often killed.

roseum. 1920. This hardiest of the Pentathera group is also a lovely one. Its color is distinctly superior to *nudiflorum* as is also its carnation-like fragrance. It occurs in this locality only on the tops of the low mountains west of Gettysburg and northeast to the Susquehanna, below Harrisburg, where it is not common. It is plentiful in the central and north central parts of the state. Generally, it is to be found only on the higher slopes. On the lower parts *nudiflorum* grows alone, higher up the two are intermingled, on top roseum predominates. Well-known observers whom I would not doubt state that many intermediate forms occur where these species grow side by side, but in these parts such a from has eluded all my searching. Nor have I been able to produce such a hybrid artificially. The species varies from pure pale pink to crimson. Mr. Frank L. Abbott has a scarlet flowered one and there is growing here a form with an orange blotch and throat.
(File card: *roseum* var. 1929: A form found near Pine Grove Furnace, Cumberland Co., Pa., that has an orange blotch on the upper corolla love and some yellow in the throat of the flower. Perhaps not distinct enough to be botanically important it is a very lovely form and may become of value as a parent of hybrids.)
(File card: *Roseum,* Scarlet, Abbott 1935.)

roseum x calendulaceum. 1927. Seedlings varied from less than 1.' to 6' at 20 years of age. The small twiggy dwarfs have not yet flowered, but the larger plants produce plentifully flowers of more variegated tints in the same floret than any other azalea—or rhodo—that I know. Almost as if a monkey got in the paints.
(File card: the taller plants have lovely flowers mostly striped orange and pink.)

roseum x japonicum. 1927. Another hybrid between members of the Luteum subseries which should be closely related but which, in common with many other hybrids within the subseries, show results generally associated with wide crosses by geneticists. This hybrid started with a good number of very thrifty looking seedlings, which grew well at first, then indifferently, then died. All but one or possibly two sick ones still exist. Some of these were 5' high and some were sold. Only one plant flowered here but many of them produced buds plentifully which never opened. On investigation, I found practically all of the buds of the summer dead in September.

sanguineum s: neriiflorum s.s. sanguineum. 1935-1940. All species of the *sanguineum* subseries yet tried here are extremely difficult. It is a pity because being dwarf in habit and generally of bright colors, interesting and charming hybrids might be made from them.

(File card: *R. sanguineum* var. 1935. Very slow and difficult.)

Schlippenbachii s.s. Schlippenbachii. 1927. Now coming into its own in this country but it still takes years of patient waiting until a small plant establishes itself well enough to flower at its best. It appears to best advantage in open woodland sites. In dense shade it is inclined to grow open and form rather few buds, while in full sun, though it grows into very compact shape and flowers profusely, the flowers wilt too quickly. This species is said to do well on limestone soils though I have had no personal experience in that, but I do know that it is prone to react unfavorably to chemical acidity, i.e., not too much aluminum sulfate, etc. It grows almost anywhere here, and our soil is naturally strongly acid.

(File card: This azalea is apparently adversely affected by soils that are very acid.)

serrulatum s. azalea s.s. luteum. 1927-1939. This southern species of which I flowered a plant for several years is so late as to seem almost posthumous. The plant was never injured by winter cold but became crowded and was lost in transplanting. Its flowers of the *viscosum* type are better and just as spicily fragrant. From my experience I think this species can be grown in this area. (File card: This southern species of which I have a plant from the Arnold Arboretum . . . flowering each year as late as November.)

semibarbatum s. semibarbatum. 1934. Until after 1946. So different that it is very interesting is this hardy little shrub, I have now lost it but not from winter cold. From neglect—I suspicion. The tiny florets are intricately marked in lovely pattern if one is able to discover them as they nod below the bronze green leaves, which are deciduous. So far from the typical that the profane would have trouble accepting it as either an azalea or a rhododendron. Had but one plant, a gift from Nearing.

Smirnowii s. ponticum s.s. caucasicum. After twenty five years experience with this species, one often highly recommended for our gardens in this area, I must say that in every place I have it and in every other place I have seen it growing it is rather disappointing in garden value. First of all, it seldom flowers freely, that is what one grows a rhododendron for, after all. This seems to be due to several causes: first, it does not produce the buds necessary for a real display, second, the buds are too easily started into opening by a spell of warm wet weather in the fall—mine are usually dotted with a sprinkling of flowers through September and October—and to be sure this makes the bud an easy prey to winter cold. And that even at its best, *Smirnowii* opens its florets one or two at a time and the cluster is never full, i.e., some are faded and gone or some are not yet opened and good full trusses fail to materialize. Yet as a shrub, it is a hardy rhododendron, has good plant habit, holds an abundance of foliage during the winter when in good health and produces some excellent hybrid offspring.

For at least a quarter of a century, a plant has existed in the trade as *R. Smirnowii* which is in reality a hybrid of that species. I have it here (it could be *Smirnowii* and *ponticum*?) and it flowers well in large trusses of not too welcome color. Some of my early hybrids when I had not yet flowered true Smirnowii are from this hybrid and perhaps some of the recommendation the species has received as a garden plant originated in this hybrid.

Smirnowii x arboreum x Atrosanguineum. 1936; 1941. I doubt if this lot of seedlings died—there never were many of them—but rather think they are lost among some unmarked lots. During the late war, many plants were marked with tags carrying iron wire, which rusted off in a year's time or less, and we had a bad time getting our records straight. The wires looked like copper, washed? The same tags from the same company had always had copper wires and we were caught unawares.

Smirnowii x Early Pink. 1941. This mysterious entry in my other notes does not explain itself and neither can I explain it. Nothing around here now is marked with this name. It should be crossed off.

Smirnowii x Fortunei. 1932: Flowered 1937. Have saved two plants of this hybrid and made a few grafts of each. One has been named Katherine Dalton and a very few plants have gone out. But in 1947 a spring freeze—which caught *carolinianum* in full flower and killed many plants to the ground—hurt this plant badly and it has only come back during the past summer. The flowers open pale lavender, fading to white, and are early.

Souliei x discolor x litiense. 1932. The first time these flowered in shades of yellow and cream, sometimes tinted pink, we were much excited, thinking that the long awaited good yellow rhododendron was in the bag. *But*, when planted out in the woodland they were planted on low ground, where many old rhododendrons were already succeeding very well and in a few weeks I had lost nearly all of them from blight. The remaining plants grow and flower but never like that first two hundred young plants in their first flowering. Through the years they have been fairly hardy, hurt a little at times but on the whole dependable. The trouble seems to be that all the better yellows have disappeared. A second generation should be the answer and is in the making but it will be some years before there are any reports on that. (File card: Nearly all died, Summer 1938)

Stump. 1942. A 1950 selection. Parentage unknown but possibly an F_2 seedling of *Smirnowii x Fortunei*. Has large, almost huge, flowers in pale lavender spotted dark red in the throat.

Selected in 1951. A hybrid of unknown origin with huge blue lavender flowers. It was found growing in a decayed stump (hence the name) and may be a volunteer hybrid seedling.

sutchuenense s. Fortunei. 1924. Under the label *oreodoxa*, this plant came from the Arnold Arboretum in 1924—or rather, it came through the Arnold Arboretum from another grower. It is definitely not *oreodoxa* and since it agrees with the description of *sutchuenense* in every detail except that my plant has smaller leaves and flowers than the type, I have so tagged it. The plant is hardy and fairly satisfactory but opens its flowers much too early for safety, often before mucronulatum. It has been in flower on Feb. 22. These flowers of course freeze but it is astounding how the fat pink unopened buds can freeze again and again without injury. Only the fully opened flowers are killed. Plants raised from seed from Mr. Lionel de Rothschild of England have developed into plants which are replicas of this old plant, so I feel my identification is certain. As to its garden value, the flowers would attract only casual attention in the season when it would have to compete with the rank and file (to make no mention of those in command). In its season, it has no competition and if the chance of seeing its bright pink trusses, of good size, in full flower in March or even February, about one year in three, appeals to one's sporting complex—here it is. (File card: flowered 1940, etc.)

taliense s. taliense. 1925. This species, which gives its name to the series in which it is included, is a difficult thing to grow and flower—which is typical of the entire series in as far as they have been attempted here. At least some of them are hardy enough where winter cold is concerned, but they blight badly, die back for no apparent cause, and the very few flowers this group has produced have been freakish and deformed. In such a large series, most of which are reputedly hardy, and many of which are said to bear cream and yellow flowers, others striped and spotted pink, red and crimson in varied patterns, to not be able to find a single one that can be used in the breeding program is disappointing indeed. Several years ago a small, minute, almost microscopical borer was found under the bark of this group and this could easily be the limiting factor in their cultivation. I have not seen this borer in any other rhododendron nor can I find an old plant of any *taliense* affinity that does not have it. (I must correct the above statement. There are some species of the Lacteum series that are undistinguishable from the Taliense by we who are of the profane, that are similarly afflicted.) But after writing all the above I still wish I could hybridize some species of this group with another hardy rhodo and get its "blood" into a race of hybrids. I suggest it as an objective to those fellow sufferers from my incurable affliction, would-be rhodo hybridists.

Thomsonii s. & s.s. Thomsonii. 1930. and several later sowings: I have not succeeded in flowering this species, I have not heard of its flowering in the eastern U.S. Indeed, the whole series to which it gives its name is a worthy challenge for the most sanguine grower in our part of the world.

Three Star. 1952. This is also noted under Essex Scarlet hybrids but as we intend to carry it on as a clone, we have inserted it here. It is a better plant than Essex Scarlet, though we have cut it up terribly for propagation (with meager results). Its leaves, flowers, and trusses are only medium in size but its dark red color—close to Mars—and the lasting quality and free flowering characters would seem to make it worthwhile.

Tschonoskii s. azalea s.s. obtusum. 1926. The only absolutely hardy species of the obtusum subseries with white flowers but yet not too much of an acquisition for our gardens in itself. Years ago I had visions of white flowered hybrids from this species that would prove hardy. It has proven rather difficult to mate with others of its group and to date (1950) not a single hybrid seedling has opened flowers of white. It has produced a few interesting hybrid seedling varieties with colored flowers on very dense twiggy, rather dwarf plants and some hose-in-hose forms that are first generation.

Vaseyi. This well-known native azalea which is at its best planted by stream or pond margin where it can arrange its makeup in the reflection needs no description. Hybrids of it within its own section or with any other section are as yet unknown, so it may perhaps be able to keep its person inviolate, the following two names being names only, included here solely to record the attempt.

Vaseyi x Schlippenbachii 1929 and later. Flowered as typical *Vaseyi*.

Vaseyi x Kurumes. 1929. All seedlings which were very weak, indicating possible hybrid origin, died without flowering.

vernicosum s. & s.s. Fortunei. 1957. There seem to be a number of different things on the market—or at least on the seed counters—as this species. Most of them resemble decorum and equal or exceed that species in tenderness. Rock's 25373 is a rather different plant but it too is losing out from winter cold. Another form, Rock 6929 (F.P.I. 56366) grew here for about twenty years but always suffered and failed to flower. It is a pity that we seem unable to come by a good hardy form of this interesting species belonging as it does to the generally quite growable Fortunei series. Two old plants (of which I have now sold one) were identified by Dr. Leach as *vernicosum* and are fairly satisfactory When flowering well, the pale pink florets tumbling over the foliage are both original and beautiful.

vernicosum aff. 18139 Rock. 1930. This variety endures but is extremely slow to flower having now been a pensioner at my board for some twenty years without producing a single bud. There should be a reason for this and I suspect the following, which also applies to R. houlstonii and others with this habit: The new growth is produced so early in the season that it is regularly killed by late spring frosts. The flower buds which would appear in any season are already formed in these buds and the secondary growth which follows will produce no flower buds. This species is rather more susceptible to blight than the average, and the best of drainage is imperative.

Saw this number in flower at Bill Dauber's nursery and it was good enough to rate the green eye, very, very lovely.

(File card: sad to say it has proven subject to blight and few plants are left—1938.)

1956: These seedlings have finally flowered here and were indeed worth waiting for. Though the variation is considerable, practically all have flowers of some shade of apricot pink about 3½″—4″ across in fair trusses. The plants—or most of them—are slow in growth and wider than high. One plant has grown like a poor lanky Fortunei to a height of nearly 10′ and with inferior flowers and only 4-6 in a truss (if indeed it could be called a truss). This looks more like a chance seedling than a typical 18139.

Its extreme slowness in flowering will no doubt be a drawback to raising it from seeds and will perhaps cause hybrids of it to be slow in blooming but it roots easily from cuttings and these should not be too long in flowering. 40 cuttings placed in early July of this summer (1956) were rooted and potted off in September—100%.

The flower buds of this number are sometimes injured, though they have never been completely killed and we have not noticed any injury to the plants by winter cold. It is lovely enough and not too tender to be of importance in plant breeding. Hardier and of better color than R. decorum, though slower in growth and with duller foliage.

viscosum s. azalea s.s. luteum. The late white fragrant azalea of north eastern America once thought to be plentiful here but afterwards found that what we had thought to be this species is all Atlanticum and probably there is no viscosum in these parts. As a garden plant it is surpassed in the same color effect and the same season of bloom by arborescens, though in very cold gardens viscosum will be found the hardier species.

Wardii s. Thomsonii s.s. Souliei. 1930. If protected in winter, this species will endure and flower though it is prone to all the maladies of its *(Thomsonii)* series. Such numbers as have flowered here are pretty but by no means a true yellow in color. They are cream, pink and cream, etc. (File card: much more adaptable to conditions in this section than *R. campylocarpum* or *R. lacteum.*)

Wardii x discolor. 1935. This has been growing in the open and flowering long enough to be considered a standby. The buds have been slightly injured on at least one occasion. It is in the very first class of its kin, being better in plant habit than *Souliei x discolor* and about equal in flower. Grown from seeds from Rothschild. Still needs a wee ray from the lamp of Aladdin! to make it more hardy.

1958: Old plant died but not from cold. Have no clonal progeny.

(File card: these seedlings from Lionel Rothschild as L. R. 791.)

Weyrichii s. Azalea s.s. Schlippenbachii. 1933. From Magor. I must really revise my older notes on this species. Coddled along and protected, it always looked sick. I never had many plants. But planted in the open woodland to take its course it produces its *Schlippenbachii*-like flowers of brilliant brick red in early July. It is as conspicuous as a group of lobelia cardinalis. Spring 1950, a small forgotten plant in an open bed flowered in pale brick red late May. Tag reads, *Weyrichii.* (File card: 1933. Finally through the kindness of Mr. E. J. P. Magor, from whom I have so many fine things, I have succeeded in obtaining this azalea true to name and have plants in flower bud. Fall 1935. This has not yet flowered but has buds for 1939. These older plants all died without flowering. Now have other small seedlings in bud for 1945.)

Weyrichii. 193? Dr. Hirosha Hara's article, "The

Occurrence and Distribution of Rhododendrons in Japan" (page 112 of the 1948 *Rhod. Yearbook* of the R.H.S.) would seem to be a logical solution of the incompatibility of the various descriptions of this species one notes.

This classification would put my late flowering, deep red, plant in R. amagianum and the lighter colored, early flowering sort would presumably be the subject of this note. If only a sizeable stock could be built up, these two azaleas should prove quite popular, and here would seem to be a possible source of a new race of hybrids of good color and fair hardiness.

R. amagianum is perhaps the finer species but *R. Weyrichii* is also showy and unusual.

yakusimanum. 1953. My two plants of this species have been variously classified by my rhododendron loving friends but I think Dave Leach is right in saying they do not represent the type at any rate. They look like a species however—but what? This is not too hardy in the open in winter.

Gable's Evergreen Azalea Notes

1G La Premier. 1930[*(poukhanense x Kaempferi) x indicum* (double form) (macrantha florepleno. Hort.)] First azalea to be numbered here and named. Medium late double pink. The original plant still growing on the lawn acquits itself nobly spring after spring but I think there are later numbers of more merit to take its place now.

111G. Mary Dalton 1930. Of the same parentage as Chinook and was numbered and introduced at the same time. After these years I am inclined to think Mary Dalton the better of these scarcely distinguishable sorts and that Chinook will eventually become obsolete.

13G Louise Gable. indicum x (poukhanense x Kaempferi). Double salmon pink, medium late in flowering and very hardy and dependable. Of good plant habit without pruning. One of my first introductions and I still regard it one of the finest.

21G Elizabeth Gable. indicum x (poukhanense x kaempferi). Salmon pink, evergreen. First selected for its evergreen character alone this proved to flower freely in time. For evergreen character it is still the best we have in a dependably hardy variety.

38G Maryann. indicum x (poukhanense x kaempferi). Midseason double pink. From the same lot of seedlings as Louise Gable. After first selection this was neglected for a time until a row of plants in the open

field grew into fine little specimens and proved its ironclad hardiness. The color is not too bright, though pleasing, but the flowers are good size for a hardy double, and the plant is of about ideal habit unpruned. It is healthy, hardy, and easy to grow. About the only grouch we can think up is that the rabbits are extremely fond of its twigs and buds in winter. So call in the hunters—and cats. Here a good fox terrier does wonders.

47 G Herbert poukhanense x Hexe. Hose-in-hose magenta or light purple. In spite of this description, those who see it in flower buy it—about nine times out of ten. We are confronted with the "sold out" stage on this one as often, if not oftener, than with any other azalea. My own sense of color values, unhampered by the educational efforts of the orthodox, and influenced only by what I see and what I like, finds no more quarrel with a good magenta shade than with a good red, yellow, pink, blue, or what have you. Obviously, also, many of my customers' ideas of color are untrammelled by educational allergies.

50G Viola, 51G, 52G Charlotte. All seedling of *poukhanense* x Ledifolia Alba—more properly, *mucronatum*—and all much alike. One is enough to grow and I prefer Charlotte. The original seedling of Charlotte is 8'–10' high and close to 20' wide so give it room. Lavender, single, spotted red. There is some evidence that commercial growers may have these named 50G-Charlotte and 52-Viola and my own records are inconsistent, but not in the appearance of the two plants.

The following entries are for 1932.

60G/63G/66G/67G Disc.

69G Mildred Mae. A selection of *poukhanense* x *mucronatum* same as 50G, 51G, 52G, but a much more compact dense growing plant which will require as much room as the other three selections and which bears equally lovely flowers. It is the best seller of this group with me.

96G Caroline Gable (poukhanense x Hexe) x (Kaempferi x poukhanense). Same parentage as 34G, 35G, and 86G, this number proved the hardier. Though its buds have been hurt here in very cold winters it is, on the whole, satisfactory. When the old original plant of Caroline Gable is in full flower, it is the brightest thing in the landscape.

111G Mary Dalton. Also described in this list, following 11G. Named for my wife who regards this number better than Chinook, which it closely resembles. The slight points of difference noted are: the interstices of the corolla lobes are exactly, almost formally, filled in by the lobes of the "hose" or corolloid calyx, the plant is a little more dense in habit, and the flowers of Mary Dalton are inclined to be more lax in habit (almost pendant when wet with rain).

117G White Star and 118G Polaris. These two named varieties have the same parentage and are so alike that one description will well do for both. Their parentage is (*poukhanense x Kaempferi*) x Snow. They bear white hose-in-hose flowers much like Snow but both plants and flowers show a gain in hardiness over that variety. They are not quite hardy enough to be a success with us but they are in the trade and proving hardy in some nurseries where Snow is too tender. We have abandoned their propagation here.

120G Indian Summer (October). Pure *Kaempferi.* as far as I can ascertain, flowers regularly in late fall. It is peculiar in that all of the flower buds formed are two or three times the normal size of *Kaempferi.* On the average, about half of these open in autumn and the remainder will still produce flowers in spring. In seasons of plenteous rainfall, this azalea is strikingly colorful even into November. The fall flowers last a long time if there is no hard freeze.

As to the name October which is sometimes attached to this number by some growers, it may be my fault. We had considered both names and I am just erratic enough to have written a tag—especially while talking to a customer.

A11G Springtime. Another *poukhanense x Kaempferi F₂* seedling. Very early clear pink. The best azalea we know of in its season. Difficulty in propagation holds it back. In front rank for hardiness.

B5G Rosebud 1938. Minature roses on a dwarf slow growing plant, it is especially beautiful in stage of the opening bud. Of A1G parentage.

B8G Carol. Flowers much like Caroline Gable but plant more dwarf and spreading. A promising sort.

C1G Purple Splendour. poukhanense x Hexe 1939. Rose purple hose-in-hose much resembling Herbert.

C3G Mary Frances. A particular favorite of mine, this tall growing type has medium size, deep pink hose-in-hose flowers that glow with some indefinable yellow or orange suffusion. Small plants are leggy and it requires room and several years to develop its true character.

C6G Jessie Coover. Fully double pink. A good double.

C8G Lorna. Fully double pink. One of the best of this group with profuse very double florets covering a low spreading plant with branches touching the ground all around.

D3G Rose Greely. 1940. White hose-in-hose and so far hardy. The Russians have their Five-Year-Plan, etc., but this is the result of a Sixteen-Year-Plan, though no one knew how long it would take in the beginning. Many people, including some plantsmen, think that hybridization is just a matter of crossing species and varieties and then waiting for something to turn up. Maybe all too often it is conducted with the wrong name on it. Otherwise I can not explain it. But they are the one and same plant.

D3G's plan was as follows:

1. *poukhanense x mucronatum* (Led. Alb) to get a hardy white. 400 seedlings. No whites.
2. Above cross-selfed, 240 seedlings flowered. Three single whites.
   a. *poukhanense* x Hexe to get a hardy hose-in-hose. All seedlings rose purple.
   b. (*poukhanense* x Hexe) x (*poukhanense x Kaempferi*) to obtain lighter colors, in hose-in-hose form. Several fine pinks.
3. Crossed white from #2 with hose-in-hose pink from #2a. Flowered nearly 200 and got one hose-in-hose white which is D3G or Rose Greely, easily a hardier white than we ever grew here before. Still think I made this cross in a country cemetery, dark of the moon, with a rabbit foot in each pocket.

176G La Roche. Hinodegiri x *poukhanense.* Hardy, vigorous, floriferous and magenta. Recommended for trial where hardiness is Azalea's "Public enemy" #1.

A1G. 1937. Fully double pink. The double flowered Louise Gable was crossed with 34G in the effort to obtain azaleas with the flower characters combined, i.e., the corolloid calyx of 34G and the petaloid stamens of Louise Gable on the same flower. This number was the first to flower in which the attainment of these objectives was noted; it was sparingly propagated and disseminated. We no longer have a plant of this but Rosebud—B5G and C8G carry on this along those lines. Neither will I commit perjury! But if knowledge is lacking *experimentia docet*, it is little short of tragic if a would-be hybridist spends too many years of the only life he has in attending only her school. Definite objectives should be set and whether we attain them or not a comprehensive long time plan (but as short as we can make it) will bring us a lot closer to that attainment a lot sooner in this "onliest" lifetime.

F1G James Gable. 1942. Cardinal red hose-in-hose. Seems to be proving hardy and is close in color to the ideal we have been working for. It might bear more flowers and better foliage.

F3G Campfire. Flowers almost identical with F1G but plant more vigorous and larger leaves. The color in these two varieties will be hard to improve on, in clarity and pureness of red.

G1G. 1943. A late red flowering azalea from Jim Gillin. Hence all the Gs. This is much different from our familiar type of flowering late and among the new growth and about brick red. The azalea fancier will make room for this one. (Gillin's Red—Ed.)

H12G. Late double red. A Beni-kirishima hybrid. Much hardier, brighter, larger flowers and more attractive foliage than that variety. A Long Island nurseryman named it. What?

J11G Jimmie Coover. Late macratha hybrid with deep red flowers. Very showy but flowers too late for customers to see it in bloom. It is very good.

R56 The Stewartstonian. 1956?. Introduced last fall to the trade, we have at last been able to offer this variety which we have been testing for several years. We offer it as an extremely hardy red—and then hope we are correct. Time will tell how well it will be received. Some report that it is not as hardy as first reported. Here it is never hurt.

Wilhelmina Vuyk-Palestrina. 1952. This two-named white azalea is proving hardy here and perhaps the best white where hardiness is the prime factor.

R4G Margie. A hose-in-hose pink much like 34G (which was named Edna but discarded here for tenderness.) This is a quite hardy variety with good foliage and free flowering.

The Study Group Report

It was Joseph Gable's complete devotion to the miracle of beauty in rhododendrons that drew so many people to him. His appreciation of the spiritual and aesthetic was shared with all who came to visit him. His creations were a relief from everyday life, where people are bombarded by advertisements trying to make nonessential things seem desirable. Joe never tried to fool anyone, and was the first to point out the plants that were not up to his standards of hardiness and quality. This complete honesty is what kept people coming back— that and a delightful sense of humor. His desire to have others continue his work was his major concern in his later years, even though Joe had been partial all his life to those having an interest in hybridizing.

Some years ago Mr. Gable gave a talk in New York on nut tree hybridizing, and at the beginning said, "I know very little about nut trees; and it would probably be better if I should keep my mouth shut and let you folks think I knew nothing, than to open my mouth and remove all doubt from your minds." He then proceeded to present a very thought-provoking talk on nut tree hybridizing and on plant breeding in general. One quote especially worth mentioning is, "Life at best is uncertain in length; and while the individual may be very capable and, starting, accomplish something quite worthwhile, he will be fortunate indeed if those who follow keep up the work." This was in 1936 when Mr. Gable was only 50. He lived to be 86.

Ignited by a talk given to the Potomac Valley Chapter of the A.R.S. in 1973 by Capt. Dick Steele, an old friend and admirer of Mr. Gable, the chapter formed a Gable Study Group. Its purpose was to research and document Mr. Gable's work from his notes and correspondence and to catalog the known Gable plants. The original committee, included Caroline Gable, George Miller, Jane and Ray Goodrich, and George Ring. Later Russ and Velma Haag from North Carolina, long-time admirers and collectors of Gable plants joined the group.

In 1973, the Study Group developed a preliminary list of known Gable rhododendron hybrids and selected species, which they sent people known to have Gable plants requesting them to identify the Gable plants in their gardens, and to provide them with additional data they might have. In response, some 40 replies were received from growers and collectors. Many of the replies included ratings, comments, and lists of other Gable plants the group didn't know existed. All those who sent replies received grateful thanks for this important information.

When the information was collated: 100 named rhododendron hybrids were identified; 90 more (mostly group crosses) were described by their parentage, and more than 50 species that had been obtained from Mr. Gable were listed. This information was compiled and forms the body of the report that follows. The listing contains: (1) rhododendron names; (2) parentage; (3) flower color; (4) blooming period; (5) hardiness; and (6) ratings, where all the information was available. A separate listing of evergreen azaleas includes 30 named varieties, which Mr. Gable selected as his best; and more than 200 others, some numbered by Mr. Gable, and some named and propagated by others.[3]

In 1929, Gable was growing seedlings from several plant-hunting expeditions, and his records indicate more than 100 rhododendron species and another 100 hybrids were growing at Stewartstown, Pennsylvania. Gable worked alone, and without the convenience of plastic bags, knowledge of growing seedlings in sphagnum, airplanes to transport plant material, or refrigeration to store pollen. When pollen arrived from England, it was immediately used on whatever was in bloom. Perhaps this is why we have his beautiful *R. maximum x R. haematodes* hybrids today, and the cream colored Catalgla x *R. wardii.*

In the 1920's, Joe Gable and Guy Nearing met and began an exchange of letters, plant material, and enthusiasm that lasted 40 years.[4] They had a common bond of enchantment with the lepidotes and soon produced Conewago, Windbeam, and many others which give faithful annual performances in thousands of American gardens. Joe and Guy combined hundreds of exotic tender types with the ironclads in the hope that they would get hybrids both exotic *and* hardy. As a result, thousands of undistinguished seedlings bloomed—but occasionally it worked. A classic example is Joe's Mary Belle in which he combined *R. decorum x R. haematodes* with Atrosanguineum x *R. griersonianum.*

In later years, Henry Yates of Frostburg, Maryland became Joe's hunting friend and raised many seedlings of Gable crosses which they shared. Henry eventually made his own crosses and selected many hardy clones. In the early days at "Little Woods" in Stewartstown, Pennsylvania, as the Gable seedlings matured, each spring became a season of excitement to see the survivors bloom.

To introduce the Study Group report, the following are brief comments on some of the plants. Among the most widely grown Gable clones is Caroline, which has a white flower, edged mauve. It is reported to be very root-rot resistant. The progeny include Cadis and the reverse cross Disca. David Gable is Atrosanguineum x *R. fortunei,* which blooms early. Pioneer is probably the widest grown of the scalies. It is a seedling of *R. mucronulatum,* most likely pollinated by *R. racemosum.*

There was a bit of confusion about Conestoga, *R. carolinianum x R. racemosum,* Rock 59717. Mr. Gable's notes say that it apparently dies out in 5 to 10 years, both for him and his customers. He said in 1954, "I do not know of a single living plant of true Conestoga." Therefore we assume that the respondents who said they have Conestoga probably have Conestoga Improved, a seedling which was also propagated. Mayflower is a little-known second generation seedling.

Conewago is *R. carolinianum x R. mucronulatum.* Conewago Improved has better flowers and foliage, and does not break so

---

easily under snow loads. There is also Conewago Special and Conewago #2, the latter having lighter colored flowers. A seedling of #2 is Conewago #3 with larger flowers and lighter coloring. The Conewago tribe often escapes late frosts in this area while Pioneer may not.

The Keisrac group varies from pale pink to pale yellow to almost white. Nearing finally got one of these to take *R. keiskei* pollen and the result was Mary Fleming.

R. carolinianum (album compactum) is dense growing and has short annual growth. Another good one is called Bowman's Carolinianum Alba. Carolid is a cross of *R. carolinianum x R. olieifolium x R. davidsonianum*. Gable's *R. augustinii* blooms in late April and is reliably hardy. Mucram is also early, as is Conemaugh and *R. keiskei*. These last four are all good early bloomers, but you do take a chance that they might be caught by an April frost. *R. racemosum* is later and safer. Gable's notes indicate that his stock grown from seeds were hybrids of the two varieties of *R. racemosum,* Forrest 19404 and Rock 59717, the latter being by far the hardiest of the two.

We are indebted to Mr. Gable for a hardy strain of *R. fortunei*. He grew a great number in the woods, the weaker perishing in harsh winters. Seed was saved from the survivors, shared with Guy Nearing, and the two evolved through the years a strain which will stand -15°F. These pale mauve to almost white hardy species were parents of the Madforts. The seed parent, Madonna was *R. decorum x R. griersonianum* x America, having a large white trumpet-shaped floret. Unfortunately, Madonna is difficult to root, and we found only 3 surviving clones of this plant in the survey. Crossed with *R. fortunei,* it produced Yelton's Choice, Big Bells, Bellfort, Hardy Madfort and White Lily. Many of the Madforts were sold by Mr. Gable, and the recipients regarded them as so superior that they made cuttings and sent them back to Gable at Stewartstown ... almost always with the notation, "You sold me the best one, and surely a cutting should be growing in your woods." Among the many species Gable grew in those woods is *R. houlstonii.* It blooms early and sometimes gets caught by late frosts, but it's well worth the gamble.

Another outstanding species is *R. vernicosum, Aff., Rock 18139.* These were grown from seed of the 1929 Joseph Rock expedition to China. It took years for them to bloom from seed; from cuttings, they are not so slow. Gable propagated the best two. Clone #1 is the more peach-colored of the two, and Clone #2 is the pinker. *R. vernicosum, Aff.* 18139 is a good parent. Crossed with *R. houlstonii,* it gave Dr. Rock. With Mary Belle as the seed parent, we have Isabel Gable. Isabel is coral in bud, opens to flesh pink, and is hardy to -10°F. *R. vernicosum* with *R. fortunei,* cream, resulted in Mary Garrison, a salmon yellow with blends of brownish red colors. Mary Garrison has been difficult to root, but is a good parent of yellows. Another hybrid is *R. brachycarpum x R. vernicosum* 18139.

Now we come to the Catalgla x *R. wardii* crosses. Mr. Gable repeated this cross many times, always seeking a good hardy yellow hybrid. Progeny of his first cross tend to be early season bloomers. Moonshot is the best known of these. There are also Cat-wardii #1 and Cat-wardii #2 (2-66). Cat-wardii #2 usually blooms in ivory-yellow with green spots, but depending on the weather it can look pale pinkish cream. From a later Cat-wardii cross came Joe Gable, perhaps the best of these. Henry Yates may also belong in this group, however there is some indication that it is a *R. litiense* hybrid.

Catalgla, which is a shortened form of *R. catawbiense album,* Glass, came from seed of a white form of *R. catawbiense* found by Powell Glass in the mountains of Virginia. Here was the hardy element of rhododendron hybrids without the magenta tint of the ordinary *R. catawbiense.* Gable used it extensively as a parent. He also sowed seed from his Catalgla, and when some customers observed that their plants bloomed lavender, he withdrew the item from his listings, and all the customers had a white *R. catawbiense* refunded to them! He said, in explanation, "you can't tell what those bees will do." We surmise that after hand pollinating, the stigma was still receptive when the bees came around with pollen from a neighboring *R. catawbiense* in the woods.

The cross which gave Pink Twins was from a red flowered *R. catawbiense* and a *R. haematodes* from the Arnold Arboretum. Many people reported to us that "Joe always told them his *R. haematodes* was a hybrid, and so it may have been. He also used pollen from another form of *R. haematodes*—from Magor in England—and this he regarded as more typical of the species. The pollen from Magor was used to develop the Maxhaems; #7 is salmon, #10 is yellow, and there is also a clear red. The Maxhaems are fairly small flowered, but have excellent foliage, and some are very hardy.

A sibling of Pink Twins, called Cathaem #1 was an important parent for Mr. Gable. He crossed this with Mars several times. He is quoted as saying of Mars hybrids, "Some are tender, some are awful, but the remainder are magnificent." The Marcats, as they are called, include Frazzles, Red Sox (a hose-in-hose red), Marcat 4, Marcat 58, and Tom Thumb, a dwarf red. Tom Thumb, selfed, produced the Tommies. In researching the Tommies, a member .of the Study Group questioned whether Tom Thumb was indeed the parent, since all of the Tommies were of good stature, with none of the dwarf characteristics of Tom Thumb. The explanation did not lie in a hereditary fluke at all. It was much more simple. Gable had all the dwarf seedlings lined up together, and they were all "lifted." The Tommies are numbered #1 through #12. The bicolor is #2, and #3 is called Plain Pink. Flower color of the Tommies is good and clear. Even on a grey day they look bright. Two unnumbered Tommies are called Bonnie and Little Bonnie—buff-colored like the collie dog after which they were named. Mary Yates is a Tommie named by Henry Yates, and his Shazaam may also be a Tommie since the seed was shared.

Mars was also used with Catalgla to produce some superlative plants. This cross was made with Henry Yates' help. Perhaps the best seedling is Running Deer which is bright pink with a white throat. Dr. Bess is a vigorous growing dusty rose that also blooms late midseason. Strawhat is a glowing pink bicolor with green and white markings. It was so named because its truss fills a straw hat. Many of the Catalgla—Mars group are bicolors, as are some of the Tommies. Mars seems to be the influence for the bicolor.

Another parent used extensively by Mr. Gable was the old *R. catawbiense* hybrid, Atrosanguineum, a hardy red. Crossed with R. *griersonianum*, it produced the Atrier group. Redhead is Atrier #10. Gable wrote that the cross was originally planned only as a stepping stone for later crosses, and he was pleasantly surprised to find hardy plants surviving in his woods. Of course, about 90% did prove to be tender, but the survivors were considered hardy enough to propagate. Besides Redhead, there is also Atrier Hardy, Atrier Oak, Atrier #7 and lastly, William Montgomery which was the tenderest of the group and had the largest florets. The Atriers range in color from rose-red to red, and vary in hardiness from -5°F. to -10°F. One of the Atriers, when crossed with *R. decorum x R. haematodes* produced Mary Belle. From the same cross came Shrimp and Flamingo, a bright salmon pink.

Now we come to Atroflo which is recorded as Atrosanguineum x *R. floccigerum*, Rock 18469. This *R. floccigerum* was in the "almost hardy" category, so Gable kept it in a tub which was moved into the barn each winter. Atroflo #2 is the hardier clone. The clone of Atroflo which received the A.E. (award of excellence) is a bit more tender. Foliage of Atroflo is dark green with suede-like indumentum on the underside. The Study Group has hypothesized that the cross might have been *R. smirnowii x R. floccigerum* because of this heavy indumentum and other plant characteristics. The cross has been repeated this year on Atrosanguineum with pollen of *R. floccigerum* from the west coast, although pollen of the original Rock form of *R. floccigerum* would have been preferred if available. Seedlings will be grown on and results reported later.

As mentioned earlier, Gable used his white Catalgla extensively as a parent to impart clear color *and* hardiness. Crossed with *R. decorum* he produced Anne Glass. The large white flat trusses are surrounded by a collar of good green foliage. Crossed with Madonna, came Lisa and Lisa siblings. Mary K is Catalgla x *R. fortunei*.

In the Gable woods were other selected forms of *R. catawbiense*, Red Cat among them, and there was also a good rose he used extensively. An early cross of one of these with *R. fortunei* produced the Clone C-11. This isn't around much, but it showed up in the A.R.S. Potomac Valley Chapter's 1976 cut truss show, and won a ribbon! We believe that C-11 was the Catfort used as a parent for the plants known as Catfortcampys, *R. campylocarpum* being the pollen parent. There are only three selections, Salmon Bamboo which is coral, rated 4/2, Catfortcampy #2 (same as 6-62) which is apricot pink, rated 4/4, and Du Ponts Apricot (also 28-60) is a pale apricot, and is difficult to distinguish from Catfortcampy #2 except by the foliage. It was so named because Mr. Henry du Pont wanted to buy the plant, but Joe wouldn't sell it to him.

Mr. Gable seeded the species *R. decorum* 14 different times. He liked the Forrest 30887 group very much, but the flower buds lost out in severe winters. There is a hardy *R. decorum* growing in the Gable woods today from one of the early seedings. In the survey, Ross Davis of Wayne, Pennsylvania, and George Harding of Germantown, Maryland both reported to be growing hardy *R. decorums* they bought as seedlings from Gable.

R. discolor proved to be a good parent for Gable. For instance, Cadis, which we have already seen, and its sibling, Robert Allison, are two of the *R. discolor* progeny. The reverse cross, *R. discolor* x Caroline, was named Disca which he regarded highly. In his notes, he commented that Disca might be but a superior form of *R. discolor* itself. Disca has been hand pollinated, and the seedlings are well over knee-high. When enough have bloomed, results will be reported.

There are a number of clones which are regarded as Gable-Nearings. The two men shared seed and plants so frequently that it is often difficult to determine who made the cross. For example, the cross Degriff x Kettledrum was made by Nearing who shared seed with Gable. The one selected by Gable was named Gretchen. Rochelle, a sister seedling, was grown and selected by Nearing.

Nearing's Pink, Degriff x *R. williamsianum* x *auklandii*, growing in Gable's yard was from Nearing, and Gable wrote in 1956 that he regarded it as the finest of this group of hybrids.

Nearing's Catanea was originally from Gable, whether a sister seedling of Catalgla, or a second generation, isn't known. Both Ramapo and Purple Gem were from a Gable cross and seed shared with Nearing.

There are a few clones believed by some to be Gable's hybridizations, which are not. Pygmalion x *R. haematodes* was a Dexter cross sent to Gable which Gable thought was good. A named Dexter clone from this group is Dorothy Russell. Despite many disclaimers which may be forthcoming, we accept this as a matter of fact, for it was so recorded in Gable's notebooks. Also, Russautinii is not a Gable, but a gift from the Haags. It is an English cross.

There are other Gable clones rated highly

by respondents to the survey. Milo blooms fairly early—a handsome plant with pink and cream blends. Bosutch is very early, before mid-April in the middle Atlantic region. It has good dark foliage, although the florets are not of the caliber of the Gable midseason hybrids. Pink Bosutch is a sister seedling, blooming about a week later. Albert Close blooms late and is hardy to -20°F. Mac Kantrus is Degram x Atrier and blooms midseason. Its flowers hold up well in the heat. The plants numbered 14-59 and 15-59 are Annie Dalton hybrids. The latter (15-59) is a low grower.

Blackie blooms late midseason and was considered superior to its better-known brother, Kentucky Cardinal which sometimes tends to brown on the edges of the florets. Blackie has a delicious fragrance of fruit salad. Another clone, 1-67, called Renaissance was rated 4/3 and is hardy to -15°F. Smirfort and Carol's Superwhite are both large-flowered plants and quite hardy.

Although Beaufort is reported by some to be a shy bloomer, it puts on a real show when given sufficient sun.

Some unusual forms of species grown by Gable include: (1) a pinkish white variant of *R. campanulatum* with heavy indumentum, blooming very early. (2) *R. brachycarpum*, Nottcutt, a free bloomer which may be a hybrid despite its typical *R. brachycarpum* foliage, and (3) a white *R. vernicosum*, which is both fragrant and early. It was grown from a different seed lot than the Rock *R. vernicosum, Aff.* 18139.

These are just a few descriptions of the rhododendrons and azalea legacy left to us by Joseph Gable. There are still many seedlings in "Little Woods" as yet to bloom and be evaluated. Some are already showing promise, with tentative names such as Upper Right, a late discolor hybrid with a huge bicolor truss. And a Mary Belle hybrid, a good yellow with an excellent plant habit. Annie '70 is a brilliant pink Annie Dalton hybrid which promises to be a real winner.

As important as these new hybrids is the extremely valuable collection of selected hardy species which includes: a yellow *R. brachycarpum*; a hardy *R. decorum*; a hardy *R. campanulatum*; a *R. racemosum* hardy to -15°F.; an *R. adenopodum* for early bloom; a red *R. catawbiense*; a red *R. maximum*; the *R. vernicosum*; *Aff.* Rock 18139; and many others. The gene pool of hardy species and selected hybrids at "Little Woods" is unique, and recognized by hybridizers as a solid base for the future. To quote from a talk by Mr. Gable, "We are sure to realize sooner or later that creation is not yet complete."

APPENDIX A _____

Best Known Gable Rhododendron Clones*

Albert Close. Rating 3/2; hardy to −10°F; late. (*R. maximum* x *R. macrophyllum*) Somewhat straggly and open with attractive blue-green foliage; flowers medium size, bright rose pink with throat heavily spotted chocolate red; compact conical truss; can take sun. (Seed from Fraser).

Anne Glass. Rating 4/2; Hardy to −20°F; late midseason. (Catalgla x *R. decorum*) Plant grows tall and full; vigorous; flowers pure white; large lax truss surrounded by collar of dark green leaves.

Atrier g. Rating 3/2; hardy to −5/−10°F.; late midseason. (Atrosanguineum x *R. griersonianum*) Rose-red to red in a flat truss; plants rather open;

_____

*All plants of average growth unless otherwise noted.

several forms of the Atrier group have been named; Atrier #10, named Red Head is superior to other forms, but not quite as hardy as Atrier Hardy; others are William Montgomery and Atrier Oak; prefer afternoon shade.

Annie Dalton. Rating 4/2; hardy to −15°F.; late midseason. [(*R. decorum* x *R. griersonianum*) x America] leaves long and narrow with a slight twist; very open plant; large blooms of good glowing apricot pink in a large lax truss; a good substitute for Azor in cold climates.

Atroflo. Rating 4/3; hardy to −10°F.; midseason. (Atrosanguineum x *R. floccigerum*) Somewhat open habit when young, foliage dark green, suede as above, heavy fawn indumentum; flowers rose madder, good substance, large, trumpet shaped, 10 to 12 in a lax flat truss; roots easily; forms vary in hardiness; A.E. form (A.R.S. 1960) not quite as hardy as Atroflo #2; a good grower; (Editor's note: Mr. Gable's notes suggest that his seedlings of this cross may have been confused with those of another cross, *smirnowii* x *floccigerum,* made about the same time. The heavy indumentum and dark green veined leaves tend to support this.)

Beaufort. Rating 3/3; hardy to −15°F.; midseason. (Boule de Neige x *R. fortunei*) Plant compact with large leaves; flowers, 2 ¼″, open; faint mauve, fading to white; fragrant; 12-14 flowers to tall truss; may be a shy bloomer in shade; blooms profusely in more exposure and when mature; insect resistant.

Bosutch. Rating 3/4; hardy to −5°F.; very early. (Boule de Neige x *R. sutchuenense*) One of the first rhododendrons to bloom, just after *R. praevernum* and *R. mucronulatum.* Blossoms withstand a few degrees of frost; flowers white with lavender spotting, campanulate; good plant habit with excellent dark green foliage; roots easily from early July cuttings. Sibling, Pink Bosutch blooms one week later.

Cadis. Rating 4/5; hardy to −10°F.; late midseason. (Caroline x *R. discolor*) Good habit, dense foliage; flowers light pink with yellow flush, 3³/₄″, frilled, in a flat truss; very fragrant; will bloom well in light shade; grows more compact in sun but flowers do not last as long; an outstanding grower; A.E. (A.R.S.) 1959.

Caroline. Rating 3/4; hardy to −15°F.; tall spreading; midseason. (Parentage unknown) May be *decorum* or *brachycarpum* hybrid; plant vigorous; will grow in poor soil; fairly upright; dense; leaves large with wavy margins; flowers pale orchid, large, pleasantly scented, easily damaged by insects.

Catalgla. rating 4/2; hardy to −25°F.; late midseason. Selected F₁ seedling of *R. catawbiense* var. *album.* Open habit, leaves medium green; grows best in some shade; flowers white, pale pink in bud, in a tall, many flowered truss; very cold hardy. Used by Mr. Gable and others in hybridizing to impart cold hardiness without usual magenta tint of *catawbiense.*

Catfortcampy, g. Rating 4/4-4/2; hardy to −5/−10°F.; midseason. [(*R. catawbiense* x *R. fortunei*) x *R. campylocarpum*] Flowers apricot pink to coral; the three named clones are: Salmon Bamboo; Catfortcampy #2 (6-62) apricot pink; and DuPont's Apricot (28-60) also apricot pink. Catfortcampy #2 is the hardiest and the strongest grower.

Conemaugh. Rating 4/3; hardy to −15°F.; low; early April. (*R. racemosum* x *R. mucronulatum*) Plant rather open when small, becomes dense when grown in sun. Semi-deciduous; flowers lavender pink, star-shaped in ball truss, about 2″ in diameter; floriferous; flowers sometimes caught by late spring frosts; introduced 1934.

Conewago. Rating 3/2; hardy to −25°F.; early April. (*R. carolinianum* x *R. mucronulatum*) Plant fairly open, making long shoots from base; leaves 2½″ x 1″; flowers lavender rose; needs morning sun to grow and bloom well; airy, graceful appearance in bloom.

Conewago Improved. (R. *carolinianum* x R. *mucronulatum*) Similar to above but more floriferous; larger blossoms and slightly more pink color.

Conestoga. Rating 3/2; hardy to −20°F.; early. (R. *carolinianum* x R. *racemosum*) Pink. F₂; seedlings are Conestoga Improved and Mayflower.

County of York. Rating 4/4; hardy to −15°F.; midseason. (Catawbiense Alba x Loderi g.) Previously exhibited under name of Catalode. Plant rather open with long convex dark green leaves; flowers of good substance, graceful, pale lavender pink in bud, opening white with pale green throat; grows well in a wide variety of conditions; roots and grafts easily; best in light shade; very plant hardy; A.E. 1960.

David Gable. Rating 4/4; hardy to −15°F.; early. (Atrosanguineum x *R. fortunei*) Good plant habit; large medium green leaves; flowers bright pink with red throat, in a large dome shaped truss; floriferous and easy to grow; Synonym is Gable's Pink #1; blooms with many early midseason azaleas, just before *R. fortunei;* A.E. 1960.

Disca. Rating 4/3; hardy to −10°F.; late. (*R. discolor* x Caroline) Vigorous grower with good plant habit in open exposure; blooms are better and last longer in light shade where plant is somewhat open growing; flowers, 4″, scented, slightly frilled, in a large truss; new growth does not appear until blooming is completed.

Dr. Rock. Rating 4/4; hardy to −10°F.; early midseason. (*R. houlstoni* x *R. vernicosum* aff. Rock 18139 #1) 4″ peach pink flowers when well grown; much like its vernicosum parent, but better plant habit.

Frazzles. Rating 4/3; hardy to −10°F.; midseason. (Mars x Cathaem #1) Pink to salmon rose flowers with shaggy calyx; good medium green foliage; siblings are Marcat #4, '58', Tom Thumb, and Red Sox.

Freckles. Rating 3/3; hardy to −10°F.; midseason.

(Jacksonii, pink x *catawbiense-haematodes*) Flowers pink with brownish spotting; deep green foliage; tall, vigorous; easy to root.

Gretchen. Rating 4/4; hardy to −15°F.; midseason. [(*R. decorum* x *R. griffithianum*) x Kettledrum] Good foliage and plant habit; flowers pink with red throat, in a large dome shaped truss; very floriferous; does not root easily; a livelier pink than David Gable, but much later; seed from Nearing; sibling is Nearing's Rochelle.

Haag's Choice. Rating 3/4; hardy to −10°F.; midseason. (Parentage not recorded) Synonym is Haag #1; flowers rose pink; densely clothed with dark green leaves; somewhat slow to bloom from cuttings, but floriferous when mature.

Henry Yates. Rating 4/5; hardy to −15°F.; early midseason. (*R. wardii* or *R. litiense* hybrid) Flowers pale yellow; retains leaves more than one year; difficult when drainage is not adequate.

Joe Gable. Rating 4/4; hardy to −10°F.; midseason. (Catalgla x *R. wardii*) Creamy ivory; pale yellow in morning or evening light; highly regarded by Mr. Gable.

Katherine Dalton. Rating 3/4; hardy to −15°F.; early midseason. (*R. smirnowii* x *R. fortunei*) Flowers very pale pink; excellent plant habit, densely leaved; traces of indumentum; flowers open gradually from bright buds; some tendency to fall bloom.

Kentucky Cardinal. Rating 2/3; hardy to −15°F.; low; midseason. (*R. brachycarpum* x Essex Scarlet or *R. fortunei*) Plant has open habit when young; a beautiful foliage plant when older; flowers small, very dark red with tendency to browning of edges; best used as background. Blackie, a sibling, is better.

Ladifor. Rating 3/3; hardy to −10°F.; midseason. (Lady Clementine Mitford x *R. fortunei*) Flowers pink with bicolor effect; fragrant; pleasing shiny convex foliage. (Grown by Gable from a Nearing seed—Ed.)

Lisa. Rating 3/3; hardy to −15°F.; midseason. (Catalgla x Madonna. White; tall; slow to root.

Madfort, g. Rating 4/3; hardy to −5°F.; midseason. (Madonna x *R. fortunei*) Flowers very large, heavy texture, pale pink to white, fragrant; leaves dark green; a sturdy appearing plant; blooms when young. Named clones: Hardy Madfort, Yelton's Choice, Bellfort, Big Bells, and White Lily.

Mars x Cathaem, g. Rating 3-4/3-4; hardy to −10°F.; medium to low; midseason. (Mars x *R. catawbiense*, red, x *R. haematodes* A.A.) Deep red to pink. Frazzles, Marcat #1, Marcat #4, '58', Tom Thumb, and Red Sox are selected clones. Haematodes pollen parent from Arnold Arboretum thought to be a hybrid.

Mary Belle. Rating 4/4; hardy to −15°F.; midseason. (Atrier x Dechaem) Flowers open salmon pink, fading to buff yellow; heavy bloomer; leaves have a distinctive twist. Flamingo and Shrimp are sister seedlings.

Maxhaem Salmon. Rating 3/3; hardy to −15°F.; late midseason. (*R. maximum* x *R. haematodes*) Synonym

Maxhaem #7. Flowers salmon, medium to small, in well-filled truss; floriferous; dark green foliage, moderately veined. True *haematodes* from Magor was pollen parent.

Maxhaem Yellow. Rating 3/3; hardy to −5°F.; late midseason. (*R. maximum* x *R. haematodes*) Synonym Maxhaem #10. Flowers pale yellow, small; good dark green foliage with interesting bronze new growth.

Milo. Rating 4/3; hardy to −10°F.; early midseason. (*R. brachycarpum* x Dechaem) Flowers cream and pink blend; handsome plant; cuttings slow to grow on.

Moon Shot. Rating 4/4; hardy to −10°F.; early midseason. (Catalgla x *R. wardii*) Creamy white flowers combined with dark green foliage; best selection from Gable's first cat-wardii cross.

Pink Twins. Rating 4/3; hardy to −10°F.; low; midseason. (*R. catawbiense*, red, x *R. haematodes*, A.A.) Plant is slow growing, compact when young. It opens with age; leaves ovate elliptic; flowers hose-in-hose, light shrimp pink, fleshy, or good substance; 15 or more in truss; sibling, Cathaem #1.

Pioneer. Rating 2/3; hardy to −20°F.; late March to early April. (A chance hybrid between *R. racemosum* and *R. mucronulatum*, pink) Plant habit upright, responds well to cutting; semi-deciduous, 1½″ x 1″ leaves; flowers light mauve pink, about 1″ across, very freely produced; often flowers before last frost, after *R. mucronulatum* and before Conewago.

Robert Allison. Rating 4/4; hardy to −10°F.; late midseason. (Caroline x *R. discolor*) Plant rugged, upright, leaves waxy green, large; flowers pink with golden throat, scented, up to 3½″ across, in a flat topped truss; floriferous, roots easily; blooms a week later than Cadis, its sister seedling.

Red Sox. Rating 4/4; hardy to −10°F.; low; midseason. (Mars x Cathaem #1) Unique flowers, bright red, hose-in-hose; very open habit; slow grower; needs some shade; foliage and color like Mars; none other like it.

Sir James. Rating 3/3; hardy to −10°F.; midseason. (*R. fortunei* x ?) Flowers light pink, floriferous; medium green foliage; (Hicks-Gable); selected by Gable from Planting Fields.

Skylark. Rating 3/3; hardy to −5°F.; very late. (Parentage not recorded) Flowers rose pink, will withstand summer heat; eye-catching because of lateness of bloom, early June in Philadelphia. Introduced by Baldsiefen.

Strawberry Swirl. Rating 3/3; hardy to −10°F.; low; very early. (Jacksonii x) Synonym Jacksonii #5; flowers pale pink with darker, pink stripes, frilled; restrained growth habit, almost recumbent; flowers just after Bosutch with briefly glorious two-toned trusses.

Tom Thumb. Rating 4/4; hardy to −15°F.; low; midseason. (Mars x Cathaem #1) Very slow growing, semi-dwarf; good clear red flowers; distinctive leaf form has "indented waist" at midsection; root system could be more ample; needs watching in dry weather; parent of the Tommie group; buds up young from cuttings.

Vernicosum aff. Rock 18139 #1. Rating 4/3; hardy to −5°F; early. Selected from seedlings of *vernicosum affinis* grown from seed from 1929 Rock expedition to China. (R.H.S. #03788). 4″ peach pink with no trace of blue; full lax truss very graceful; depth of color may vary with the warmth of early May; medium to light green foliage; best in high shade.

Vernicosum aff. Rock 18139 #2. Rating 4/3; hardy to −10°F; early. The second selected seedling from the Rock expedition; 4″ pink, less peach shading than #1; mound shaped at maturity; medium to light green foliage; easy to root from July cuttings.

Auriculatum x Discolor g. Rating 3/2; hardy to −5°F; large; late. (*R. auriculatum* x *R. discolor*) F₂. Flowers white; large, open plant with very long leaves held one year; shy bloomer until some maturity attained.

APPENDIX B

Other Named Gable Rhododendron Hybrids.

Table 1. COMPILED BY GABLE STUDY GROUP, 1976

Name of Clone and Cross	Color	Bloom Period	Hardiness	Rating	Remarks
Anna Caroline Gable (*adenopodum* x *metternichii* var. *tsukusianum*)	pale pink	early	−10°F	3/4	good tight plant form.
Annie Dalton [(*decorum* x *griersonianum*) (Syn: Degram Pink) x America)]	glowing apricot pink	late midseason	−15	4/2	A.E. 1960.
Atkar (Atrosanguineum x Kentucky Cardinal) (group name)	red?	midseason	−10	3-1/3-1	Highly variable; a few clones very good; AS1 Best Atkar; AS2, Atkar Star.
Atror Atrosanguineum x (*orbiculare* x *williamsianum*)	rose	very early	−5	2/3	
Bamboo (*catawbiense* x *fortunei*) x *campylocarpum* syn: Salmon Bamboo; Catfortcampy#1	coral	early—midseason	−5	4/2	no stamens.
Beechwood Pink (Atrosanguineum x *fortunei*)	bright pink	midseason	−5	4/3	Gable-Herbert.
Big Bells (Madonna x *fortunei*)	blush-white	midseason?	0	4/2	
Blackie (Essex Scarlet x *brachycarpum*,?)	very dark red	late—midseason	−5	3/3	Kentucky Cardinal sibling; 9-56; better than Kentucky Cardinal; fruit salad fragrance.

Name of Clone and Cross	Color	Bloom Period	Hardiness	Rating	Remarks
Bonnie (Mars x (*catawbiense* x *haematodes* #1) F₂	pale buff, edged pink	midseason	−10 °F		10-65
Brachdis (*brachycarpum* x *discolor*)	flesh, copper marking	late	−10	4/3	
Bramax (*brachycarpum* x *maximum*)	white	late	−20	2/3	
Camich (*catawbiense* x Michael Waterer)	cerise-red	midseason	−15	2/2	cross by Fraser; floriferous; very slow growing.
Caroline Cream (Caroline seedling) (syn. Mrs. H. R. Yates)	opens pale mauve; fades to cream	midseason	−15	3/4	very floriferous.
Carol's Super White (Catalgla x)	white	late midseason	−20	4/2	plant very sturdy, like a loosely branched tree; difficult to root.
Catdis (Catalgla x *discolor*)	white?	late?	−15	4/3	
Cathaem #1 (*catawbiense* red x *haematodes* A.A.)	rose red	early midseason	−10	3/3	corolloid calyx reflexed; lax truss. Gable: "This was an important parent." Haematodes A.A. thought to be hybrid.
Cathaem #4 — see Pink Twins					
Cathaem #7 (*catawbiense* red x *haematodes* A.A.)	red	early	−5	3/2	single.
Cherry Vanilla (Mary Belle x *vernicosum* 18139)	striped pink and cream		0		
Coplen's Pink (perhaps 'E.L. Ames' x *fortunei*)(5-56)	pink	late		3/2	a selection by M. G. Coplen; much like Amphion (E.L.Ames)
Coplen's White (*catawbiense* x *fortunei*) (-58)	white	late midseason	−15	4/3	
Decatros (*decorum* x Atrosanguineum)	pink/white	early	−10	3/3	two clones propagated; premature aging.
DeWilde's Yellow (*wardii* x *discolor* x *discolor*)	cream to pale yellow	late midseason	−15	3/3	Hardy in Nova Scotia.
Double Dip (Catalgla x *yakusimanum*)	white	midseason	−20	4/5	durable flowers; like oversized yak.
Double Dip sibling (Catalgla x *yakusimanum*)	white	midseason	−20	4/4	
Du Pont's Apricot—see Catfortcampy					
Dr. Bess (Catalgla x Mars)	dusty rose	late midseason	−10	3-4/4	Gable-Yates; vigorous.
Five Inch (Atrosanguineum x *fortunei*)	light lavender pink	midseason	−10	3/2	
Flamingo (Atrier x Dechaem)	bright salmon pink	midseason	−5	4/2	a Mary Belle sibling. pinching helps shape.
Flat Top (*catawbiense* x ?)	red	late midseason			low; spreading.
Floribundum ?	pale pink	early midseason	−5	3/2	

Name of Clone and Cross	Color	Bloom Period	Hardiness	Rating	Remarks
Fraser #3 (*macrophyllum* x *maximum*)	pink?	late	−15 °F*	?	cross by Fraser.
Gable's Best Purple (20-60)					Nearing.
George Fraser (*macrophyllum* x *maximum*)?	light red	late	−10	2/2 ?	shy bloomer; Fraser Red is better.
Gretchen #2 and #3	rose red	midseason	−15	3/4	Nearing-Gable.
Herbert's Find (Annie Dalton x ?)	pink, flushed orange	midseason	−10	?	striking in color.
Hopewell (Degram x Atrier)	?	?	?	?	
Isabel Gable (Mary Belle x *vernicosum*, aff. 18139)	coral bud; flesh pink	midseason	−10	4/3	floriferous; good rooter.
Jacksonii #6 (*caucasicum* x)	red	very early	−10 ?	3/2 ?	
Judith Boyd (Cadis x Kluis Sensation)	bright pink	late	0	3-4/4	
Little Bonnie (Tom Thumb x)	pale buff, edged pink	midseason	−10	?	like Bonnie but plant lower.
Mac Kantrus (Degram x Atrier)	pink, red eye	midseason	−10	?	flowers hold up well in heat.
Madonna (*decorum* x *griersonianum*) x America	white	late midseason	−5?	3/4	almost extinct.
Marcat #1 Mars x (*catawbiense* x *haematodes*)	light red	midseason	−10	4/3	slow yearly growth.
Marcat #4 Mars x (*catawbiense* x *haematodes*)	pinkish red	midseason	−10	3/4	slow grower; corolloid calyx.
Mary Garrison (*fortunei*, cream x vernicosum, aff. 18139)	salmon yellow and brn. red blend	early-midseason	−10	4/4	difficult to root; take cuttings from young plants or take early.
Mary K. (Catalgla x *fortunei* #5)	pinkish mauve	midseason	−15	4/4	
Maxecat (*maximum* x *catawbiense*)	pink	late	−25	2/4	
Maxhaem Red. (*maximum* x *haematodes*)	dark pinkish red	late midseason	−10	3/3	haematodes pollen from Magor and was true species.
Maxie (*maximum* x ?)	pink with heavy spotting	very late	?	?	Fraser-Gable.
Mrs. Ensor (Catalgla hybrid)	lavender	midseason	−15	3/4	large truss.
Mrs. H. R. Yates (Caroline seedling) (syn. Caroline Cream)	open pale mauve, fades to cream	midseason	−10	3/3	very floriferous; tight plant; blooms young.
Mt. Mitchell (maximum hybrid or var.)	pink	late	−25	3/2?	original plant prob. c.w. North Carolina. Found 1930. Gable's is a layer.
Orbwill (*orbiculare* x *williamsianum*)	pale pink	early	−5	?	seed from Magor; plant sent to West Coast by Gable.
Papillon (fortunei hybrid)	lavender	early-midseason	−5	4/2	large, reflexed flowers.
Peaches (49-64)	peach	midseason	−15	4/3	flat truss; striking.
Pink No. 3 (*catawbiense* x *discolor*)	rose pink	late midseason	−5	3/3?	undistinguished

Name of Clone and Cross	Color	Bloom Period	Hardiness	Rating	Remarks
Plain Pink (Tom Thumb x) (syn. Tommy #3)	clear pink	early-midseason	−10°F	4/2	no throat marking.
Red Head (Atrosanguineum x *griersonianum*) (Atrier #10)	red	midseason	−5	3/3	prefers afternoon shade; buds early f. cuttings; reddest of this group. Gable-Yates.
Running Deer (Catalgla x Mars)	bright pink, white throat	late-midseason	−10	4/4	
Salmon Bamboo — See Catfortcampy					
Shell Pink (*houlstonii* x *vernicosum,* aff. 18139)	light pink	early-midseason	−5/−10	4/1	sibling of Dr. Rock; distorted foliage.
Smirhaem (*smirnowii* x *haematodes*)	red	early	−10	3/2	sometimes blooms in fall.
Straw Hat (Catalgla x Mars)	glowing pink-bicolor; green and white markings	mid to late	?	?	truss fills a straw hat Gables-Yates.
Sunset Tommy (Tom Thumb x ?)		midseason?	?	&	
Super White #2 (Catalgla x)	white	late midseason	−20	3/2	easier to root than Carol's Super White.
Tommy (Tom Thumb, self) #1-pink, earliest; #2-red, bicolor; #3-plain pink; #5-pink with prominent blotch; #9-pale pink w. deeper pink edge; Numbers 4, 6, 7, 8, 10, and 12 not described.	red, pink, pinkish salmon	midseason	−10	3 to 4/3	Bonnie and Little Bonnie are Tommies; all are Gable-Yates crosses; Mary Yates is a Tommie grown by Yates.
Tinker Bell (Camich x Elizabeth)	light red	early midseason	−5	3/3	Gables-Yates cross.
White Lily (Madonna x *fortunei*)	white	midseason	−5	3/2	
William Montgomery (Atrosanguineum x *griersonianum*)	red		−5?	?	more tender than other Atriers.
Yellow Bells (Mary Belle x Toodeloo)	lt. yellow	?	?	?	named by Haags.
Yellowthroat (Catalgla x)	white w. yellow center Reflexed				sibling of Carol's Super White; hard to root.
Yates #1 and #2 (ungernii x auriculatum), F₂ perhaps	pink	late	−10	?	seedlings of *ungernii* x *audiculatum;* vigorous growers.
Yelton's Choice (Madonna x *fortunei*) (syn. Dr. Yelton)	white to very pale pink	midseason	−5	4/4	very large florets.
Zig Zag (*decorum* x *griffithianum*) x hardy red	pale lavender	?	?	?	

Table 2. GROUP NAMES OF KNOWN GABLE CROSSES

Name of Clone and Cross	Color	Bloom Period	Hardiness	Rating	Remarks
adenopodum x *metternichii,* var. *tsukusianum*	pale pink	early to midseason	−15°F	3/4	Rich green narrow foliage, rust indumentum.
Amath x *fortunei*	?	?	?		
Atrier x Disca					
Atrier x Kentucky Cardinal					
Atrier x (*orbiculare* x *williamsianum*)					
Atroflo x Atrier					
Atroflo x *fortunei*					
Atrosanguineum x *haematodes*	pink		−10		
Atrosanguineum x Toodeloo					
auriculatum x *ungernii*	white	very late			Yates #1 and #2 may belong in this group.
Azor x (Catalgla x *decorum*) (16-64)	pink with maroon blotch	midseason	−5	3/3	
Boule de Neige x *fortunei*			−15		some forms rated better than Beaufort.
brachycarpum x *catawbiense*			−30	2/2	being used for hardiness & frost resistance.
brachycarpum x Decatros			−10		plant hardy to −25°F.
brachycarpum x *decorum*	pink		−10		
brachycarpum x *discolor*			−10		
brachycarpum x *fortunei,* cream					
brachycarpum, cream x *vernicosum,* aff.	mostly cream to pink	midseason	−5		some clones excellent.
Bramax x Romany Chai					
Cadis x Kluis Sensation	pinks ?	late midseason	−10		
Camich x Elizabeth	red	midseason	−5		mostly low.
Caroline x Disca					
Caroline x *discolor*	pure white	late midseason	−5/−10		Cadis and Robert Allison are named clones.
Caroline x Essex Scarlet	pink	midseason	−5		Tall
Caroline x *fortunei*					
Catalgla, selfed	white	midseason	?	3/3	
Cadis x Catalgla	near white	midseason			vigorous foliage.
Catalgla x Caroline					
Catalgla x County of York					
Catalgla x Dechaem	pink	late midseason	−10		
Catalgla x *decorum*					Anne Glass is named clone.
Catalgla x Disca					
Catalgla x *discolor*	white		−15		one named Ned Schrope.
Catalgla x Essex Scarlet					
Catalgla x *fortunei*	almost white		−15		Leach rates *super;* Mary K. is named clone; rose pink.
					(cat-fort #5).

Name of Clone and Cross	Color	Bloom Period	Hardiness	Rating	Remarks
Catfortcampy x *vernicosum,* aff.					
Catalgla x (*griersonianum* x *fortunei*)			−15°F	5/2	
Catalgla x Mars (Gable-Yates)	reds and pinks and bicolors		−20		Running Deer, Straw Hat, and Dr. Bess are named.
Catalgla x Maxhaem					
Catalgla x *wardii* (at least 4 clones propagated: 1, 2, 4, and 6)	cream to ivory (Earliest season bloomers are from first cat-*wardii* cross)				plant hardy for Pride; cross repeated many times. Moonshot, and, Joe Gable, and Bufy.
Catalgla-*wardii* x *fortunei,* cream					
Catalgla x *yakusimanum*					Double Dip is named clone.
catawbiense compactum x *discolor*	poor pink	late midseason	−10		
catawbiense, red x *haematodes,* A.A.	pink; red	midseason	−10		see Pink Twins.
catawbiense compactum x Mayday	pink; red	midseason	−10		sterile?
catawbiense x *discolor*	pink		?		very bud hardy Gable's Pink #3 is named clone.
catawbiense x *fortunei* (C-11 is selected clone)					
catawbiense, var. *rubrum* x (*griersonianum* x *fortunei*)			−15	5/2	
caucasicum x *fortunei**					
David Gable x *forrestii,* repens					
decorum x *discolor*					
decorum x *griersonianum*	pink	midseason	−5/0	4/4	
(*decorum* x *griersonianum*) x America = Degram	good bright pink	midseason	−10	3/2	sibling of Annie Dalton.
Degram, Pink Lily	pink	midseason	−10	3/2	
Degram x Atrier	pinks?				Mac Kantruss, Hopewell, and 6-60 are clones.
Degram x Cathaem					
Degrier x Charles Dickens	pale orchid		−5	3/2	huge trusses; floriferous.
Degriff x Purple Splendour					Gable lists Degriff x Purpureum Elegans —from Nearing.
Disca x Madonna					
Discamp x *yakusimanum*	pale pink	midseason	−5		only 1 clone has been propagated.
discolor x *campylocarpum*	cream				

*Note: "fortunei x caucasicum, seed from Magor, prob. F_2...a
single plant marked to save because of superior dwarf form and
excellent foliage," Gable Notebooks.

Name of Clone and Cross	Color	Bloom Period	Hardiness	Rating	Remarks
discolor x *catawbiense,* var. *album*			−15.°F	3/2	
Essex Scarlet x *fortunei*	pale pink with red blotch	midseason	−5	3/3	11-56 is named clone.
Essex Scarlet x *discolor*					
fortunei, cream x *vernicosum,* aff.	peach	early		3/3	also reverse cross, q.v.
haemaleum hybrid	almost black; pink				Gable crossed with Red Cat. & America (see 7-57).
haematodes x *fortunei?*	rose red	midseason	−10	2/2	
houlstonii x *vernicosum,* aff.	pink; apricot		−5	4/3	Dr. Rock is selected clone.
Jacksonii seedlings	pink	very early	−5/−10		dwarf size; Haag reports a midseason sdlg.; red flecks on yellow; 4/5
Jacksonii #1 (apud)	red flecks on yellow			4/5	highly rated by Haag.
litiense x Crest					
longesquamatum, pink hybrid					Gable crossed species with Gretchen, D. Gable, Cadis, Catalgla, and auriculatum-discolor.
longesquamatum, red					
longesquamatum, white hybrid					10-67 a selected clone?
longesquamatum, yellow hybrid					52-64 and 26-65 are selected clones.
Madonna x *fortunei*	pale pinks and white				Hardy Madfort, Bellfort, Yeltons Choice, Big Bells, and White Lily are named.
Mars x Cathaem	reds	midseason	−10		cross made at least twice.
Mars x (Catalgla x *wardii*)	pink		−15		one clone highly rated by Pride; good substance to blooms.
Mary Belle x *fortunei,* cream	deep yellow; pink	midseason	−5		no stamens.
Mary Belle x *vernicosum,* aff.	pale peach; pinks and creams				Isabel Gable is selected clone. Also Cherry Vanilla.
Mary Belle x *yakusimanum*	pink, fades white	midseason	−10		
Maxhaem x Caroline	pink	mid-May	−5	3/2	
maximum x Atrier	deep pink	very late	−20	3/3	5-57 is selected clone.
maximum x *discolor* clonal names proposed by Dr. John C. Wister: Alumni Day (9015-2) white, Nearing-Gable; Baccalaureate	pink; white	late	−10		first cross from Nearing; repeated by Gable.

Name of Clone and Cross	Color	Bloom Period	Hardiness	Rating	Remarks
maximum x *discolor* (cont.)					
(13251-1) pink; Diploma					
(13251-5) white.					
maximum x *fortunei*					
maximum x *griersonianum*	red; deep pink	late midseason	−25°F		
maximum-discolor x Catalgla-discolor					
maximum x *haematodes*					see under Maxhaem; Pride has an excellent red form.
metternichii x *degronianum*	pale pink	early midseason	−15	2/2	
metternichii var. *tsukusianum* x *adenopodum*	pale pink	early midseason	−10	3/4	(this is the correct order of the cross) Anna Caroline Gable is named clone; good indumentum.
Romany Chai x *discolor*					
smirnowii x *arboreum*	crimson to mauve				Gable seeded 1931.
smirnowii x *griffithianum*					
smirnowii x *yakusimanum*	white	midseason	−10	−/5	Haag's Selection rated highly.
(*soulie* x *discolor*) x (*discolor* x Caroline)					
Two Tone Pink	pink		−10		
vernicosum, aff. x *fortunei,* cream	cream?		−10		101-70 listed as selected clone; cross was made both ways.
yakusimanum x *metternichii*	dk. pink fading white	early midseason	−15	4/4	
Vulcan hybrid (13-63)					
wardii x *discolor,* F₂	rose to peach	early midseason	−5	4/4	
(*wardii* x *discolor*) x *discolor*	pale yellow?				'DeWilde's Yellow' is named clone.

Table 3. SPECIES GROWN BY GABLE AT STEWARTSTOWN

Name of Clone and Cross	Color	Bloom Period	Hardiness	Rating	Remarks
adenopodum, West Coast	pale pink	early	−10	3/4	Good indumentum, hardy.
albrechtii					
amagianum	orange-red	late midseason			
ambiguum		midseason			
augustinii	light lavender	early	−5		
auriculatum	white	late	−5		
brachycarpum	cream to white; peach (HR)	late	−25	3/3	very slow to set buds; hard to root.
brachycarpum #5	white	late	−10		
brachycarpum, pink, Nottcutt	bright pink	midseason			may be a hybrid; Free bloomer.
campanulatum, pinkish	pink-white	very early	−20	3/4	a hardier variant; 2 forms at Gable's.

Name of Clone and Cross	Color	Bloom Period	Hardiness	Rating	Remarks
carolinianum (Owl Tree)	pink	midseason	−25°F		
carolinianum album compactum	white	midseason	−25		
carolinianum, alba, Bowman (syn: Bowman's white *carolinianum*)	white	midseason	−25		original plant in Mr. Bowman's yard.
carolinianum, Red Twig	pink	midseason	−25		deep red twigs in winter.
catawbiense (Catalgla seedlings)			−25		Nearing's Catanea was originally from Gable (white with lavender stamens)
catawbiense			−25		
catawbiense, compactum	rose pink	midseason	−10	3/3	
catawbiense, rubrum	red		−25		Nearing: "not quite equal to the best red hybrids, but hardier, and nearly pure red."
caucasicum	cream white	early	−25		
chapmanii	pink	midseason			
chrysanthum var. niko-montanum	pale yellow				close to *brachy-carpum.*
decorum	pale pink to white		+5/−5/ −10	5/3 (for hardy white form)	Gable sowed 14 times.
detonsum					Haag: "this could be a hybrid." Gable had this x Thomsonii, seed f. Magor.
discolor					Gable: Arnold Arboretum seedlings truest; used in most of his crosses.
fargesii	pink?	very early			The following Rock numbers seeded by Gable: 23325, 23326, 23324.
(apud) *fastigiatum*	bluish lavender	early midseason	−10	3/3	Gable: could be a hybrid with *augustinii;* resembles Blue Tit.
ferrugineum	lavender	late	−10	3/3	
fortunei	pale pink-mauve	early midseason	−10		
fortunei, cream		early midseason	−10		
fortunei, white					
haematodes	red	midseason		3/4	two plants recd. from Arnold Arboretum were hybrids; pollen from Magor used in most of Gable crosses.
hemitrichotum					

Name of Clone and Cross	Color	Bloom Period	Hardiness	Rating	Remarks
hippophaeoides	pinkish purple				
houlstonii	pinkish white	early	0 °F		#5 is very good; also Basic Houlstoni.
intricatum (Rock 03757, which = 18144)					
keiskei	pale yellow	early	0		
litiense	pale yellow		0		
longesquamatum	pink w/crimson blotch	midseason			sparse bloom; leaves tend to mottle.
makinoi	pale pink	early	−10?		very slender leaves. late new growth.
maximum, rubrum					
metternichii, var. *tsukusianum*	pink	early	−10	4/4	Gable, 1952: plant from Larsen; good foliage; density.
mucronulatum	pale mauve	early	−25		
mucronulatum, pink	pink	very early	−25?		color clearer and deeper than species; brighter than Cornell Pink.
orbiculare					
oreodoxa	pink and striped	very early	0		
ovatum	white to pale lavender	late midseason	−10		plants: P.I. 124719
racemosum	pink	early	−10		
sanctum					
schlippenbachii					
smirnowii	pinkish mauve		−15		
vernicosum, white	white	early	−5?		Rock 25273 grown at Gable's; fragrant.
weyrichii	orange red				
yunnanense	pink to white?		−5?		

Table 4. LEPIDOTES, NAMED CLONES, AND GROUP CROSSES BY GABLE

Name of Clone and Cross	Color	Bloom Period	Hardiness	Rating	Remarks
Blue Jay seedling of Blue Tit	blue	early	−5?		Gable rated: "fine blue where hardy".
Carolid [*carolinianum* x (*racemosum, oleifolium* x *davidsonianum*)]	pale rose, crimson spots		−5?		flowers like trailing arbutus.
carolinianum x *augustinii*					
carolinianum x *hippophaeoides*	purplish pink				Gable lists cross as *hippophaeoides* x *carolinianum*.
carolinianum var. *album* x *keiskei*					Both Gable and Nearing seedlings grown at Gable's.
chapmanii x *mucronulatum*	mauve pink	early midseason	−10	3/3	a week after Conewago.
chapmanii x *mucronulatum* x *racemosum*	pale lavender	early	−30	3/3	Early Bird is named clone.

Name of Clone and Cross	Color	Bloom Period	Hardiness	Rating	Remarks
Codorus(*racemosum* x *minus*) pink			−28°F		flowers like trailing arbutus.
Double Decker (*minus* x *carolinianum*)	pink	midseason			
hemitrichotum x Conewago					
hippophaeoides x *minus*					
Keisrac *keiskei* x *racemosum*	pink; pale yellow; almost white		−5		most are sterile.
Mayflower *carolinianum* x *racemosum*, selfed	pink				seedling of Conestoga.
Mincar *(minus* x *carolinianum)*	lav. pink; white; apricot	midseason	−15		several forms propagated; Double Decker is named clone.
Mucram (*mucronulatum* x *ambiguum*)	rose	early	−15	2/2	only one plant raised from this cross.
Pioneer (*racemosum* x *mucronulatum*, selfed)	mauve pink	early	−15	3/2	Gable Notebooks: a seedling, a chance hybrid of mucronulatum pink. Introduced by Baldsiefen.
Rosie *chapmanii* hyb.	pale pink	early midseason	−5	3/3	Original plant died.
Muchamp	mauve pink	early	−15	2/2	
spiciferum x Conewago	pale pink				

APPENDIX C ——————————————

Gable Azaleas

GABLE EVERGREEN AZALEAS

Introduced by Joseph B. Gable and kept in, or restored to his listing

Barbara Hille. (T7G) (Louise Gable hybrid). Flowers single, salmon pink, midseason. Exceptionally slow grower in contrast to many other Gable azaleas. One to two feet tall and three feet wide in 12 years. Sometimes confused with T4G which is more dwarf and slightly different color.

Big Joe (42G). (*poukhanense* x *kaempferi*). Reddish violet, HCC 29/2, with brown blotch, single 2-1/2", early midseason, large open growth, very hardy and floriferous. Nine feet tall and twelve feet across in 32 years.

Plant covered with flowers before new foliage appears. Barely evergreen.

Campfire (F3G). (Caroline Gable x Purple Splendour). Flame red, HCC, 022, with darker blotch, hose-in-hose, late midseason. Larger in leaves, flowers and twigs than James Gable. Five feet tall and six feet wide in 25 years. Hardy in Buffalo, N. Y. Introduced 1942.

Carol (B8G). (Louise Gable x Caroline Gable). Violet red, HCC 025/1; flowers single, 1-1/4", hose-in-hose, late midseason, spreading. About six feet tall and 8' wide in 25 years. Fine autumn foliage coloration. More floriferous with age. Cuttings must be taken early to root easily. Introduced 1938.

Caroline Gable (96G). [(*poukhanense* x Hexe) x (*poukhanense* x *kaempferi*)]. Red, HCC 623, with darker blotch. Late midseason, medium tall, 7' by 7' in 25 years. Introduced 1933.

Elizabeth Gable (21G). [*indicum* x (*poukhanense* x

kaempferi)]. Salmon, HCC 022/1, with darker blotch, flowers single, 2-1/2″, frilled; late, medium spreading. 5′ tall and 9′ wide in 25 years. Very hardy and vigorous. More evergreen than most. Introduced 1930.

Gillin's Red (G1G). (parentage unknown). Flowers deep maroon red. Leaves partially hide flowers. Not a typical kurume or *kaempferi* hybrid. Late. Gable obtained from Jim Gillin, Ambler Nurseries, Ambler, Pa. Seven feet x seven feet in 22 years.

Herbert (47G). (*poukhanense* x Hexe). Flowers reddish violet, HCC 31, with darker blotch, single, 1-3/4″, hose-in-hose, frilled. Early midseason, medium spreading, six feet tall x ten feet wide in 19 years. Twiggy growth. Introduced 1931.

Howard Anderson (145G). (syn: H. W. Anderson): (*mucronatum* hybrid). Flowers pale blush, spotted red. Low spreading, dense. Introduced 1934.

Indian Summer (syn. October) (120G). (a form of *kaempferi*). Flowers coral pink with lighter throat, single, hose-in-hose, late fall and spring flowering in some locations. Upright but not tall. Not as easy to root as some. 7′ tall and 6′ wide in 19 years. Introduced 1934.

James Gable (F1G). (Caroline Gable x Purple Splendour). Flowers red (HCC 022), with darker blotch, single, hose-in-hose, late midseason; medium spreading. 6′ by 7′ wide in 19 years. Color exceptionally sun resistant. Introduced 1942.

Jessie Coover (C6G). (Louise Gable x Caroline Gable). Flowers deep violet red, double, hose-in-hose. More spreading than Rosebud and more open growth. Roots easily. Introduced 1939.

Jimmy Coover (J11G). (*macrantha* hybrid). Flowers red, sometimes semi-double; late, low, spreading. Hardier than *indicum*. Roots easily. 6′ by 5′ wide. Introduced 1944.

Judy (J4G). (parentage unknown). Flowers rose pink, single, hose-in-hose, late, medium tall. Flowers last well in sun. Introduced 1944.

Kathleen (200G). (*poukhanense* x *kaempferi*). Flowers small but of very clearest pink, single, medium tall. 7′ tall x 6′ wide in 11 years. Early midseason. Introduced 1956.

La Roche (176G). (Hinodegiri x *poukhanense*). Flowers magenta red, single; very early, vigorous. About 5′ tall by 5′ wide in 25 years with upright habit. Very hardy. Makes excellent hedge. Introduced 1935.

Lorna (C8G). (Louise Gable x Caroline Gable). Flowers rose pink, HCC 25/2, double, hose-in-hose, medium low, densely growing. 3-1/2′ tall and 5′ wide in 25 years. Almost as dense as Rosebud but lighter pink

flowers. Late, Very hardy. Has been referred to as Koster's Rosebud. Introduced 1939.

Louise Gable (13G). [*indicum* x (*poukhanense* x *kaempferi*)]. Flowers salmon pink, HCC 0625, with darker blotch; semi-double; late midseason, six feet tall x eight feet wide in 25 years. Referred to by many as Gable's best azalea. Introduced 1930.

Margie (R4G). [(*poukhanense* x Hexe) x (*poukhanense* x *kaempferi*)]. Flowers deep pink, single, hose-in-hose, late midseason. 7′ tall x 6′ wide in 19 years. Much like Edna, but hardier. Introduced 1952.

Maryann (38G). [(*indicum* x (*poukhanense* x *kaempferi*)]. Flowers lavender pink with darker blotch, semi-double, late midseason. Low, spreading. One of the more evergreen. Easy to root. Introduced 1931.

Mary Dalton (111G). (*kaempferi* x Yayegiri). Flowers orange red, HCC 020/1, single, 1-1/2″, hose-in-hose. Early midseason. Upright, tall. 13′ tall by 9′ wide in 32 years. Best in part shade, as flowers will fade in sun. Should be pruned when young. Roots very easily. Introduced in 1930.

Mary Frances Hawkins (C3G). (parentage not recorded). Flowers pink with yellow or orange tinted center, single, hose-in-hose, midseason. Vigorous, needs room to develop. 6′ tall by 7′ wide in 25 years. Introduced in 1939.

Mildred Mae (69G). (*poukhanense* x *mucronatum*). Flowers pale orchid purple, HCC 31/1, single, large. Early midseason, spreading. Original plant is 5′ tall and 30′ across in almost 50 years. Field hardy. More fragrant than most. Easy to root. Introduced in 1932.

Miriam (A10G). (*poukhanense* x *kaempferi*)F2 Flowers rose bengal with darker blotch, single. A week later than Springtime with conspicuous blotch. Vase shaped plant. Very vigorous and colorful. 8′ tall and 12′ across in 32 years.

Polaris (118G). (Springtime x Snow). Flowers white with faint chartreuse throat, single, 2-1/4″, hose-in-hose; midseason, compact, slow growing. Mr. Gable went back to growing this fine white after dropping it from earlier listings. Hardier than either Snow or Delaware Valley in some locations. Very floriferous. 4′ tall by 8′ across in 19 years.

Purple Splendour (C1G). (*poukhanense* x Hexe). Flowers reddish violet, HCC 31, single, fringed; midseason, open, larger growing than Herbert. Very hardy. Best in full sun. 6′ tall and 10′ wide in 19 years. Introduced in 1939.

Rosebud (B5G). (Louise Gable x Caroline Gable). Flowers rose pink, HCC 25/2, double, hose-in-hose, petaloid stamens and corolloid calyx. Like miniature roses on a very dwarf compact growing plant. 4' by 4' in 25 years. Much confused with several similar clones in the trade, including Lorna. Award of Merit, Royal Horticultural Society, 1972. Introduced in 1938.

Rose Greeley (D3G). [(*poukhanense* x *mucronatum*)F₂ x (*poukhanense* x Hexe) x (*poukhanense* x *kaempferi*)]. White with chartreuse blotch; single, 2-1/2", hose-in-hose, frilled, sweet scented. Early midseason. Dense, spreading. Hardy, becoming more so with age. 6' wide and 7' tall in 25 years. Introduced in 1940.

Springtime (A11G). (*poukhanense* x *kaempferi*)F₂. Flowers rose pink, HCC 25/1, with darker blotch, single, 2", very early. Plant upright spreading. 8' by 8' in 19 years. Very hardy. Introduced in 1937.

Stewartstonian (R5G). (parentage not recorded). Flowers clear red, single, midseason. Compact spreading. Striking bronze winter foliage. Reddish stems. Roots easily. One of Gable's finest. H.C., Royal Horticultural Society, 1971. 6' tall and 6' wide in 19 years. Introduced in 1952.

Viola (50G). (*poukhanense* x *mucronatum*). Flowers petunia purple, HCC 32/2, with darker blotch, single 2-3/4", early midseason. Wide open growth. 8' tall and 13' across in 25 years. Confused with 51G, and with 52G (Charlotte) which are similar.

Yorktown (A17G). (*poukhanense* x Hexe)F₂. Like an early, hardier Hino-red. Hose-in-hose, compact red. Becoming very hardy with age. Propagated and distributed extensively by Dauber's Nursery, York, Pa. For planting when Hino won't stand. Recently added to Gable list.

EVERGREEN AZALEAS NAMED AND INTRODUCED BY GABLE BUT LATER DROPPED

(Most were extensively propagated by Mr. Gable for a while, and some continue to be propagated by various nurserymen.)

Apricot (80G). (parentage not recorded). Apricot pink, very hardy. Flowers fade.

Cherokee (30G). [Hinodegiri x (*poukhanense* x *kaempferi*)]. Orange red; attractive to rabbits at Gable's.

Chinook (11G). (*kaempferi* x Yayegiri). Orange red, early. Dropped in favor of Mary Dalton.

Ethylwyn (49G). (parentage not recorded). Light pink, single. Not hardy enough to satisfy Gable.

Forest Fire (H6G). (*tschonoskii* x Caroline Gable). Flame red, single, hose-in-hose, flowers tiny in size. Compact, dense branching. Introduced 1942.

Fuchsia (F4G). (*linearifolium, macrosepalum* x Carolina Gable). Flowers violet red, HCC 28/2, single, hose-in-hose, frilled, somewhat pendant. Late midseason. Gable liked this very much, but it is not as hardy as some of his other introductions. Introduced 1942.

Glow of Dawn (115G). (*poukhanense* x *kaempferi*)F₂. Light pink, good, very early, but dropped in favor of Springtime which has a better habit.

Iroquois (45G). (*kaempferi* x Maxwelli). Fine large red. Too tender for Gable.

La Lumiere (100G). (Hinodegiri x *poukhanense* x *kaempferi*). Flowers flame red, single, small, on small upright plant. Similar to Hinodegiri but less compact. Roots easily.

La Premiere (1G). ((*poukhanense* x *kaempferi*) x *indicum*, double form). Flowers fuschine pink, double, late.

Linda Ann (C2G). Pink, double, hardy. A good azalea which Mr. Gable said was much like others he introduced.

Mable Zimmerman. (parentage not recorded). Flowers brick red, single; late midseason. Medium upright plant habit.

Pyxie (F2G). Similar to Forest Fire. Named by but not introduced by Gable. *Tschonoskii* hybrid. Pink, hose-in-hose.

EVERGREEN AZALEAS RAISED BY GABLE—NAMED AND MAINLY PROPAGATED BY OTHERS.

(Some propagated by Gable under number)

Billy (37G). (*poukhanense* x *kaempferi*). Showy violet red; low, dense.

Boudoir (18G). Rose pink with darker blotch, single. Roots easily. (Cannon)

Cameo (2G). (*poukhanense* x *kaempferi*) x *indicum*, double form . Pink, hose-in-hose, late. A tendency to double. Not as hardy as some.

Cameroon (97G). (*poukhanense* x Hexe) x (*poukhanense* x *kaempferi*). Red, with darker blotch, single.

Claret (10G). (*poukhanense* x Hexe)F₂. Dark red, single, hardy dwarf.

Charlotte (52G). (*poukhanense* x *mucronatum*). Lavender, single, spotted red. Sibling of Mildred Mae and Viola. Very large plant.

Corsage (16G). Orchid lavender, large, single, fast growing, very hardy, needs lots of room. Almost deciduous. Fragrant with age. (Cannon)

Deep Pink. (*kaempferi* x *poukhanense*). (O. S. Pride)

Edna (34G). (*poukhanense* x Hexe) x (*kaempferi* x *poukhanense*). Excellent pink, hose-in-hose. Similar to Carol but large flowers and not as hardy. (Tingle)

Fringed Beauty. Pink, single, fringed. (Tingle)

Gable's Flame (C4G). Syn: Gable's Scarlet. Orange red, single, hose-in-hose, frilled, medium spreading, late mid-season. Not as hardy as some.

Garda Joy (H12G). Beni-Kirishima hybrid. Flowers salmon coral, semi-double, 2-1/4", spreading, late. Similar to Beni-Kirishima, but hardier. (Griswold)

Grenadier. (perhaps 53G) Scarlet, single, very early and dependable. The first upright red to bloom. Not named or propagated by Gable.

Isabel. (Hexe x Pink Pearl). Apricot-rose, hose-in-hose. Not hardy for Gable. Greenhouse forcing variety.

J. C. Bowman. (*mucronatum* hybrid). Pink, single, fast growing.

Little Indian (83G). Dwarf red with coppery sheen. Similar to Claret.

Marjorie. (*kaempferi* x *poukhanense*). Bright orchid. (O. S. Pride)

Mauve. (*kaempferi* x *poukhanense*). Bright orchid. (O. S. Pride)

Mary Hohman. (*kaempferi* x *poukhanense*). Bright coral. (O. S. Pride)

Mrs. C. C. Miller. (parentage unknown). Flowers opening orange pink, fading to pink, 2-1/2", long lasting, very late. Original planted on Frick (Miller) estate, Waynesboro, Pa., with other Gable seedlings obtained from Dauber Nursery.

Nadine. (*kaempferi* x *poukhanense*). Light clear pink. (O. S. Pride)

Norbert. (*kaempferi* x *poukhanense*). Salmon red. (O. S. Pride)

Old Faithful (136G). (*poukhanense* x *kaempferi*). Rose, early mid-season. Earlier than others in this group. Hardy. Cuttings must be taken early to root easily.

Olive. (after Mrs. G. S. Lee, Jr.). Similar to Mildred Mae, but more compact. Hardy, vigorous, roots easily, flowers at young age. Propagated and distributed mainly in Connecticut. (Lee)

Peach. (*kaempferi* x *poukhanense*). Light peach pink. (O. S. Pride)

Pink Rosette (C5G). Reddish pink, double, late, low growing. (Tingle)

Royalty (A27G). Orchid purple with darker blotch. (Cannon)

Shell. (*kaempferi* x *poukhanense*). Light shell pink. (O. S. Pride)

Susan (54G). (*indicum* hybrid). Excellent single pink, hardy, roots easily. Late. (Tingle)

Vicky. (*kaempferi* x *poukhanense*). Bright coral. (O. S. Pride)

Victoria. (*kaempferi* x *poukhanense*). Salmon red. (O. S. Pride)

Watermelon. (*kaempferi* x *poukhanense*). Pink. (O. S. Pride)

White Star (117G). [(*poukhanense* x *kaempferi*) x Snow]. White, hose-in-hose. Sibling of Polaris. Hardier than Snow.

SEQUENTIAL LISTING OF NUMBERED EVERGREEN AZALEA CLONES BY GABLE

(Note: Many of those not named may be in the trade or private gardens)

1G   La Premiere
2G   Cameo
3G   semi-double pink
4G   lavender
5G   lavender, hose-in-hose, dwarf
6G   (record lost)
7G   pure pink (*poukhanense* x *kaempferi*) (difficult to propagate)
8G   scarlet, double (macrantha hybrid)
9G   maroon red, odd color, not hardy
10G   Claret
11G   Chinook
12G   carmine red
13G   Louise Gable
14G   pure pink
15G   (no record)
16G   (no record) may be Corsage
17G   pink, single, large growing, hardy; may be Boudoir
18G   (record lost)
19G   lavender, hose-in-hose, large fls., not bud hardy
20G   pink

21G   Elizabeth Gable
22G   like Elizabeth Gable, but tender
23G-29G   (no record)
30G   Cherokee
31G   bright red, tender
32G-33G   (no record)
34G   Edna
35G   similar to Edna
36G   White, hose-in-hose
37G   Billy
38G   Maryann
39G   (*poukhanense* x *kaempferi*)F$_2$, flame,
        and
40G   poor foliage.
41G   salmon pink, double
42G   Big Joe
43G   (no record)
44G   dark purple, tender
45G   Iroquois
46G   (*poukhanense* x Hexe) magenta, hose-in-hose
47G   Herbert
48G   showy bright, double pink, tender
49G   Ethelwyn
50G   Viola
51G   sibling of Viola, similar
52G   Charlotte, sibling of Viola, similar
53G   (no record) perhaps Grenadier
54G   Susan
55G-59G   (no record)
60G   pure pink
61G-62G   (no record)
63G   flame
64G-65G   (no record)
66G   pink, evergreen
67G   pink, fine winter foliage
68G   (no record)
69G   Mildred Mae
70G   rose
71G   discarded
72G   (no record)
73G   discarded
74G   bright magenta
75G   discarded
76G   lavender
77G   rose, double
78G   discarded
79G   dark purple, poor grower
80G   Apricot
81G   white, hose-in-hose
82G   red, large flowers, very vigorous
83G   Little Indian
84G   discarded
85G   (no record)
86G   hose-in-hose deep pink; sibling of Caroline
        Gable
87G   (no record)

88G   discarded
89G   discarded
90G   flame; seedling of Koster's *kaempferi* x Malvatica
91G-a   pink
91G-b   discarded
92G   pink, large flower
93G   dark red, mysteriously disappeared
94G   (no record)
95G   discarded
96G   Caroline Gable
97G   Cameroon
98G-99G   (no record)
100G   La Lumiere
101G-110G   (no record)
111G   Mary Dalton
112G   discarded
113G   pale lavender with yellow throat, tender;
        sibling of 126G
114G   clear pink, hard to root; sibling of 115G
115G   Glow of Dawn
116G   pink
117G   White Star
118G   Polaris
119G   pink, sibling of 117G and 118G, tender.
120G   Indian Summer (October)
121G   salmon, early
122G   pink, fastigiate; similar to Hinodegiri except in
        color
123G   pink, small flowers
124G   (no record)
125G   scarlet, late
126G   lavender with yellow throat
127G   carmine pink, early, very hardy
128G   pink, early
129G   rose pink
130G   pink, late
131G   light rose, spotted
132G   lavender, red throat
133G   scarlet, late
134G   red
135G   scarlet
136G   Old Faithful
137G   carmine, late
138G-139G   (no record)
140G   pale lavender
141G   pink, late
142G   discarded
143G   (no record)
144G   (J2G) red, large flowers
145G   H. W. Anderson
146G   red, hose-in-hose, late
147G   pinkish lavender, double
148G   pink *macrantha* hybrid, late tender
149G   (no record)
150G   pink *macrantha* hybrid, late
151G   pink, double

152G   pink, single, evergreen
153G   red, late
154G-175G   (no record)
176G   La Roche
177G-199G   (no record)
200G   Kathleen
201G   *mucronatum* x *kaempferi*; Discarded
202G   discarded
1115G   pure pink, large flowers; (*kaempferi* x *maxwelli*)F$_2$.
A1G   pink, fully double; (Louise Gable x 34G-Edna)
A2G   pink, fully double
A3G   red
A4G   rose purple
A5G   rose, very hardy
A6G   salmon pink
A7G   pink
A8G   pink
A9G   flame
A10G   Miriam
A11G   Springtime
A12G-A13G   discarded
A14G   coral pink, dwarf, not hardy
A15G-A16G   discarded
A17G   Yorktown
A18G-A26G   discarded
A27G   Royalty
A28G-A52G   discarded
B1G-B4G   discarded
B5G   Rosebud
B6G   discarded
B7G   flame scarlet, hose-in-hose, hard to root
B8G   Carol
B9G-B11G   discarded
C1G   Purple Splendour
C2G   Linda Ann
C3G   Mary Frances Hawkins
C4G   Gable's Flame
C5G   Pink Rosette
C6G   Jessie Coover
C7G   pink, fully double
C8G   Lorna
C9G   (no record)
C10G   red
D1G   red, good but tender
D2G   discarded
D3G   Rose Greeley
D4G   discarded
E1G   white, single

E2G-E9G   (no record)
E10G   discarded
E11G   white, single
F1G   James Gable
F2G   Pyxie
F3G   Campfire
F4G   Fuchsia
G1G   Gillin's Red
H1G-H5G   (no record)
H6G   Forest Fire
H7G-H11G   (no record)
H12G   Garda Joy
J1G   (*kaempferi* x Yayegiri)F$_2$, double
J2G   same as 144G
J3G   red; sibling of James Gable and Campfire
J4G   Judy
J5G-J10G   (no record)
J11G   Jimmie Coover
J12G   (no record)
J13G   similar to Mary Dalton, but lighter
K1G   no description
K10G   flame red, beautiful foliage
M1G   similar to K10G
M2G   no description
M3G   no description
O5G   no description
O7G   salmon red, semi-double
P1G   salmon red; very close to Jimmy Coover
P2G   flame red, single
R1G   deep purple, single
R2G   similar to Mary Dalton, but darker
R3G   no description
R4G   Margie
R5G   Stewartstonian
R6G   brilliant purple red
R7G   pink, single
S1G   no description
T1G   no description
T3G   no description
T4G   similar to T7G but more compact
T5G   no description
T6G   no description
T7G   Barbara Hille
T15G   no description
U1G   no description
V1G   Louise Gable seedling
macrosepalum hybrid #1 rose, red, single, vigorous
macrosepalum hybrid #2 violet red, vigorous, less
outstanding

This chapter was written with the collaboration of several persons comprising the "Gable Study Committee". Members were George W. Ring, Chairman, Caroline Gable, Colonel and Mrs. Raymond H. Goodrich, Mr. and Mrs. Charles Haag, and George Miller.

CHAPTER III

Benjamin Yeo Morrison
1891—1966

On the afternoon of May 3, 1954, Frederic P. Lee, Chairman of the
National Arboretum's Advisory Council, welcomed the many friends of
B. Y. Morrison who had gathered at the National Arboretum in
Washington, D.C. to dedicate the Morrison Azalea Garden.* Lee
remarked that it had always puzzled him that while Mr. Morrison was a
bachelor, he designated many of his azaleas with feminine names. Mr.
Lee introduced Dr. Henry T. Skinner who had succeeded Morrison as
the director of this 300-acre arboretum by the Anacostia River in the
District of Columbia.

   Dr. Skinner spoke to the representatives of many groups and
organizations which had encouraged and assisted the establishment of
this institution.

   "Just four years ago, I was a guest here at a rather similar event—the
dedication of Cryptomeria Valley of the Garden Club of America, and
was among those welcomed by Mr. Morrison. Little did I dream that
the tables would be turned and so quickly.

   "This earlier occasion was my first view of Mr. Morrison's azaleas in
full flower on this hillside. I shall never cease to marvel at them, and
can only hope that, with other plants and in other lines of plant

---

*Dedication from the transcript courtesy of The Hunt Library for Botanical Documentation,
Carnegie-Mellon University, Pittsburgh, Pennsylvania.

research, this National Arboretum will remain ever mindful of the standards set by its first director.

"This clonal azalea garden is already unique. Perhaps never before have the authentic products of a single breeder's skill been assembled as a permanently maintained master set for future observation and comparison. It will be of immeasurable value for continuous reference for azalea growers the world over that the fruits of his twenty-five years of careful breeding and selection are growing in this garden.

"Planned at this arboretum are a series of gardens to contain ultimately all the named azaleas susceptible to cultivation in this climate, to be used to determine correctness of name, cultural desirabilities, and their peculiarities on a testing basis. It is eminently fitting that the first unit of such a project should be the Glenn Dale hybrids, and equally fitting that the garden should be named for the originator of one of the finest races of azaleas we have yet seen . . ."

After an introduction by Lee, J. Earl Coke, then the Assistant Secretary of Agriculture, stated his pleasure in attending this meeting in recognition of the outstanding accomplishments of a former department worker.

J. Earl Coke's Tribute

"This pleasure is multiplied today, because the achievement we are honoring represents a work of art as well as a scientific accomplishment.

"In these days of national and international tension, it is a rare privilege to gather in a spot where there is so much natural beauty. As we look around us, we cannot restrain a certain amount of envy for those who have the privilege of working here every day. I have that feeling every time I visit the Arboretum.

"Many people seem to feel that the best thing about a job with the government is the security it affords. You sometimes hear people say that a career in the government does not offer enough opportunity for really creative accomplishment. Those people would change their minds if they could have witnessed the transformation of a very ordinary hillside into one of the most beautiful spots in America. It is entirely fitting, therefore, that we should be here today to recognize the work of Ben Morrison, and to dedicate to him the azalea clonal garden that will serve as a living tribute to the work of this extraordinary man.

"I suppose the starting point of our story goes back to a trip to the Orient made by Mr. Morrison on a Sheldon fellowship awarded by Harvard in 1916. There he saw what had been done with azaleas and visualized possibilities of what might be done in this country.

"In carrying on the work of plant introduction, ornamentals were included along with our food and fiber crops. Some of the introduced azaleas appeared to have many desirable qualities, but most of them did not have the hardiness needed in the Washington, D.C. area, or the flower size of the Indian azaleas in our southern gardens. At that time, the late 1920s, there was very little interest in azalea breeding in this country; so Ben Morrison decided to begin a breeding program to develop new varieties with large flowers and sufficient hardiness to be adapted for general eastern planting. He also wished to extend the flowering season, and to fill in some of the gaps.

"As with most plant breeding work, this job required many years. Those who knew Ben Morrison during this time tell me that he went about the new task with great thoroughness. He had to become familiar with every known species of azalea throughout the world and arrange for introduction of those which had the qualities needed for his breeding work. In those days, department people worked $5\frac{1}{2}$ days a week, but Ben went on a 7 day week. The first fruits of his work were distributed in 1939 and 1940. Something like 50 new varieties were released at that time under the name of Glenn Dale hybrids. Some of these new forms were distinct improvements over the older varieties adapted in this area but they were only a hint of what was to come later.

"During World War II, all the greenhouse facilities and manpower at Glenn Dale were turned over completely to special wartime jobs, and the new azaleas had to wait. After the war, Morrison returned to evaluate his breeding work. Most of the crosses had already been made, and the big job at this time was to make selections. You can realize what a big job this was when you learn that he grew 75,000 seedlings and selected 454.

"The creation of so much beauty for its own sake is a significant achievement. But a horticulturist such as Ben Morrison would not be satisfied to stop at that point. One of his earliest plans for the Arboretum called for a clonal garden in which one or more examples of each variety of azaleas would be included. As it now stands, the garden represents primarily the Glenn Dale azaleas, but future plans call for adding individual plants from all available species and varieties that will grow in this area. Here, then, will be a place where students, plant breeders, and plain ordinary folk can come to study azaleas. This garden will serve as a "card catalog" to one of the most notable collections of azaleas to be found anywhere. We meet here today to pay tribute to this remarkable man by naming this the Morrison Azalea Garden."

Morrison surrounded by his Glenn Dale Azalea creations

Morrison's Response at the Dedication

With his characteristic modesty, B. Y. Morrison responded to J. Earl Coke's address by saying:

"At this moment the one item which seems most important to me is to assure you that I do not feel distinguished; that I do not feel important; that I feel extraordinarily humble.

I would like to say that it has been a privilege to work for the government. I still well remember the day, a good many years ago, when I signed my name to a sheet of paper as a newly appointed government employee. I signed that very seriously and very ceremoniously, and I promised to give loyal and faithful service to my country as I began this service. And, I can assure that there were times when some of my colleagues thought that perhaps I had brought forth too much and too fast. If I have brought too much, then I can say it has been a great privilege to work where I did see a great variety of plants, and also to see them in the hands of great colleagues, and to work with persons who were willing to give me their faith and trust in my accomplishment in the developing of the things that you see about us; and that you see and enjoy them today—and you will likewise be able to appreciate and enjoy them later on.

"The thought that comes to me that is most important is that there was the proper timing in the breeding program in the stepping up of time and place. These same things would have been accomplished at some other time by someone else anyhow.

"I am greatly touched by the honor and extent of your garden dedication. I owe a great debt to a great number of persons, some of whom I know and some of whom I shall never know, for I have never been able to find who they were. For instance, I have no way of knowing the names of the Japanese gardeners who were so kind and helpful in passing the azaleas through our hands. I owe a debt to those unknown persons and a debt to the persons who lived years ago in England, China, Belgium, France, and to many others in this country, and an enormous debt to my colleagues at the Station and at Glenn Dale where they were grown, where they raised them for me so that they lived and so that they were increased. I also owe still greater debt to all of those faithful employees who did the hard jobs; who cut down the trees, suffered with the poison ivy and the chiggers and various other inconveniences. I even owe a debt to those who built the old school along our boundary—for nearly all the brick from the school was used in the buiding of this garden. And, I owe still another debt to Sir Edward Luytens, an English architect after whose pattern for formal gardens in England this garden was planned. So, if there is any beauty in the brickwork of this particular garden, I am happy to acknowledge it.

"As I stand before you today, I would like you to realize that I am honored, I am moved, and I am touched by what you are doing.

"In my mind, I am here often, and even when I am not here, I hope you may feel my presence in this garden. Eventually, I hope to be able to send you, from my own new garden, other azaleas which I do believe will grow and be hardy here.

"I, too, believe in the values and beauty of human life, and as one enjoys it to the degree of is own person; but I myself like to think that I am only one link in the great chain in the Department of Agriculture. So, if I could, as a conductor of a symphony orchestra does, I would ask you to stand and share the acclaim for his performance."

His Many Talents

Benjamin Yeo Morrison, while professionally a horticulturist, geneticist, plant breeder, and plantsman extraordinary, had diverse artistic talents. They encompassed many of the fine arts: he was a painter of landscapes, architectural renderings, flowers, and technical botanical drawings; a musician, accomplished at the piano and organ, a vocalist who gave many professional concerts, usually of sacred music or German lieder, a composer of an opera libretto *Salve Regina*. In the practical arts, he was known as a landscape designer with acute sensitivities for color, form, and texture; and by temperament, varying with the mood—charming, ebullient, gracious, taciturn, or vituperative.

He was born in Atlanta, Georgia, on November 25, 1891, the son of Lyle Morrison. He was quite close to his brother George, but agreed to disagree with his sister Phoebe. He attended the University of California, Berkeley, where he earned a B.Sc. in 1913, followed by an M.A. in Landscape Architecture from Harvard University in 1915, and a Sheldon Traveling Fellowship to the Orient in 1915-16. Later, he served as a Second Lieutenant in World War I, then briefly practiced landscape architecture with a New York City firm until 1920, when he joined the U.S. Department of Agriculture as assistant to David Fairchild. Beginning as a horticulturist, he became Chief, Division of Plant Exploration and Introduction, at Glenn Dale, Maryland from 1934-48. Morrison, from 1937-51, was Acting Director and then Director of the U.S. National Arboretum at Washington, D.C. On his own time, he was an indefatigable gardener, testing many plants on his home grounds at Takoma Park, Maryland, and later in retirement at Pass Christian, Mississippi. He was the principal founder of the American

Morrison (right) with sister Phoebe, brother George, and parents

cuts, when we dared not find a more expensive cover, and all such. An endless petitioning of personal friends and acquaintances for copy, all went into the whole.

Morrison received numerous horticultural awards. Among them were: the Gold Medal of the American Horticultural Society (A.H.S.); the Gold Medal of the American Daffodil Society; the Veitch Memorial Gold Medal; the Peter Ban Memorial Cup of the Royal Horticultural Society for his work with daffodils; the Distinguished Service Medal of the American Iris Society; the Arthur Hoyt Scott Horticultural Medal and Award; and the Sarah Fife Memorial Trophy of the Garden Club of America. He was a vice-president of the Royal Horticultural Society (R.H.S.) from 1945 until his death in 1966. He remained a bachelor all his life. One of his closest friends speculated that he shunned marriage because he heard so

Horticultural Society in 1924, and served as editor of its magazine for 37 years until 1963, and as President of the American Horticultural Society from 1936-40. Through all those years, his enthusiasm, almost limitless energy, extensive correspondence with horticulturists, gardeners, and botanists, and his remarkable number of horticultural lectures and articles enabled the society to grow and take a leading position in American horticulture. Morrison spoke and wrote with an excellence of style that included a special verve and charm. Of his work as editor, Morrison reminisced in a letter to a friend in 1965:

> Whatever I learned in the years of working with the Quarterly was learned from the old system of trial and error with some welcome assistance from the printers and from a few critical friends who were connected with publication work in other fields, one a newspaper man in Chicago.
>
> This plus an ambition that had a dubious base, were spurs of sorts. No one of my colleagues in the beginning had much courage, and the fact that I was repeatedly told that "it could not be done" were my goads.
>
> Many of the things done were determined by costs. This was particularly true in relation to illustrations. Drawings, when we had no photographs; linoleum

The NATIONAL HORTICULTURAL MAGAZINE

JOURNAL OF THE AMERICAN HORTICULTURAL SOCIETY, INC.

JANUARY 1954

Cover of "National Horticultural Magazine," January 1954. Morrison edited this journal and made the cover drawing.

From Morrison's sketch book, Japan trip 1916

much parental quarreling, even though he was fond of women and gave feminine names to many of his hybrids.

How he got started with azaleas is not known. Surely he saw them during his traveling fellowship in Japan, but they did not feature prominently in the sketchbook he filled that year with landscapes, garden architectural details, and quick, candid impressions of Japanese women and children he saw there. It is likely that his azalea fever began when he joined the Department of Agriculture in 1920 as horticulturist with the Division of Plant Exploration and Introduction of the Bureau of Plant Industry, Soils, and Agricultural Engineering (D.P.E. & I.). This division received vegetables, grains, fruits, shrubs, and trees from all over the world; grew them in test gardens to evaluate their suitability in our climate, or incorporated their genes in breeding programs. During his long service

in D.P.E. & I., over 92,000 plant introductions from all over the world were brought in for study. About 1 in every 250 of these contributed to advances in horticulture and farming, either as new items for the garden or as breeding stock carrying some new quality of value to the hybridizer. Morrison firmly believed in and spoke publicly of the value of his Division's efforts:

Reintroduction of wild stock is valuable. Plant life may well become too refined, too cultivated after a time. From India have come virile new stock from the pumpkin-squash family, citrus fruits of the mountains with cold resistance, and peaches at home in hot climates. From Mexico, Central and South America arrive new tobacco seeds. From China come soybeans, the Chinese Elm of great beauty, a crested wheat grass of merit in the dust bowl for a cover crop. From Japan and South America come blight resistant chestnuts, alfalfa, and peanuts. Each country has its contribution to awaken slumbering stocks, and inject the necessary virility for their far-flung American homes.

Among these myriad introductions were cuttings of Japanese azaleas sent in by R. K. Beattie, in 1928, including *R. indicum, mucronatum,* and *phoenicium* which may have caught Morrison's eye as likely candidates to help create a race of large-flowered evergreen azaleas.

The Project Begins

The Glenn Dale azalea breeding project began "on a serious scale" in 1929, "with the end in view of creating races of azaleas that should be winter hardy at Washington, D.C., and that should have flowers as large as those borne by the varieties of Indian azaleas which were the great ornament of southern gardens," Morrison wrote in the *Agriculture Monograph No. 20,* published October, 1953. The article also contained the following:

In looking over the materials, it was found that a rather greater number of species and garden forms was available than had been anticipated. However, there was not only a definite lack of information about these plants, but also much difference of opinion as to the hardiness of some of the members of the section and their progeny.

Two species were cold-hardy in the Washington area beyond all question: Kaempfer's azalea (*R. kaempferi* Planch.) and the Korean azalea (*R. poukhanense* Lev.). Equally hardy under nearly all local conditions, but occasionally suffering, were the Satsuki azaleas (Azalea macrantha of commerce, R. indicum of the botanists); the forms of *R. mucronatum* (Blume) G. Don (A. *indica alba,* A. *ledifolia,* A. *rosmarinifolia,* of trade); several forms of *R. phoeniceum* (Sweet) G. Don, with Maxwell's azalea the most reliable (R. *phoeniceum f. maxwellii* (Millais) Wils.); and the Kurume azaleas (clonal variants of R. *obtusum f. japonicum* (Maxim.) Wils.). Open to question were various "Indian azaleas" from the South, some of which have since proved to be much hardier than was first expected. Root-hardy but regularly plant-injured in some localities and exposures has been Oldham's azalea (R. *oldhamii* Maxim.) from Formosa.

To this group were added later plants raised from Chinese seed of what is considered R. *simsii* Planchon, although the seedlings do not agree perfectly in all details with taxonomic descriptions; the Japanese horticultural clones reported as 'indica x macrantha'

hybrids, some of which appear to be mere color variants of R. *indicum* (L.) Sweet (A. *macrantha*); some hybrids that may involve blood of the plant that Hayata described as R. *indicum* var. eriocarpum.

The hybrid seedlings that had been carefully grown under greenhouse conditions through one summer and winter and whatever part of the second summer that elapsed before all transplanting was completed to well-prepared beds with high deciduous shade. The seedlings were by no means uniform in size, but nearly all had sound woody stems at ground level.

After this initial care, the plantings were left to thrive or fail under natural conditions, in order that all weaklings might perish.

An examination of those that did fail (winterkill) showed that greater losses occurred where the tree cover was inadequate, and in those seedlings that had the thinnest woody stems. The greatest damage to tops showed on those plants that did not ripen new wood sufficiently before the first killing frost, which commonly occurs in this area in mid-October and frequently is followed by a month without other killing frosts. There were relatively few cases in which the deaths might be explained solely from the use of one parent of known or of presumed tenderness.

The first winter passed judgment on the transplanted seedlings. All weaklings were killed, and none that barely survived was coddled back to health. The rest were allowed to grow normally and with no special care in the woodland where the seed population had been planted. No choice was ever made from a plant that did not grow vigorously. Propagations by cuttings made in a coldframe under good, but not better than nursery, facilities produced the thousands of plants that were sent to the National Arboretum for permanent display. The nursery there was exposed, with no tree cover. A few hedges of California privet were planted to break the full force of the wind. Ample peat moss was plowed and harrowed into the soil. After 5 years, it was possible to tell that all would grow well in field conditions, but a location free from late spring frosts would have produced even better plants. No training or pruning was given, and eventually much overcrowding resulted before transplanting to permanent location was possible. A review of these plants showed that no weaklings had been chosen and none on which the foliage was poor.

Personal taste has much to do with one's preference between the glistening pointed leaves of the *indicum* type, the sometimes glossy, often obovate leaves of the Kurume type, the larger softer leaves of the *simsii* x *kaempferi* derivatives, or the longer, obviously downy leaves that stem from *mucronatum.* The essential point is that the plant should, at maturity, appear well clothed with foliage.

Although it should be obvious from all the foregoing,

the azalea work was carried out on the basis of plant breeding, and no genetic studies were made. No care in pollination was used that would justify genetic conclusions, but one or two observations may be useful to other plant breeders.

It has already been stated by other workers that crosses can be successfully made between any two species within the section. This has been true in every case tried.

In the inheritance of striping, several observations were made. In all cases save one, where a colored flower and a striped flower were crossed, approximately a 1:3 ratio is obtained if the whites are counted together with the striped whites. Unfortunately, the white plants were not grown on to see if striping appeared later.

Although they are known to exist in various races and the writer has one Japanese clone in which a dark stripe occurs on a colored ground, this pattern was not observed until 1947, when a clone that never before had shown any stripes gave a few flowers in which a rose-colored stripe appeared on the pale pink ground. Several more appeared as bud sports, flowering in 1948.

In the majority of cases, the stripe on the upper surface of the petal is not directly over the stripe on the undersurface, but in all cases in which the stripe is broadened into what might be called a sector, this color is the same on both surfaces.

In some clones in which the flowers show no striping, the leaves at time of autumn coloring show blotches of much deeper color that are distributed almost like stripes on the petal tissue. These are clones with a striped parent in the immediate ancestry.

The most unusual striped flower in the collection resulted from the cross Vittata Fortunei X Louise. (Louise is a good rose-colored clone of *kaempferi* X Malvatica blood.) This particular seedling bears two different types of striped flowers consistently on the separate branches, and also throws entire branches of self-colored deep red flowers. The lighter striped flower has a dull-white ground somewhat green-toned on the upper lobe, the entire flower irregularly and completely striped with light red; the darker striped flower is similar, but has a preponderance of dark, somewhat broader, red stripes. The leaves of this plant show very definite blotch colorations of crimson as autumn approaches, though during the rest of the year leaves appear normal.

Self-colored flowers crossed with white flowers bearing colored margins or white flowers with stripes gave only one patterned flower out of several hundred in the F_1 generation. The pollen parent was dominant in bush habit.

White flowers crossed with the same set of striped and bordered flowers returned practically all the patterns, but mostly gave dominance of the white

flower growth habits and only slight reduction in size over the patterned flower.

No definite suggestions can be offered as to the inheritance of a highly pigmented blotch. There is apparently a special type of cell that holds the pigmentation, and the effect may be clearly drawn, as in many of the *poukhanense* hybrids, or diffuse, as in some of the *simsii* hybrids. Only in some individual cases was the F_1 blotch resulting from the mating of two blotched parents stronger than that of the parents.

In contrast to this pattern of the upper lobe, mention might be made of the pattern of *R. oldhamii* in which the flower color is salmon to orange, and the area where the blotches would be is not blotched but pigmented with a definitely lavender pink. This combination was noted in several old but unnamed varieties at Magnolia Gardens, Charleston, S.C., none of which are likely to have blood of *R. oldhamii* in their ancestry, since they were produced before that species was in cultivation. No crosses have been made to show the manner of inheritance of this type of blotch.

For the worker who is concerned with the breeding of azaleas, various unknowns appear to be beyond present solution. Most of them have been mentioned indirectly in this monograph. For example, the precise origins of the clonal variations of the Kurume azaleas are not known, and the steps that lead to their present range of variations are also unknown; the latter are essentially of horticultural rather than taxonomic significance. Again, it appears unlikely that there will ever be available a complete and accurate record of the much more modern races of Japanese azaleas, of which the much advertised clone, Gumpo, may serve as an illustration. The "Indian azaleas" surviving in the southern gardens and their descendants, which are somewhat divergent from the older clones and are represented by what nurserymen of today call "Belgian" azaleas, will probably never be determined except by inference, which never provides a completely safe criterion.

The writer has produced some flowers that in one way or another approximate the "Indian azaleas" of the South, and several that definitely approximate the modern "Belgian" type. Some evidence exists that the combination is most likely to appear in progenies that involve three blood lines, usually with blood of some form of *mucronatum* or its close kin in addition to the to-be-expected *indicum* and *simsii*.

The further problem remains—what element was introduced and when, that brought tenderness into this race whose progenitors all are cold-hardy here? This has not yet been revealed by such studies of the literature as have been possible or surmised from experience, but Vittata Fortunei has given a fair percentage of cold-tender progeny in almost every combination.

Not all the Vittata Fortunei hybrids were cold-tender, as the following abstract of Morrison's work sheets on these crosses shows.[1] It also gives evidence that considerable study was made before the final selections were determined:

At Glenn Dale, or later in Takoma Park, when a seed harvest was made from a cross, a Bell number was assigned to the entire population under which it was grown to flowering. If selections were made from that population, individual Bell numbers were given to each plant. Later, those plants that were selected to be given PI numbers were chosen from these selected clones. Most of these were determined on the basis of individual performance not only at Glenn Dale but also at Takoma Park, where a small clonal propagation was also grown. The number of PI selections, however, was greatly increased by studies in 1945-47 on the materials still growing at Glenn Dale and not represented in Takoma Park. These last were from crosses made at Takoma Park, germinated at Glenn Dale, and sent to the National Arboretum as whole populations (Bell nos. 33337-67 inclusive).

One of the definite projects given to Mr. Gunning in the earliest stages of the azalea breeding project was to cross "Vittata Fortunei" with everything available. This was carried out on the plant bought from Fruitland Nurseries (Bell 10159) the spring following its purchase. The plants were potted and the work was done under glass.

Notes were taken in May, 1939, in the woods planting on the populations covered by the following numbers in the Bell series. The notes were taken primarily to record if striped flowers would appear in F_1 generation.

13555 Vittata Fortunei X HEA#38, 25 plants. No whites or stripes.

13556 Vittata Fortunei X Amoena, 42 all strong purplish.

13557 Vittata Fortunei X Kaempferi, 52 all pink.

13558 Vittata Fortunei X Ho-oden, 33 plants, 7 whites.

13559 Vittata Fortunei X Marta, 25 in population. 13 white and white with stripes. Flowers smaller than those of Vittata, about Kaempferi size. Very good form. Bush of considerable height and more twiggy than most Vittata Fortunei seedlings. (Later observations show us no notes on the earliest selections, B. 27416-18, only that a second lot, 32148-50, were all chosen for earliness and their delicate colorings.)

[1]From the Hunt Library for Botanical Documentation, Carnegie Mellon University, Pittsburgh, Pa.

Caress PI 141769 was originally B. 27417.

Dayspring PI 141780 was originally B. 32149.

13560 Vittata Fortunei X Maxwelli, 50 plants. No whites or stripes.

13561 Vittata Fortunei X Bridesmaid, 20 all pink.

13562 Vittata Fortunei X HEA#34, 10, no whites.

13563 Vittata Fortunei X Amoena (see 13556 above), 38 plants in population, 11 whites and whites with stripes. (At this writing, I have no recollection as to why the cross appears twice, nor why there were no whites in the other series.) From this series were selected:
B. 27419-25 inclusive; also 32151 and 32152.
PI 141770 (B. 27422) = Alabaster.
PI 141771 (B. 27424) = Stardust.
PI 141772 (B. 27425) = Minuet.

13564 Vittata Fortunei X Alice, 75 plants in population. A very fine lot, **strong colors and strong blotches—no whites.** (B. 32476-86) inclusive were selected for further examination. Only one of these, B. 32481, were given *PI No. 14197,* and named Jongleur.)

13565 Vittata Fortunei X Willy, 38, no white.

13566 Vittata Fortunei X indica alba *(R. mucronatum),* 53, 32 white or striped.

13567 Vittata Fortunei X Omurasaki, *45 plants in population, six stripes altogether,* mostly weak growth, fairly largish flowers. B. 27415 given PI141768 named Mavourneen.

13568 Vittata Fortunei X Gibiyama, 22, 10 white with stripes.

13569 Vittata Fortunei X Surisumi, 20 plants, 8 white, 1 flaked.

13570 Vittata Fortunei X Asahi, 18 plants, 12 striped or white.

13571 Vittata Fortunei X Miyagimo, 23 plants, 7 white or striped. One plant, saved as B. 27445, has been named Geisha and released as PI 141774.

13572 Vittata Fortunei X Kurai-no-himo, 19, none white.

13574 Vittata Fortunei X Louise, *59 plants in population; 22 of these white* or striped. Plants essentially like Kaempferi in habit; stripes all within color range of Kaempferi. Another population of 21 plants under this same Bell number, with 2 whites and 4 striped flowers, showed many dead, flowers all brilliant and often blotched.

13575 Vittata Fortunei X Koraini, 11, 3 white or striped.

13576 Vittata Fortunei X Kyu-Miyagimo, 39 plants in population, 16 whites and striped whites. A very nice lot. Medium-sized flowers, some tendency to form ragged petaloid calyx. (Ten individuals were propagated for examination, B. 27451-60, with a later choice of others, 32269 and 32301-05. From the first series, B. 27460, has been introduced as

Pixie, PI 141777. One of the others was given PI 141790, and named Pastel.

13609 Vittata Fortunei X Louise (see also 13574), 36 plants in population. Notes not very full, it is indicated that many plants had died and many were poor. Two whites and three striped plants. (Apparently no selections were made from this population.)

13622 Vittata Fortunei X Sunstar, 40, no whites.

13628 Vittata Fortunei X Hinodegiri, 48 plants, brilliant colors.

It is regretted that no record was kept of the number of seedlings originally put out in the woodland nursery. The population figures represent the survivors as of May, 1939.

A Friend Recalls

There were some difficulties and interruptions in this azalea breeding project, according to Eugene Hollowell, a longtime friend and neighbor in Takoma Park.

"Ben Morrison was actively interested in ornamental plants, but this group had stepchild status in the section on fruit and vegetable crops. He collected azalea species and hybrids with parent potentials for his breeding project only when time was available from his higher priority agricultural plant work. During the mid-1930's, a newly appointed Chief of the D.P.E. & I. ordered Morrison to 'get rid' of his azaleas at Glenn Dale Station, and forbade him to do any additional work on them. Stung but not defeated, he moved the plants to a two-acre garden near the Takoma Park home where he lived with his parents. There, the last Glenn Dale crosses and selections were made. Later, when that chief resigned, there was much rejoicing in the division, but Ben's wounds were slow to heal. When the next bureau chief saw Ben's hybrids at Takoma Park, he agreed they should be released to the public. Moved back to Glenn Dale Station, the selected plants were propagated and released to the nursery trade as 'Glenn Dale' azaleas.

"Two Maryland nurserymen in particular, Tingle and Hohman, propagated them extensively and were thereby instrumental in their wide distribution in the eastern United States. Tingle's efforts were so large-scale and persistent that Ben turned to him to propagate his 'Back Acres' hybrids that were selected in Pass Christian after his retirement in 1951."

Eugene Hollowell's friendship with Ben Morrison had begun in 1928, and in their many conversations over the years, the former came to know much about the man and his plants. In Hollowell's view:

Those who knew Ben Morrison well, loved him. He was kind, witty, helpful, and charming, but could be irascible to those who disagreed. He did write scathing letters when in reality he meant to be forthright. He was sometimes maligned by people who did not know him and his characteristic way of challenging statements that were inaccurate was evident in his correspondence and editorials. Ben's artistry, appreciation of colors and their combinations, and his landscaping training and experience formed the basis of his selection of parents for the Glenn Dales. Ben did allow that he may have named too many clones—but those nearly identical in flower color or form *did* differ in blooming period or plant habit. Many excellent hybrids were not named. For example, Albert Close, who did most of the propagation, gave me a collection of one cross which he called the sweet pea group. Albert wanted to save them from being burned, and I think some of them ought to be named.

After living with the Glenn Dales for over twenty-five years, Ben had these comments: "Parade is a large flowered fine purple. F. C. Bradford is a strong crimson red. For a smaller-flowered purple, Damaris is good. Sappho and Zulu are good purples with strong dots on the upper lobes. Welcome is a beautiful pink with white center and more dependable than Helen Gunning." Among the large whites, he liked Artic, Everest, and Nativity. Among the brownish reds, Carmel, Gladiator, and Galathea. Burgundy he thought especially fine. Once, when asked for a list of choice cultivars, he recommended Helen Close, Martha Hitchcock, Fountain, Pearl Bradford, Acrobat, Bravura, Terese, Wildfire and Moonbeam. When asked by novice breeders what parents he would recommend, he would advise that, Selection should be based on those sorts which do well under your conditions.

Hollowell especially recalled how thoroughly Ben enjoyed singing:

He had a fine, sensitive baritone voice and he often was his own accompanist. He sang as a soloist with choirs, and occasionally gave voice lessons. I have been

Springtime   West   31   *Big Joe*   Ring

Gable's azalea creations were bred for hardiness. Springtime (30) the first of his hybrids to bloom; Big Joe (31) a flamboyant show in early spring; Rose Greeley (32) a very evergreen hose-in-hose; Carol (33) and a fall leaf display of Campfire (34) in the same blazing red as the flowers.

Rose Greeley   West

3   *Carol*   West   34   *Campfire*   West

Gable's Rosebud (36) is a favorite double pink azalea with wide distribution; Conewago (35) and Pioneer (38) extend the blooming season of *R. mucronulatum* by two weeks; Flamingo (37) is a striking sibling of Mary Belle (see 54).

35 *Conewago* Wes

36 *Rosebud* Suggs

37 *Flamingo* Ring

38 *Pioneer* Leac

Cadis   West

40   *R. brachycarpum x vernicosum Rock #18139*   Ring

Four exemplary Gable rhododendrons: Cadis (39) received the Award
of Excellence from the A.R.S. in
1959; *R. brachycarpum* x *vernicosum*
Rock #18139 (40); Strawberry Swirl
(41) formerly known as Jacksoni #5;
Albert Close (42) a hybrid of eastern
and western species *R. maximum*
and *R. macrophyllum*.

1   *Strawberry Swirl*   West   42   *Albert Close*   Suggs

The wide variety of Gable rhododendrons is demonstrated by three hybrids named for his family — Caroline (43), David Gable (44) and Isabelle (45). County of York (46), previously called Catalode, was named for his home county. It received the Award of Excellence in 1960.

44   *David Gable*   Leac

43   *Caroline*   West

45   *Isabelle*   Miller

46   County of York   Sugg

Maxhaem Salmon   Goodrich   48

Moonshot   Ring

Tommy #2   Goodrich

Beaufort   Suggs

Another selection from Gable's rich legacy: Maxhaem Salmon (47); Moonshot (48); Tommy #2 (49); Beaufort (50); Catfortcampy (51) and Tom Thumb (52). Hybrids making up the Tommy series are Gable-Yates grown seedlings of Tom Thumb (Mars x (*catawbiense* x *haematodes* #1) selfed.

Catfortcampy   Ring   52

Tom Thumb   Miller

53   *Catalgla*   Miller

54   *Mary Belle*   Su

Five major Gable plants with genes for the future: Catalgla (53) a valuable parent for hardy whites; Mary Belle (54) an exceptional hybrid named for Mrs. Gable; Mary Garrison (55) parent of good yellow offspring; Pink Twins (56) with hose-in-hose flowers; Henry Yates (57) noted for its excellent deep green foliage.

55   *Mary Garrison*   M

56   *Pink Twins*   Suggs

57   *Henry Yates*   Sug

59   *Mary Fleming*   Grothaus

e 40 year collaboration of Guy Nearing and Joseph
ble (58) was commemorated in 1964 by the New York
apter of the American Rhododendron Society. Mary
eming (59) a *racemosum/keiskei* cross, is among the
ost popular Nearing lepidote hybrids; Rochelle (60) a
e pink.

60   *Rochelle*   Leach

Guy Nearing and Joseph Gable   Sleezer

61   *Windbeam*   Livingston

62   *Windbeam*   Livings

Nearing's Windbeam (61 and 62) received the
A.R.S. Award of excellence in 1973; a hybrid
of Conestoga, as is Wyanokie (63) with
larger leaves and whiter blossoms. Purple
Gem (64) is similar to Ramapo, but not as
dwarf. Nearing Pink (65).

63   *Wyanokie*   West

64   *Purple Gem*   West   65   *Nearing Pink*   Su

told that he was offered an opportunity to try out for the Metropolitan Opera. I have heard him sing "Ave Maria" several times and each time my eyes got misty.

When he moved to Pass Christian, Mississippi, his friend Ivan Anderson's house was not large enough to accommodate his piano. So he gave it to the neighborhood church, and became choir director and soloist. The church had to build an addition a few years after Ben's arrival there.

He put much energy into everything he did. He started a commercial nursery at Pass Christian, which he claimed was his greatest mistake, mostly because he wasn't able to get the help to do things with the degree of excellence that he demanded. He frequently refused rides in automobiles, claiming to get both exercise and time to think and plan from walking. I can still see him striding along in his long, loping walk.

Morrison's Ladies

Who were some of the women that Ben Morrison honored by giving their names to his azaleas?

Janet Noyes had been very helpful to Ben in his efforts to get sufficient funds to maintain the newly established National Arboretum. (Her family controlled the *Washington Star.*) She also helped Ben engineer an agreement to supply azalea cuttings to the National Capital Parks System.

Grace Freeman, the wife of a botanist at the National Arboretum.

Helen Close, the wife of Albert Close, Ben's chief propagator, who came to Glenn Dale from Kew Gardens and was honored by Joseph Gable who named a rhododendron hybrid for him.

Helen Gunning, the wife of Harry Gunning, Superintendent of the United States Plant Introduction Station at Glenn Dale, who also helped Ben at the arboretum.

Leonore, the wife of F. J. Hopkins, an assistant at Glenn Dale.

Louise Dowdle, wife of Frank Dowdle, a propagator at Glenn Dale, who worked briefly for Morrison at Pass Christian.

Martha Hitchcock, the wife of A. S. Hitchcock, principal botanist of D.P.E. & I. and author of the classic *Manual of Grasses of the United States.*

Mary Helen, Harry Gunning's daughter.

Phoebe, Ben's sister.

Pearl Bradford, the Glenn Dale Superintendent's wife.

Corrine Murrah, of Memphis, Tennessee, who collected Ben's azaleas and corresponded voluminously with him.

May Blaine, his secretary who helped him both at Glenn Dale and the National Arboretum.

Marion Lee, the wife of Frederick P. Lee, author of *The Azalea Book.*

A Visit to Pass Christian

In the 1966 *Gardener's Forum* of the A.H.S., Mrs. Francis Patteson-Knight wrote of her visit to Morrison in Pass Christian:

After several letters and telephone calls we had set off for Pass Christian, well provided with instructions regarding the route. We managed to over-run the turn, and called Mr. B. Y. Morrison to tell him where we were and when we expected to arrive. After more detailed instructions, we finally drove into Pass Christian. At the turn for Back Acres, standing in the middle of the road was a tall, sparse, white maned figure waving frantically. Close by, in a Volkswagen, sat Ivan Anderson and their constant companion Doug, a charming well-fed Dachshund. Not only did we explore the garden, going over every inch of it, seeking out all the treasure, and all the species and forms of zephyranthes and habranthus, of which he had written me so often, and which now flaunted their delicate pastel blossoms. We also saw the now introduced "Back Acres" azaleas, magnolias and Ny Tiawan cherries of which he had told me in a letter, "Ny Tiawan have had a few short sprays of bloom, very interesting in that the color appears to deepen with age; what happens is that the calyx darkens and the base of the stamens as well, so that the light area there appears to vanish, ruddy! I'll check the Ridgeway color in the morning, if I get up in time." We spent many pleasant hours poring over slides (the azaleas were out of bloom) and his delicate drawings—and just talking. Each day brought new surprises, for not only was he a great plantsman, and an able artist, but his love and knowledge of music added to our enjoyment. He gave us a wonderful evening in the little church where he worked and prayed—here he sang for fully two hours accompanying himself on

Morrison in Pass Christian, Mississippi

the piano. We listened spellbound to ballads, Jewish chants, the songs of John Ireland and Brahms . . . it was unforgettable.

Ben Morrison never ceased to amaze me; his volume of correspondence was quite unbelievable. He was deeply interested in plants and people; he spent many hours in serving A.H.S. even after his name disappeared from the masthead of the magazine. But, I think that the quality which endeared him the most (at least to me) was his childlike simplicity and humility, here was no puffed up *I am better than you man* but a gentle, understanding wholly delightful companion, making you feel at one and the same time on an intelligence level with him (this in my case was purely imaginary), and I am so very grateful for the privilege of his friendship.

How did Ben Morrison perceive himself? A few quotations gleaned from his retirement correspondence preserved in the Hunt Library for Botanical Documentation in Pittsburgh give an impression of his self-awareness. Writing to an apologetic and delinquent correspondent in 1949:

Descriptions of my disposition would vary enormously depending on whom you asked! Having been an idiot all my life, who thought he could do more than any one person should attempt, I have spent most of my life in hot water, so I couldn't be nasty about non-acknowledgements should I want to.

Two years later, confiding to a close friend about personal matters, he wrote:

My own (physique) is excellent in spite of my 60 years, and except for the neck muscles that are definitely showing age, getting stringy, the body itself does not betray it. And it has served me well for many years of active work and promises to serve me well for years to come. I have used barbells, carefully for some time, with some interruptions, but I look forward to renewing my routines. I use them for my health, and they have done all that is claimed for them.

What I hope I can do, once I am safely past the details of getting settled into the new home and garden in Mississippi, is to go back to drawing and painting again. Aside from making scientific drawings and some horticultural drawings, I have had no time to consider it since high school days. Then I did well enough, but it was all brushed aside in the necessity of earning a living.

My difficulty at the moment is that this week I am concluding my lifelong career as a worker in the U.S. Department of Agriculture, and while I myself should much prefer to slip out of my past with no more than the cordial relations that I have always enjoyed with my colleagues, they feel that I must be feted in all the embarrassing ways that attend "final days!"

Writing to a nurseryman in Oregon about his want-list of camellias and magnolias for his retirement home:

Apparently I shall continue to live for some years, since I come of tough stock and long-lived, but when I buy any plants I have an argument with myself, about the wisdom of each purchase. I do not always yield to my persuasive inner man.

There is a story that I recall, imperfectly of course, about George Bernard Shaw, who said that when he went to Heaven he was certain that he would be greeting all the thousands of animals and fowls that he had NOT eaten. To turn it about, I am confident that when I arrive in Hell, I shall be confronted by the myriads of plants that I have killed. So, while I list the things that inflamed my interest when I read them in *Plant Buyers Guide,* under NO circumstances pay the slightest attention to anything that you consider problematical or too precious to risk.

Now after all the pros and cons have been stated, I am going to append the list of the names of Camellia and Magnolias that made me sit up with joy and you need not pay the slightest attention to any of it if in your opinion it should be sure death!

Also, I should much prefer to pay for them, please. Plants cost money, and labor and maintenance come high. I know! Also, aside from the fact that the plants will be cherished, I must admit that while we have many visitors here (I have overrun a place which is owned by a bachelor friend of mine who no longer gardens much), very, very few of them are horticulturally alert. The nurseries of this whole area grow only standard stuff and sell most of it to the NORTH! Now that old man Sawada of Overlook has retired and his modern trained sons are "streamlining" the place, that nursery which was my one Mecca is scarcely worth a trip!

To sum up: Morrison is old, has no future plan for the place, has indifferent visitors, lives in a climate that has high summer temperatures but good air drainage, and occasional, very occasional frosts in winter. It looks to me as if you should reply—NO! Nothing from here.

Of his correspondence in the Hunt Library, the following two letters (written in 1958 to an aspiring nurseryman who had asked Morrison's advice about going into business) especially demonstrate Ben's warmth, sagacity, and charm.

10 October 1958

Dear Mr. Pennington:

Thank you for *your* nice letter! There really is no reason why you should worry to weigh the pros and cons of bachelorhood against matrimony! I hold not one single reservation against it, believe me, and my only reason for telling you about it all, was the fact that I discovered that another man who wanted to visit here, and who did, would really have liked to have brought *his* wife along, but did not know whether to or not! As he had never indicated whether he was married or not, I had not had the wit to ask, although our letters had been informal enough. So, my dear sir, if Mrs. Pennington comes along or would like to come along, please do!

Now about the nursery set-up here. My own personal objection to the whole thing is that we did not get all the mutual understandings clearly and out in the open from the very beginning! It was proposed to me, when I was north the last time that there should be formed a group to make a nursery (on Anderson's land) with my stock, my know how, and all, (and I blush to add, my reputation), and that one family would provide certain monies and another man who had worked with me in the U.S.D.A. be brought down to do all the work, and that the income would allow me to keep up the place and finance my breeding work.

The man of the family and the former colleague had presumably worked out all the details, to their mutual satisfaction. I told them on the first day that I wanted no work in it all, and that I had no money to invest. "Do not give it a thought." . . . Well, it turned out the family man and the other did NOT understand things mutually, with the result that there has been bad blood between the two, since 1955, and I have been in the middle! It has also turned out that I have done more manual labor, and general drudgery than I have in years and I have always worked and have always believed in work. I have also expended all my savings and borrowed to keep the thing afloat. I have now reached the limit of my willingness to borrow, at my age, which will be 67 next month. I am in excellent health, but at my age there is no point in assuming that I shall live forever. . . This summer I brought things to a head, and got rid of the family group, who still remain friends, and who still have not the dimmest idea of what they have done that has been damaging to the other chap. I am old enough so I can shrug my shoulders and hoe my row and forget the rest. The younger man cannot.

So, IF you plan to have anyone in with you, whatever you do, have everything in writing early in the game so there can be no possible misunderstanding.

Next. You may or may not realize it but once in a nursery, you are never free to go or come anywhere when you might like it, sometimes not even with advance planning. . . . Never! You are tied to the spot. There is no place that I particularly would like to go, but I do not like the idea of not being able to pick up and go, should I wish it! I am very serious about this aspect of the work.

Next, unless you have already established a clientele, do have enough money to live on for three years, without depending on sales. I do not know how much soil preparation you have to do, but here we have to have from 100 to 200 jumbo bales of peat a year. Fertilizers are not so dear. Our peat comes wholesale of course, trucked from the importer in Mobile who has given excellent service.

If you plan on shipping, containers are important and we had to find our type of crate by trial and error, as the manufacturers of crates would not consider making one to our specification unless we had about 5 thousand at one time. We get our burlap squares from Philadelphia, and as they come by motor freight the cost is not as unreasonable as it might seem. No local suppliers.

There is practically no local market in these parts. We knew that in advance and foolishly thought we could swing it all on the wholesale level, but we could not grow enough to warrant such a program.

Our initial propagation was almost 100% successful. The next year for no reason that I can understand even now with hindsight, it was practically 100% a failure in the usual midsummer, or late summer, early autumn time; and pretty good with the winter propagation. Now, we find that it is better to contract with Dr. Tingle to grow cuttings of the things we want, and put our whole attention to the things that we are propagating of my new seedlings and such Glenn Dales as he has in short quantities. The first year all such are grown in one area, where we have facilities for reed mat shade, that can be rolled back when we work and rolled over in winter for protection. We do not mulch with leaves as we found too much blowing resulted in killing a fair lot of well rooted cuttings.

Now we depend on winter propagation in the cold greenhouse that I had built for entirely different uses, and have had to give over, with electric cables in the beds for bottom heat. This works very well here.

My own breeding work has been brought practically to a standstill. This year I had time and energy for only about 10 pollinations, and very few of them took which did not surprise me. I have a fair lot of small seedlings from last year's work, a moderately good lot from the year before and those from 1954 and 1955 are right this moment buried in weeds, not irrevocably, but buried just the same.

Help is almost impossible in this area, and we could not afford it if we could find it! So it is one man, and myself who count more or less as half a man now! We have about 26,000 plants for sale, and about 22,000 coming on, with smaller numbers of various things that we will not offer for sale for several years now.

The small plants have all the flowers removed as soon as they open and show that the plant is correctly named. All the rest of the place had to be sprayed for petal blight, nursery and garden, about three times a week for about three months. Power sprayer of course.

I have kept my assistant at $400.00 a month, and I have had NOTHING... He has earned it all too, as he is a fine worker and never spares himself. He has had a phenomenal amount of sickness in his family and the hospitalization has by no means covered the costs. So, though unmarried myself, I know all about family details, even to lengths that would astonish you!

I do our simple bookkeeping and all the letter writing. I have had to plan what little advertising we have attempted and now have to plan the follow ups. This year we are selling at retail, and thank God most of it, little enough has been by mail.

I have not the least doubt about the value of the plant and varieties and I have some new things coming along that are truly spectacularly new and different. They include a lot of things that beat the Chugais, and are in that category and also several series of true doubles that are quite handsome. This and the beauty of the whole place do compensate. Nevertheless I tell you all this stuff, so that you will consider very carefully whether or not you want to tie yourself down,

for that is what it will be. Your finances may be quite adequate to cover all the needful, but if you do not foresee all the needful, there can be surprises at the wrong moment.

15 December 1958

Dear Mr. Pennington:

Our thermometer is low this morning, 28 at 7:30 a.m. and that means that my helper is a total loss, in spite of the fact that there are still things he *could* do. But, poor man, his wife is ailing this morning and I have sent him off, and plan to devote the morning at least to catching up on various letters that I have acknowledged but not answered most of them letters that I should have preferred to answer on the moment!

Re your experiment. All of it sounds fine to me. My only personal objection to any of it, is the use of pure peat in any bed. There is absolutely no question but that the plants grow superbly in it: but when the plants go on to John Doe, who probably will not prepare the ground properly for them, there is always the chance that either of two things may happen: one, that the hole he digs will become a sump and the plant will drown; or that the peat moss may dry out sometime when he is not fully aware of it, and then it is pretty difficult to get moisture into the center of the root mass again. John Doe won't know any of this and ... But I may be crying in the dark. There is absolutely nothing wrong with your theory re the salts. I know another nurseryman who does approximately the same thing. Merely a variation in the routine. My assistant here, was raised to grow all cuttings in pure sand, under the hand of a Kew trained man who was a martinet. In the USDA greenhouses, it worked like a charm so ... There is another nurseryman near here who raises all his in vermiculite; but I am up against a prejudice and when I am peremptory, there is a—baking, shall I say, that is comical if it were not so aggravating.

Our plants here raised in such sandy soil face something of a similar problem when they go off to live in heavier soils, and it is for that reason that on the catalogues to retail people, I made the point for preparing the soil to offset this. In my old garden I had the benefit of a mica schist soil, that was easily permeable, but when I bought plants from Tingle who lives on sand, if I did not remove most of his soil and get the roots well established in mine, the plants died 100%. I had a similar experience in USDA with a shipment of material grown in sphagnum for air transport during the war, that went to a country with heavy soil. The idiots there did not remove the sphagnum mass and the plants died almost to the last one, drowned in the soggy mass of moss.

The one nursery detail that I have not mentioned to you that perhaps you should think about, is that all the

Glenn Dales do not grow at the same rate of speed. Helen Close is so slow, I doubt if she will ever be a commercial item, and there are many others that are what I call normally slow. They are not dwarfs.

I find that people who do not know azaleas, about 99% of my callers, will not look at them. If I want to sell Eros, I should grow it for 4 years in order to get a plant comparable in size to, say, Vespers in two growing seasons. Jubilee which is valuable ONLY because of its late bloom, makes a very poor looking plant in the first bedding, and not much better in the second move, but in time it is a very decent bush blooming here in JUNE, later in the north. No one looks at it. Then there is another set that are nearly erect in habit when young, e.g. Copperman. In time this makes a fine flat top, but not when young. People do not look at it, unless it is in bloom!

Another lot, particularly Helen Gunning and Martha Hitchcock, make stringy-looking little plants and no one will look at them. They also lose more leaves when young than they do when old and established, another point against them, but the flowers are so wonderful, anyone would be a fool to pass them by, but pass them by, the average buyer will and does!

Of course there are plenty of other clones that lose more leaves in winter when young than they do later in life, but those mentioned are conspicuously naked!

So far, most of the people who have wanted later flowering azaleas have been people who knew something about azaleas. While I was still in U.S.D.A., Fruitlands to whom we had sent plants of the Glenn Dales, said that in their area no one wanted any azalea that bloomed after roses came into flower. I do not know the validity of that judgment, but you might keep it in mind.

Then of course, people have had a wonderful time, telling me that there are "too many" Glenn Dales. There are for the average person, and I will never go on record to anyone, which I consider the "best" a ridiculous request at best, as people have already made it plain on occasion, that they did not agree with me! I heartily endorse that practice, one of the pleasures of living in the U.S.A.

I also know, from reading the trade papers, for the last few years, that the trade when it is "successful" looks to a factory type production, in huge quantities of a very small number of almost foolproof items. The average nursery trade list that comes to me, might be almost identical whether the address is Texas or Tennessee, or in some cases, Florida. This is more or less the doom of good nurseries except in the cases of people who grow only one item, and I often wonder how well they fare. There are endless iris lists, hemerocallis lists, camellia lists and of course the "orchid" people are fabulous for their lists and their prices, but from what I have seen of them, far from a wide survey, they, the nursery people are in the same pattern as the bearded iris and the hemerocallis people, every man producing his own seedlings and clamoring for attention! (In a way, I am in the same position re azaleas, but what I look forward to is a time when I can close the door on the dear public and be like the old recluse in Japan, who collected and improved the Kurumes, and died safe from all attention.) Actually there is no chance for me arriving at that state.

If you plan to sell retail and from the yard, when the plants are in flower, many of my type of problems will not arise, but just for the record, here they are. If I should think of others, I'll add to these.

In a wide-ranging letter to Frederic Lee in 1951, Ben Morrison gave his candid opinions on several issues:

From my own experience in the breeding of azaleas, I have absolutely no faith whatever in the opinion, expressed here by Dr. Hume, but stated elsewhere by others, Bowers in particular, that *calendulacea* could have anything to do with the earlier "Azalea indica" such as Duke of Wellington, Coccinea Major, and Glory of Sunninghill. I have already stated my opinion in regard to these and see no reason to alter it. I have yet to hear of anyone anywhere, who has succeeded in bringing to flowering size any single plant that represented a cross between a pentanthera and an obtusum. This I state in spite of the so-called Vuykeana hybrids and the "Belgians" recorded in the Tuinbouw, which are supposed to have "mollis" blood. It would be a very easy matter to self any of the three mentioned and raise the seedlings, but I hate to waste my time and space on such a silly business!

Merely as a personal opinion, I feel that Dr. Hume has a very vague idea of macrantha. The illustration in his book is not "macrantha" but a hybrid of it, probably of the same type of cross as that of Fashion. The actual plant shown, I suspect but do not know, looks like one of the Japanese clones that are grown by Sawada.

What Dr. Hume does not say is that in the South including Florida, all the "Belgians" bloom intermittently throughout the year, except in the coldest months. I am not prepared to back up the statement at present but I believe that this is due to the plant's habit of making short but continuous flushes of growth throughout the entire year. I would expect such a habit to come from a species that was native in the southern part of a climatic range, and personally I suspect R. *indicum (macrantha)*.

On the second page of this same letter, he gives a tip useful to breeders interested in producing double-flowered hybrids:

From working with double plants I have found that it is almost always possible to find some single and semi-double flowers on almost every variety. This is of interest to me as a breeder, as the single or near single flowers usually betray the stamen number and that, with the type of winter leaves, gives a rather fair indication of the predominating strain of blood in the "mongrel". I have not included in my write-up all the little notes that I made for myself as a breeder, as I see no point in handing over to the lazy geneticists what they should have done for themselves—ages ago, with their super techniques! Sorry to be such a crab but there is a limit to what I expect to hand out from now on! A further clue to the dominant strain also appears in the character of the leaves on the new shoots, which I believe I can read from having handled so many thousands of seedling plants of which I know the ancestry.

Morrison Sees A.R.S. Problems

In a letter written in 1949, Morrison declined a request to write an article and delivered an outspoken discourse on the problems faced by the American Rhododendron Society in meeting the needs of its eastern members.

Your problem is basically understandable since for 22 years I have been beating the bushes for materials for a quarterly magazine that needs some rather careful writing (even if it has not always had it). I know all about promises.

I do not have good illustrations of the Glenn Dale azaleas. That is one of the chores that hangs over me for the coming spring when I am planning to bring together all the material that some day will be called "historical" about the Glenn Dale clones that will eventually get introduced into trade, even if many are later on dropped. The writing of descriptions that will give all from an obituary standpoint and still evoke some visual image, are driving me mad! The obituary details sound very much alike; but the plants are not.

All the wonderful things that can be grown in the Pacific Northwest are of no use to us. Many of them I find ugly. No one in Great Britain has had the courage to say in print, that plenty of the species are UGLY, and as far as I am concerned all that stuff about the purity of a species, etc. and their pristine beauty is the BUNK. A thing is beautiful or it isn't beautiful no matter whether it once grew wild or was born in a greenhouse. The things that I would know about wouldn't be of any interest to the majority of your members and quite properly so. I do not believe that the Glenn Dale azaleas will be of much use in the Puget Sound area; they will sigh for a good hot summer and maybe a little for a cold winter! All of this does not mean that I am not perfectly and sincerely delighted that all the things I cannot do, can be well done out there! I am not that stupid!

One living in another climate (than that which covers the majority of membership) hesitates to say anything about practices. I do not *know* that the method of seed-sowing described in one of the yearbooks is the one and only for the conditions out there, but it certainly is antiquated as far as we are concerned. We never use soil; only sphagnum moss. We do *not* use vermiculite or any of its allied materials though they are good enough for some things, but not rhododendrons. We do not look with pleasure on—*** or **** or ***** or ****** varieties that put-down the varieties that are the very best we have here and not only for here but for five-sixths of the rest of the country as well. Your problem as I see it, is either to turn the A.R.S. into a purely local outfit (which it is to all practical purposes) or else offer that same majority stuff that won't be of the slightest interest to them, an equally untenable position! You have the reverse of the problem that we have. The West cries out that we neglect them, and there is more than a little excuse for it, but we publish what we can persuade the westerners to write for us. Westerners don't want (and in fact shouldn't have) stuff written here, unless it relates to practices or methods or taxonomy or some other matter equally without locale. Now if you want to dump the Glenn Dale piece, you have my blessing!

"I belong to the American Rhododendron Society, not because I care about the Society doings, not one whit, but because I believe that all organizations do stimulate the sum total of national horticulture! I have managed to grow practically all the azalea species that can be had, and that are hardy. One by one I have gotten their pictures and published them in the *National Horticultural Magazine*. Does anyone care? As far as I know, *they do not.*

I'm sorry as I can be but I have no *good* suggestion. Not one. Now if you want to throw me out, as I have said before, you have my blessing! Meantime, God help you, the members won't and I know!

Another refusal, this time in a letter to Norvell Gillespie in 1961:

Nothing in the world would induce me to make a zone map! That is something that would be so full of errors, every one would shout for joy.

It simply cannot be done. Too many micro-climates, too many different parents among the Glenn Dales, too many stupid people who do not know how to grow azaleas and blame the plan, not themselves for the failures.

Clem Bowers stuck his neck out once, and said that anywhere one could grow a Kurume, he could grow a Glenn Dale, but he did not say which Glenn Dale. I have already given you all the outlying areas where I *know* some Glenn Dales will grow and thrive. I have already told you, I believe, that as they go north, the heights decrease in many cases and the spread increases, so that a plant that has a normal growth habit here may look like a cushion there. Mr. Oliver of Scarsdale, N.Y., thinks Cygnet is a low mound; not here, just a slow upright bush.

One cannot compare them to the "southern indica" either as they are not equally cold tender. While we do not know their parentages, it can be safely deduced in many cases, from the number of stamens, the degree of evergreenness of the foliage, the growth habits, and so on.

The one safe generalization seems to be, note that nasty word seems, that the farther inland one goes, the less hardy any evergreen or semi-evergreen azalea is. But no one, to my knowledge could produce any proven figures on this. My one former correspondent in Oswego, Kansas, kept many alive with slat protection, but that is no way to handle azaleas. The St. Louis man had no such precautions and did some that I should have thought doubtful. I am still puzzled by the sucesses in Oklahoma City and Tulsa. The lack of summer heat is what ruins the optimums in Seattle. Miss Brandt thought well of them and there are reported to be some good plants in the Stribing Arboretum, planted for effect.

Frankly I cannot see why any person who wants any plant and does not know in advance its behavior in his own area, does not do what I do: buy it and find out. I am not rich, believe me, but I have had to do it that way, and I certainly do not feel abused. I know others who use the same system. And as for the usual zone maps . . . pfui! They give a northern limit and there are just as terrific southern limits too.

Advice to Hybridists

And finally, in an unpublished paper, Ben Morrison described how he would advise any azalea hybridist to grow his seedlings, starting with the gathering of seed:

It used to be customary to say that when azalea seed is ripe, the capsule opens naturally. Observations here suggest that the capsules, if ripe, open only after a frost. Since the writer was primarily concerned with the harvest of seed resulting from crosses, he had no wish to risk any possible loss of seed by a frost-triggered opening. It seemed preferable to risk one year's harvest about October 10, a safe date before the

usual "first frost." The capsules were full size, but entirely green in color.

The capsules were put in small coin envelopes and left at room temperature. A gradual darkening to brown color followed on the capsules themselves, but many of them showed no signs of opening after two months. They were then opened by crushing, and the seed poured out. They were different only in color, the hue being slightly less intense than bush-ripened seed. At germination there was no visible difference. An October harvest has become routine.

TIME TO SOW SEED. As far as has been observed, there is no best time, other than that time which fits best into the grower's routine. The newly germinated seedling should have as long an uninterrupted first year's growth as possible. If one has the facilities and the space, the seed can be sown immediately after harvest. By providing extra light in winter, they will grow continuously.

Mr. Albert Close, using greenhouse space at the U.S. Plant Introduction Garden, Glenn Dale, Maryland, kept two lots of hybrid seedlings of the Obtusum subseries in constant active growth and they produced their first flowers in 14 months.

Working as an amateur, without greenhouse facilities and only after office hours for work, the writer has found it more convenient to sow his seed in March by which time there is sufficient sun-heat to warm a cold frame or unheated pit greenhouse. Germination and subsequent growth rates are slower than are found in heated houses. If the seed is sown earlier and if no additional light is provided, the seedlings tend to remain dormant from late December to late February, and it is not always easy to rouse them into growth.

The writer admits that his working routine builds up delays since the seedlings are slower to reach transplant size and he is slower to get all the work done. Some work that should have been completed in April is barely finished by the end of July if there are thousands of seedlings to handle.

METHOD OF SOWING. To use any other method than that of sowing on sphagnum moss seems complete folly.

A shallow flat or pot of convenient size is filled to $3/4''$ from the brim with tightly packed chopped sphagnum moss that has never been used before. The flat or pot is set in a container of water and allowed to stand over night. It is then stood aside to permit all excess water to drain away. Press the surface level and then cover it with a $1/2''$-layer of sphagnum that has been scrubbed through a sieve mesh of $1/8''$ square. This must stand until it is uniformly moist. The seed is then sown on the surface, the receptacle covered with a pane of glass and a sheet of newspaper. No more attention will be needed until long after germination has taken place.

Temperatures ranging between 60-70°F. bring on

germination within two weeks for most azaleas. Lower temperatures produce slower results. One may watch the seed absorbing moisture and fattening before the tip of the radicle begins to show. It is interesting to watch the seeds through germination as occasionally one finds a lot that are not uniform in time.

If the moss is fresh, there will be no losses from any of the damping-off fungi common in this area. The writer learned by experience that an old flat, even if completely resurfaced with a deeper layer of sifted sphagnum no longer protects the germinating seedlings.

PRICKING OFF. This again is a matter of convenience, related to facilities. For the worker in the greenhouse where atmospheric humidity can be maintained, it is perfectly safe to transplant the seedlings before any true leaf has formed. With conditions similar to those of the writer, it is much better to wait until 2 or 3 true leaves have formed.

The soil mixture for the transplant flat should be the usual azalea soil mixture with about one third by bulk of coarse sand to insure rapid draining. The flats can be filled, watered copiously and drained before using, or they may be used at once, and then be removed to their place on greenhouse bench or frame. Shade must be given. Additional water will not usually be needed for several weeks when there should be active signs of growth. Greenhouse temperatures should average 65°F.

Each worker handles the seedling according to his own skill. The tiny seedlings are remarkably tough. They can be pulled out of the sphagnum and dibbled into the prepared transplant flat. Even if the root or hypocotyl should be damaged, plant it as if sound and whole, but a little deeper than normal. New roots will be thrown out from the hypocotyl. If by accident a seedling falls over on the seed flat, roots can be observed all along the hypocotyl, as well as from the growing radical end. The one requirement is that soil moisture and atmospheric humidity be kept constant.

Any seedlings not needed can be left in the original seed pan almost indefinitely now without feeding. To prevent too rapid growth, the degree of moisture should be much less than that given to seedlings in active growth.

Where space is not at a premium, broadcast sowing of seed is easiest. The writer works under limited space conditions and sows his seed in broad rows that are spaced about one inch apart. Germination is excellent but the seedlings are seriously crowded. If it is possible to prick out the seedlings quickly, no harm follows. When it is not possible to transplant promptly, many seedlings become seriously elongated before they are handled, but no damage results if they are planted more deeply than they had been growing. These facts are included to show again that the azalea is not as difficult as certain older texts would suggest.

Space between seedlings in the transplant flat must be determined by the space at one's command and the speed with which they can be rehandled for the next shift. At the Plant Introduction Garden they are usually spaced about two inches apart each way; in the writer's home garden, never over one inch apart and a few extras for good measure. Widely spaced plants are ready for permanent nursery beds the same season— the crowded ones should wait until the following spring.

NURSERY-TRANSPLANT. This will be influenced by the severity of the local climate and the amount of hard wood present at the base of the plants. When there is almost no hard wood, the first winter should pass in a cold frame. Lacking frames, a light mulch of leaves and a cover of brush will suffice. The crowded, smaller seedlings must go through the winter in a frame, but need no special protection. They can be set out as early in the spring as desired and if they are assiduously cared for will almost catch up with the better plants after the summer's growth is finished. The young plants should be spaced at such distance that they will touch one another by the end of summer and provide mutual protection the following winter.

Transplanting is the easiest of operations. One merely cuts between the rows and between the plants in the row and lifts out the individual plant with its square prism of roots. Occasionally in the crowded system, a plant will have made a crooked main root that is cut off too close to the plant. In that case the top should be cut back two-thirds. In general practice, one may plant out the young seedlings at any time of day in any temperature, provided about one-half pint of water is poured into the hole as the plant is set and the hole closed as the water disappears. A light shelter to provide broken shade for a week will hasten the adjustment, but the writer has moved small seedlings successfully in mid-July with no shading whatever. Rarely is there any wilting and when it does occur, it disappears after the first night. The more quickly the plant is established, the more quickly it can resume the summer's full measure of growth. Subsequent nursery care is the same as for any small plant, with regular attention to moisture and food.

Well-grown plants will give almost 100% bloom the third year whereas the plants produced under the writer's more casual system give only an indication reading in the third year.

FIRST FLOWERING. In all cases observed by the writer, the flowers that are poor in size or form can be immediately discarded. Color sometimes improves a little and large flowers sometimes appear larger, but the small bloom, with pinched corolla lobes, usually stays just that way.

Ben Morrison's influence in American horticulture will continue to be felt for a long while. Azalea enthusiasts may think of him when they contemplate the glories of his Glenn Dale and Back Acres hybrids, but especially when visiting the garden dedicated to him at The National Arboretum in Washington, D.C. There he said, "In my mind, I am here often, and even when I am not here, I hope you may feel my presence in this garden." His azalea children are his most eloquent memorial.

Two Studies of The Glenn Dale Azaleas

The Glenn Dale azaleas were created with the climatic requirements of the Middle Atlantic states in mind—particularly those of the Washington, D.C., area.

When the plants became commercially available, and azalea buffs tried them out in gardens located far from their birthplace, it was evident that many of the 400-odd named cultivars were at home from Richmond to Cape Cod, and, as noted above, in many western areas. Testing programs are beginning to reveal the extent of the territory suitable for many cultivars, and a number have emerged as candidates for wide sale by nurseries as replacements for the over-propagated "fruitstand" varieties.

An extensive testing program was conducted for the Philadelphia, Pennsylvania, area under the direction of three members of the Philadelphia Chapter, A.R.S. Several microclimates and several azalea series were involved. The results were published in the American Rhododendron Society's 1967 publication, *Rhododendron Information.*

Another study, restricted to the Glenn Dales, has been tabulated and reported by Roy Magruder, Ph.D., a member of the Potomac Valley Chapter, A.R.S. Dr. Magruder recommends varieties (chosen from the 454 Glenn Dales) for use in small gardens in the

Washington, D.C., area. They all meet these requirements:

1. They retain enough leaves through the winter to be considered evergreen shrubs.
2. They have a dense or compact habit of growing requiring little or no pruning.
3. They grow relatively slowly (with short internodes).
4. They bear an abundance of good quality flowers, mostly single.
5. They all are adapted to the Washington area.

Almost all of Dr. Magruder's selections rate high in all of the five characteristics noted; the others possess outstanding qualities on most points.

To aid in selection, the varieties are arranged by (1) color groups, (2) according to season of bloom, (3) height, (4) recommended border position (front, middle, rear), (5) fall foliage color, and (6) winter foliage color. Data on season of bloom comes from records of observations made over eight years of the same plant or plants at the National Arboretum in Washington, D.C.

The importance of leaf color in the small garden is stressed by Dr. Magruder, as follows:

Observations also have been made, during the last ten years, of plantings containing the Glenn Dale azaleas in Maryland, Virginia, North Carolina, Tennessee, Georgia, Mississippi, and Florida.

Among the Glenn Dale azaleas there is a wide range in leaf color during the autumn as the days get shorter, night temperatures get lower, and the first light frosts occur.

On white flowered varieties, as fall approaches, the older leaves which developed on the new growth during the late spring and summer turn yellow and usually fall off. Those which persist are some shade of green and keep it throughout the winter.

Some of the colored varieties follow the pattern of change of the white flowered varieties. Most of them, however, make a spectacular show of color changes during the fall—from yellow to orange, then to different reds, and finally to a maroon or bronze red either partially or completely covering the plant.

The period of bright attractive leaf color is usually longer than the flowering period and should be considered in planning the garden.

Glenn Dale Azaleas for Small Gardens

BY ROY MAGRUDER, Ph.D.

Key

Season of Bloom		Border Position	Leaf Color		
			Value:		Hue:
E=Early	A=April	F=30'' max	Med=Medium		G=Green
M=Middle	M=May	F-M (see text)	Dk=Dark		M=Maroon
L=Late	J=June	M=40'' max	Leaf Area Covered:		O=Orange
		R=40+''	Sl=Slight (about 25%)		R=Red
			Hvy=Heavy (about 50%)		Y=Yellow
			Sol=Solid (100%)		

Example of how to read the information below: The variety Nobility will be in good bloom for about three weeks, starting from middle to late May; it is suitable for a position at the front or toward the middle of the border; in fall, its leaves will start medium green, and then turn to yellow, to orange, and to red; in winter, its leaves will turn maroon at the edges. Variety Anchorite will have dark green leaves in fall, turning from yellow to orange to red, and in winter its leaves will be half to all maroon.

Name of Variety	Season of Bloom	Border Position	Fall Leaf Color	Winter Leaf Color
WHITE				
Helen Close	EM-MM	F-M	Med G+Y	Med G
Glacier	LA-EM	M	Dk G+Y	Dk G
Swansong	EM-MM	F	Dk G+Y	Dk G
Vestal	LA-EM	R	Dk G+Y	Dk G
Wavelet	MM	M	Med G+Y	Med G
WHITE THROAT OR BASE, PINK TO RED PETALS AND MARGINS[1]				
Aztec	LM-EJ	F-M	Med G+Y	Sol M
Bopeep	MA-LA	F	Med G+Y	Med G
Dayspring	MA-LA	M-R	Med G+Y	Med G
WHITE THROAT OR BASE, LAVENDER TO PURPLE PETALS AND MARKINGS[2]				
Fawn	LA-EM	F	Med G+Y	Sl M edges
PINK TO RED THROATS AND PETALS WITH WHITE MARGINS				
Helen Fox	MA-EM	F-M	Med G, Y-O-R	Med to Sol M
Refrain	LA-EM	F-M	Med G, Y-O-R	Sl to Hvy M
Surprise	EM-MM	M-R	Med G, Y-O-R	Med to Sol M

Reprinted with permission of the editors of "Successful Gardening in the Greater Washington Area", Second Edition, 1975. Men's Garden Club of Montgomery County, Maryland.

---

[1]Bravura, Helen Gunning, Pied Piper, and Valentine also have this color and pattern but occasionally throw sports with solid colored flowers. If interested, purchase plants of them when in bloom to be sure you have the desired color and pattern.

[2]Boldface, Martha Hitchcock, Picotee, and Susannah also have this color range and pattern but occasionally throw sports with solid colored flowers. If interested, purchase plants of them in bloom to be sure you have the desired color and pattern.

Name of Variety	Season of Bloom	Border Position	Fall Leaf Color	Winter Leaf Color
LAVENDER THROATS WITH WHITE MARGINS				
Nobility	MM-LM	F-M	Med G, Y-O-R	Sl M edges
LIGHT SALMON PINK				
Argosy	LA-EM	M-R	Med G, Y-O-R	Med to Sol M
Crusader	EM-LM	F	Med G, Y-O-R	Med to Hvy M
Eros	MM-LM	F	Dk G, Y-O-R	Med to Hvy M
Grandee	EM-MM	M	Dk G, Y-O-R	Med to Sol M
Peerless	LA-MM	M	Dk G, Y-O-R	Med to Sol M
Sagittarius	LM-EJ	F	Very Dk G, Y-O-R	Med to Sol M
MEDIUM SALMON PINK				
Fashion	LA-EM	F-M	Dk G, Y-O-R	Sol M
Kashmir	EM-MM	F	Dk G	Sl to Med M
Swashbuckler	EM-MM	M	Dk G	Sl to Hvy M
Wildfire	MA-LA	F	Dk G	Med to Hvy M
LIGHT ROSE PINK				
Anchorite	EM-MM	F-M	Dk G, Y-O-R	Med to Sol M
Bagdad	EM-MM	F	Dk G, Y-O-R	Med to Sol M
Gaiety	EM-MM	F-M	Dk G, Y-O-R	Med to Sol M
Masterpiece	LA-EM	F-M	Dk G, Y-O-R	Med to Sol M
Suwanee	LA-EM	F-M	Dk G, Y-O-R	Med to Sol M
DEEP ROSE PINK[3]				
Corsair	LA-EM	F	Dk G, Y-O-R	Med to Sol M
Corydon	LA-EM	F	Dk G, Y-O-R	Med to Sol M
Cranford	LM-EJ	F-M	Med G, Y-O-R	Med to Sol M
Dazzler	EM-MM	F-M	Dk G, Y-O-R	Med to Sol M
Jessica	EM-MM	F-M	Dk G, Y-O-R	Med to Sol M
Pearl Bradford	LM-EJ	F	Dk G, Y-O-R	Med to Sol M
Sterling	LM-EJ	F	Dk G, Y-O-R	Med to Sol M
Vanity	LA-EM	M-R	Dk G, Y-O-R	Med to Sol M
ROSE COLOR[3]				
Con Amore	EM	F-M	Dk G, Y-O-R	Med to Hvy M
Demure	LA-EM	F	Dk G, Y-O-R	Med to Sol M
Effective	LA-EM	F	Med G, Y-O-R	Sl to Med M
Epicure	LM-EJ	F	Med G, Y-O-R	Sl to Med M
Fairy Bells	EM-MM	F-M	Dk G, Y-O-R	Sl to Med M
Harbinger	LA-EM	M	Dk G, Y-O-R	Sl to Hvy M
Prudence	LA-MM	M	Dk G, Y-O-R	Med to Hvy M
ROSE RED[3]				
Firedance	LA-EM	M	Med G, Y-O-R	Sl to Med M
Dragon	LA-EM	F	Dk G, Y-O-R	Med to Sol M
F. C. Bradford	EM	F-M	Dk G, Y-O-R	Med to Sol M
Glamour	LA-MM	M-R	Dk G, Y-O-R	Med to Sol M

---

[3]These color names are from Ridgeway: *Color Standards and Nomenclature,* 1912. See articles on Color Chart and Color Wheel in Wyman's *Gardening Encyclopedia.*

Name of Variety	Season of Bloom	Border Position	Fall Leaf Color	Winter Leaf Color
ORANGE RED				
Beacon	LA-EM	F-M	Dk G, Y-O-R	Sl to Med M
Copperman	LA-MM	M	Dk G, Y-O-R	Med to Sol M
Greeting	LA-EM	F-M	Dk G, Y-O-R	Med to Sol M
BROWNISH RED				
Galathea	LA-EM	M-R	Dk G, Y-O-R	Sol M
Kobold	LA-EM	F	Dk G, Y-O-R	Med to Sol M
Trouper	LA-EM	F	Dk G, Y-O-R	Med to Sol M
MAUVETTE[3]				
Simplicity	EM-MM	M-R	Med G, Y-O-R	Med to Sol M
LIGHT PURPLE				
Content	LA-EM	M-R	Med Dk G, Y-O-R	Med to Sol M
Matins	LA-MM	R	Med G, Y-O-R	Med to Sol M
Reward	MA-EM	F-M	Med G, Y-O-R	Med to Sol M
Violetta	LA-MM	M	Dk G, Y-O-R	Med to Hvy M
RHODAMINE PURPLE[3]				
Nocturne	EM-MM	M-R	Med G, Y-O-R	Med to Sol M
ASTER PURPLE[3]				
Dauntless	MM	F	Dk G, Y-O-R	Med to Sol M

[3]These color names are from Ridgeway: *Color Standards and Nomenclature,* 1912. See articles on Color Chart and Color Wheel in Wyman's *Gardening Encyclopedia.*

Source List for Glenn Dale Azaleas

Although the first releases of the Glenn Dale azaleas were made to commercial nurserymen over 30 years ago, relatively few varieties are available from any one nurseryman. The National Arboretum in Washington, D.C. has a Glenn dale Azalea source list of commercial nurserymen who sell plants or offer custom propagation. On request, the National Arboretum can furnish the name and address of one or more sources for virtually every variety of Glenn Dales in the following lists. The source list request should be addressed to the Curator of Education, National Arboretum, Washington, D.C., 20002.

An abbreviated list of sources follows:

W = Wholesale Only

*Does not ship nor publish a catalog

The Azalea Garden
Hugh A. Caldwell, Jr.
Star Route #1, Box 419
Doctor's Inlet, FL 32030

Bon Air Nursery
1416 Bon Air Road
Bon Air, VA 23235

Brooksite Nursery
10804 Braddock Road
Fairfax, VA 22030

Columbia Nursery
1903 Martha's Road
Alexandria, VA 22307

Tom Dodd Nurseries, Inc.
(w)
U.S. Highway #98
Semmes, AL 36575

Gladsgay Gardens
6311 Three Chopt Road
Richmond, VA 23226

Robert G. Hailey
3467 Gallows Road
Falls Church, VA 22042

George W. Harding
22525 Wildcat Road
Germantown, MD 20767

J. D. Mitchell
2424 Sunny Meadow Lane
Vienna, VA 22180

Oliver Nurseries
1159 Bronson Road
Fairfield, CT 06430

Rees Evergreen Gardens
3908 Madison Street
Hyattsville, MD 20781

Spartansburg Landscape
Nursery Co.
2265 East Main Street
Sparta, SC 29302

Clyde M. Stewart*
4112 Accotink Parkway
Annandale, VA 22003

Sweet Gum Farms
Route #2
Alma, GA 31510

The Tingle Nursery (w)
Pittsville, MD 21850

J. E. Whalley Nursery
22000 N.E. Halsey Street
Troutdale, OR 97060

Frank B. White, Jr.
6419 Princess Garden
Parkway
Lanham, MD 20801

Marcus A. Zehel
7407 Pepper Lane
Clifton, VA 22024

Morrison's Glenn Dale Azaleas

The editors have arranged the 454 named clones* of Glenn Dale azaleas according to (1) flower form and color, (2) plant size, and (3) season of bloom. The tabulation is primarily derived from Morrison's monograph published by the U.S.D.A. in 1953. While errors in this compilation are inevitable, we hope it will serve as a practical guide to this otherwise bewildering abundance of hybrid evergreen azaleas.

In the climate of the mid-Atlantic region of eastern North America (40 degrees North latitude), evergreen azaleas have a blooming season of over seventy-five days. After dividing this time period into three arbitrary portions, we arranged the Glenn Dales into *early, midseason,* and *late* flowering groups. Since the actual blooming dates can vary by one or two weeks from year to year, this table should be used as a guide to blooming sequences rather than *blooming dates.* (At Philadelphia, in a normal season, the *early* group blooms April 10-May 5; the *midseason* May 6-24; and the *late* group from May 25 through June.) Blooming dates are also influenced by altitude, slope aspects, and other site characteristics.

The *number* after the variety name refers to the diameter of the flower in inches; and *R* after this number indicates a frilled or ruffled flower. It may come as a surprise that Morrison did not select clones to fit all the slots provided for in this table. The blanks offer creative challenge to contemporary hybridizers.

---

*Editor's Note: The reader is referred to *The Glenn Dale Azaleas,* B. Y. Morrison, Agricultural Monograph No. 20, U.S.D.A., or *The Azalea Book* by Frederick P. Lee, for an alphabetical list, and detailed descriptions, parentages, etc. of the Glenn Dale azaleas.

Note: When a name is boldfaced, this indicates the variety was recommended by Dr. Roy Magruder or the Philadelphia Azalea Study Group.

THE EARLY GLENN DALE AZALEAS

	Tall (over 5')	Average (3'-5')	Low (under 3')
WHITE			
Flowers single	Marmora 2½"	Cantabile 2½" Ivory 4"	—
Single with blotch	—	Bridal Veil 3"	—
Flowers hose-in-hose	Samite 2"	Cygnet 2½"	—
Flowers double	—	Barchester 2" Ranger 2½"	—
Flowers striped, sanded, margined, or blotched in color)			
Single, with pink or red	Dimity 2" Festive 2½" **Geisha** 2½" Limerick 2"	Alabaster 2½" **Bopeep** 2½" Caprice 2" Caress 2¼"	—

	Tall (over 5')	Average (3'-5')	Low (under 3')
Single, with pink or red	Refrain 2" Satrap 2¼"	Fantasy 2" Pied Piper 3" Pixie 2¼"	
Hose-in-hose, with pink or red	Mother of Pearl 1¾" Pastel 2"	Cascade 1½"	—
Single, with lavender or purple	Delight 4" Minuet? Quakeress 2¾" Stardust 2¼"	Duenna 1½" Portent 1¼"	—
Hose-in-hose, with lavender or purple	Capella 2½"		
ORANGE-PINK			
Single	Aladdin 2"-2¼" Ambrosia 2½" Delilah 2½" Touchstone 3" Troubador 2"	Nectar 2¾" Shannon 2½"	—
Single with blotch	Astarte 3¼" Bacchante 3" Brangaene 2½" Colleen 2" Marionette 2" Tango 3" Velvet 2½"	Argosy 3½" Bowman 2½" Cathay 2" Freedom 2½" Pippin 2½" Trilby 3"	—
Hose-in-hose	Tartar 2"	Lullaby 1½" Souvenir 1¼"	—
PINK, ROSE, or LAVENDER SHADES			
Single	Allure 2½" Carbineer 2½" Dayspring 2" Rising Sun 3½" Serenade 3" Serenity 2¾" Vision 3"	Abbot 3" Camelot 3" Chloe 3" Circe 2¾" Dawning 3" Desire 2¾" Effective 3" Horus 2¾" Katinka 2" Mavourneen 2¼" Mayflower 2" Quest 3" Reward 3" Roselight 2¾" Scout 2" Vintage 2" Witchery 2¾"	—
Single, darker margin	Sheila 3½"	—	—
Single with blotch	Arcadia 3" Constance 3½" Dream 3"R Faith 3" Madeira 3" Morning Star 2"	Con Amore 3" Concordia 2" Consuela 3" Darling 2½" Echo 2¾" Oracle 3"	Refulgence 1¾"

	Tall (over 5')	Average (3'-5')	Low (under 3')
Single with blotch	Prelate 2½″ Tokay 2½″ Tristan 2½″	Pilgrim 2½″ Signal 2¼″ Sprite 3″ **Suwanee** 3″ Temptation 2½″ Twinkles 2″	
Hose-in-hose	**Fairy Bells** 2½″ Sebastian 2½″ Sligo 1½″	Melanie 1½″ Noreen 2″ Romance 1½″ Whirlwind 1½″	—
Semi-double or double	—	Modesty 3″	—
ORANGE-RED and SCARLET			
Single	Cavalier 2″ **Kashmir** 3″	—	—
Single with blotch	Burgundy 2″* Clarion 3″ Emblem 2″ Mascot 2½″ Pontiff 2½″R	Grenadier 2″ Jamboree 2½″	
Hose-in-hose	**Ballet Girl** 2″	Opera 1½″	—
ROSE-REDS and CRIMSON			
Single	Acme 3″ Alexandria 2¾″	Araby 2″ Bettina 2″ **Galathea** 1½″* Illusion 2½″ Jingle 2″ Red Hussar 1½″ Robinhood 4″ **Trouper** 1½″*	—
Single with blotch	Antares 2¾″ Jongleur 2¾″ Ladylove 3″ Minstrel 3″	Bishop 1½″ Carmel 2″* Gladiator 2½″ Jeannin 2″ Marvel 3½″ Red Robe 2¾″	—
Hose-in-hose	—	Candlelight 1½″	—
Double	—	—	—
PURPLE, VIOLET-ROSE, LAVENDER, or MAGENTA			
Single	Afterglow 2″ Gypsy 3¼″ Jubilant 2½″ **Simplicity** 3″	Matins 2½″ Medea 2″ Valkyrie 3″	—
Single with blotch	Padre 2¼″ Sappho 2½″ Seneca 3½″ Templar 3″ Warrior 2″	Angelus 2½″ Astra 3″ Viking 2¾″ **Violetta** 2¼″	—
Hose-in-hose	—	—	—
Double	—	—	—

*Brownish red.

THE MIDSEASON GLENN DALE AZALEAS

	Tall (over 5')	Average (3'-5')	Low (under 3')
WHITE			
Flowers single	—	Driven Snow 3" Glacier 3" Helen Close 3"	—
Single with blotch	—	Mary Helen 2" Nativity 2½" Polar Sea 3½"R Silver Moon 3"R Treasure 4" Vestal 2½"	Carrara 3" Eucharis 3"R Niagara 2½"R Seafoam 3"R
Flowers hose-in-hose	—	Damask 2"	—
Flowers double	—	—	—
Flowers striped, margined, or blotched in color.			
Single, with pink or red	—	Bravura 3" Chum 2½" Cinnibar 3" Cocktail 2" Defiance 2" Furbelow 2" Gallant 2½" Helen Gunning 2½"R Madcap 2" Paprika 2" Pinocchio 2½" Pinto 2½"	Lacquer 3" Motley 2"
Hose-in-hose, with pink or red	—	—	—
Single, with lavender or purple	—	Altair 3" Boldface 3"R Chameleon 3½" Glee 2½" Harlequin 2" Herald 2" Joker 3½" Martha Hitchcock 3" Novelty 2" Picotee 2" Polonaise 2" Requiem 2" Rogue 3" Sonata 2½"R	Conquest 2¾" Grandam 3"R
Hose-in-hose, with lavender or purple	—	—	Futurity 2½"
ORANGE-PINK			
Single	Blushing Maid 2½" Sentinel 3"	Caraval 3" Luminary 2¾"	—
Single with blotch	Bagatelle 3¼" Evangeline 3" Zingari 2"	Alight 2½" Challenger 3" Coral Sea 3"	—

	Tall (over 5')	Average (3'-5')	Low (under 3')
Single with blotch		Cordial 3"R Dulcimer 2½" **Grandee** 2¾" Stampede 2½" **Swashbuckler** 2¾"	
Hose-in-hose	—	Captivation 2" Coquette 2" Coralie 1¾" Damozel 2" Enchantment 1¾" Fanfare 2" Favorite 1½" Magic 1¾"	—

PINK, ROSE, or LAVENDER SHADES

	Tall (over 5')	Average (3'-5')	Low (under 3')
Single	Ganymede 2½" Morgana 2¾"	**Anchorite** 2" **Aphrodite** 2" **Corydon** 2¼" Cytheria 3" Daphnis 2½" **Grace Freeman** 4" Joya 3" Merlin 3" Naxos 2¾" Orpheus 2" Peter Pan 1¾" **Prudence** 2" Revery 2½"	Cupid 3"
Single with blotch	Felicity 3" Pinkie 2¾"	Bountiful 3" Celestial 2¾" Content 3" **Corsair** 2½"R Demure 2" Ember 3"R Evensong 2¼" **Gaiety** 3" Gorgeous 2" Gracious 2" Lucette 2" Nerissa 1¾" Phoebe 3" Rhapsody 3"R Ursula 2½" **Vanity** 1¾" Wanderer 2½" Winner 2"	**Dazzler** 3"R Mandarin 2¾"
Hose-in-hose	—	**Peerless** 1¾" Satin Robe 2½" Thisbe 1½"	—
Semi- or double	Andros 2½" Delos 2½"	—	—

	Tall (over 5′)	Average (3′-5′)	Low (under 3′)
ORANGE-RED and SCARLET			
Single	—	Beacon 2″	—
		Buccaneer 2″	
Single with blotch	—	Carnival 4″	—
		Commodore 3″	
		Greeting 2½″	
		Picador 2½″	
		Redbird 2½″	
		Tanager 2½″	
Hose-in-hose	**Fashion** 2″	Paradise 2″	—
	Pirate 2″		
ROSE-REDS and CRIMSON			
Single	Hopeful 1¾″	Advance 2″	—
		Anthem 3½″	
		Berceuse 2½″	
		Campfire 1½″	
		Dragon 2″	
		Glamour 3″	
		Janet Noyes 2½″	
		Kobold 2″*	
		Luster 2½″	
Single with blotch	Granat 2″	**Bagdad** 3″	**F. C. Bradford** 2½″
	Isolde 2½″	**Darkness** 3″*	**Madrigal** 3½″
		Token 3″	
Single with white margins	—	**Surprise** 3″	**Helen Fox** 2½″
Hose-in-hose	—	—	—
Double	—	Kenwood 2¾″	—
PURPLE, VIOLET-ROSE, LAVENDER, or MAGENTA			
Single	—	Dandy 2½″	—
		Etna 2″	
		Progress 2″	
		Prosperity 3″	
Single with blotch	Cherry Spot 2½″	Commando 2½″	—
	Damaris 2¾″R	Fandango 3″	
		Gawain 3″	
		Litany 2¾″	
		Muscadine 3¾″	
		Nocturne 3″	
		Parade 3½″	
		Remembrance ?	
		Veteran 3″	
		Volcan 2″	
		Zulu 3½″	
Hose-in-hose	—	—	—
Double	Rosette 4″	—	—

*White margins of petals

THE LATE GLENN DALE AZALEAS

	Tall (over 5')	Average 3'-5')	Low (under 5')
WHITE			
Flowers single	Snowscape 2"	Angela Place 3" Everest 2¼" Moonbeam 5"R Safrano 3½"	—
Single with blotch	—	Lyric 3" Moonstone 3" Omen 2½" Snowclad 3½"R Snow Wreath 3½" Swansong 4" Undine 2½" Wavelet 2½" Wisdom 2"	Arctic 3"
Flowers hose-in-hose	—	—	—
Flowers double	—	—	—
Flowers striped, sanded, margined, or blotched with color			
Single, with pink or red	—	Aviator 3" Cream Cup 2" Fawn 2½" Folly 3" Frivolity 2½" Gnome 2½" Goblin 2" Kohinoor 3"R Masquerade 2½" Moira 2" Presto 2½" Puck 3" Shimmer 2" Spangles 3" Swagger 2½"	
	—	Talisman 2½" Tomboy 2" Trinket 3" Trousseau 3"R Vanguard 2½" Yeoman 2½"	—
Hose-in-hose, with pink or red	—	—	—
Single, with lavender or purple	—	Acrobat 2½" Allegory 3" Antique 3" Ave Maria 3"R Baroque 3" Blizzard 3"R Cadenza 2"R Cavatina 3¼" Consolation 3"R Dowager 3"	Memento 2" Prodigal 3" Roundelay 3"

	Tall (over 5′)	Average (3′-5′)	Low (under 3′)
Single with lavender or purple		Egoist 3″ Galaxy 3″ Killarney 3¼″ Niphetos 3″ Orison 2½″ Patriot 3″ Punchinello 3½″R Sarabande 3″ Satyr 3″ Scherzo 3″ Scholar 3″ Silver Cup 3¼″ Silver Lace 3″ Silver Mist 2″ Sorcerer 2″ Susannah 2½″ Taffeta 2½″ Vespers 3″R Whimsical 2″ Winedrop 3″ Zephyr 3″	
Hose-in-hose, with lavender or purple	—	—	—
ORANGE-PINK			
Single	Fenelon 2½″	June Glow 1¼″ Kathleen 2½″ Pink Star 2½″	Eros 3″
Single with blotch	—	—	Crusader 3″ Jubilee 2½″
Single, violet blotch, stripe, white margin	—	Teresa 2½″	—
Hose-in-hose	—	—	—
PINK, ROSE, or LAVENDER SHADES			
Single	—	Lillie Maude 3″R Manhattan 2½″ Seashell 3″	Sagittarius 3″
Single, with blotch	—	Adorable 3½″ Bolivar 2¾″ Bravo 1½″ Catawba 2¼″ Cremona 3″ Crinoline 3″R Epilogue 1¼″ Fakir 3″ Louise Dowdle 3″ Luna Masterpiece 3½″ Mavis 2″ Megan 3″ Oriflamme 3″*	Cranford 3″ Epicure 1¼″ Fountain 3″ Mountebank 3″ Pearl Bradford 3″ Radiance 3″ Saga 3″R Sterling 3″

*White margins of petals

	Tall (over 5′)	Average (3′-5′)	Low (under 3′)
Single with blotch		Regina 2¾″	
		Rose Ash 3″	
		Samson 3″	
		Valentine 2½″*	
		Welcome 3″	
		Zealot 2″	
Hose-in-hose	—	—	—
Double	—	—	—
ORANGE-RED and SCARLET			
Single	—	—	Wildfire 2½″R
Single with blotch	—	**Copperman 3″**	Aztec 3″
		Elizabeth 3″	
		Mary Margaret 3″	
Hose-in-hose	—	—	—
ROSE-REDS and CRIMSON			
Single	—	Bohemian 2½″	—
		Jessica 3″	
Single with blotch	Loveliness 2¾″	**Firedance 2″R**	Harbinger 3″R
		Leonore 2½″	
		Marjorie 3″	
Hose-in-hose	—	—	—
Double	—	—	Aries 3″
PURPLE, VIOLET-ROSE, LAVENDER, or MAGENTA			
Single	—	**Chanticleer 2″**	Dauntless 2″
		Meteor 3″R	
		Paladin 2½″R	
		Rosalie 3″	
		Sambo 2″**	
		Youth 2″	
Single with blotch	—	Bonanza 2½″	Guerdon 3″
		Trophy 3½″	Nubian 1½″
Single, violet blotch and stripes, white margin	—	Nobility 2½″	—
Hose-in-hose	—	—	—
Double	—	—	—

**Brownish effect   *White margins of petals

Morrison used a number of satsuki azaleas in his crosses, particularly when late blooming was sought. In his work "The Glenn Dale Azaleas", Morrison referred to this group as "Azalea macrantha of commerce, R. indicum of the botanists." He gave no list.

It can be assumed that the lack of information about the group loosely known as satsukis, Chugais and Gumpos would pique the curiosity of Morrison. The result of his studies was the draft of a proposed article, in which he puts down his thoughts and the results of his use of these plants.

The draft, which was prepared in the mid-1960's, while he was in retirement at Pass Christian, Mississippi, was made available to the editors by the Hunt Library, Carnegie-Mellon University, Pittsburgh, Pennsylvania. It is not a finished manuscript, but the subjects covered will interest the student of the Glenn Dale azaleas, and of the Back Acres group which follows this discussion.

Notes on the Satsukis

As yet, the writer has not been able to persuade any of his Japanese friends to define a satsuki azalea in terms that would save him labor. The word itself, as all know, indicates a "fifth month" azalea, i.e., a late blooming kind, for May or June. This is characteristic of wild forms of both *indicum* and *eriocarpum*. It also appears from the plants of *R. eriocarpum* in the garden here, that the flowers are not large, as compared to such as *mucronatum* though they are large as compared to flowers of ordinary Kurume clones.

One may start then, with the idea that Satsukis are a race of late blooming azaleas. In general this is true, but there is at least one clone, Kei-setsu, that blooms well ahead of all the others and even in late April here. As normal blooming becomes established in the collection here, others may appear as early, for not all clones have had normal flowering as yet.

The next generality that may be safely offered is that the foliage is evergreen and lasts about two years per leaf, as is the case with *R. indicum*. The foliage, in no clone as yet observed would suggest that *R. mucronatum* has ever been used, but this is not an altogether safe conclusion as among the Glenn Dale azaleas such clones as Angela Place show heavy foliage of comparable type though not always lasting two season. *Mucronatum* figured in the ancestry of Angela Place, together with a Satsuki. The typical leaf form of *indicum*, which Wilson gives as "short-petioled, narrow-lanceolate, lanceolate to oblanceolate, mucronulate," does not appear in many of the clones.

Wilson's description of the plant habit, "The plants though often decumbent, are naturally upright and very densely branched" is certainly correct for all the clones observed. He also mentions the fact that in the only place where he observed the plant truly wild, it grew "from a half to two meters high and

forming dense masses in open country". Certainly in cultivation, in habit according to the nature of the site, free standing and upright to four or five feet in ordinary positions, lower and prostrate to semi-prostrate in exposed positions, and these characteristics seem to be true of the named clones of satsukis as well. The species apparently grows less and less tall as it is grown in colder parts of this country often with wide spreading habit, similar in character to that which it shows when grown in sunny exposed positions here.

From all this plus the present condition of the oldest collection of the named clones in the garden here, plants now about twelve to fifteen years of age, one may safely say that the satsukis are not dwarf. It is important to establish this fact early in their history in this country, so that we need not allow the error that plagued the Kurumes for years, as dwarfs when they definitely are not such. Here the oldest plants reach as much as eight feet in height and this is not due to crowding as they were planted at least forty inches apart, some have died out, so that the distances are even greater. It is true, however, that some clones show a tendency to greater lateral growth than vertical and only a few appear to be approximately columnar.

If one dare use merely casual observation, it may be said that the majority of the named clones have leaves that approximate those of *R. eriocarpum,* heavy in substance, dark green in color, and rounded on the tips, often obovate in form. Whether or not this may safely be assumed as an indication of the free use of this species in the total progenies, is doubtful. In the writer's work with *R. indicum* as one parent in various combinations, widely differing leaf forms have resulted, some of which would belie the possible use of *indicum*. None, it is true, are as small or as rounded as those in the Japanese clones of satsukis.

It would appear therefore, that until some Japanese authority will write on this subject, we cannot be too certain of the total ancestral background of our plants.

It may be said, however, that they constitute, a group of clones with flowers of singular beauty, and beauty not only of color and form, but of pattern. They make up a race that will add at least one month to the blooming season of azaleas in all places where they are cold hardy.

In Japan, the species and some few clones are most commonly used in the landscape gardens, as ground covers, as hedges or as individual specimens, usually so severely trimmed as to curtail all flowering and provide only accents from foliage masses.

The other great use appears to be in the special cult of Bonsai, in which the special clones of satsukis are magnificently done, and are exhibited annually at Utunomiya.

Judging from the illustrations in the annuals in the writer's hands (yearbooks for about ten years in the mid-thirties) the plants grown as bonsai are more valued for the actual training of the plant itself than for what flowering it may have at the moment showing.

The passion for the production of an early establishment of a plant habit that will simulate that of age, is paramount in much of the bonsai work, as well as in training practices in the regular gardens. It is a form that should present, philosophically, the idea of maturity, with a sense of the achievement of the ultimate poise and serenity that will come or should come with the matured plant—or individual.

One may well ask, "what do the flowers look like?" Judging from the collection as known to the writer, there seem to be three major types of bloom in regard to shape; the smaller, more or less funnel-shaped blooms, rarely over an inch and one half, larger flowers often to three inches that are flatter, and among the last importations even larger flowers that are absolutely flat, so that they appear to show their total widths at five inches or so. Private correspondence suggests that flowers of the first type are preferred by the purists. Those of the last type while causing great admiration are often on plants that require or seem to require more years in establishing a

strong framework of branches, so that the sheer weight of the blooms does not pull the plant out of shape.

As to colors, one may have almost anything one wishes, save true yellows and pure blues, the usual limitations of the evergreen azaleas of any type. The colors may be pure selfs, but more often are represented either as stripes and derivatives of striping to be discussed later on, as marginal colors on a white or tinted ground, and as a variation on this last in which the white center is not equally distributed on all lobes, and is often accented by the darker color of the small dots that make up the blotch on the upper lobe. Since all these patterns are related to somatic variations, any one plant, may, and often does exhibit more than one type of bloom. In this lies the delight of the bonsai grower and from it, the despair of the nurseryman in this country when it comes to propagation.

As an example of what is meant, one plant of the clone, Gobi-Nishiki, in this garden produced a fine plant of good proportion on which all flowers were the proper white with an occasional fleck of rose pink. One single branch appeared on which all flowers were solid rose pink.

The still more common type of variation, is that of the clones that are essentially white flowers, marked with dots, flakes or stripes of color. This is the type of plant that may produce, and frequently does, branches with colored flowers margined irregularly with white, and more rarely with flowers that are white, margined with color. In so far as the writer's experience allows any statement, propagations from the typical part of the plants, i.e. the striped, freckled or otherwise marked branches, will continue as such and will continue to produce all the sports mentioned above. Propagations from either of the two types of sports have so far continued as such without reversions. This does not mean that reversions cannot occur. In so far as the writer has observed, the two major types of sport occur only on clones with striping or one of its forms. In such clones as have white eyes, the reversion to solid color, usually the color and not to white is more frequent. There seems to be no time element involved, if one may judge from the experience with one clone (here, unfortunately unnamed) that has been producing pure white flowers for at least ten years. Two years ago, a few flowers showed a very few, very small rose pink stripes. In 1962, one branch produced one flower, that was of the white margin type, with a light rose pink ground, darker stripings, deep rose dots in the blotch area, and the irregular white margins. This after ten years of whiteness.

In correspondence the writer has been told that the chief sport of the satsuki growers who are concerned with bonsai production as well, is the annual hunt among their plants for sports of any kind that can be propagated and named. As soon as the sport can be grown to a size where it in turn may be used as a source of cuttings, it becomes a source of income, by sales to other bonsai growers who wish as "complete a collection as is possible."

Because of this constant interest in new forms, it often happened that old varieties drop out of cultivation, just as old kinds of any plant may do in this country. One would particularly like to see plants of the clone known to British growers years ago and given varietal status by Wilson, the clone known as Tanima-no-yuki. Dr. Creech was able to find this in Kyoto, but as yet plants have not been successfully brought to this country. It is said to be very old, and it would be fine to see it and ponder as to whether or not it represents the original source of all the variegations that have come since. Since it is described as having "salmon-red flowers whitish at the base" it may not be the source; and one would also like to see the clone named by Wilson as common about Osaka, and known there as Shiki-takane-satsuki. This is a "red spotted" white flower and would appear to this writer as a more probable ancestor. One would also like to get replacements of some of the clones first brought over by the Department of Agriculture, as the plants now in cultivation of at least two clones appear to be identical, which should not be the case. The writer's inquiries have brought back word that neither is now known.

Morrison's Back Acres Azaleas

These hybrids probably result from a blending of late flowering azaleas (a specific interest of Morrison's), with bright colored, single flowered sorts that have sharply contrasting white or light colored centers. Most of this breeding work was done at Pass Christian, Mississippi. Parentages of these hybrids have not been previously published.

Low, under 3'; Average, 3'-5'; Tall, over 5' (As registered with R.H.S. in 1965 and 1966)

Apricot Honey. (Kagetsu x *indicum*) x *(mucronatum* x *kaempferi)* x Tama-Sugata. Plant low; single, light center, margins orange pink, carmine blotch, 2¾".

Badinage. (Vittata Fortunei x *mucronatum*) x *(kaempferi* x Shinnyo-no-Tsuki) average size; double flowers, white centers, margins broadly rose pink, 3".

Bergerette. Seedling 32666 x Musashino. Plant average size; flowers single, white, washed at edges shrimp pink, 2½".

Bouffant. (*mucronatum* x pink *simsii* clone) x Gunrei. Low plant; flowers single, ruffled, rose pink centers fading to white margins, pink blotch, 2½".

Bourdon. (Vittata Fortunei x Warai-Gishi) x Pluto (old S.I. clone) average size plant, early flowering, double, 1½"; light purple, re-blooms in fall.

Brides Bouquet. (Warai-Gishi x Kagetsu) x Rogetsu. Somewhat columnar plant; flowers double, 2½", gardenia-like white. Late midseason.

Cayenne. (Vittata Fortunei x Warai-Gishi) x Pluto. Average size bush, flowers orange pink, rose color blotch, double, 1 $^3/_4$″, with 12-16 petals.

Cora Brandt. Kagetsu x Warai-Gishi. Scarlet double flowers, occasionally with garnet brown blotch, 20 petals, late blooming.

Coral Ace Troubador x 158057. White centers, rose margins, reddish blotch, 2 $^3/_4$″, single flowers.

Corinne Murrah. Kagetsu x (Hazel Dawson x *indicum*). 4′ in 10 yr. Flowers single, 3 $^1/_4$″, deep rose pink, ruffled, sinuate margins, white centers. Late midseason.

Crescendo. Parentage unknown. Late double flowers, imbricated as a camellia, orange red.

Debonaire. Copperman x Hakatashiro. Single 3″ flowers, deep pink borders, pale pink center, washed greenish, very late bloom.

Elise Norfleet. Kagetsu x Warai-Gishi. Very low growing, single flowers, scarlet red with pink centers, 2 $^1/_2$″, carmine blotch.

Encore. Kagetsu x Warai-Gishi. Low to average bush, double flowers, with 14-18 petals, rose color, 3″, late.

Extravaganza. Seedling #32629 x Tama-sugata. Average size plant, conspicuous autumn bloomer, 3 $^1/_2$″, single flowers, white with stripes, flakes and dotting of rose pink. No 2 flowers the same.

Fire Magic. (Vittata Fortunei x Warai-Gishi) x Pluto. Evergreen, average size plant, early blooming orange pink, with red blotch, double, 1 $^1/_2$″, 16-22 petals.

Folksong. Seedling 36/45 x Shikun-ow. Low growing, single flowers 2 $^3/_4$″, white with showy pink blotch, rare rose color stripes.

Friendship. Kagetsu x Copperman. Single 3″ flowers, rose color with blotch of same color, late.

Garnet Royal. (Vittata Fortunei x Warai-Gishi) x Pluto. Average size plant, double flowers 1 $^3/_8$″, purple with centers lighter; carries as brownish red, darkest early flowering double.

Gratitude. Kagetsu x Warai-Gishi. Very low growing, double, rose pink with slight blotch of pink near base of petals, late.

Habanera. (Indicum Orange x Hatsushima) x Tama-sugata. Average sized plant, single flowers, 2 $^1/_4$″, white centered pink flowers with prominent blotch. As floriferous as Kurume hybrids.

Hearthglow. Kagetsu x Warai-Gishi. Average size plant, late flowering, double, orange pink, flushed scarlet from center, 10-15 imbricated petals.

Heigh-ho. Seedling 32629 x Tama-sugata. Circular form, single flowers with overlapping lobes, rose color, darker on margins, heavy rose blotch.

Heirloom. Kagetsu x Seedling 32666 (*indicum* x Hazel Dawson). Average sized plant with single flowers, 3″, pale margins and white centers, brownish purple blotch.

Ivan Anderson. (Warai-Gishi x How-raku) x Kokoku. Low growing, double flowers, 2 $^3/_4$″, white centers and broad rose-pink margins.

Keepsake. Kagetsu x Seedling 32666. Average size plant, single flowers, 3 $^1/_4$″, starry white base, pale lavender pink margins, brownish blotch.

Largesse. Kagetsu x Warai-Gishi. Low to average growth, double flowers, 2 $^1/_4$″, deep rose pink with rose red dots at bases of upper petals, loose form; late.

Lost Chord Dream x Luna (mucronatum x simsii pink clone) x (kaempferi x Shinnyo-no-Tsuki). Columnar growth, to 5′ in 15 years; single flowered, circular form, rose red margins, 50% with pale pink centers, blotch of small pink dots at base of upper petals.

Malaguena. (Vittata Fortunei x Warai-Gishi) x Pluto. Early double 1 $^1/_2$″ flowers, brilliant coral pink, rose blotch. Fall bloomer.

Margaret Douglas. (*indicum* x Hatsushima) x Shinsei. Average growth, single flowers, 3″, centers pale pink, margins orange pink.

Marian Lee. Kagetsu x (Hazel Dawson x *indicum*). Average plant, 3″, flowers with white centers, Nepal red borders. Late May bloom. Good cold-hardiness, garden effect "like butterflies".

Marion Armstrong. Kagetsu x Warai-Gishi. Average size plant, double 20 petaled flowers like a camellia, orange pink.

Maud Jacobs. Kagetsu x Warai-Gishi. Low growing, double flowers, 3 $^1/_4$″, rose pink, very floriferous.

May Blaine. Kagetsu x Warai-Gishi. Low to average plant, late flowering double, 3″, light lavender purple.

Merrymaker. Kagetsu x Warai-Gishi. Late double blossoms, 2 $^1/_4$″, orange red.

Miss Jane. Kagetsu x Warai-Gishi. Low growing, double flowering, 2 $^1/_4$″, irregular white centers, pink borders.

Misty Plum. Kagetsu x Seedling 32666. Single 2 $^3/_4$″ flowers, funnel shaped, white centers, purple margins and blotch.

Moresca. (Vittata Fortunei x Warai-Gishi) x Pluto. Average height plant, double flowering, early, 1 $^1/_2$″, lavender pink with rose blotch, effect is purplish rose. Fall bloomer.

Orange Flare. Kagetsu x Warai-Gishi. Very low growing, double 3″ flowers, base of petals pale pink, deepening to orange pink on margins, no blotch or stamens; flowers are striking, late blooming, pistils occasionally with petaloid flags.

Painted Tips. (Seedling 38/45 x Cavendishi) x Shinnyo-no-Tsuki.) Low plant, wide spreading, single 3″ flowers, off white, pale pink flush to tips of petals carrying orange pink blotch. Late flowering.

Pat Kraft. Copperman x Hakatashiro. Low growing, single 3 1/4″ flowers, occasionally 6 lobed, scarlet red, rose blotch, very late.

Rachel Cunningham. Seedling 32619 x Pluto. Average size bush, double 20 petal flower, pompom shaped, orange pink margins deepening to scarlet bases of petals.

Red Slippers. (Andros x Parade) x Keisetsu. 2′ plant in 10 years, single 3″ flowers, with occasional petaloid stamens, rose red with purple blotch; some autumn flowers.

Rejoice. Kegetsu x Warai-Gishi. Average height, open growth. Late double flowers, 12 petals opening widely, rose pink, slight blotch.

Rose Brocade. Kagetsu x Warai-Gishi. 4′ tall and broad at 15 years, double flowers, 3″, 20 petals, rose color, trace of blotch, no stamens.

Saint James. Cross 23/45. to 4′ in 10 years. Single, late 3″ flowers, orange pink washed peach red, rose blotch, white starry centers.

Spring Bonnet. Unknown parentage. Excellent foliage, 5′ in 10 years, single 2 1/4″ flowers, centers white, deepening to pale pink margins; pink blotch, mid-season.

Starfire. (Vittata Fortunei x Warai-Gishi) x Pluto. 4′ in 10 years, double 1 1/2″ flowers, early, bright coral pink, rose blotch; also blooms in fall.

Storm Cloud. Kagetsu x Warai-Gishi. 4′ in 10 years. Late double flowers, appears single with inner crest of small irregular petals, purple with purple blotch near bases of upper petals.

Target. Parentage not recorded. 4 1/2″ in 10 years. Single, late midseason flowers 2 1/4″, orange pink shading to scarlet on margins, red blotch.

Tharon Perkins. Parentage not recorded. 3′ in 10 years. Single, late, 2 3/4″ orange pink flowers deepening to orange red on margins, with heavy carmine blotch.

Waltztime. Kagetsu x Warai-Gishi. Slow growing and low. White centers appear only on mature plant. Late, double 3″, petals narrow, irregular, loose appearance, 20 petals, rose pink margins.

White Jade. Helen Gunning x Rei Ro. 4′ in 10 years, late midseason 3″ single, ruffled white flowers with pale green flush on upper lobe.

CHAPTER IV

G. Guy Nearing
1890-

Introduction

Guy Nearing's place in the history of rhododendron breeding rests on a modest number of introduced clones and on a number of other hybrids still under study. As a man he is noted for thoroughness, for courage in the face of repeated adversity, for his capacity for friendship, and for the wide diversity of his interests.

The term "genius" has long been applied to this man who, in addition to his accomplishments in hybridizing, is also a botanist, an artist, a chess master, a poet, an inventor, and a folk dancer.

The early life experiences, tragedies, and successes, of Guy Nearing are presented by Dr. David G. Leach in the March, 1961 edition of *Flower Grower*. In this article Leach wrote that Nearing, in defiance of repeated disasters so appalling they call to mind a classic tragedy, has achieved the kind of life admired by Leach. In addition, Nearing has the distinction of being outstanding in fields so varied that his talent is awesome to contemplate. To observers, he is the most remarkable man to appear on the horticultural scene in this generation.

He is a slight, graying man, lean and fit. Visitors receive an immediate impression of alert intelligence and energy that is like a coiled spring. His conversation is as brisk as his walk.

Guy Nearing was born January 22, 1890, at Morris Run in Tioga County, Pennsylvania, into a well-to-do family marked by colorful characters and strong intellectual interests. As a boy, he became an amateur naturalist, roaming the countryside, examining and collecting plants in the woods and fields, showing the same enthusiasm and curiosity for the natural world which is so evident in him today.

When he entered the University of Pennsylvania in 1908, the brilliance of his work soon drew attention. His election to Phi Beta Kappa was almost routine for a student of such conspicuous talent. Not so routine was his athletic ability. By his senior year, the famous track coach, Mike Murphy, had him headed for the Olympics as a champion miler. Then came the first jarring blow of a malignant fate that was to lash out at him again and again, for decades: blindness. Nearing's mother read the assignments—and the senior year was finished with a graduation of distinction.

Nearing's vision slowly improved. He worked for several national magazines, served in the Army, and began a promising career in advertising. This came to an abrupt end when his doctors advised him to change his work to an outdoor activity. In 1928, he opened a nursery at Arden, Delaware. Within a year, Nearing had become a recognized expert on hollies. The nursery acquired a reputation as a source for new, rare and fine plants, and the owner a widening prestige as a reputable advisor on horticultural matters.

In 1929, the Guyencourt Nurseries absorbed Nearing's enterprise and together they began to propagate own-root rhododendrons on an immense scale. Once again, however, the man was struck down. The Guyencourt firm was dissolved. A program that had begun so promisingly ended in bleak defeat, just another victim of the great depression.

From this period, however, came an invention, the Nearing Propagating Frame, that has since become a standard device for rooting cuttings in the nursery industry. An outdoor frame of special design with a sloping hood superstructure, in Nearing's hands it became the first commercially successful method of rooting rhododendron cuttings, freeing the nursery industry of dependence on imported grafted plants. Nearing was the first to propose the wounding of cuttings; he also pioneered other propagation techniques that have enriched the professional growers of America.

After the collapse at Guyencourt, Nearing once again started a small nursery, this time at Ridgewood, New Jersey. His creative talent turned to the production of new and more beautiful rhododendrons. The hybridizing work Guy Nearing undertook was on a large scale. Hundreds of crosses were made, and tens of thousands of plants were grown. In an attempt to isolate forms that would be hardy in the New Jersey climate, Nearing tested scores of species newly discovered in Asia. Again his nursery became a focus of interest for gardeners throughout the East, and Nearing added to his other accomplishments an international reputation as a rhododendron authority.

In the meantime, he had been studying fungi as a hobby and had written some popular articles about them. His characteristic drive produced such a comprehensive knowledge of the subject that he wrote *The Lichen Book*. Seven hundred of his own line drawings illustrated it; and he printed and published it himself, a project that took almost ten years. Today the work is considered a classic. Another accident in Nearing's long series of disasters struck again in 1945, when a flash flood destroyed his nursery. The splendid rhododendron hybrids that he had created in ten years of concentrated effort were almost all lost. It is incredible to realize how the Nearing hybrids that are now so highly regarded by specialists were brought on to the market. They were salvaged and sold after the general disaster and eventually introduced commercially solely through the recognition of their value in the gardens of their owners. A

Guy Nearing, author of The Lichen Book.
*Photo courtesy of the Hunt Library for
Botanical Documentation.*

tribute to those superlative creations of one man's genius and persistence!

For the next four years, Nearing was a resident naturalist at Greenbrook Sanctuary on the Hudson River's Palisades. His present nursery at Ramsey was opened in 1950. For a third time, he has assembled a remarkable array of rare rhododendron species and exotic hybrids of his own creation. Specialists all over the world know his work, visit his nursery and keep in touch with him by mail.

Gardeners everywhere sadly ponder what might have been whenever they think of the few Nearing hybrids that escaped the 1945 flood. The survivors that did finally come on the market are universally admired: Ramapo and Purple Gem, the first "blue"-flowered dwarfs to capture in hardy form the charms of the alpine species from the mountain passes

of Asia; the delightful pink-and-white Windbeam and Wyanokie, two more valuable additions to the small list of dwarf rhododendrons available to meet modern landscaping needs in cold climates; and the Guyencourt series: Brandywine, Chesapeake, Delaware, Hockessin, Lenape, and Montchanin, small-leaved hybrids rarely over two feet tall ranging in flower color from white through pale yellow to rose.

Nearing's friendship with Joseph B. Gable, their cooperation in hybridizing and evaluating, and their eagerness to share seeds and cuttings when one or the other met adversity form a bright spot in the rhododendron world.

A modern impression of this versatile plantsman has been written for this volume by his friend and neighbor, Paul E. Sleezer, a fellow member of the American Rhododendron Society.

Guy Nearing As I Know Him

Those who have met Guy Nearing remember him. This is the hallmark of his remarkable personality. Now in his eighty-eighth year, this man continues an active life, maintaining the ongoing propagation of rhododendrons, managing his specialized nursery at Ramsey, New Jersey, and participating each week in square dance clubs that he helped organize years ago. He reads, he studies, and he attends meetings of the New Jersey and Tappan Zee chapters of the American Rhododendron Society (A.R.S.), with complete disregard to inclement weather.

A hallmark needs descriptive terms and so does the word "personality." Thus many adjectives are required and indeed are due Guy Nearing: still a dynamo of work and

Guy Nearing celebrates his 83rd birthday.

enthusiasm; a purist—tough and resolute that insecticides will not be employed in his garden; that artificial growth stimulation must be avoided and, above all, that plants he breeds and grows must survive in their environment which is rigorous in Ramsey, New Jersey.

The first thing I learned from Guy Nearing was that "an acceptable, worthy rhododendron must be *hardy.*" After twenty years of experimentation (with some thought of breaking "Nearing's Law" of hardiness), I join the growing line of those convinced!

The New Jersey chapter of the A.R.S. is richly endowed in having Guy Nearing as an active participating member. He has lectured, taught, and counseled us for many years on those species and their hybrids that can or might be grown in north New Jersey. Informally, he has been designated dean of the chapter. Indeed, he is a dean of our confraternity—nationally and internationally.

This material is based on the author's acquaintance with Guy Nearing. However, it cannot be written without introducing other honored A.R.S. confreres. In Nearing's long history as a nurseryman, breeder, and propagator of rhododendrons; artist and photographer; acute observer and reporter there appears the name of Joe Gable of Stewartstown, Pennsylvania. My research reveals that Guy's first letter, on Guyencourt letterhead, to Mr. Gable is dated March 31, 1930. A delightful, exhilarating, and highly illuminating correspondence developed between Messrs. Nearing and Gable. (Gable to Nearing letters appear in the Supplement at the end of this volume.)

In the ensuing years, the Nearing letters to Gable repeatedly carry the theme of collaboration and reciprocal sharing of pollen, plants, seeds, and information. In such an atmosphere of enthusiasm and respect for each other, it was inevitable that as I became acquainted with Guy Nearing I also came to know Joe Gable even before I had the pleasure of meeting him at Winterthur, Delaware, during the first national meeting of the A.R.S., "East of the Rockies." This dissertation might aptly and more correctly be entitled The Nearing-Gable Saga.

Guy Nearing has an energy that still drives him to work long hours and at hard jobs. Early in his letters to Gable he reported "we are taking out 4000 rooted cuttings, and a couple of thousand additional will root later." Later, he informs Mr. Gable "Crickets cost me several thousand of the most desirable seedlings this year. . . ."

Early in my contacts with Guy Nearing, I found that he is vigorously inventive. In his pioneer nurseryman days at Guyencourt, he had discussed with Gable the need and problems of affording a proper windbreak for small plants. On December 15, 1931, he wrote to Mr. Gable.

"We bought some lengths of rye straw mat, which is now being sold for wind screen, and erected against steel posts. It stands 3′ high and cuts off all wind very satisfactorily, also looks well. But I thought I could do better and save money. I made a crude loom on which I am weaving a mat of eulalia stems. The effect is much finer than the rye straw. I could make it any width up to 6′ or 7′, but am using a 5′ width at present. It is slightly open, which takes off the wind resistance, but tight enough to stop everything except a faint breeze. This condition is really better for rhododendrons than stagnant air. The work of weaving is slow, but I have felt that I ought to do it myself as a demonstration before asking the corporation to put any of our men on it."

The inventiveness, the sense of thrift, quality, and control of his product! I will wager Guy carried out this innovation "after work."

The volume of his letters to Gable alone is impressive. However, to any of us who may have sown a dozen or so pots of rhododendron seeds, pricked off the seedlings and grown them on, the lengthy communication of April 6, 1933, is overwhelming. He lists carefully and with identity numbers, 200 or so crosses or species all sown in 6″ pots—full of seedlings. These are to be returned to Mr. Gable "with all that grows in them—except for a couple of plants of things that I do not have."

Thus, it is apparent back at that early date that, as Phil Livingston once waggishly put it, "It may be pretty difficult to determine sometimes whether Gable or Nearing wielded the brush."

The Nearing interest in rock garden plants, in particular the dwarf species of rhododendron, began to take shape during experiments at Guyencourt. After many problems and disappointments in 1934, early in 1935 he wrote: "I can now call the experiment of growing dwarf rhododendrons in wet ground a complete success."

Most of us know Mr. Nearing for his interest

in and contribution of dwarf and smallish hybrids—the conception of the Guyencourt hybrids.

During these pioneer days, the names of Dexter, Rothschild, Bowers, the Rock expedition, Kingdon Ward, and others began to appear in Mr. Nearing's letters—so the "giants of those days" had begun to exchange information and produce impact one on the other!

In the summer of 1935, the arrangement at Guyencourt had been dissolved, and Guy Nearing became an independent rhododendron grower at Ridgewood, New Jersey. This certainly was a turning point and Guy has often spoken of his "antediluvian days" at the Ridgewood nursery. In November 1935, a letter to Joe Gable notes: "I have been doing more work than ever before in my life." This was a reference to a crash program of digging and building a new cold pit to winter the more tender species and hybrids moved from Delaware. Since the majority of these specimens were small, it meant the propagation and breeding program was being started all over.

Many a reader will, no doubt, ask "Why wasn't power equipment brought in to help with this digging and earth-moving?" Remember that 1935 was the midst of the Great Depression. No one had much money! Guy had just moved and invested in property. Additionally, he had the personal traits of thrift, stubborn adherence to fending for one's self, a loathing of debt, and a fierce pride in accomplishment by the sweat of his brow.

In this new "northern environment," he launched into keen observation of winter damage and continued to report faithfully and in detail to Mr. Gable.

Early in 1936, floods inundated propagation frames set low in the new nursery site. "I have had to use a boat in getting around my nursery altogether about ten days this spring." This was an omen of the devastating flood that hit in 1945.

Early in acquaintance with Guy Nearing, I learned there are several variants of Roseum

Elegans on the market. He taught me (and many more of his confreres) that the clear pink hardy form is alone worthy of living space. In November, 1936 Guy wrote:

> I have not had the courage to write recently because I didn't want to talk about the October freeze. After a frostless month, the thermometer suddenly dipped to 15 degrees, destroying species which I had thought hardy—*fictolacteum, Bureavii,* etc. Even Roseum Elegans was badly damaged, but I find it was a spurious form and not the true one that was injured. Of course I have resolved to weed the tender Roseum Elegans out of my nursery, if indeed that hasn't already been done by the cold.

Both were impressed—and dismayed—at the effects of early hard frosts at Ridgewood compared with the climate along the Mason and Dixon line near which both Guyencourt and Stewartstown, Pennsylvania, are located.

It required quite a few years before Guy Nearing called me Paul; certainly, I did not address him as anything other than Mr. Nearing. It took a decade of letters before on December 29, 1940, Guy Nearing wrote to Joseph Gable:

> I have been addressing you as Mr. Gable for a long time, but as we both have three-letter names, maybe we ought to save ink.

During 1945, the demise of his Ridgewood nursery came on the crest of a flash flood. Most of the stock plants and the Ridgewood hybrids as well as nursery installations were carried away. Surviving larger hybrids planted at Mountain Lakes, New Jersey, have grown into venerable specimens.

From 1945 to 1950, the Nearing-Gable letters dwindled to a trickle. By early 1951, Mr. Nearing was back in business at his present nursery location in Ramsey, New Jersey. He had acquired a sizable piece of higher ground, gently sloping to a rocky ridge on the northerly side. It was barely spring plowing time when Guy took much pride in showing the new property to Joe Gable, during his visit and delivery of many plants to the Nearing nursery at Ramsey. A few years later, I had the pleasure and honor of being personally escorted by Guy on my first tour. Once again the prodigious amount of work of clearing, building, planting, and rock moving was evident in results on every hand. Soil removed for the new cold pit was in excess of 60 cubic yards. Once more, Nearing had done it alone, literally, with pick and shovel!

By the autumn of 1951, Nearing reported a crop of 10,000 seedlings at his new nursery enterprise. Guy once told me he frequently potted plants during consecutive 16 hour days! This is no way daunted him. His interest and participation in square dance clubs increased. He expanded his activities in mycology, rock garden interest, built more Nearing frames, constructed 10' high fences to keep deer from destroying field plantings, even took time off to paint, write, and lecture.

Guy would simply say that the labor was necessary to the end, and good for his physical well being. I know him as a man who believes this and further believes in and lives on a very simple (low in carbohydrate) dietary regimen.

Since Mr. Nearing did not stop hybridizing and raising his generations of seedlings, he now has countless plants, with all degrees of greatness. These are the progeny that he eagerly watches and guards, looking forward to those "all too short days" when some will bloom and display their merit.

A dozen years ago, I had the pleasure of taking Guy to Long Island for a special dinner event given by the New York chapter of A.R.S. Guy Nearing and Joe Gable received special plaques honoring them, singly and yet together, for a lifetime of devotion and dedicated work, in the improvement and propagation they pursued and shared, with the genus *Rhododendron.** This indeed was a high water mark of the Nearing-Gable saga!

---

*See plate no. 58

In order to sustain and perpetuate those hybrid progeny, selected forms, and large stock plants, Guy Nearing's will provides that the ownership and preservation of such plants will be the task of the committee comprising members of the New Jersey, Princeton, Tappan Zee, and New York chapters of the A.R.S.— heading the Nearing committee are Dr. William F. Sullivan, President and Emil V. Bohnel, Vice President.

Thus, by handing the torch to friends and confreres, this singular being demonstrates his supreme generosity and understanding— which may be the nearest approach that any person can make in man's effort to "look around the corner of time."

Letters from G. Guy Nearing to Joseph B. Gable (1930-50)

The following extracts are from the letters of Guy Nearing to Joe Gable, a voluminous correspondence that spanned the decades from the 1930s to the 1950s. Most were typed on hand-printed letterheads—at one time Guy Nearing had purchased a small printing press and some type and taught himself the art of printing: one more addition to his vast repertoire. The few letters not typed were usually handwritten because Nearing was in hospital—once to have an eye removed, another time for an appendectomy. Both operations are referred to with brevity and a matter-of-factness which left no room for comments other than wistful allusions to time lost from working on the hybridizing of Nearing's thousands of rhododendrons, work which was a self-perpetuating cycle of labor—a labor of love, for it certainly was not financially successful (the writer himself refers to it with the usual Nearing pungent succinctness as "a religion").

The staggering record covers the years of patient work, the plateaus and the many chasms of disasters, some natural: floods, frosts, worms, and quirks of propagation, when apparent "chaff" produces seedlings, even when the maestro has "decided there were positively no seeds"; some manmade: the Depression, World War II, and finance— the eternal lack of funds evokes the wry comments on what the future *could* promise *if* sufficient finance ever did materialize.

The letters brim with an exchange of ideas and methods, as well as a nonstop, two-way flow of seeds, pollen, cuttings, and flower trusses. Occasionally, the details are personal: graduate work at Columbia University in mycology, articles written and in preparation, comments on the Nearing classic book on lichens. Lengthy though the following collection of extracts may seem, it is merely the exposed tip of the iceberg. It reveals the overwhelming labor of one man whose primary objective in hybridizing rhododendrons was to instill hardiness, and to develop superior plants to withstand the rigors of the climate in the northeastern United States.

In 1943, Guy Nearing analyses his philosophy when he writes to Joe Gable that some of the rhododendron plants are flowering "... almost too late for me to benefit by them. However, as you may guess, I intend to go right on crossing as though I had two hundred years to live."

April 28, 1930

You should have charged us for all the rhododendrons, but since you prefer it this way, I assure you I will share up everything I am able to raise as soon as it is large enough. My *lacteum,* the only species where I have the advantage of you, is still almost microscopic but bright and healthy.

Also if it develops in the future that we can make an advantageous business arrangement, I will do my best for you.

June 12, 1931

With the unexpected good behavior of my seedlings and the evidence of a successful year with our cuttings ... I think I will not lack backing in the work. In that respect, you are much more fortunately situated than I, for I must have continuous success or perhaps be left stranded. It looks now like success.

Need for an A.R.S.

July, 1931

We really need a Rhododendron Society in this country. After I have joined the British Society, I will try to stir up interest in the project here. I need not undertake any exhibitions at the start. If it were no more than a list of names of those who grow rhododendrons, so that we could exchange information, that would be a great deal.

June 19, 1932

I am trying out some more of the other dwarfs in the boggy rock garden—*drumonium,* primulinum, *ravum, russatum, ramosissimum,* some unnamed Rock numbers, and *saluenense. Hippophaeoides, orthocladum, impeditum, setosum, chrysanthum* and *lepidotum* continue to thrive there in nearly full sun.

Of all the five- and six-year *decorums,* only one remains in anything better than a dying condition, and that one is fairly good. It lost two branches out of five, but seems not to have split its bark. There is also the hybrid in that lot, which is plainly *decorum* X stray pollen, a plant which was injured somewhat by the fall of the lath house, but did not lose any bud or discolor any leaf from weather. It looks exactly like a *decorum* hybrid at Longwood. It is now growing magnificently, seems remarkably free from any pest, and if it holds its flower buds, which it ought to form this year, may be a more satisfactory parent to work with than pure *decorum.*

The more data I get on hardiness, the plainer it is that plants from Szechuan or northward take much more kindly to our climate than those from Yunnan, Southeast Tibet and southward. I am making a large-scale map of that country, just for study, as drawing a map emphasizes it in your mind much more impressively than merely examining the map. Have you ever noticed how much farther north the western ranges of the Himalaya reach than the eastern? *R. campanulatum* stretches from Bhutan to Kashmir. No wonder reports of its hardiness vary, for that range covers 7 or 8 degrees of latitude and an immense difference in precipitation. I wonder whether seeds have ever been collected in Kashmir. But probably that strain is the worst color.

In all our crossings, I think it will not pay to bother with hybrids of two tender species unless there is some reason why we cannot cross each with a hardy one direct. Our successes are most likely to come from crosses of a hardy species or hybrid with one nearly hardy, and the more I think of it, the more I am convinced that it is better to use hybrids than species. A cross of two species will give rather uniform results, where the cross of a species with a hybrid should show a wide range of form in most cases. Have you noticed in the English writings that some of the finest hybrids show a pedigree of a species and a hybrid, frequently unknown?

June 26, 1932

A few days ago, I received the enclosed letter from Mr. Dexter. I wrote in reply that I hoped we could do something about the hardiness by hybridizing with *carolinianum, racemosum, ferrugineum,* and perhaps some of the Triflorum and Azalea series. He wrote again, offering pollen in the spring, though he says blooming takes place very early, and even plants which are held back will flower by early April. If you have any forced *racemosum* at the time, I think that might make a very desirable experiment.

I would send you his second letter, but after a two-day hunt, cannot find it. Mr. Dexter has a misconception of the effect of hybridization, remarking that since *moupinense* has such large flowers, it would be a shame to cross it with a small-flowering species. But I feel that with a subject having a two-year generation, we ought to get eventually a fertile hybrid, by which subsequent variations would enable us to breed a plant essentially *R. moupinense* with the hardiness of, say, *carolinianum.* It is with that idea in view that I hope to cross the Lapponicums with *racemosum* and other vigorous things. That is, if I can ever get flowering plants of some of these things, I hope to start.

June 16, 1932

Mr. G. G. Nearing
Guyencourt, Pa.

Dear Mr. Nearing:

I recently received an article written by you, taken from the *Florist's Exchange* in regard to *Rhododendron moupinense.* I would like to advise you that I have several dozen of these plants that were two years old this spring and most of them were in bloom. The flowers of nearly all the plants were white, some having a greenish throat, and a few were shaded with bright crimson and had red spots on the upper petal. None of these were fragrant, at least I could not detect the slightest fragrance, but the flowers are very beautiful and quite large for so small a rhododendron. They varied somewhat in size from about 2″ to 2-3/4″.

I am afraid you will be disappointed in regard to their hardiness. A year ago, I planted out in the open ground, in a location that should have been favorable, about two dozen of these plants, but not a single one survived the winter. They are inclined to start growth very early. January and February were very mild with us, and March very cold so it is quite possible that these may have started during the mild winter and then been destroyed by the extreme cold of March. When the plants are larger next year, I shall try them again.

Yours sincerely,
Chas. O. Dexter

No Date

... Would you care for some more cutting-grown hybrids? I forget which kinds I took to you last spring. We are likely to have suitable plants of any of the following, or at least, I could be sure of including most of them in two groups, one now, the other in late August or September: Caractacus, Album Grandiflorum, Kettledrum, Lee's Dark Purple, Candidissima, Delicatissimum, Minnie, Chas. Bagley, Boule de Neige, Cunningham's White, Purpureum Elegans, Album Elegans, Catawbiense Album, Ignatius Sargent, Roseum Superbum, General Grant, Luciferum, Everestianum, Lady Armstrong, E. S. Rand, and perhaps some others which I don't think of at the moment. Also Laetivirens and Myrtifolium. And I have seedlings of the following: *Ilex* "Rotunda", Sugeroki, *integra, Oldhami* (purpurea), *vomitoria, cassine.* And did I ever take you one of our *Ilex Pernyi?* I know I haven't yet furnished the Camelliaefolia which I promised some time back. I had one set aside, and it was sold in my absence, but this year, and hereafter, we will undoubtedly have plenty.

If there are any of this year's rhododendron species which you have not, let me know, and I will make a special effort with them. As some of last year's which I held over in the pots have seen fit to germinate, I may have a stranger or two for you. But I think you have practically everything I have. *R. adenopodum,* Amesiae, *anthopogon, Baileyi, brevistylum, campylocarpum, ciliatum, cyanocarpum, diacritum, erastum* (2 very tiny), *erubescens, eximium, Falconeri, Fargesii, fastigiatum, Fauriei, fictolacteum, Hodgsonii, hemitrichotum, hormophorum, irroratum* (Rock 59581), *lacteum?, lanatum, lepidotum chloranthum, manipurense, microphyton, Morii, neriiflorum, niveum, ochraceum, oreodoxa, orthocladum, paradoxum, pubescens, radinum?, rigidum, setosum, sperabile, strigillosum, Thomsonii, trichocladum, Wallichii, zaleucum.* I omit, of course, the things I know you are plentifully supplied with.

The Loss of an Eye

September 12, 1933

I am writing from Baltimore where I have just had an eye out. Probably the rhododendrons have been suffering in my absence, but it can't be helped. I potted up a good many of the new Rock numbers, dusted, and tucked them away before leaving. One looked like *fictolacteum.* One was apparently *moupinense,* and there are two other pots like it which I did not disturb. There are some exactly like *calostrotum,* but seemingly hardier. *Calostrotum* seems very subject to disease. Some of the Lapponicums, I think, are new. I am not clear on the Cephalanthums, though. Sometimes I think I can recognize them; sometimes not.

I expect to be back on the job about the beginning of next week, and maybe the removal of the bad eye will restore the good one to normal, so that I can get something done again. I just dropped everything.

The operation was not much, and of course I won't miss the eye which has been blind so many years. I shall probably be a lot better off and more comfortable from now on.

July 31, 1934

... I am also anxious to have you take a few hundred or thousand plants of the Rock numbers in 2″ pots. Some of them already need repotting, or will very soon. I spoke to Mr. Phelps about the situation, and he said by all means you should have a share of these plants. I am particularly anxious for you to take enough of the rarer things so that there will be less likelihood of our losing them if anything happens here. Last week a big worm got into one frame and ate a hundred *R. phaeochrysum,* practically wiping out the species here. If you had had a dozen or so of those, I could know where to get them.

... The situation here is still full of dynamite. If anything happens, I may have to walk out and leave all these thousands of rhododendrons to die. In fact, I believe it would rather amuse Mr. Phelps in that case to destroy the lot. As he said not long ago, "If you have to fuss with the damned things, why bother?"

I think I have done some good work here, and you will do me a great favor if you will take a share of all the rarer things, enough to let me have a few back some time if necessary.

I can't explain all the complications that have come up. Just take my word for it that a great load will be lifted off my mind if you come down immediately and take a substantial share of the rhododendrons. Whatever happens, I don't want my work to go to waste.

I want you to see the rock garden experiment too. *R. hippophaeoides, impeditum, orthocladum, chrysanthum,* and others growing like weeds in full exposure, *saluenense* 1-1/2″ high perfectly cheerful without shelter after all that heat. I am hoping for flower buds on *chrysanthum. Pubescens* has set seed, in the lath house. *Campylocarpum* and *Thomsonii* are as much as 6″ and 8″ high.

September 3, 1934

I went up to see Dexter, and think the trip was worthwhile. The most important thing I found out was a matter of soil. He showed me some seedlings of the Rock numbers, as well as other rhododendrons, many of which were badly affected with Pestalotia, and evidently with the other leaf trouble, the hardening and turning black which we so often notice on Talienses.

He said he has never had that trouble before (not distinguishing between the two diseases). He has definitely decided that it is due to insufficiently acid soil. For the first time this year he used a Florida peat, practically neutral, about 6.5. The soil he ordinarily uses is about 4.2 ... I have been checking over my plants since then, and it looks as if the recent pottings where I ... increased the acidity show practically no disease of the leaves.

Dexter's place is full of *Fortunei* hybrids, which to him are the whole rhododendron story. All others are incidental ... His *Williamsianum* clumps look for all the world like trailing arbutus. He is not outstandingly successful with anything except *Fortunei* hybrids, which he grows practically in full sun.

Nov. 6, 1934

It is hard to work with much enthusiasm toward a future which looks so unstable. I am going through the motions of caring for all these plants, yet without much plan or method. After the success I have had recently with seedlings, it seems a pity not to push ahead, but I am really only marking time, living in the current season, and hoping that some deal will be made whereby my plants will be taken care of. For a while, I saw hopeful signs that the whole rhododendron project would be sold to one of the duPonts, and me with it, but nothing seems to have come of the idea.

Mr. Phelps is now interested in hollies, and I put in about 6,000 cuttings of the Arden tree this year. It is a good thing, too, but the possibilities compared with the rhododendron work are pathetically limited.

With such ominous signs about, I am furbishing up my writing as something I can turn to if the nursery business crashes under me altogether, since it was by writing that I made my living before I took up nursery

propagation. I do not want to go back to it because it is not a dependable source of income, and when I write for a living, it is impossible to write for pleasure on the side, as I have done for years past. But such is the pinch of the depression, hitting me a little late—perhaps it will not hit after all. Anyway it is giving me a long-drawn-out scare. I had actually made preparations for the Guyencourt organization going to pieces this fall, and afterward verified my suspicions that this had actually been discussed by the others. Now I feel pretty sure things will stay together till late spring at any rate.

Nearing Leaves Guyencourt

March 24, 1935

I am leaving Guyencourt Nurseries, and taking my pick of the rhododendrons to Ridgewood, N. J., where my father has some land. I shall have to go ahead on a small scale there, but think I can work it out satisfactorily.

The preparations begin this week, and the moving will spread over three months.

In the long run, I am sure it will be greatly to my advantage to take this step. There was so obviously no future for the work here, and if I had let the rhododendrons get a couple of years older, I couldn't have afforded to move them.

There will be plenty of problems to solve at Ridgewood, but I have thought them over carefully, and believe I can meet them all. The temperature there does not go as low as here, and there are plants of *Vaccinium corymbosum* and some Azaleas on the grounds, the soil must be reasonably favorable.

It is altogether likely that I will take up some other work to earn a living, if I can find something, because it will take time to establish the propagating system and get plants up to salable size. But I will not lose the 1935 seedling crop, as I intend to sow over there instead of here. I am taking a couple of thousand rooted cuttings of named hybrids, which will be my mainstay for a year or two. It will not be practical for me to take plants of any size, because, after I had moved them 130 miles, which is expensive, I should have to hire help to prepare enough room for them and handle them. It would run into so much money that I should have to break my neck selling to make any profit out of them.

Starting small and building up again will be slow work, but at least I will have a collection and a lot of experience. I imagine I will be able to take over about 10,000 plants.

In moving, I find a number of strong young plants of *decorum* X Atrosanguineum, your cross, and the foliage looks very good. They should all come different, I imagine, and I am hoping some will flower next spring. Also my cross of Giganteum X *Fortunei* shows a good many strong plants, some with good foliage, and I am selecting only the best of those to take with me—the ones that show *Fortunei* influence in the foliage. Some plants of your Atrosanguineum X *Thomsonii* look so much like *Thomsonii* that I thought they were that species. I also discovered a plant of *Falconeri* that was left out in the lath house all winter, apparently uninjured, and only a trifle smaller than the ones in the deep frame.

May 22, 1935

I am weeding out the crop of Giganteum X *Fortunei,* taking with me only the forms with good foliage and those that show definite *Fortunei* influence. Also the *maximum* X *discolor,* but I cannot be quite sure which of these are hybrid. Many are definitely not *maximum,* but of others I can't be sure, because I used an unusual *maximum,* the pure white form with heavy indumentum, and the seedlings of this probably vary. I am not taking any hybrids from chance seed unless the foliage is extremely good.

A couple of thousand plants in 3″, 4″, and 6″ pots must be left behind. I am nearly worn out with what I have undertaken.

Sorry I can't drive over to see your plants in flower, as it must be a very interesting show this year, but I have worked all day, every day including Sunday since early in April, driving all evening three times a week.

From now on, I shall have to be extremely economical until I can build up some sort of business, which will be slow, difficult work in these times. My main reliance, of course, will be on cutting-grown plants of standard hybrids.

On my little printing press (I printed this stationery on it), I intend to work up an original catalog, going into considerable detail with the new things that have been thoroughly tested out. I do not intend to push the experimental stuff much, but things like *Fortunei* I can feature with some confidence, and more confidently after we have a race established from seed grown in this country.

I do not like to sell new crosses until I have seen them in flower and picked out the best to keep. And with the species too, I should hate to sell the one finest plant of all, when by keeping all, I can take my pick to propagate from. In that respect our businesses will be largely of a different nature, since mine is founded on cutting-propagation. . . .

August 28, 1935

. . . If we are to sell rhododendrons, we must tell people as much as we can about them, and make them sound interesting. It would be an expensive undertak-

ing, but a couple of years ago I bought a hand press for $10, as well as type and simple equipment for, perhaps $20. I got a book on printing from the library, as I had never printed, though familiar with printing from having so long written advertising matter. Now all I have to buy is paper and ink. The total cost of a couple of thousand catalogs in the present form is about $10.

Therefore, I am going to put as much reading matter in the catalog as time will permit, and see if I can't do my share toward educating the gardening public.

To tell me about rooting cuttings is no coals-to-Newcastle idea at all. I am eager to learn all I can about experiences in that connection. My own method is so highly specialized that I have a lopsided viewpoint on the whole subject, and while I can do things that apparently are difficult for others, others can do things difficult for me. Furthermore, I am still trying to improve and speed up my own system.

September 28, 1935

I received your handsome gift yesterday, and thank you for it. You might at least have let me pay the express charges. How do you get such small plants to set flower buds—by exposing them to sunlight? At this elevation, I should have to expose carefully indeed, or the sun would burn them up.

All these plants will go into my new greenhouse for the winter. I suppose the Decatros are bud-hardy, but the fall handling might cause winter injury. The *carolinianum* X (*oleifolium* X *Davidsonianumum*) looks like a remarkable plant. Do you know whether it is hardy? The massed flower buds look most promising, and the foliage is excellent.

This year, you sent me some seed of Conestoga which germinated well. (I now leave the seedlings in the seedpots till I am ready to pot them off—a year or so later if necessary. I don't even look at the pots oftener than once in a week or two.) But germination continued in that pot till the seedlings stood much too thick, and I decided to transplant part of them and of a couple of other thick stands.

Down among the characteristic Conestoga seedlings, and apparently the latest germination of all, I found the "Stewartianum" oddities reproduced exactly, about half a dozen plants. I am almost sure there was a pot or two of Conestoga in the flooded frame.

Conestoga, then, is evidently one parent, but what is the other? An azalea? They do not start at all like *carolinianum* X *Kaempf.* which I remember distinctly. What else would have been in flower at the same time as Conestoga—something unrelated to any cross you have yet made? Would you suspect *micranthum?* That seems to me most likely.

I do not know whether you have found these oddities in your seedlings, but if you have not, it may be because you do not leave them in the seedpots long enough to get this late germination.

I lost your latest list in the moving, and have no clear idea of your prices or of the species you are offering. My list, which I print a page at a time, will soon include *Fortunei, oreodoxa, Fargesii, decorum, vernicosum,* and *calophytum,* and *discolor.* I know we will overlap on at least half of these. Would you care to give me an idea of which of these species you are offering? I don't know how we compare on the rock garden species, of which I sent you the list.

My tentative prices:

calophytum	4" pots	1.50		
decorum	4	1.00	6"	2.00
discolor	4	2.00	6	3.50
Fargesii	4	1.00		
Fortunei	4	1.00	6	2.00
oreodoxa	4	1.50		
vernicosum	4	1.00		

December 30, 1935

Your seeds just arrived, and I am so very much obliged for them. There are only two or three things of my own that I can send you, but I am getting Ward's, probably early in January, and will send you half of those.

I agree with you that your *Smirnowii* X *haematodes* may result in something very fine. If the color of *Smirnowii* can be intensified without loss of the compact habit and the interesting foliage, you will certainly get an important hybrid. All crosses involving *haematodes* and *haemaleum* will be well worth having a look at. *Maximum* X *litiense* and *maximum* X *dichroanthum* also suggests interesting possibilities.

Macrostemon I don't recognize. Is it one of your origination?

Regarding your note on *fastigiatum* X *carolinianum,* no doubt you have experiences like one I had last year. A single capsule matured on *pubescens,* and after examining the contents with a glass, I decided there were positively no seeds in it. I had not made any cross, but was willing to sow more *pubescens,* so made a sowing of the chaff for good luck. About two dozen seedlings came up, looking enough like *pubescens* so that there was surely no mistake.

January 26, 1936

Spent a whole afternoon in the herbarium, studying rhododendrons. On one of Rock's specimens of *R. fictolacteum,* he notes leaves up to 60 cm. *R. crinigerum* seems to be a rather striking species, with dark brown felt and good sized flowers. A Forrest specimen of *R. lacteum* raises hopes that my plant is true after all, especially when compared with the run of *fictolacteum.* But the flower bud scales on *lacteum* are very blunt, while the scales on my leaf buds taper to a point like *fictolacteum.* I must find a Millais and get the description there of the leaf buds. Two cuttings of my supposed *lacteum* were still alive before the snow fell. If they root, I will have a plant of something for you, even though we don't know what. *R. catacosmum* looked exactly like your hose-in-hose *haematodes. R. Forrestii* is a magnificent dwarf, many very small specimens showing the character. It has plenty of leaves too, which is more than I can say about most of the Neriiflorums. But *fulvastrum* and *himertum* are perfect. The flowers of all the Neriiflorums look much like yours, with surprisingly little variation in the size of the corolla, though the calyx is extremely changeable. *R. haematodes* must be an uncertain species. One specimen of it had leaves just about the shape of a *Thomsonii,* heavily felted and full 3" long, not at all like the leaf from England which you sent me.

...*R. brachycarpum* does not look at all like what we have raised, yet I am perfectly sure that we have raised *R. brachycarpum.* For one thing the petiole is much longer in the flowering-size plants. We are going to find that both *brachycarpum* and *chrysanthum* undergo a change of foliage as they approach maturity—not as great as *leptothrium,* but much more than *maximum* or *catawbiense.*

Many of the Taliense Series have small, poor flowers, earning them few stars, of course. *R. adenogynum* in some species has flowers very much larger than most of the series. But here again I noted something worth thinking about. There was great variation in the size of all parts between different specimens attributed to the same species. Some *aganniphums* and *Balfourianums* were much better than others. It seems as if the botanists have gone too deeply into the matter of leaf indumentum, and have not stopped to consider whether the plants to which they give the same name are really the same. Looking hastily over what I have seen so far of the Taliense series, I should say that while there may possibly be as many species as there are names, somebody ought to regroup them, putting plants of the same kind together under the same name—something our worthy botanists seem to have failed to do. Of course I have seen very little, and would not venture such a statement to an outsider. But when we find out more about these and other rhododendrons, I think we will see a change of heart about the indumentum feature.

February 24, 1936

My argument about the *carolinianum* X *Kaempferi* is that it is unlikely to amount to anything because, being so haphazard about its leaves and its manner of growth, it will probably be the same about its flowers. Of course, I hope otherwise ... Few praiseworthy rhododendrons lack a good vegetative habit.

By the way, the cross has a name. It happened that just as I discovered the presence of the hybrid seedlings under the *carolinianum,* a society girl dropped into the potting shed to chat with me. The plants were difficult to distinguish, and I had no glass with me, but her eyes were sharp, so I got her to pass on the plants. I held up each one as I pricked it out, and if she said "Freckles," threw it away. If she said "Whiskers," I potted it. The result—every one potted turned out hybrid. I promised her that if they came to anything, they should be named after her: Rachel Biggs.

The seed parent was as good a plant as we had, the *Kaempferi,* the best I could find, a true salmon. If the hybrid ever flowers, it will be interesting to see what it does about holding its color. The one parent starts pale and intensifies. The other fades rapidly as it ages. Will the hybrid average the parental tendencies and retain its color, I wonder?

Goals for Hybrids

The prevailing idea that hybrids should have a pedigree means little to me. If you will examine the rating of the hybrids in the Association yearbook, you will find the key to their apparent amazing inconsistency in this prejudice against the so-called mongrel. The Waterer hybrids, no matter how fine, are marked with a Y, but the trashy Album Elegans, because its parentage is known, escapes, and even gets a star. We consider it hardly worth growing at Guyencourt.

To my mind, the only measure of merit is beauty. A hybrid without a pedigree makes as good a garden plant as one with. Perhaps the origin of the prejudice is that rhododendron men think of a plant in terms of its offspring. Any rhododendron which gives a high percentage of good hybrids in a cross gets honorable mention from the association. And of course we know that very many mixed hybrids tend to produce a rather uniform mediocrity of offspring. Hence the rating.

But that should not blind us to the merit of the plant itself, though of course we should avoid the poor parents in making our crosses. The second generation is probably the best to pick hybrids from, hence our choice of parents should be predominantly first crosses, that is, when crossing a first cross with another first. When using a species on one side, I don't see why a very mixed parent shouldn't be an advantage in some cases....

We have long ago decided that Catawbiense Album is not a natural variety of the species, but a hybrid. Do you think it possible that Bowers' clone is different from ours? That is his only chance of being correct. I have checked ours against those in other nurseries, and never noticed any difference.

The form I used to call Cunningham's White (the name was given me by a very good propagator) is probably not the Cunningham's White of the books but Caucasicum Album. It almost certainly is the Cunningham's White of the continental nurserymen. It is certainly a *caucasicum* hybrid, and judging from appearance and behavior, couldn't possibly be *maximum* X *cinnamomeum.* Also I venture a guess that *maximum* X *cinnamomeum* would not root freely from cuttings.

Caucasicum Album is *caucasicum* X *ponticum album* as I remember it, though Bowers doesn't list it. That answers the description of the plant I was mistakenly induced to call Cunningham's White. Now what was the plant Bowers used? I should like to see it, but he confided to me that most of his plants have died.

There is certainly confusion here, and I am sure I was not the one to start it. The man who identified Cunningham's White for me is one of the country's best propagators. Could the mistake have originated with Cunningham?

March 19, 1936

The plants out in nearly full sun, mostly named hybrids, have been badly injured this winter, but in the grove it was a different story. I put a few of the best plants of each species in the cold-pit-frame, where, as remarked before, they behaved almost perfectly. Since the flood, I have had to handle over most of the plants left outdoors....

Taking stock, out of a good many *barbatum,* half are in good condition, some perfect. Three *crinigerum* all live, two are perfect. One aeruginosum perfect. *Campanulatum,* nearly all good. *Wallichii* good, but most of them are hybrids. *Cephalanthoides* all good. *Cinnabarinum* poor but all alive. One *Falconeri* dead, the others good in frame. *Fictolacteum* many plants nearly all practically perfect. *Rex* fair. *Ferrugineum* fine. *Calophytum* good. *Decorum* fair. *Discolor* fine, including one plant that stuck above the snow. *Fortunei* fair. *Vernicosum* fair. *Oreodoxa* fine. *Fargesii* good. One *fulvum* good, all the rest did less well in the frame. One hypolepidotum good. *Rubiginosum* rather good. Others of the Heliolepis Series not yet examined. *Dryophyllum* good. Levistratum fair. Sigillatum good. *Traillianum* fair. Lapponicum Series all rather good. *Lepidotum* bad as usual. *Baileyi* poor. *Adenopodum* rather good. *Brachycarpum* good. *Chrysanthum* fine. *Fauriei* fine. *Metternichii?* fine. *Smirnowii* good. Californicum practically gone. *Maximum* fair.

Saluenense good. *Chameunum* good. *Hemitrichotum* and *pubescens* not examined. *Adenogynum* fair. *Balfourianum* good. *Bureavii* good. *Agglutinatum* good. *Sphaeroblastum* good. *Wasonii* good. *Caloxanthum* fine. *Campylocarpum* fair. *Dasycladum* good. *Rhaibocarpum* fine. Croceum and *litiense* good. *Wardii* good. *Eclecteum* fair. *Cyanocarpum* mostly dead. *Thomsonii* poor, smaller plants fair to good. *Mekongense* poor, perhaps dead. *Trichocladum* good. Few Triflorums examined. *Racemosum* fine.

One of the best things I saw at the herbarium was *R. proteoides*. From the pressed specimen, it looked like the best of the dwarfs except *repens* and *Forrestii. R. pronum* is not nearly so good. My one plant of *proteoides* is probably a rogue, and not likely to live in any case. For that matter I don't seem able to keep any of the Roxieanums except recurvum and perhaps poecilodermum and aischropeplum.

Of crosses, a good percentage of Moonstone were good, but some practically died. Same with *orbiculare* X *Williamsianum.* One plant of Androcles came through perfectly in the open too. *Souliei* X *discolor* X *litiense* were all left in the open and practically all look very good, but some have spotted foliage. Some plants of *carolinianum* X *cuneatum* were badly hurt, which convinces me that the cross was successful. Most seedlings of Conestoga badly hurt, but some good. *Minus* X *chartophyllum* good. I have decided that one of my unknowns is probably *impeditum* X *racemosum* (chance cross) perfectly hardy, but very dwarf and no suggestion of flower buds. I threw away nearly half of *maximum* X *discolor* for winter injury and leaf spot, but some look very good. Some Decatros are good, other injured. Those you sent with buds on are in the cold-pit-frame.

June 19, 1936

My hopes are high for getting new things in bloom next spring. *R. auriculatum* is now as large as plants I have seen in bloom. One *discolor* is about 2′, with a good spread. When it puts out its new growth, which should be about the end of this month, it will be close to 3′, which might be large enough for a flower bud or two. The largest *campylocarpum* is only about 16″—too small for any hope this year, but another season may bring it out....

The new seedlings continue to thrive. A spot of damping did get into a pot of croceum, and has cleaned out most of the middle, continuing to run after I had scooped out the infected dirt. But I have another pot of *croceum,* and a good many larger plants doing fine. That is the only damping so far. And there being no sign of crickets, I have not needed to dust or spray. When crickets do appear, I shall probably give a weak spray and then dust in addition. But the crickets don't like pots which stand in water, giving no place to hide. *R. horaeum* and *citriniflorum* continue to come up, some lots better than others, but as many as 50 to 75 in the best pots. They start so small, it is hard to tell how many there are. Germination goes on to some extent all summer and increasing in the fall, so that I look for more of nearly everything.

Only one Goldsworth Yellow X Decatros. Conemaugh X *Keiskii* has shown nothing, but I think all the other crosses of *Keiskii,* Conewago and Conestoga are up in force. There is a good pot of *Smirnowii* X *haematodes. Oreotrephes* X Conewago has given only a couple of small seedlings so far. *Maximum* X *dichroanthum,* X *litiense* and X mixed English pollen are all up plentifully considering the amount of seed, that is a dozen or more plants each, some very yellow. *Maximum* X *haemaleum* is up well. There are a few *fastigiatum* X *carolinianum* just up and very small. *Catawbiense* X *haematodes* makes a good showing. Blue Tit is up thick and growing fast. *Haematodes* X *Kingianum* plentiful. *Augustinii* X *Roylei* plenty. *Apodectum* only 2 or 3. *Ungernii* X *auriculatum* doing fine. *Dichroanthum* pretty good. *Neriiflorum* X *apodectum,* it seems to me has shown no life, and I think it is the only lot from Magor that has failed. About four of Ward's failed. Of Rothchild's seeds I believe every lot has come up, mostly thick. There must be 150 *Williamsianum,* while *orbiculare* produced only a dozen or so. *Keleticum* is up thick, *tsangpoense* rather thin, while *radicans* and *fragariflorum* show only a few plants.

August 11, 1936

In the catalog of K. Wada, Numazu-shi, Japan, appears: "Rhododendron brachycarpum montanum lutescens, alpine form of the type of dwarf creeping habit with sulphur coloured flowers." Plants, not seeds. Does this sound like our *chrysanthum?* I suspect that it is. However, I think I should rather have it than *R. chrysanthum,* because the truss should be a better shape than the flat-topped cluster of that species. I am going to state in my new catalog that this *chrysanthum* is probably a dwarf form of *brachycarpum.*

The Japanese beetle inspectors have been unable to find any beetles on my ground, and I hope they will let me ship next spring.

Buds on *R. muliense* are now opening. Too bad they could not wait till spring, but forming so early on such a small plant, I did not expect them to last. The expanding bud looks greenish. My young plants of both *muliense* and *chryseum* are doing nobly. Ward says they are nearly the same.

An Early Freeze

November 27, 1936

I have not had the courage to write recently because I didn't want to talk about the October freeze. After a frostless month, the thermometer suddenly dipped to 15°, destroying species which I had thought hardy: *fictolacteum, Bureavii,* etc. Even Roseum Elegans was badly damaged, but I find it was the spurious form and not the true one that was injured. Lee's Dark Purple was badly cut even in the lath house. But here again, I find there is some uncertainty as to the true variety. There is a form much like Purpureum Grandiflorum which is sometimes called Lee's, and is perfectly hardy. Of course I have resolved to weed the tender Roseum Elegans out of my nursery, if indeed that hasn't already been done by the cold.

The only other hardy hybrid to suffer was Lady Grey Edgerton, though Luciferum and Candidissimum have black spots on the leaves, and of course Cynthia is slightly injured.

Maximum X *discolor* was almost ruined. Why is it that *R. maximum* cannot pass its hardiness to its offspring? In the end, we may find that all our hardy hybrids must derive from other species. Delicatissimum is less hardy than either parent. But the fact is that young plants of *maximum* were killed by the cold.

I notice that *carolinianum* X *cuneatum* is not on your list, and will include a plant with those I take you in the spring. This winter I put several indoors to recover from the beating they took last winter. I have also *carolinianum* X *Edgeworthii* which took the same beating, but that cross simply can't be correct, or it wouldn't have lived through last winter at all. *Edgeworthii* is one of the tenderest things I ever tried to raise. Anyway, I put them indoors and will watch them very skeptically as they develop.

Certainly it means we will have to breed for hardiness above all things. I am looking forward to your *Smirnowii* X *haematodes* as a likely parent for new reds, though it may suffer from some unforeseen drawback, such as sterility. Since you mentioned the resemblance between *Smirnowii* X *arboreum* and Caractacus, I have been looking at the two and have come to the conclusion that this is the true parentage of Caractacus, more especially because Caractacus sets seed so poorly, which is not usually the case with second crosses. Looking at the foliage of Chas. S. Sargent (I have never seen the flowers), I am wondering whether it also may not be a *Smirnowii* hybrid, also hoping it is, because, if so, the cuttings of it should root handily.

Last summer, I put in one cutting of *campylocarpum* X *Williamsianum,* and it rooted so quickly that I conclude both *campylocarpum* and *Williamsianum* hybrids will be rootable. Previous experience with the Thomsonii Series has been confined to an unsuccessful attempt to root *Thomsonii*. My attempts to root the Fortunei Series are few, but *decorum* has struck easily.

January 14, 1937

I am sending back your list with checkmarks on, and feel ashamed that I have practically nothing to offer in return. Have not been able to get in touch with the missionary at Chengtu. Ward has promised me a set of his seeds from this coming trip. He is going into unexplored territory between Yunnanfu and Talifu, then north "into a drier region." Of course, I shall be glad to divide these seeds with you, but that will not be until next year. This year the best I can do will be plants.

The only seeds of my own which could possibly interest you are the enclosed Decatros (a form with many virtues) X H. W. Sargent, Atrosanguineum & Kettledrum. It was hand-pollinated under glass.

May 30, 1937

Sorry I couldn't make the trip with you, but I simply haven't the money. I have never seen Dexter's rhodos in flower, which must be an inspiring sight, and there is a lot I could learn by studying the named varieties at the Arnold Arboretum, where they should be true. Some other year, perhaps.

When I visited Dexter's, he had not enjoyed much success with the Lapponicums, but told me how he was arranging a special place for them. They need a special place, and I have not been able to give them a really satisfactory one so far.

He has thrown almost all his energies into the *Fortunei* hybrids, and considering his age, that was probably wise, for he can do a definite, important piece of work and more or less complete it before he dies. He had a lot of *discolor* and *discolor* hybrids when I was there, but only in small sizes. Also I remember *croceum, rufum, Williamsianum, Fargesii*. The *Fargesii* were fine big plants and flowered every year. But his and Everitt's are different from the *Fargesii* I have, which is Rock 23326.

He can select very fine and fairly hardy individuals from his *Fortunei* hybrids just as they now stand, and no doubt we shall have some named and on the market before long. But the pursuit of yellows and of better reds must go on a much longer time.

Need for Hybridizers

One of the women at the Horticultural Society suggested that they might get up a group of amateurs to undertake hybridizing. They asked who was engaged in the work, and for the life of me I couldn't think of anybody in the east except you and Dexter and Brower. Bowers and Gillin have dropped out and, I believe, Kelsey. Hicks is not active. I have not heard whether H. F. duPont intends to do anything constructive. I offered to give them all the necessary instructions.

Now that the country is pulling out of the depression and out of the cold-winter cycle, perhaps we can build up some interest again. There ought to be a hundred people working at the production of new hybrids. I almost gave up when everybody lost interest, because three or four people are not enough to make things move.

The rock garden society were after me to stage an exhibit, which I had to refuse for two reasons: (1) I hadn't the plants in condition to show; (2) I couldn't stand the cost or the loss of time.

In a couple of years, if I have pulled out a little ahead of the game, perhaps we could stage an exhibit in the New York show together—or perhaps in the Philadelphia show, as a compromise in distance. Flower show exhibits do more to popularize a plant than all other means combined. . . .

His Rooting Method

July 10, 1937

In working out my rooting method, I tried many kinds of medium, perhaps a hundred all told, and finally arrived at a formula which works better than any other. After fixing upon it as standard, I went on trying variations in small plots marked off by panes of glass, but no variation worked as well as the standard. It works every year almost uniformly, so I have given up trying to improve the medium except as some new idea comes along. Strange to say, any considerable departure from the formula results in a very considerable reduction of efficiency. . . .

My original experiments ranged from pure peat to pure sand, and I noticed that each had its advantages, although neither worked well. Then I began stratifying. The disadvantage of pure sand is that when the cuttings have to stay in it so long, they die from lack of nourishment. Peat has nourishment, but the cuttings can't get it until they callous, and they don't callous well in peat. The surface of peat lends itself to sudden runs of fungi which wipe out whole blocks of cuttings, while a sand surface tends to check fungus growth.

To begin then: contrary to all extablished usage, my beds have no drainage. I build a tight wooden box just as big as a cold-frame sash, and the depth of a twelve-inch board, as you have seen. The bottom is rough tongue-and-groove flooring, and while tight, allows water to drain away in time through the cracks and joints. I have also used watertight galvanized pans with pretty good results, and intend to use more of them in future, as they do not require watering nearly so often. My latest has holes punched in the side here and there, down to within an inch of the bottom, but no lower, ensuring an absolutely swamp condition in the bottom, but a certain degree of drainage higher up.

The Nearing Frame

The shade arrangement you of course understand. All possible indirect light is admitted, but no direct sunlight, as that would spoil everything. At least the sun does touch the glass in early morning and late afternoon, when too low to build up any heat inside. To test the importance of exluding sunlight, three of the units at Guyencourt were turned 15° toward the east instead of due north. That is not much of an angle, but every cutting in those frames burned to a crisp. I line my frames by the north star now. Having the frames in tiers, and all painted white, the back of each shade throws reflected light into the frame to the south of it. The frames farthest north never work as well as the others, because of this lack of reflected light.

In the 3' x 6' box . . . I use the following stratified medium:

1st layer: 1 bushel measure of mushroom manure, screened, and 3 bushels peat, thoroughly mixed and leveled. I have used both German and Michigan peat. There is not much difference, but I prefer the German. The mushroom manure is a convenient material, but I think it would be all right to substitute very, very old, well rotted manure with a little good top soil mixed in. . . .

This first layer lies below the butts of the cuttings. If the cuttings penetrate it, they usually rot and do not callous. It is there for two reasons—to act as a sponge filled not with water, but with a nourishing liquid, which can be sucked up slowly when growth begins, and also to become a growing medium as soon as the roots penetrate it.

2nd layer: 1/2 bushel screened Michigan peat, 1/2 bushel fine sand, mixed together outside, and spread on the first layer carefully, so as not to disturb the levels. To make this easier, I usually water the first layer heavily before spreading on the second. Sometimes I do not screen the peat, and the sand need not be very fine, but I think the grade known as plasterer's sand is best.

This is the rooting layer. Most of the cuttings just reach it, and in it or just above it they callous well. Once calloused, they can live two or three years if

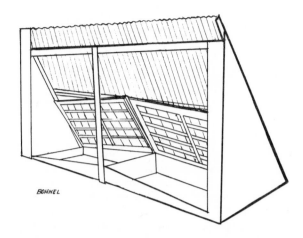

The Nearing Frame. *This structure may be built by any handyman. The wood should be 1" stock of redwood or cypress; the sloping rear wall of corrugated aluminum. Full instructions and detail drawing will be found in "Rhododendrons of the World" by David G. Leach, pp. 322-323. Note that the frame must face true North and that the sloping rear wall must be kept 2" above the ground to prevent the accumulation of hot air during the summer.*

necessary until they decide to root. German peat is not nearly as good as Michigan.

Top layer: three bushels of sand. I have tried many different sands, some of which are no good. The plasterer's grade is too fine for this layer. My best results are from the grade known as concrete sand, a round-grained pit-sand with acid or neutral reaction, acid of course preferred. One year I bought glass-sand on a tip from someone, but the grains were angular and all coarse. There must be fine sand mixed with the coarse, or it will not hold enough water. If the sand is too fine, it holds too much. By good fortune, we have sand right here in our orchard which is just right. I merely dig down a couple of feet and get all I want.

The top is leveled carefully, and the whole thing watered very heavily until water stands on it half an inch or an inch deep. When this drains away, the sand has packed somewhat, and I make the holes with the template you have seen, rows of 20d nails in a board. The cuttings are set about 2" apart, totaling about 250 to each sash. I trim the shanks so that when I hold them across the palm of my left hand, or rather at the roots of the fingers, with the petioles resting against my forefinger, the butts just reach across my little finger. This makes about 3-1/4", all of which goes in the sand, right up to the petioles, as you have seen. Sometimes the frost pushes them up during the winter, and when the frame thaws they have to be pressed back, but if the earth level is high on the outside of the box, this seldom happens. I usually trim off all the leaves except three, or if they are small, up to five, never more. One leaf is sometimes enough. Where the leaves are very large, I have sometimes cut them in half, and the results were fairly good. When too many leaves interfere, the lower ones rot.

As soon as the cuttings are placed, I water heavily, and water about twice a week for a month or so. During the winter and even in late fall, I reduce the watering. In October it is perhaps once a week, and in midwinter once a month or so, only when completely thawed. When spring opens up, it is important to water two or three times a week. At each watering, I keep sprinkling till water stands all over the sand at once. In June, I rather reduce the watering again, but not much. In July, the cuttings are ready to take out, having put up top growth. The ones which have not rooted, but are still in good condition are put in a new frame to root next year.

The rooted cuttings are potted in 4" pots (sometimes the best require 6", when the roots won't squeeze into a 4"), and kept in a partly shaded frame till the following June, wintering under glass, then bedded out in the lath house.

I forgot to say that I occasionally spray the beds with arsenate and Bordeaux, and in case of fly or aphids, either dust or spray as elsewhere. I used to lose a good many cuttings to leaf diseases, but the Bordeaux takes care of them.

This is the only written record of my formula, and as it is based on years of work, it ought to be kept, though for the present, privately. You will find it very simple and easy in practise, and I have had practically no failures in seven or eight years, except the varieties which refuse to root.

Success varies a little from year to year with the different varieties, but they usually rank something like this, beginning with the best: Roseum Elegans, Catawbiense Grandiflorum, Purpureum Elegans, Caractacus, Lee's D. P., Album Grandiflorum, Catawbiense Album, Kettledrum, Atrosanguineum, Lady Armstrong, Everestianum, Cynthia, Boule de Neige, Charles Bagley, Memoir, Album Elegans. All these, and perhaps some others I can't think of at the moment, are dependable for 50% or better on the average. Judging by the few cuttings tried, *Fortunei* hybrids should root with the best. The worst rooting is among *maximum* hybrids. Charles Dickens, Amphion, Mrs. C. S. Sargent,

Delicatissimum all give poor results, though I have rooted some cuttings of them. There will be several more to add to the list when this year's returns are in.

August 6, 1937

I neglected to say in my last letter that my cutting system is not much good for Azaleas, conifers, etc. It is a highly specialized method suited only to the large-leaved rhododendrons. I doubt if it does as well as yours with the Lapponicums and such. But I feel sure it is the best system yet devised for its purpose, and is so easy to operate that you will find it convenient when you want to propagate your new varieties. At any time of year, I can lock up my nursery and go away for three or four days, and can leave the propagating frames unlooked-at for a week without injury.

My cuttings do not root well unless they are deep in the sand. This is true also of hollies. I imagine the difference is due to slow rooting, but you cannot root rhododendrons fast by any method yet devised, and by letting them take their own time you can root them both easily and cheaply.

June 16, 1938

It looks as if you had at last achieved the hardy yellow, over which so many have labored for so long. All of that cross is plant-hardy here, and even if yours doesn't keep its buds in the worst winters, which is possible, it will be worth a lot as the only hardy yellow known. Of course, I have not seen the plant, and the flowers had blackened considerably, but if the yellow is as bright as these flowers indicate, and if there are no glaring defects in the plant, it ought to be worth at least a couple of thousand dollars. I should not expect more than 10% of that cross to come yellow, and most of the yellows will probably be very pale, so your plant is not likely to have many rivals.

Whether it will have value as a parent, remains to be seen. I have been considering it a final cross, but as it is only once removed from a primary, have intended to use it in future crosses also. Too bad there is nothing but *maximum* to try the pollen on this year.

Your new yellow will probably grow well from cuttings, and it will be safest for you to propagate it yourself. I have listened to a great deal of advice from propagators hereabouts, and it all adds up to something like this. If you want to make money out of a new thing, propagate it yourself, and don't let any plant of it get out of your hands till you have built up a considerable stock. There are a surprisingly large number of nurserymen who are not completely honest, and if you let anyone else propagate for you, be sure to patent

first. Even then, you may have to sue. If I had it, I should build up a stock of at least a thousand plants before even talking much about it. . . .

I am going to publish my cutting-propagation method some time this year.

September 22, 1938

The New York hurricane brought a flood 4″ higher than the highest previous one. The havoc is staggering, and I hardly know what to do about it. Things as I had them were safe from an ordinary flood, and I had begun to feel easy about most of my plants, but I had not expected anything like this. It is surprising what a difference a few inches can make.

This is certainly a bad place for rhododendrons, but I have gone so far with them that it is hard to see how to move or where to move to. Having put in thousands of dollars and an enormous amount of labor, I suppose I'll just have to keep going and take my losses, like the neighboring market gardeners whose losses were much larger in money than mine.

January 28, 1939

. . . With first crosses there is no use raising many plants, because they are likely to be much alike, and there is no great range to select from, but with second crosses, it will pay to grow as many as you can take care of, throwing away as soon as possible all that obviously cannot produce good garden subjects, but keeping all that show promise, for the variation will be wide. I have a great many seedlings of Conestoga, and the range of habit is simply astonishing, as I suppose you have noticed in your own seedlings. Your seed of Conestoga produces better results than mine, because you have more for it to cross with, and almost anything it crosses with should produce good results. The only fault with the original Conestoga was that it lost its buds at 20 below. It might produce a seedling of its own type but fully hardy, but it is also giving many plants of totally different habit. On the same pattern, I am trying to visualize the offspring of (*Smirnowii* X *Fortunei*) X (*orbiculare* X *Williamsianum*), all of which I know in growth and in flower, and I can picture some fascinating possibilities.

The plant I want most to see, however, is (*Smirnowii* X *haematodes*) X (*haematodes* X *arboreum*) which should produce a hardy red of great merit. Another (*maximum* X *discolor*) X (*calophytum* X *arboreum*) gives me a good mental picture. The use of *calophytum* itself rather than the cross would be still better, but the cross will probably bloom many years before the species. If we can get *maximum* X *auriculatum* this summer, I hope some day to cross it with

Griffithianum X *Griersonianum,* and of course the use of *maximum* X *discolor* in that cross need not be far distant, as I have large plants of *Griffithianum* X *Griersonianum.* By the way, could you use one of them? I have about three, all growing out of bounds.

September 9, 1939

. . . So many crosses grow here in small sizes that I have never made any attempt to list them. Almost every lot of seed you have sent in the past three or four years has produced something. The ones I consider most important are the *haematodes* crosses. I have a good lot of *Smirnowii* X *haematodes,* some very interesting *maximum* X *haematodes,* but only one of this last cross has shown real vigor. The crosses with *dichroanthum, arboreum,* etc., have good possibilities as parents. A few *maximum* X *litiense* look good. *Auriculatum* X *Ungernii* has done poorly, seeming very tender, but is still around. A tremendous thing is *calophytum* X *arboreum,* which I hope may flower in a couple of years, to be crossed with something hardy. It ought to come into bloom much sooner than *calophytum.* The plants of it that have been exposed in winter have mostly died off, but two or three are still alive, and I think I shall stow them in the pit this winter.

Imagine the possible combinations for second crosses, and if that isn't a lifetime's work for anyone, then I'm Napoleon Bonaparte. Dexter was wise to devote himself to the *Fortunei* and *discolor* hybrids, because they are so near realization, and give such good results with one crossing. But I haven't seen any on the market in this country. I am not forgetting Waterer's statement that the best results have come from the crossing of two first crosses. If for instance we can cross *maximum* X *discolor* with *maximum* X *haematodes,* the offspring should show many different combinations of those three species. But to be sure of getting the best out of this race, several hundred plants should be raised. By the time I get to raising many such crosses, I will need a much bigger place than I have here.

If I were sure of staying here, I should accept your offer of *catawbiense* X Michael Waterer, but what with floods and quarantines, this may prove too much for me in the end.

March 31, 1940

I have often thought that it would be very pleasant to join forces with you at Stewartstown, but there is no present possibility of making such a move. I don't like it here, but am tied down so that leaving would be far too difficult.

Instead, I am now a writer, with a little rhododendron nursery on the side. I have a book ordered, will continue to write magazine and newspaper articles on horticulture, and perhaps other things. When I get the book finished, there is another possible one in which a publisher has signified some interest. Every morning I write until noon, then have lunch, and spend the afternoon at the nursery. There won't be any more expansion, and not much new construction until I have built up a system of dikes that will really protect my operations. What I do after that will depend on how well the writing goes, and whether prospects in the nursery business brighten.

Some day perhaps, I may get into a position where I can do what I like, and then I may open up the discussion of a possible move to Stewartstown, but it cannot be until I have a good many thousand dollars ahead. Thanks, anyway for suggesting the possibility.

June 3, 1940

I can't quite agree with you about the Triflorums. They are of course entirely different from the Carolinianums, but I have plans for a whole race, or rather series of races, one founded on Conestoga, with yellow from *Keiskei,* blue from the blue Lapponicums and the *Augustinii* crosses, and perhaps crimson from *cinnabarinum.* I am also waiting patiently for my *carolinianum* X *Edgeworthii* to bloom, in the hope that it will prove fertile, and introduce a large flower into the hybrid strains. I want a series of smaller sizes too, as small as I can get them, and I hope that *keleticum* X *racemosum,* now germinating, will help in that direction. Also a larger race based on *rubiginosum,* of which I think I have an accidental hybrid. This year a white *Augustinii* was covered with long-pediceled flowers of generous size, appearing before the foliage. The effect was striking, and suggested what longer pedicels could do for *carolinianum.* As the plant has wintered outdoors in the past, I crossed it with *carolinianum v. album,* and hope for a hardy hybrid from which to work further.

Only one plant of *racemosum* X *Keiskei* flowered for me, and it was cream colored, with pale pink edge. Plants left outdoors appear perfectly hardy, and of good habit, so next year probably I shall have plenty. That cross should be the basis for yellows, if it is fertile. My one plant did not hold its capsules, and produced no pollen, but due to the excessively damp conditions, it and some other inhabitants of the cold pit were attacked by mold, which destroyed entire flower heads, and just to cap it off, a flood three days ago tumbled them around and buried most of them almost completely under wet peat. Most of them survived, however, and no doubt will ripen seeds.

The lepidote hybrids could never be more than a

side-issue with me and especially with the public. They lack the dignity of the larger leaved Rhododendrons. They will have to compete with the Azaleas, and the public will always look upon them as evergreen Azaleas. Therefore, they must have good colors. In fact, no hybrid strain of anything can get very far without a good range of color. Conestoga seedlings tend to go white, and are lamentably lacking in hardiness. The flowers are almost invariably small and few, nothing so far to compare with Conestoga itself. Whether the curse will be carried to the various Conestoga crosses, remains to be seen.

Two years ago, I grew a lot of supposed seedlings of *racemosum,* only to have them all turn out very much like Conestoga seedlings, but with a tendency to larger leaves. Where the seed came from, I don't remember at all. Most of them had all the leaves burned off last winter, but one with a very narrow, pointed leaf, came through as green as summer. I think it is a *micranthum* hybrid. It is certainly not *micranthum,* or anything else that I have seen, but doesn't suggest any feature of *racemosum.*

Unfortunately, I have been throwing the rejected plants where they could be seen by visitors to the nursery, and these have insisted on dragging off the remains, hoping to bring them back to life. Hereafter they are going to be thrown out of sight. Gardens are too full of worthless trash as it is. I am not going to let anything go out of my nursery except first-class material. Plants which have possibilities will be grown on for two or three years before being propagated, although some which look very promising may be propagated experimentally to see how they respond. After nearly fifteen years of breeding, I have fewer than a dozen plants kept for observation, and most of those will pretty surely be thrown away.

Suggests Forming A.R.S.

September, 1940

The war overseas is going to play hob with all progress in rhododendrons. I tried to buy some seed from the British Rhodo. Association, but my letter seems to have taken over a month to cross the ocean, arriving too late, after the seeds had been distributed. Then my money was returned, but how much of it I will ever collect, with foreign exchange the way it is, remains to be seen. It will be impossible to get pollen from there. Also we will certainly miss the information which the yearbook has always contained.

Under the circumstances, it might be worthwhile to launch an American Rhododendron Association, and try to keep up the interest until the British one resumes, but I can't spare the time to do anything about it. Perhaps, too, our own country will soon put

us in a situation where the best we can do for the rhododendrons is try to hold on to what we have. Do you think it would be worthwhile to sound out the former members of the Rhododendron Association, and find out whether there is anyone willing to organize the group?

After Ten Years!

December 29, 1940

I have been addressing you as Mr. Gable for a long time, but as we both have three-letter names, maybe we ought to save ink.

On receiving your letter, I brought out my seeds and threshed them, which wasn't much of a job, as out of the 80 or so attempted crosses, only about 20 had perceptible seeds. I mean to sow the rest, ten or twelve lots in one 4" pot, just in case there is a seed or two that I can't see. Most of them are not important anyway, but some were real disappointments. The trouble was mainly incessant rain at flowering time. Next year, I'll provide some cellophane bags for bad weather. In some cases, I applied pollen three or four times, only to have showers come up within a few hours and wash it all off. Whether the bags will do much good, remains to be seen.

None of my successful crosses look very important, but the *discolor* X *auriculatum* (plenty of seed) ought to be worth trying as a promising parent. For final results I hope to get something worthwhile perhaps, out of Kettledrum X (*decorum* X *haematodes*) or (Caractacus X *Fortunei*) X (*decorum* X *haematodes*). From your description of this plant (*decorum* X *haematodes*), I am anxious to see something from it, but the hardiest things I used on it yielded mostly no seeds. Perhaps, H. W. Sargent X *discolor*, of which there is a good seed crop, may show some class, as the cross is not unlike Caractacus X *Fortunei*, which produced a good plant, lacking only the ability to carry all its florets. The lateness of *discolor* might result in less bud injury.

I like several of your crosses, especially those using *decorum* X *haematodes*. In this climate, I am not so hopeful of offspring from Britannia and Essex Scarlet, because both have complex and probably not too hardy parentage. I would rather use simpler crosses and hope for a hardier parallel to these reds. . . .

July 8, 1941

My cuttings this year look better than ever before. I expect to get 2500 rooted, perhaps more, and think also that I have learned something. Leaf-bud cuttings struck much sooner than stem cuttings. I found that I could take a leaf-bud cutting off the side of my stem cutting, sometimes two or three or more, leaving a shank with one or two sides partly sliced off. This ought to give the advantage of the leaf-bud cutting—a large area of cut, combined with that of the stem cutting—bulk. About half of my cuttings were made that way, and though I am not yet sure of the results, there are evidences of much quicker strike in the slow ones.

Three of my boxes will probably do better than 90%, not including the leaf-bud cuttings placed around the edge. As they are a new experiment, it is hard to say how they will come out—evidently well in some varieties, very poorly in others. Pridham, who has taken Skinner's place at Cornell, paid me a long visit the other day. He wanted to see what a plant looked like after having been grown from a cutting. His project is to find out how to make his rooted leaf-bud cuttings break, as it appears they confine their activity to root-growth, and do not put up any shoot. I was able to show him leaf-bud cuttings in pots with two lengths of wood and a third starting. These interested him greatly, evidently a novelty.

August 23, 1941

The flower arrived in perfect condition. It is a fine color. As I botanize it, without seeing the leaf, it is certainly *R. didymum*. When you have a little leisure, run through the key in The Species of Rhododendron, and see if there is any other possibility. All the details of hairy, glandular, and wrinkled ovary, and the glabrous red style and red filaments are exactly right for that species and suit no other. All my *didymum* have died, I believe. I have few left of the whole Neriflorum series. Most of the losses are due to flooding. Anyway, if they do live, they blight easily.

As I have pinned strong hopes on the hybrids from this series, I am most grateful for the many good crosses you have made, some of which are thriving nicely here. As soon as they flower, I want to work them on the Boule de Neige type. If this *didymum* could only be captured in a hybrid, it might extend the color range all the way to black.

. . . It is inconceivable that the breeding of nut trees should bring any financial return during the lifetime of the man who begins it. I am beginning to think that rhododendrons are nearly the same class, but at least we didn't know that when we started. Or if we did, the work seemed so tremendously worthwhile that we had to go ahead with it anyway. E. H. Wilson said, when I told him I did not expect to live long enough to profit by breeding work, that he thought it could be made to pay if carefully planned. I still don't see how. Seven to ten years to bring a seedling to a state of maturity at which you are sure it will be worthwhile, then six or eight more years to build up a stock big enough to make even a moderate financial return. And that all comes after you have raised countless possible candidates from which to select. If Wilson knew any other way, he failed to tell me about it. And now after fifteen years of work, I still haven't raised a first class seedling. Next year, however, that part of the story may be changed.

January 26, 1942

I think I see a real chance to stab at a hardy yellow. What appear to be flower buds have set on a plant of *campylocarpum* X *Williamsianum* in the cold pit. Crossing that with things like Goldsworth Yellow would probably yield some yellows for English conditions, but no good here. However, if you have flowers on your *maximum* X *campylocarpum* this season, or on any cross of *campylocarpum, litiense,* or other yellow, with *maximum, catawbiense* or *Smirnowii,* in other words any primary cross of a yellow with a cast-iron hardy species, a cross between that and *campylocarpum* X *Williamsianum* should give some hardy yellows. (*Maximum* X *campylocarpum*) X Goldsworth Yellow would be even better, I would think, but of course very different. Your seeds of (*maximum* X *campylocarpum*) X (*decorum* X *haematodes*) may give something very fine and unexpected, but with less chance of a yellow. I suppose *maximum* X *campylocarpum* will bloom later than *campylocarpum* X *Williamsianum,* so that it will be best to send you the pollen, but as my plant will be in the cold pit until about the middle of May, perhaps we can make the cross both ways. The cold pit holds back all my flowers. Last year hardly anything opened there until May. In a warmer season, flowering usually begins there about the middle of April. There is no danger of insects, as I do not have to ventilate, and the stigmas usually stay receptive about two weeks, perhaps three.

There is an antiaircraft gun being set up about a hundred yards from my nursery, which may mean shell fragments falling around and breaking glass, etc. That is one item you probably won't have to worry about.

Nearly all my lepidotes are budded for next season. There is a whole bed of Conestoga seedlings, *racemosum* X *Keiskei* and such things mostly with buds. Some of the seedlings of your apud *hormophorum* are surprisingly hardy, and unusual in habit, one of the least attractive with buds this year, and evidently intending to winter them.

March 17, 1942

On Botanical Names

I don't use the author's name because I think that is the origin of a situation which is ruining the whole of botanical taxonomy. The botanical politicians decreed that usage so that they could make themselves famous, and incidentally clean up some money. They name thousands of useless and meaningless species simply to get their own names spread around, and to compel people to buy their new books in order to find out what changes they have made. In my introduction, I proudly state that I have not named one new species, and throughout the book I point out which are real species and which are segregated on insufficient grounds.

I could of course have included the authors, but was specially anxious to avoid the format of the conventional monograph. My book is written to explain what lichens the professional botanists have referred to in their highly technical treatises, for they have scrupulously avoided letting anyone in on this little secret. When the book is finished, they will flail it with scientific curses and common sarcasms, and the more credulous botanists will believe them, but about that time I'm planning to have some unexpected ammunition ready for them.

The best procedure in *naming an unknown* of your own is to work it out in the manual, then press a bit, and at your convenience take it to a herbarium for comparison. I should think you could reach the Smithsonian without too much traveling, and it is there, I believe, that the material is located, also probably much of Wilson's. Perhaps you have been there.

One thing I'm sorry I didn't do is keep a few seeds of each species. The seeds differ a lot, and would be useful as an aid in determination. Many specimens have flower, capsule and seeds all present, and though seeds are not included in most of the descriptions, they might well be. If a fellow had a good collection of the seeds, he could take those of Feng, etc., and match them up nearly enough to make some sort of guess before sowing.

April 7, 1942

I had an experience with *Smirnowii* which may interest you. After a series of nightly hard frosts, with frost very deep in the ground, I examined a number of buds of *Smirnowii* and decided that they were hopeless, so limp and soft that it seemed impossible they could have survived. *Smirnowii* X *arboreum,* the old faithful, not only had its buds mushy soft, but the whole plant seemed to have collapsed, the twigs shriveled. I gave it up for dead. Today that plant is as sturdy as ever, all its buds firm and full, as are the buds of *Smirnowii* which looked hopeless. So far as I have observed, no other rhodos except *Smirnowii* and its hybrids can play dead and later come to life. I had the same experience with a *Smirnowii* hybrid last year.

The buds seemed completely ruined, so I tried to uproot the plant to throw it away. The ground was frozen so hard, however, that after a couple of yanks I decided to wait until I could get rid of the plant without going for the axe. Then I forgot it. In due season, it opened every floret with a fine display of really good trusses. But because the foliage had been badly injured, I threw it away then.

June 14, 1942

I certainly appreciate the trouble you took to send me all those flowering specimens. The *Fortuneis* arrived just as I was starting a demonstration of rhododendron breeding for the Torrey Botanical Club. I had very little of my own to show, so made the most of what you sent. One *Fortunei* opened three florets for me, all other buds being killed completely. But nearly everything lost its buds. The only rhododendron in the open to open buds at the top of the bush was Charles Dickens, and it had lost many florets. . . .

Of the specimens you sent, *atlanticum* X *calendulaceum* is one of the most brilliant shades I ever saw in an Azalea, while your Rosebud, if the specimen was typical, ought to be a magnificent show. The second *catawbiense* X *haematodes,* with the bright color and paler calyx was the outstanding large rhodo, so far as I could judge. It will make a striking novelty. The last *maximum* X *haematodes* is a fine shade of salmon, but not quite showy enough. All *Fortuneis* are worthless up this way, because the first abrupt freeze after a warm fall will split the bark even of mature plants. But you surely have some fine flowers of the species.

On Naming Plants

The question of what plants should be named and propagated is a perplexing one. Of all the flowers you sent (exluding Azaleas, of which I know little), the only one sure of a good reception is that *catawbiense* X *haematodes.* Selection is the most important part of plant breeding, and I give it a good deal of thought. When you breed a striking novelty, it does not compete with any other variety directly, and if it is attractive, it can be propagated with confidence. But a slight improvement over some existing variety should be scrutinized with great care before being backed with money and effort. The success of any variety depends not on its introducer but on the response of the public, and the public consists not only of groundowners, but of landscape gardeners, nurserymen, propagators, and horticultural writers, some of whom exert powerful influence. As a propagator and nurseryman in one of our busiest horticultural centers, I see the problem this way. My sales are largely Roseum Elegans, Caractacus, Catawbiense Grandiflorum, because these propagate well, so that I can build up a supply of them. Atrosanguineum will be my leader as soon as the supply is built up. Boule de Neige sells faster than I can propagate it, but presents some difficulties, which may always prevent it from being a leading seller. Lady Armstrong and Kettledrum are straggly and hard to shape, but sell fairly well. I have practically discontinued Album Grandiflorum, Album Elegans, Luciferum, Minnie, Ignatius Sargent, President Lincoln, Lee's Dark Purple, and others because of lack of bud-hardiness, or difficulty of shaping. H. W. Sargent, Charles Dickens, Henrietta Sargent, and some others are difficult to propagate, therefore will never be important in my business. All of which boils down to about five leading varieties which get most of the attention, and which I can recommend with confidence. Each has its faults, but I have learned to handle each one satisfactorily. Now a new variety would have to take its place alongside these, crowding them more or less, because I can raise only so many plants. Before I would want to adopt an improved Roseum Elegans (I believe I have the original clone), I should want to handle it experimentally and watch it for a number of years, and so would any propagator in my position. A non-propagating nurseryman would often be willing to take my word for the superiority of a variety but, for that reason, I should want to be very sure of my facts before recommending one. You may notice that I am discontinuing many of the varieties listed as the best sixteen by the Arnold Arboretum and Rochester Park. They are being dropped gradually, or simply crowded out of the propagating frames.

But, of course, the introduction of new varieties, when I undertake it, will help to keep the customers interested. . . .

I don't know how you feel about plant patents. I don't like them because they cost too much, but if I originated a striking variety, and if anyone wanted to propagate it on a large scale, I should be willing to patent it and sell him the patent along with all the stock of it. That, however, is not likely to happen until I have brought out at least two or three highly successful varieties. But for me to propagate a variety which was a slight or debatable improvement over an existing one would be simply throwing away money. The matter must be considered with all possible judgment. I should not care to push a bud-tender clone unless it had some very striking quality not found in other clones except those that were more bud-tender. For instance, I have a Charles Bagley X *Fortunei (giganteum X Fortunei)* which is fragrant and looks like Pink Pearl. It has been crowded in a clump of those seedlings for several years, and I don't remember whether it has failed to set buds, or lost all its buds, or whether, perhaps, its first flowers were not so good,

which sometimes happen. It opened one cluster this year, which was more than any of the others of that cross did, and the cluster had no dead florets. Now I don't know of any hardier fragrant hybrid, so I am keeping it under observation, tearing out the plants which have crowded it, probably transplanting it to a more favorable situation next spring, putting in half a dozen or a dozen cuttings. Within two or three years, I will know whether it has good enough habits to handle satisfactorily, whether it is hardier or tenderer than now appears. Then I will have to judge whether its fragrance and well formed cluster are important enough to outweigh whatever drawbacks it has. I may decide to propagate a limited number as a fragrant novelty, and recommend it chiefly for planting farther south. But you undoubtedly have many fragrant clones, and there are English varieties half-hardy and better. Every year I select at least two or three plants for observation, and soon it will probably be two or three dozen. Thus far none of them have improved on acquaintance. Therefore, I will not give them space in my propagating frames.

All this is purely a business consideration. I can't see any other basis for judgment. Eventually the public is going to decide whether it likes my clones. I know what it likes of the present standard hybrids, and by comparison, I can make a guess as to its reception of any new one. A red the color of Essex Scarlet (which is truly magnificent), as hardy as Charles Dickens, and as compact as Boule de Neige, would of course meet with public approval and overwhelming volume of sale. Short of that are many desirable things. Your *catawbiense* X *haematodes* will sell well unless it has decided faults that are not apparent, but I don't think the duller one, although it has the larger calyx, would win nearly as much favor.

Fortunei hybrids have been hanging fire for twenty years or so to my knowledge, pushed by Dexter, Kelsey, yourself, and others. So far as I am aware, not a single one has captivated the public. Many of them are pretty good. Perhaps some are excellent. I just don't happen to have seen anything outstanding. Some nurserymen have said to me, "*Fortunei*—don't touch it," or words to that effect.

To conclude, I think we should be pessimistic about moderately good clones, optimistic about striking novelties, but the measure of our success will be our ability to judge which is which.

November 6, 1942

A good number of buds are setting or have set. All the *maximum* X *discolor* have buds, all but one for the first time. This was because I had neglected to give the plants room. One has foliage like *maximum,* and last year it flowered, though only 1' and with 3 tips. I noted that the flowers were unusually good for *maximum,* and that they were pink, although the parent *maximum* was pure white. This season it has set two lateral flower buds jammed under two terminal ones. This is a *discolor* trick which I don't remember to have seen on *maximum.* Evidently this is not, as I had supposed, a *maximum* which had failed to take the cross, but a cross with an exceptional distribution of the genes.

Eight of my hardy *Griffithianum* hybrids have buds, some a good number. The plants have demonstrated reasonable hardiness. Now it remains to be seen whether the buds are hardy, and then whether the flowers look like anything.

A plant labeled *eriogynum* has three buds. It is a fine looking plant which I think you gave me many years ago. At first it botanized about right, but recently a persistent indumentum under the leaves rules out that species. It has red glands like *maximum,* and resemblance enough to that species to suggest that it may be a *maximum* hybrid. It winters well in the cold pit and will probably do something toward clearing up its parentage when spring comes.

December, 1942

My customers too want red, but will take pink as a second choice, and other colors when a shapely plant is the chief idea, as it often is. I put in all the cuttings possible of Caractacus, Atrosanguineum, Kettledrum, which are my leading hybrid varieties in that order. Later, Atrosanguineum will take precedence over Caractacus, though so far I can't grow enough of either. I have set aside 15 plants of Atrosanguineum for stock plants, but none of these are yet large enough to give more than a dozen cuttings. A dozen, however, is all I can take from each of the two original grafted plants. When the cutting-grown plants are of equal age, they will be producing perhaps 50 cuttings a year each. Except these 15 stock plants, I have sold every plant of Atrosanguineum larger than 8". There are a good many plants of Caractacus, because when I came here, I brought nearly 2000 rooted cuttings of it. . . .

Every time I get a chance to move in the direction of a compact red, I take a try at it. Perhaps *brachycarpum* will be an important element in this breeding. So far I have never had a *brachycarpum* set a bud, let alone flower, and no primary cross of it is large enough to notice. Catawbiense Compactum X *brachycarpum* ought to make a good parent. *Smirnowii* X *brachycarpum* could be important too. It is my ambition to get all possible primary hybrids of *catawbiense,* Catawbiense Compactum and *Smirnowii,* so as to have them ready for the primary hybrids that winter in the cold

pit. So far my list of these primaries is microscopic. I seem to make good progress in every direction except the one I want.

The hardy *Griffithianum* hybrid, which I hope to be able to select out of my *decorum* X *Griffithianum* crosses, would of course be a fine show plant, but it would probably not stand full sun, would not have dense foliage, and could not be expected to behave perfectly in this climate. I want it badly of course. However, it could never attain the popularity that a smaller compact red could if thoroughly hardy.

Crosses which require two generations can do me no good in my lifetime if started now, and yet I want to go ahead with all that give promise. Rhododendron breeding is a sort of religion with us. If it weren't, we would certainly not put so much time on it, for it doesn't pay.

January 28, 1943

Your trick of forcing buds with a wire is worth trying. It ought to work, as it is the same idea anciently used on fruit trees—tying a chain around the trunk, spiral girdling, etc. I will try it this season, using heavy wire, so that this can be removed in November, and the branch probably recover after flowering. The small wire gets lost in the bark and can't be taken out. Also, I think I'll use a central top branch, because that is the sort I want pruned out if it should die from the injury. I have to head back several of the cold-pit plants anyway, because they get too tall for the pit.

My knowledge of genetics is only such as I have picked up by reading. I have been taking graduate work at Columbia lately, in mycology, not genetics, with a thought that perhaps I might take genetics later. However, I feel sure that my general principles are sound. In any case, it would be necessary to proceed by trial and error, for the science cannot do more than guide us in a general direction, the unknown factors being so numerous. Burbank had the right idea. He fell down merely because he didn't live long enough to work out the projects he had undertaken, and of course he publicized his intentions, representing them as results. Too bad he had to smear himself as a fake and a charlatan when he really knew how to work in the right direction.

Rothschild learned only the first steps, and does not seem to understand the purpose behind them. He wants primary crosses and so do I. He wants them because they yield a large proportion of pretty good plants nearly alike in that generation. I want them because they can be crossed together to produce Mendelian split-ups usually 90% bad, but with the possibility of the really immortal hybrid always present. It is true there have been good hybrids in the primary cross, and all primary crosses are therefore worth exploring. In this climate, however, the chance of a fully hardy primary is extremely limited, even *maximum* X *catawbiense* being somewhat bud-tender. I grew about 300 *maximum* X *discolor* and am now down to about ten, all the rest being on the trash heap. Several of the ten will take the trash heap this season, as they show leaf-burn now and will undoubtedly fail to open many of their buds. At most I expect to keep not more than three of this cross, for I don't want it except to use in hybridizing. . . . Their flowers however, are likely to show the same dirty white shade, though there was some pink in their *maximum,* while my *maximum* of the original cross was very white and with an unusually persistent indumentum, a strain from the summit of the Smokies. A pink in the larger flowered forms of this cross might turn a mediocre plant into something worth naming.

February 20, 1943

I was glad to see the good write-up of you and your azaleas in *Horticulture.* Also, I noticed Gable's azaleas in a catalog that came in the other day. I hope this means that you are getting a proper return financially.

The azaleas may belong with the rhododendrons botanically, but horticulturally they don't go together. They won't do anything for me here, because of the cold. Even *A. nudiflora* and *A. viscosa*, which I found growing here within a few yards of my driveway, suffer badly from late frosts, which destroy new growth nearly every year.

I agree that, according to descriptions, *haematodes* should be the ideal source of red. (*decorum* X *haematodes*) X (Catawbiense Compactum X *caucasicum*) might be a good combination. The *decorum* bloom might bring earlier flowering to neutralize the late flowering of *haematodes* (early and late in life, I mean), and the other elements might provide good foliage and plant-habit. I want Catawbiense Compactum X *Metternichii,* but have so far failed in attempts to get it. (*catawbiense* X *Jacksonii*) X (*decorum* X *haematodes*) would be a good substitute for the above formula.

For large rhododendrons, which I look upon as less capable of important success than the Boule de Neige type, I think my best material at hand is *Griersonianum* X *eriogynum,* which is wintering successfully in the cold pit. It may never be able to winter its buds there, but I have in mind for the future a shaded house in which there will be just enough heat to prevent freezing. As I see it, the combination of these two superb red parents may yield something hardy by crossing with a primary cross of two hardy species, or even one. Crossed with (*catawbiense* red X *haematodes*), which I have from your seed, and hope to raise, the offspring would almost have to be all red,

and according to my idea, a certain percentage would have the hardiness of *catawbiense,* though it might be only 5%, or perhaps 1% or even only 0.1%. It is in such a cross as that I place my chief hope.

Reasons for Leaf-burn

April 6, 1943

My plants have shown a lot of leaf-burn, *especially in the lath house.* The explanation of leaf-burn, it seems to me, is that it does not proceed from any one cause, but from any one or more of several conditions which prevent the roots from supplying enough sap to the leaves at critical times. Impaired root development the previous season may cause it, or lack of mulch, deep frost with high wind and bright sun, or perhaps ordinary intense cold. My plants in the lath house have very shallow root systems this year because the ground was very wet all last season, my drainage system being incomplete, not ready to function until next November. One plant of *maximum* X *discolor* was left in the lath house, all the others planted in the open. The one in the lath house has its leaves burned more extensively than any of the others. *R. discolor* in the open has been battered most pitifully, but the leaves which are not torn off are not discolored, while nearly all the leaves of *discolor* in the lath house are dark brown all over. No plants of *R. Fortunei* have seriously burned leaves.

My experience agrees with yours that light snow is beneficial but ice harmful. I have always felt that the damage done by ice was mostly root-suffocation. When the ice-cap lasted several weeks, I have known it to kill large red cedar, but only on lawns. Where sticks and tall weeds stand around, the sun quickly melts holes, and forms little caves around tufts of coarse grasses, through which air can reach the ground. I don't agree with those who attribute leaf-burn to sunshine. The only harmful action of the sun would be drying out the sap by transpiration. Of course, leaves grown in the shade and exposed to the sun by transplanting, almost invariably burn because not properly pigmented. My microscopic measurements also show that the leaves grown in the sun are 20% thicker. Properly pigmented and thickened leaves do not burn unless exposed to violent wind with the roots frozen. I wrote an article for *Real Gardening* a couple of years ago, claiming that the old idea of transplanting by compass is sound, since the leaves put out on the north or shady side of a tree are not adapted to the south or sunny side, and vice versa, and the tree determines months in advance what kind of leaves it will put out. I supported my contentions by making microscopic studies of rhododendron leaves from sun and shade and from different parts of the same plant. I still don't pretend to have covered the subject, but hope that sooner or later some college may put a graduate student on the job of investigating this idea.

April 21, 1943

My *racemosum* X *Keiskei* are exactly like yours, but all buds above the snow are completely destroyed every year. Xenon Schreiber was here last fall and insisted on buying one plant for a rock garden. He said it didn't make any difference about the buds because he would protect the plant. It does bud profusely. Have you noticed that none of the flowers on intermediate forms have any stamens whatever? Evidently the primary cross is fertile, as we may see for ourselves in a couple of years, and I am expecting a hardier plant. Magor evidently used one of the tender English forms of *racemosum,* which naturally would not pass on much hardiness to its offspring.

It is likely that none of the crosses I make now will ever do me any good. So many years must elapse between the sowing of the seed and the building up of a sufficient stock, that only plants already growing give much promise of yielding me anything during my lifetime. Unfortunately, they were made before I had much choice as to parents. Now that the really desirable parents are beginning to flower in sufficient variety to give some freedom of choice, it is almost too late for me to benefit by them. However, as you may guess, I intend to go right on crossing as though I had two hundred years to live.

July 13, 1943

If your new blood-red *obtusum* is hardier than Hinodegiri, it ought to replace that variety within a few years. No *obtusum* varieties are fully hardy here, yet they are very popular. People replace them time after time when a specially bad winter has wiped them out. Here's hoping you have the answer to the azalea problem!

I am glad you feel as I do about the naming of clones. Someone is sure to come along after a while with a long list of meaningless names, and so start the gardening public on the road to disgust with rhododendrons. Meanwhile, we can set a good example, and use what influence we have to hold back the deluge. I think Rothschild has started a bad practice in the peculiar program of naming inclusive hybrids that are not clones. It seems to me that the purpose of a name is to enable gardeners to get the exact duplicate of something they like. If it were possible to breed rhododendrons that would come true from seed like tomatoes, this practice might be justified. In the case of a primary cross between two stable species, where the offspring come fairly uniform, I suppose it is all right. But many species are highly unstable, especially those

. . . from western China and Burma. Your comment on the variability of *maximum* X *haematodes* is evidence that *haematodes* has no stability, and I think the same probably applies to most of the Neriiflorum Series. In this case, I think each clone should be considered separately, for *haematodes* must be a complex natural hybrid, with the result that its progeny follow the tendencies of the progeny of an artificial hybrid. . . .

October, 1943

As more and more things come into flower, the possibilities look dazzling. Yet I think we have already grown all the plants that will do us any real good in our lifetimes. By the time next year's seed is turned into flowering plants, we'll be old men, and still facing the long task of giving a thorough trial, building up a stock, then trying to convince people that what we have done is worth their money. However, if I were not interested in this work for its own sake, I wouldn't be in it at all. It certainly isn't an easy road to riches.

My situation is as difficult as ever. Father doesn't try to make things any easier for me. He muddles along secretively with his affairs, which are probably at a low ebb. In the end, he will probably have little or nothing to leave his children. My aunt assured me the other day that she was leaving me some money, of which she seems to have plenty, but the joker in that is—she is only about ten years my senior and will probably outlive me. Well, the nursery is beginning to pay a little at last. By next fall, I'll have lived down the effects of the hurricane flood, and unless some other catastrophe comes along, should have a dependable, modest income, which is much better than money inherited. I won't need much.

A Season's Breeding

December 25, 1943

I enclose a list of this year's seeds and breeding attempts, recording the failures to show what I have tried, because failures are sometimes important information. Those which appear to be only chaff, I plant anyway, several in a pot, dividing the pot like slices of a pie by laying nails on the surface, their points meeting in the center. This is a pretty good way of isolating the kinds, especially because I usually alternate lepidotes and elepidotes, and saves a good deal of pot space. Four times out of five, nothing comes up, but there are many cases in which a couple of seedlings will come up from what I thought was a failure, and in the instance of a primary cross, that is frequently enough.

Complete list of 1943 crosses   G. G. Nearing

1. *maximum* X Catawbiense Compactum   failure
2. *maximum* X *brachycarpum* . . . . failure
3. *maximum* X *campylocarpum* . . . . , . . failure
4. *maximum* X *Wardii* . . . . failure
5. *maximum* X *auriculatum* . . . . failure
6. *maximum* X *Griersonianum* . . . very few seeds
7. *maximum* X *haematocheilum* . . very few seeds
8. *maximum* X *Fortunei* . . . . failure
9. *(maximum* X *discolor)* X *(catawbiense* X
    haemotodes) . . . . failure
10. *(maximum* X *discolor)* X *(Smirnowii* X
    arboreum) . . . . fair crop
11. *(maximum* X *discolor)* X (Decatros X
    Goldsworth Yellow) . . . . failure
12. *(maximum* X *discolor)* X *(maximum* X
    Fortunei) . . . . fair crop
13. *(Smirnowii* X *arboreum)* X *(decorum* X
    haematodes) . . . . very few seeds
14. *(Smirnowii* X *arboreum)* X *(catawbiense* X
    Fortunei) . . . . small crop
15. *(Smirnowii* X *arboreum)* X (Decatros X
    Goldsworth Yellow) . . . . few seeds
16. *(Smirnowii* X *arboreum)* X Orbwill
    . . . . very few seeds
17. *(Smirnowii* X *arboreum)* X *(catawbiense* X
    haematodes) . . . . small crop
18. *campylocarpum* X *(Smirnowii* X *Fortunei)*
    . . . . very few seeds
19. *campylocarpum* X *sutchuenense* . . . . small crop
20. *campylocarpum* X *haematocheilum* . . fair crop
21. Catawbiense Compactum X *dasycladum* . failure
22. Catawbiense Compactum X *Griersonianum*
    . . . . failure
23. Catawbiense Compactum X *discolor* . . . . failure
24. Catawbiense Compactum X *Fortunei* . . . . failure
25. Catawbiense Compactum X *haematocheilum*
    . . . . failure
26. Catawbiense Compactum X *campylocarpum*
    . . . . failure
27. *decorum* X *Griersonianum* & open . . good crop
28. *rhaibocarpum* X *haematocheilum* . . small crop
29. "*eriogynum*" X *maximum* & open . . . . fair crop
30. *(Griersonianum* X Aucklandii) X *(catawbiense*
    X *Fortunei)* . . . . failure
31. *(Griersonianum* X Aucklandii) X *(maximum* X
    haematodes) . . . . failure
*32. *(Griersonianum* X Aucklandii) X *(Smirnowii* X
    arboreum) . . . . small crop
33. Delicatissimum X Orbwill . . . . failure
34. Delicatissimum X *(Smirnowii* X *Fortunei)*
    . . . . failure
35. Delicatissimum X Goldsworth Yellow . . . . failure
36. Delicatissimum X *(campylocarpum* X
    Williamsianum) . . . . failure

37. Delicatissimum X *(Griersonianum* X
    Aucklandii) . . . . failure
38. Delicatissimum X *(decorum* X *haematodes)*
    . . . . failure
39. Delicatissimum X *Griersonianum* . . . . . . failure
40. Maximum Roseum X Orbwill . . . . failure
41. Maximum Roseum X *(Griersonianum* X
    Aucklandii) . . . . failure
42. Boule de Neige X *campylocarpum* . . . few seeds
43. Boule de Neige X *Griersonianum* . . . . . . failure
44. Decatros open . . . . small crop
45. Orbwill X *(catawbiense* X
    haematodes) . . . . small crop
46. Atrosanguineum X *(Griersonianum* X
    Aucklandii) . . . . failure
47. *racemosum* X *Searsiae* . . . . small crop
48. *racemosum* X Amesiae . . . . . . very few seeds
49. *racemosum* X *yunnanense* . . . . small crop
50. *racemosum* X *aechmophyllum* . . . . . . few seeds
51. *racemosum* X Xanthinum . . . . small crop
52. *racemosum* X *Keiskei* . . . . fair crop
53. *racemosum* open . . . . small crop
54. *(racemosum* X *Keiskei)* X *aechmophyllum*
    & open . . . . failure
55. *(racemosum* X *Keiskei)* X *(moupinense* X
    lutescens) . . . . very few seeds
56. Conestoga X *(moupinense* X *lutescens)* . failure
57. Conestoga X *Searsiae* . . . . small crop
58. Conestoga X Amesiae . . . . failure
59. Conestoga X Xanthinum . . . . small crop
60. Conestoga X *Keiskei* . . . . fair crop
61. Conestoga X *oreotrephes* . . . . few seeds
62. (Conestoga X *Keiskei)* X *Searsiae* & open
    . . . . failure
63. (Conestoga X *Keiskei)* X *yunnanense* & open
    . . . . failure
64. (Conestoga X *Keiskei)* X *oreotrephes* & open
    . . . . failure
65. Conestoga X *aechmophyllum* & *yunnanense*
    . . . . fair crop
66. *Keiskei* X *trichocladum* . . . . small crop
67. *Keiskei* X *Searsiae* . . . . good crop
68. *Keiskei* X Amesiae . . . . small crop
69. *Keiskei* X *yunnanense* . . . . small crop
70. *yunnanense* open . . . . good crop
71. *(carolinianum* X *Keiskei)* open . . . . . good crop
72. *(carolinianum* X *cuneatum)* X *aechmophyllum*
    . . . . small crop
73. *(carolinianum* X *cuneatum)* X open . . fair crop
74. *(carolinianum* X *cuneatum)* X *Searsiae*
    . . . . fair crop
75. Carolinianum Aureum X *Augustinii* BLUE
    . . . . few seeds
76. Carolinianum Aureum X *Searsiae* very few seeds

77. oreotrephes X *(carolinianum* X *cuneatum)*
.... failure
78. oreotrephes X (Conestoga X *Keiskei)* ... failure
79. *eriandrum* X *(carolinianum* X *Keiskei)* . failure
80. *Bodinieri* X Carolinianum Aureum
.... very few seeds
81. *micranthum* open .... few seeds
82. *russatum* X (Conestoga X *Keiskei* & open)
.... failure
83. *russatum* X *racemosum* & open .... failure
84. *(fastigiatum* X *carolinianum)* X *Keiskei*
.... failure
85. *(fastigiatum* X *carolinianum)* X *moupinense*
X *lutescens)* .... failure
86. *(fastigiatum* X *carolinianum)* X (Conestoga X
Keiskei) .... failure
87. *(fastigiatum* X *carolinianum)* X (Conestoga X
Keiskei) .... failure

October 22, 1946

I have sold off nearly all my nursery and closed the place for keeps. It still hurts a little to think about all the plans I had for hybridizing, but after such an interruption, there is small likelihood that I can ever take it up again, and I have resigned myself to that.

I expect to make my living by writing, because I have done that before, and it doesn't take much capital, or much time to make a start. If the returns are small, as is likely, I still won't starve. Botany will be my principal hobby.

I hope you are able to carry on where I couldn't. I always said it was a rich man's hobby, and that I was able to indulge in it only through the trick of my propagation discovery.

It is possible I may undertake a book on rhodos, something entirely different from Bowers'. After I get a little perspective I'll take the matter up with some publisher.

I hope all your family are well.

Ramapo and Purple Gem

April 11, 1951

Your record of *fastigiatum* X *carolinianum* makes it look as if Ramapo is my own hybrid, because my record shows *carolinianum* as the seed parent. Also two of my seedlings proved very hardy and vigorous. One is Ramapo, and the other Hardgrove has named Purple Gem or I think he has changed it to Violet Gem. It had not flowered for me, and as I have seen it flowering for him, it is not nearly as good a color as Ramapo, nor is the growth habit or the foliage equal. Hardgrove has not yet listed either of these, but he has a good number

of rooted cuttings, and no doubt will offer it soon. Ramapo is also being propagated by at least one other nurseryman, Ed Thuem of Harrington Park, N. J., but he is doing fantastic things with it, grafting it on Hinodegiri and forcing it with heat of over 100 degrees. Hardgrove is letting me have small plants of Ramapo and Windbeam this spring, and in time I will have it propagated.

Your experience with *impeditum* X *carolinianum* only goes to show how little we know about what to expect in hybrids. But when I drive down this spring, I hope you can let me have one of those plants which look like *carolinianum* and are from *impeditum* seed. You see, Ramapo is totally sterile, but if your cross is fertile, I can be sure it has the combined genes, and I can use it. The leaf size of *carolinianum* is evidently dominant over that of *impeditum,* but the *impeditum* leaf is there in the genes, which it may or may not be in the seedling you brought me. That is why I want to use F_1 plants rather than F_2. I know what genes are in the F_1, no matter whether they are dominant and show or whether they are recessive and don't show. But I don't know what genes are in the F_2 unless they are dominant and show.

The worthlessness or worthwhileness of an F_1 plant is of no consequence in its usefulness for hybridization. We must look through the F_1 plant, ignoring its appearance, and thinking only of its parents, for their qualities will be reconstructed in the later offspring. But the worthwhileness of the F_2 plant is everything, because the F_2 has reduced genes, and those we particularly want may be missing. I wish this rule always held true in practice as it does in theory. It doesn't, but it holds often enough so that it can save us years and years in the majority of cases. In other words, when you cross *catawbiense* and *discolor,* all the qualities of both *catawbiense* and *discolor* are there, even though they don't show, and will come out in various combinations in F_2. But in F_2 there is a selection. In one plant, the large flower of *discolor* may be totally lost, and none of its offspring will ever bring out a large flower unless a new large-flower gene is introduced by a later cross. Another F_2 will have lost the hardiness of *catawbiense,* and its offspring will never show hardiness unless a new set of hardiness genes is introduced by a later cross. And so on. Therefore much guesswork and lost motion can be avoided by using F_1, even though the F_1 may seem to have no good qualities at all. I have not taken formal college courses in genetics, but have read up and absorbed much incidental information, which I have boiled down (correctly I hope) to this practical formula—breed from F_1 plants.

Of course, if you have an F_2 or later generation plant which shows the quality you are breeding for, there is no reason why you shouldn't use it. A red hybrid surely has red genes, and a shapely, compact plant surely has the genes which carry shapeliness and compactness. But you can't plan on it ahead of time. You have to wait until you have actually seen the shape and color.

The color yellow is extremely recessive in rhododendrons. I have long had a plan for producing a hardy yellow, but whether it will work or not, time alone will tell. *Catawbiense* crossed with *Wardii, campylocarpum, croceum* or *litiense,* should do the trick if I can get an F_1 plant. And it doesn't much matter what form of *catawbiense.* All I want from that species is its hardiness. I think, however, that the Catalgla should give better chances of a good yellow, because it may lack the magenta genes, which are dominant. This would quadruple the number of yellows in a subsequent cross, unless, as I suspect may be true, white also is dominant over yellow, though recessive to magenta.

The reasons I am primarily interested in dwarfs are two. Many dwarfs can be produced for sale in fewer years than it takes to produce the larger plants. And as editor of the Bulletin of the American Rock Garden Society, I feel that I am in a particularly good position to push dwarfs. But work on the larger plants will go on just as it always has, and the results will appear later.

August 30, 1951

I don't usually take my cuttings until October or even November, as I have found over a period of years that the later cuttings do best. So I will drop down some time in October, letting you know beforehand. I want to try a few cuttings of various things to see if my method will root them. And I can take a good number of anything you want me to propagate on shares.

Of my 10,000 seedlings, 3,000 or more are now potted in 2s and placed in a wintering frame. Another thousand will fill the frame, and then I think I'll winter the rest in their seed pots.

The cold pit is coming along very slowly, so slowly that the plants will have to be put in temporary winter quarters in November while I finish it. I bought almost 1,000 eight-inch cinder blocks, and with those I can erect almost any kind of shelter in a few hours, using no mortar or foundations. Surprisingly tender things have wintered for me in such frames.

January 9, 1952

Don Hardgrove has promised me small plants of *Fortunei* X *fictolacteum* which he says are getting felt under the leaves already. He is making a great play for lepidote hybrids with the idea of bringing in blood of *Maddenii, Nuttallii, Taggianum,* etc., an idea which I

have long entertained, but toward which I have never made any perceptible progress.

We had a meeting of a local unit of the A.R.S. on Long Island a couple of months ago, attended by over fifty people. Long Island of course has the climate to winter many of the finer things, and interest there is growing faster than anywhere else except the Pacific coast.

Hardiness of Dexters

John C. Wister has stopped here several times, and has told me a lot about his investigations of the Dexter hybrids. He has discovered some thousands of them planted north of Boston, where a series of New England winters will certainly have weeded out the tender ones. He agrees with me that the best are the *discolor* and *decorum* hybrids. All that have yellow or yellowish flowers have poor foliage. There are very few reds. The foliage of *Fortunei* hybrids is usually yellowish and sparse. His committee will have labeled a total of a hundred or so from all sources by the end of this flowering season, then will begin eliminating down to 25 or 30 of the finest. I have seen only one very good one so far, and it wasn't very hardy. Out of the thousands, I haven't seen, some ought to be very good.

I was able to show him a letter from Dexter which told the species he was using, the year he started work, etc. Have you any letters from Dexter which might throw further light on the subject? . . .

January 23, 1952

My trouble this year will be to find room for seed pots and seedlings. I potted off about 4,000 of last year's seedlings, and have that many or more still in the seed pots. The winter will undoubtedly dispose of some, but still I'll have to build a lot more coldframes fast. I can devote another propagating frame to seed pots, but it looks as if I won't be able to handle what I raise in them.

I reasoned that with so few years ahead, new hybrids will do me no good unless I sow them within the next year or two, with last year more important than this, this year more important than next, and so on. So, last year I sowed practically everything I could lay my hands on. Whether there is any use going on at such a pace looks doubtful, and to step it up now might be a little crazy.

To the rhododendron planters who make up their minds in advance that nonhardy ones are going to prove hardy, almost all winters are "exceptional" and disastrous." This season certainly has not been bad here so far, with exactly half the winter gone. The middle of winter cold according to statistics, comes

Jan. 22. I always feel that rhododendrons in good condition on this date are nearly sure to winter successfully.

When I think back over the many years in the 1920s and early 1930s during which I dragged along to a slow start hybridizing, and compare them with the year and eight months here, I really feel encouraged, thanks largely to the seeds and plants I had from you.

January 7, 1953

The dwarfs were a failure this year, and I am particularly anxious to work on them because results should come sooner. It is hardly worthwhile to grow the larger hybrids, though I continue to do so. Although I made several crosses on what flowers there were, nothing much came of it except chaff. I did not list Carolinianum Album X *Keiskei, mucronulatum* open, and a couple of things like that from which I did get a few seeds, because I know you wouldn't be interested in them. I am not much interested either.

If I can winter the Bric-a-brac, Cilpinense and Racil buds, which are in a well protected frame, they will give me something to work on next year, provided they don't bloom too early, and provided *Keiskei,* which is in the open, carries its buds. It lost practically all of them last year. My young plants of *racemosum* are getting big enough to flower, and some have good looking buds, but for the last two seasons I have depended on gift seeds of that species, collected from plants originally of my raising, and growing nearby, so that they are still selected for hardiness.

I am trying to get some budded plants from the West, of such things as *radicans* and *pumilum.* The last is a most attractive dwarf which is being sent out under the name of *pemakoense.* It has a very large, upright, campanulate flowers of a good pink, whereas those of *pemakoense* should be funnel-shaped and purplish. I tried pollen on *racemosum,* but got only chaff, which I am going to sow in the hope that there may be a seed or two in it somewhere. The plant is no bigger than *racemosum,* and if it could borrow *racemosum's* hardiness, would be first class. What I really need is established plants to work with. Flowers which open in shipment usually fail to set seed, no matter how much pollen goes on them. And if I buy the plants in the fall, they don't winter well. Those bought in the spring seldom set buds for the following year. So it is a long story.

I may also offer a very few of the named clones of *pubescens* X *Keiskei,* not that I have enough plants to begin selling them, but because I want to make a start, and by the time my list gets around, there will be quite a number of small plants coming along. Ordinarily I would hold these until I had several hundred of each in good marketable size. They just happen to be the only

thing of which I have enough to even think of selling. In the spring, I will bed out ten little plants of each for stock plants, and sell the rest. They propagate fast, and I'll probably be able to make at least fifty cuttings of each clone, in 1953, practically all of which will root and be ready to sell in 1955 or later.

On Mental Telepathy

January 19, 1953

There is no doubt about mental telepathy. The waves given off by the brain, somewhat of the nature of radio waves, have been measured, and can be received by another brain, conveying probably not actual thoughts, but certainly emotions and images. This accounts for the extraordinary emotional fury which sometimes builds up in mobs, each brain exciting the others to greater intensity. Communication between people at a distance depends on long familiarity and common interests. I once knew a poetess, now dead, whose letters crossed with mine so regularly that we took the event for granted. While still very young, I made two carefully thought-out experiments to demonstrate telepathy, and both were so completely successful that I abandoned the field almost in terror, and have never intentionally tried it since.

I have a touch of the virus infection too. It seems to be epidemic over most of the country. When I was young, it would have knocked me out, but now I go on working nearly every day as usual, and don't think I missed a single evening of my favorite recreation—folk dancing, in which I indulge at least three times a week. One of my favorite dances is the Ukrainian Hopak, which only a few of the young men can do because of the agility and endurance required. I do about 150 other dances, many of them on the violent side. I am digging and walling up a new cellar under the rear of the house, and so can work in any weather.

Henry Fleming, entomologist of William Beebe's staff at the American museum, and a member of the American Rhodo Society, is anxious to see your plants, and has offered to drive me down in the spring. His wife is one of my best dance partners. By that time, the New Jersey and Pennsylvania turnpikes should be hitched up, and we may be able to make the trip in about four hours each way. I can drive it alone, but my eye always kicks up afterward. Headlights and roadside lights both get more merciless every year.

The debate with Leach in the *Rhododendron Society Bulletin* has been called off, but while it lasted, it did just what I hoped it would. It focused a lot of attention on breeding methods. Amateis sides with Leach in the idea of pin-point planning. ... Both of them are day-dreaming about raising a handful of plants and having them all rated four stars. Maybe we shouldn't interrupt their slumbers. Both point to the success of crop hybrids, and don't seem to comprehend that the hybrid vigor which is the whole idea with crops, is a debatable advantage in ornamentals. When I look at the bare stalks of *catawbiense* X *discolor,* I keep wondering if there isn't some way of depriving it of vigor. Of course increased vigor may sometimes improve hardiness, and it may be that *catawbiense* X *discolor* can stand a lot of cold. I will know more about that in a few years. However I don't see how it can pass that particular kind of hardiness to its offspring.

January, 1953

Ramapo is now on the market, and Windbeam will be in a year or two, but I won't have any to offer for at least three or four years. Propagation of these was begun about 1943 or earlier. Many of the young plants were destroyed in the flood, but in 1946 Hardgrove started working up a stock of both and Thuem of Ramapo. It will be several more years before anybody has them in real quantity. That is an old story to you of course.

Cutting Methods

February 19, 1953

You undoubtedly read J.W.'s claims to have originated commercial cutting propagation of rhododendrons, ignoring all the sources from which he got the information he hasn't yet actually begun to use. The side-slicing of the cutting, he indicates he picked up in Belgium in 1946. I devised the exact method described and illustrated in 1939, and told several friends about it, and finally passed it on to Baldsiefen in 1946. He has used it ever since. J.W. muffed the point however. The increase in percentage and speed of strike is incidental. What I devised it for was to correct the habit of cuttings putting down a single root and developing the entire root system on that, leaving a weak joint between stem and root, which the wind will some-times snap. The side-slice corrects this perfectly, and that is by far its most important function. Other recent studies in side-slicing and other kinds of wound do not ignore this purpose, but do not stress it sufficiently. I have side-sliced all my cuttings since about 1941.

Vossberg puts out a big crop of rooted cuttings fast, but Knippenberg, who buys thousands of them . . . gets better results from those Baldsiefen roots. And no wonder. A cutting forced in a greenhouse all winter is a forced plant just as surely as an Easter-forced Azalea is. Everybody knows that the forced Azalea must be handled with great care if it is to be grown afterwards as a hardy plant. But even a forced cutting is better than a graft, which is also forced, and has a lot of other drawbacks beside.

May 19, 1955

When I broke up the nursery at Ridgewood, many of these hybrids went to Mountain Lakes, others to various places in and around Ridgewood, and Hardgrove selected a few. What became of the original plant I have forgotten, but I wish I had it back. I always doubted that it was true to its label, and even if it was, there is no certainty that another plant of the same cross would produce like results.

I collected seeds which were accidentally allowed to mature on one of the best of its seedlings at Mountain Lakes, and some from a plant in Ridgewood which is very good. Now I have a second generation coming along, most of which wintered very well in the open. In fact, I don't believe a single plant died or was particularly injured, except a few which had their leaves chewed off by the deer. The split-up is extreme, almost no two plants alike, with hardiness the only thing they have in common.

Although all the original Ridgewood hybrids, as I have named this offspring of *decorum* X *Griffithianum,* are completely plant-hardy at any temperatures they have met with hereabouts, many do not carry their buds when the thermometer drops to 15 or 20 below. This is about the same bud-hardiness as Atrosanguineum. The one which carried its buds best I named Beatrice Pierce, for my sister who lives in Towson, and sold it to Hardgrove, but it seems to propagate with great difficulty, and I have never been able to get a plant of it to give to my sister. Like many of the others, it is extremely floriferous.

I feel more and more certain that the most important quality to look for in a hybrid is floriferousness, second a bushy plant habit, third ease of propagation, and after that come color, fragrance, shape of truss, and all the other matters which our English friends consider first.

January 7, 1956

I'm beginning to feel my age (nearly 66).

But it is beginning to look as though the raising of the ironclads, which I must do to make a living, will take nearly all my energy, and the hybridizing will dwindle to nearly nothing. There are about 15,000 of last year's seedlings still in the seed pots, and my frames are all full, so that I must bed out a lot of plants early in the spring before I can find a place for some of those 15,000, and before I can bed out any, I must prepare the beds. I can't just put the plants in the woods the way you do, because the deer would eat them. Deer broke into one of my enclosures a few weeks ago and did a lot of damage. I hadn't quite finished the ten-foot fence, and they crawled under it.

Before I do anything else, I must prepare a bed for 500 ironclads that must come out of 4″ pots, and next year I will be up to my schedule of 1,000. It looks as if my hybridizing has nearly come to an end. If what I want isn't in the plants already growing, I'll probably never get it.

The Knippenbergs and Dave Leach sent me a lot of pollen too, and I have just sent off the results to them, so that the work will go on, but in other hands. What I did with my own pollen was mostly repetition of what I had already done, because nothing new flowered.

John Knippenberg is preparing many acres of ground with bulldozers and tractors. He has the money to do it, and countless thousands of seedlings coming along to plant there. He can carry them through to maturity, as Dexter did. He is a friendly fellow, and although he makes mistakes, is bound to learn something in the end, and should come up with many worthwhile hybrids.

So, I think I will leave the general hybridizing to him, and confine myself to a couple of limited projects. One of those is Boule de Neige X Loderi King George. I took another Kodachrome shot if it this spring, and it is nearly a hardy Loder's White. . . .

Another project is white *catawbiense* X yellows, until I get a hardy yellow. The Catalgla X *Wardii* which I got from you looks fine in the cold pit, and should set buds perhaps next year. With that I mean to carry on the project by using all the yellow pollen I can lay my hands on. It is more visionary than project No. 1.

Somebody else must breed *Griersonianum* hybrids, for I have lost faith in them. I might work a little with repens hybrids if I can ever get anything of that line to flower. I have a lot of *Williamsianum* hybrids coming along, but few of them look good, and I doubt if I will carry on in that direction. *Fortunei* hybrids don't live up to expectations. Hardgrove showed a fine yellow *Fortunei* X *croceum* last May, but later in the season it did what my plant of that lot does every year. The leaves take on a water-soaked look and fall off, withering in such numbers that the plant is almost bare. Evidently it is a fungus disease, perhaps from the oak trees. This last year I left the plant in the frame, and the disease didn't get it. Hardgrove is undoubtedly heartbroken.

Rhododendrons Introduced by G. Guy Nearing

April Blush. *R. carolinianum* X *R. mucronulatum,* (Pink form). Hardy to −25°F. Grows 2' in 15 years. Flowers scattered, blush pink. Leaves about 1″ long, narrow and thin, most of them not evergreen.

Azonea. Azor X Catanea. Hardy to −25°F. Grows 6' high in 10 years. Flowers about June 15, truss 5″ wide, florets 3″. Color like Azor but paler.

Boulodes. Boule de Neige X Loderi seedling. Hardy to at least −15°F. Grows to 5' high by 5' wide in 9 years. Flowers red turning white with faint spotting, fragrant, openly funnel-shaped, $3^{1}/_{2}$″ wide by $1^{1}/_{2}$″ long. Truss ball-shaped, 6″ across by 5″ high of 10 flowers. Blooms mid May.

Catanea. A white flowering form of *R. catawbiense,* differing from other white forms in that the plant is shapely.

Cliff Garland. Bric-a-Brac X *R. mucronulatum.* Hardy to −20°F. Grows 3' high in 10 years. Flowers open in early April, pale pink. Leaves like Cliff Spangle but thinner and rounded.

Cliff Spangle. Bric-a-Brac X *R. mucronulatum.* Hardy to −20°F. Grows 1' high in 15 years, dense and shapely. Flowers plentiful, 2″ wide, bright pink. Leaves 1″ long, dark green, thick.

Dark Eyes. Kettledrum X *(R. detonsum X R. griersonianum)* Grows to about 5' in 10 years. Leaves to 6″ wide, rounded. Flowers bright rose outside fading to flesh color within with dark red blotch, to 4″ across, 6 to 8 lobe. Truss with about 6 florets. Blooms mid May.

Decalgla. Catalgla X *R. decorum.* Hardy to at least −15°F. Branches well, grows to 8' high by 9' wide in 21 years. Flowers white, spotted green, 2″ wide by $1^{1}/_{2}$″ long, funnel-shaped. Truss ball-shaped, 6″ wide by 4″ high, of 12 flowers. Leaves 6″ long by 2″ wide. Blooms late May.

Dexanea. Catanea X a complicated Dexter Hybrid. Hardy to −25°F. Grows 6' high in 10 years. Truss 7″ wide and high. Flowers white with brownish blotch. Leaves 6″ long by 3″ wide, yellow green. Blooms mid to late May.

Elam. A seedling of Chesapeake. Hardy to −20°F. Grows 2' high in 15 years. Shapely plant; flowers deep rose, 1-1/2″ across, clustered like *R. pubescens.* Leaves 1″ long by 1/4″. Blooms early May.

Elsmere. A seedling of Chesapeake. Hardy to −25°F. Grows 6' high in 20 years. Flowers are very small, less than 1″ in diameter, scattered rather than clustered, definitely yellow. The corolla lobes are deeply divided.

Macopin. Chance seedling of *R. racemosum,* probably pollinated by Wyanokie. Probable height in 10 years is 4' high. Leaves 2″ long by 1″ wide, dark green, shining. Flowers pale lilac, in globular clusters. Blooms early May.

Magnagloss. *(R. wardii X R. discolor)* X unknown. Hardy to at least −15°F. Plant branches well, grows to 4′ high by 4′ wide in 16 years. Flowers greyed purple with conspicuous grey red blotch extending into spots, 2¹/₂″ wide by 1¹/₂″ long, funnel-shaped. Truss ball-shaped, 5″ wide by 4″ high, of 12 flowers. Leaves 3″ by 1¹/₂″, yellow green, glossy. Blooms late May to early June.

Mary Fleming. *(R. racemosum X R. keiskei)* X *R. keiskei.* Hardy to −25°F. Grows 4′ high in 20 years, very shapely plant. Flowers bisque yellow with blotches and streaks of salmon, in clusters ane are very abundant. Leaves 2″ long, narrow, pointed. Award of Excellence, October, 1973, *Quarterly Bulletin,* A.R.S. Vol. 27, No. 4, p. 245.

Mountain Aura. Dorothea *(R. decorum X R. griffithianum)* X a red hybrid. Grows to 3′ high in 10 years. Leaves to 6″ long by 3″ wide. Flowers flax blue with white center, to 4″ across, in trusses to 7″ across and 6″ high. Blooms late May.

Mountain Flare. Boule de Neige X Loderi King George. Hardy to at least −15°F. Plant grows to 5′ high by 5′ wide in 17 years. Flowers red with faint greenish to purplish speckling, 4¹/₂″ wide by 1″ long, openly funnel-shaped. Truss ball-shaped, 8″ wide by 6″ high, of 15 flowers. Leaves 7″ by 2″, yellow green. Blooms mid May.

Mountain Glow. *(R. decorum X R. griffithianum)* X Hardy Red Ironclad. Similar to Rh. Mountain Queen, the flowers are a bright reddish purple, a striking shade. Plant densely branching, to 3′ high in 10 years. Leaves oval, to 6″ long by 3″ wide.

Mountain Queen. *(R. decorum X R. griffithianum)* X Hardy Red Ironclad. Hardy to −25°F. Grows 6′ high in 20 years. A shapely plant. Leaves oval, to 7″ long by 3″ wide. Flowers are a pale rose with a white center. Truss shapely. This and the two following are called Ridgewood Hybrids.

Pink Globe. *R. catawbiense* (Gable's red selection) *(R. griersonianum X R. fortunei).* Hardy to at least −15°F. Plant upright, branching moderately, 5′ high by 5′ wide in 8 years. Flowers red with small red blotch, 3¹/₂″ wide by 2″ long. Truss ball-shaped, 7¹/₂″ wide by 6″ high, of 12 flowers. Leaves 6″ by 2″, yellow green. Blooms late May.

Purple Gem. *R. fastigiatum X R. carolinianum.* Sun-evergreen, small-leaved lepiodote, early May, Zone 4A. A sister seedling of RH. RAMAPO. R. fastigiatum is one of the Lapponicum Series with purple flowers. Purple Gem is referred to as a blue rhododendron and is a brilliant pale violet with light blue-green foliage.

Ramapo. *R. fastigiatum X R. carolinianum.* Hardy to −25°F. Grows 2′ high in 20 years. Plant nearly globe shaped. Flowers abundant, pastel violet. Leaves less than 1″ long, nearly circular, dark purplish green, new growth pale green.

Ramsey Tinsel. Chance seedling of Chesapeake *(R. pubescens X R. keiskei).* Probable height in 10 years is 1′. Leaves to 1″. Flowers ochre yellow, 1″ across in clusters of 3 or 4, corolla of 8 to 10 separate, very narrow petals. Blooms early May.

Red Lion. Tally Ho X *R. catawbiense* (Red form). Hardy to −20°F. Grows 5′ high in 10 years. Flowers deep red. Foliage somewhat sparse.

Red Puff. Golden Horn X Catanea. Hardy to at least −15°F. Plant a dwarf, decumbent and creeping, branches well, grows to 2′ high by 2¹/₂′ wide in 10 years. Flowers red with dark red speckles, 2″ wide by 1¹/₂″ long, funnel-shaped. Truss ball-shaped, 5″ wide by 4″ high, of 16 flowers. Leaves yellow green, 4″ by 1¹/₂″, borne in drooping rosettes. Blooms late May.

Rochelle. Dorothea X Kettledrum. Hardy. Semi-shade, evergreen, large-leaved elipodote. Blooms in late May in Zones 6A or 5B. It is a Dorothea hybrid. Dorothea is a cross of *R. decorum X R. griffithianum.* Rochelle has flowers that are a lighter pink than Rh. David Gable but with a similar strawberry throat. They are fragrant, 4″ across and have a velvety texture. The truss is 7 lobed and perfect.

Signal Horn. Atrosanguineum X Goldsworth Yellow. Hardy to at least −15°F. Plant branches moderately, grows to 4′ high by 3′ wide in 10 years. Flowers red with conspicuous red spotted blotch, 2″ wide by 2″ long. Truss lax, 5″ wide by 3″ high, of 8 flowers. Leaves greyed green, glossy, 7″ by 2″. Blooms mid May.

Windbeam. Seedling from a hybrid of R. *carolinianum X R. racemosum.* Hardy to 25−°F. Grows about 6′ high in 20 years, making a shapely bush in an open position. Flowers plentiful in globular clusters, white turning soft pink. Leaves 1″-2″ long, dark green. Award of Excellence, October, 1973, *Quarterly Bulletin,* A.R.S. Vol. 27, No. 4, p. 244.

Wyanokie. Same parentage as Windbeam, and equally hardy. Grows about 4′ high in 20 years with denser habit. Flowers abundant, white. Leaves slightly larger and somewhat paler green.

The following six varieties are known as the Guyencourt hybrids. Introduced by Guy Nearing around 1950, they are creations of his from a cross between *R. pubescens* X *Keiskei*.

Brandywine. *R. pubescens* X *R. keiskei*. Hardy to −20°F. Grows 5′ high in 20 years. Not quite as hardy as Hockessin, but otherwise similar except in flower color which is pale pink as the buds open, turning rich rose.

Chesapeake. *R. pubescens* X *R. keiskei*. Hardy to −25°F. Grows 4′ high in 20 years. A well branched, shapely plant. Flowers about May 1, clustered on nearly every tip, pale yellowish pink, turning white. Leaves to 2″ long, 1/2″ wide, rich green, hairy.

Delaware. *R. pubescens* X *R. keiskei*. Shrub twice as wide as high. Foliage 1-1/2″ long, 1/4″ to 1/2″ wide covered with pubescence. Blooms late April. Able to thrive in full exposure. Mass 1/2″ blooms have lasting quality.

Hockessin. *R. pubescens* X *keiskei*. Hardy to −25°F. Grows 5′ high in 20 years. Similar to Chesapeake in every respect except that growth is larger and more open.

Lenape *R. pubescens* X *R. keiskei*. Hardy to −20°F. Grows 5′ high in 20 years. Similar to Rh. Chesapeake. Flowers are pale yellow.

Montchanin. *R. pubescens* X *R. keiskei*. Hardy to −25°F. Grows 6′ high in 20 years. Flowers are pure white, the showiest white of the Guyencourts.

CHAPTER V

Anthony M. Shammarello 1903—

Of the five "pioneer" hybridizers who created the modern, hardy rhododendrons and azaleas for eastern North America, Anthony Shammarello was the last to begin a major hybridizing program. His great contribution is a series of plants hardy in northern Ohio. Thus he extended the range of modern rhododendrons and azaleas to homes west of the Allegheny Mountains.

Equally valuable to home gardeners is the extensive Shammarello list of varieties whose compact structure is suited to the modern suburban property. They serve as foreground plantings for the generally more rampant Dexters and Gables; Shammarello azaleas can be used where most of the Glenn Dales would not fit because of space requirements.

Alfred Martin's Impressions

When I look at the complete collection of Shammarello rhododendrons and azaleas in my garden, I realize that Tony Shammarello and his plants are truly inseparable. I like to reflect on the strange trail of coincidences which brought these plants to us. The father, Angelo Shammarello of the A. Shammarello and Son Nursery, was a truck farmer and nurseryman in Calabria, Italy. At the urging of a close friend, he came to the United States during 1899 and settled in Salida, Colorado. The only employment available locally was with a railroad section gang. His son, Tony, was born in Colorado in 1903.

In 1909, the family moved to Cleveland, Ohio, where relatives lived nearby. The elder Shammarello shortly found congenial employment in Lakeview Cemetery, one of the most beautifully landscaped cemeteries in the United States. Mr. Shammarello, because of his valuable leadership skills and his knowledge of grafting, budding, and pruning soon became a foreman. The cemetery was within walking distance of his home, and young Tony made frequent visits to be with his father. He was particularly impressed with the spring season when flowering trees and shrubs were in full bloom. All of this became more fascinating to the boy as he rapidly learned the names and characteristics of the plants used in the cemetery landscaping.

The Family Business

Around 1920, Tony's father decided to leave the cemetery to begin a landscaping business. Tony desperately wanted to join his father in the business. He had a growing and instinctive love for plants and their beauty as well as an extremely strong desire to leave Cleveland's relatively unlovely ethnic ghetto. On the other hand, his father felt that Tony, because of his age and size, should seek steady employment indoors, in the tailoring trade. In the end, the son prevailed. He joined his father with a promise that he would continue his schooling at night. For several years, Tony took courses in horticulture, landscape design, and business management.

The 1920s were formative years for the young plantsman. Landscaping business during the early part of the decade was not only conventional but reasonably unimaginative. Few people could afford the taxus or rhododendrons and other plants which had to be imported from the Atlantic seaboard states. The typical landscaping at that time for a Cleveland house consisted of, perhaps, a half-dozen spirea, two forsythia, a barberry hedge and a couple of maples. There was an additional drawback, as Tony points out, in that landscaping was generally an eight-to-nine-month proposition and "what we made in the summer we ate up in the winter, so that we were always behind the eight ball." The early 1920s were apparently also an opportunity for Tony's social development and, indeed, the only chance for the sowing of wild oats. I have been fascinated by Tony's accounts of the Cleveland social scene in his area during that period. He loved fast cars and one of my favorite pictures on the wall of Tony's office shows him as a debonair young man about town standing next to his immense, impressive 1924 Wills St. Clair roadster. This era was short-lived; in 1928 the firm decided to enter the nursery business. The subsequent workload effectively pinched off the budding social activities.

The Shammarellos ventured into the nursery business because their ideas and thoughts on landscaping had become considerably more sophisticated. They were no longer happy with typical landscape work. A. Shammarello & Son began to grow pines, junipers, dogwoods, azaleas, lilacs, philadelphus, and a few rhododendrons, as well as new varieties of spirea. Each passing year brought more sophisticated designs, new material, and increased stock. Junipers and taxus, dogwoods, and lilacs, for example, were just beginning to be used for screen planting.

It is very difficult for most of us to realize that what we consider as average plant material today, in the 1970s, was confined almost entirely to large estates before 1940. The firm received their largest commission in 1930, from a Mr. C. K. Sunshine, to landscape a recreational area for a Japanese garden. The contract price of $10,000 represented almost a third of the annual income for the firm at that time. The planting is still in existence forty years later, and the work turned out to be sound, imaginative, and durable. This is true of many of their jobs that lasted for several decades without need for more than routine maintenance—the true test of landscaping excellence.

The firm outgrew their first location and in 1936 moved to the present location of A. Shammarello & Son, Monticello Boulevard in South Euclid, Ohio. Their thirty acres were practically country land at that time. At the new location, they erected a greenhouse and started propagating many of their own plants such as taxus, azaleas, rhododendrons, dogwoods, lilacs, and flowering trees. Spirea, forsythia, lonicera, and viburnum were grown in outdoor cutting beds. Perennials were grown from seeds, divisions, and cuttings. At one time, the firm had over ten acres of various types of *Ilex opaca*. By this time they employed over twenty people and the business took up all of Tony's waking hours seven days a week—this left him little time for personal social life or recreation.

America's entry into World War II in 1941 and 1942 brought an understandable decline in the landscape business, as well as a scarcity of labor. This was a very discouraging period for both father and son since they had to handle the business almost alone. In many instances, every other plant had to be destroyed so that the staff could cope with the work on the remaining plants. During 1946, business began to pick up, labor became available, and the nursery material once again came into prime shape. Tony wished to press ahead and expand the nursery business by

adding new facilities and equipment. The senior partner did not agree entirely with his philosophy and the longstanding partnership amiably came to an end when Angelo Shammarello retired. Tony continued to expand the business through 1964 and then gradually began to reduce the acreage in the nursery. By 1970, about ten acres of rhododendrons and azaleas and five acres of holly remained.

Somewhere along the line Tony did find time to become a master vintner. His white wines are products of great excellence and, according to his claim, more than one marriage of horticulturally inclined couples has been assisted by a session with Shammarello's peaches and wine. For my own part, I recall with great pleasure memories of meal sessions in the greenhouse office area with Tony and his devoted, long-time assistant, Rose Marzi. Unfortunately for me, I did not have the opportunity of meeting Tony until 1961 at the International Rhododendron Conference in Portland and shortly after that at meetings of the International Propagators' Society. During this period I began, with much pleasure, to devote a great deal of time to both Tony and his plants.

Since 1970, the nursery acreage has been gradually reduced until by 1975 Tony retained only a few acres. There he annually propagates and raises 1,500 to 2,000 small size plants—especially, he says, for his friends. In many respects, it was sad to me and surely a dismay to landscape men and connoisseurs throughout the United States to realize that tens of thousands of superior large specimen plants and garden size varieties were no longer available from this nursery. Tony himself still remains quite active. However, he feels that he must be getting older since he tends to tire about four-thirty in the afternoon after acting as a lead digger from eight o'clock in the morning.

In the early 1970s, with the thought of an eventual retirement in mind, Tony began constructing a beautiful home largely from the stone of the original farmhouse on his

Tony Shammarello prunes one of his hybrids

land; the building dated from the Civil War period. Around the house he created an informal garden and landscaped an adjoining lot, an old stone quarry. Surely this has to be the most loved of his creations! No matter where you are in the house, beauty surrounds you. Whether it be in the kitchen—where Tony might be enjoying a meal so amply provided by his mother—or in the nursery office, or in the magnificently executed living area, the true Tony Shammarello emerges. Here, he has created something of unusual design and beauty which speaks of his philosophies and true appreciation of all that makes life good.

Interest in Rhododendrons Begins

Up to this time, I have purposely said little about the Shammarello rhododendrons since this makes a chapter in itself. Late in the 1930s, Tony became very much interested in these plants because they were scarce, and a very ready market existed for whatever stock could be produced or imported into the area from sources in the eastern United States. One of the great virtues apparent to a nurseryman was that rhododendrons and azaleas required no root pruning in contrast to many other landscape materials. This was the period, too, when large estates were no longer in demand. The city lot with its two and a half story home and, later, ranch-type homes required another form of landscape design and plant varieties. Most of the Shammarello customers were beginning to look for plants of unusual merit to enhance their gardens.

By 1938, the firm had over 1,500 conventional rhododendron grafts and seedlings of flowering size growing in open fields. The winter of 1938-39 was a real killer in the area, with little or no snow cover and temperatures going to −25°F. The Ironclads—Kate Waterer, Dr. Dresselhuys, Charles Dickens, and Madame Carvalho, among others—froze to the roots. A few varieties, although damaged, survived—among these were America, Elegans Alba, Boule de Niege, Kettledrum, some hybrid seedlings, and *smirnowii* hybrids. In all, only approximately 300 plants survived.

Tony began his first experiments in hybridization during 1940, using plants that had survived that previous stringent winter. *Catawbiense* hybrid seedlings became an important factor in the process. From 1940 through 1955, over 100,000 seedlings were grown to blooming size until the first plant was named. In the heaviest years of experimentation, more than 10,000 seedlings a year were grown. In addition to regular nursery stock, all of these had to be kept in the field until they bloomed four to five years later. Plants from each cross were carefully selected for further tests and the remainder sold simply as reds, pinks, or whites. Often hundreds were destroyed. Some outstanding plants were difficult or impossible to propagate, and had to be sold with reluctance.

His Breeding Objectives

It is fortunate that as a landscape designer or contractor, Tony gained expertise and a keen sense of composition and proportion in design of plant material—advantages that enabled him to evaluate plants that were unique and would appeal to the large group of people who were his potential customers. But his principal interest was to create hybrids that would tolerate the rigors of the Cleveland winters and be adaptable to the coming trends in landscape work. This meant the creation of rather low, compact plants which would, over a long period of time, retain their permanence and aesthetic values in landscaping. The blooming characteristics of these hybrids were to be crisp, clean, and devoid of magenta, which tended to permeate a good many of the older varieties. It was evident that Tony had always worked with his plants from the viewpoint of both a landscaper and a nurseryman. Profitable operations, ease of

propagating, and short terms from cuttings to better plants were primary considerations. The plants selected were to be widely adaptable to climate and soil conditions, and able to prove their integrity of characteristics through extremely long periods of proof testing.

The basic rules Tony laid down for himself when he began hybridizing have never been subject to a great deal of deviation through the years. His father constantly admonished him that horses with stars tend to breed horses with stars. Throughout his early formative years, he was fortunate to have the friendship and deep interest of Michael Horvath, then the owner of Mentor Nurseries, and one of the leading rose geneticists of the era. Mr. Horvath provided a cardinal principle: "get out the bad blood." Tony contributed his own theory of working with series of five. In brief, the best plants available would be selected and crossed in all combinations. Whichever combination of the five produced the most uniform, dominant, and desirable characteristics was selected and used in further experiments. His own instincts—coupled with a lack of time, space, and desire to hold down expense—led him to work with primary crosses and not progress to F_2 hybrids. In his own words, he loved to stir up the genes. Only one of his named varieties is the result of crossing two of his own named plants. Lastly, according to Tony, you have to be both lucky ... and grow at least 250 seedling plants of any cross. The latter advice came, not unexpectedly, from Joe Gable.

His early work is exceptional when you consider that it was not until the 1940s that he learned from Dr. Henry Skinner, then at the Morris Arboretum, the possibility of rooting leaf cuttings and later, the technique of rooting stem cuttings. There were none of the aids now taken so much for granted: hormones, polyethylene, and mist. Almost all ericaceous plants were layered or grafted. Propagation techniques were closely guarded secrets. The present-day wide dissemination of this knowledge owes a considerable debt to the International Plant Propagators' Society, which was founded less than three decades ago on the principle that such knowledge should be shared. Even in the 1970s, sharing knowledge and techniques is a condition of membership. Without modern methods, the vast number of plants required to produce the Shammarello hybrids could not have been raised. They are fundamental to the asexual reproduction and distribution of the hybrid rhododendron.

Almost all of his named varieties were selected in the period from 1950 to 1960. However, his 1961 catalog was the first in which any of his hybrids appeared. Fourteen in all were listed but over half of them were overprinted as sold out. Each of the hybrids introduced in this catalog had something desirable by comparison to the old Ironclad hybrids, and provided a welcome addition to the extent of the blooming season.

The Shammarello Rhododendrons

Generally speaking, the Shammarello plants can be easily divided into three groups: (1) an early May blooming group, (2) a mid-May blooming group, and (3) a late May blooming group. The early May group apparently was the first to be developed in order to find a popular pink to go with prevailing white houses in the Cleveland area, as well as to produce a plant that would have branches from the ground level up instead of being bare from the ground to the graft. the earliest crosses were mostly between Cunningham's White and Red *catawbiense* seedlings, Cunningham's White and America, and Ignatius Sargent and America. There were also a number of *brachycarpum* crosses in this group that were eventually discarded despite the beauty of their habit and leaf because, from a nurseryman's viewpoint, ten years was too long to wait for a bloom.

The first group includes Cheer, Elie, Holden, Rocket, Spring Glory, and Spring Parade. All of these are hardy to at least −10° F. and have a magnificently dense structure and handsome foliage. I am sure that most readers know that one of the faults of the early blooming Shammarello rhododendrons is the fact that they tend to bloom in the fall. I have not found this to be as negative a factor as have some people. This group is the only section of the Shammarello plants with such a characteristic. Fall breaking of flowers is confined to Cheer and Spring Glory and usually is a result of a dry August and wet fall. Under these conditions, many hybrids other than Shammarello varieties also tend to flower. I have never found that this fall flowering was large enough to impair the extremely heavy flowering characteristics of these plants in the spring. Spring Parade, with its recurved leaves and dense foliage, is my favorite of the group. The plant receives high accolades wherever it is grown. Most of this group could be classified as pinks with the exception of Spring Parade and Holden, which are more on the red side.

The second or mid-May group of plants largely evolved from crosses of Boule de Neige x America. This group includes Besse Howells, Pink Cameo, Pink Flair, Prize, Sham's Pink, Sham's Juliet, and Tony. In the same group, Lavender Queen is a cross of Cunningham's White x America. Lavender Queen is one of the finest foliage plants that I have ever seen. While the bluish lavender flowers are not sensational, they are certainly not obnoxious. I would grow this plant gladly for its foliage characteristics alone.

This second group of plants is hardier than the first, and could be considered safe to −15° or −20° F., depending on the quality of the cold. Besse Howells and Tony are in the red range. Pink Cameo, Pink Flair, and Sham's Pink are, as might be expected, in the pink color group—all with attractive reddish or deeper pink blotches. Prize and Sham's Juliet are rather delicate pink with brownish blotches.

All of the midseason group are attractive in foliage and dense compact plants. Because of their very heavy flowering characteristics, they are almost self-breaking and require very little training.

The third or late blooming group of plants is probably the most versatile and varied of the three groups. Three of these plants are direct descendants of red *catawbiense* seedlings which survived the winter of 1938-39. These are Romeo, Sham's Ruby, and The General. They are quite simply listed in parentage as red *catawbiense* seedling x red *catawbiense* seedling. The three have a fair red flower truss and are extremely hardy. In relation to Tony's other plants, they are relatively tall growing.

Perhaps the hardiest in this group is King Tut, a beautifully bushy plant with a larger than average truss of deep to light pink with brownish blotch. This hybrid of *R. smirnowii* x America blooms in very late May or early June. David Leach, writing to Tony Shammarello after a disastrous winter a few years ago, said that only King Tut and Pinnacle bloomed normally. Cold was registered in Brookville to −35°. Interestingly enough, these plants the same year did not bloom very well in Tony's nursery field in South Euclid where the temperature reached a low point of −26°F. This proves that there is merit to the argument that it is the quality of the cold rather than the cold itself which is disastrous.

The other bloomer, the pink flowered Pinnacle, is a cross between Mrs. C. S. Sargent and a pink *catawbiense* seedling. Spring Dawn is a direct descendant of two surviving pink *catawbiense* seedlings from the winter of 1938-39, and it is one of the taller growing of the Shammarello varieties.

A later introduction, Sham's Candy, a late blooming pink, is the only named variety that is a cross between two of his named varieties, Pinnacle and Pink Cameo. Belle Heller, a compact grower with attractive light green foliage, is a cross between Catawbiense Album and a white *catawbiense* seedling. It is an extremely floriferous plant and sometimes has multiple flower buds on many terminals. It is a good white with a yellow blotch, a trifle less hardy than the rest of its group. It would be considered safe to minus 5-10° F. under our normal conditions. One of the finest of all of Tony's hybrids is Ice Cube, a good creamy white with a yellow blotch. This hybrid of Catalgla by Belle Heller combines the best features of both plants, comes into bloom late, and has been consistently hardy for me. Ice Cube is a rather tall but dense grower with excellent foliage.

His latest and newest group of plants originated from a cross of King Tut x *yakusimanum* F.C.C. These plants could be classified in a mid-to-late flowering date and in the pink range of color. Most of them were on display at the Pittsburgh meeting in 1973. Tony named the plants Yaku-King, Yaku-Queen, Yaku-Prince, Yaku-Princess, Yaku-Duke, and Yaku-Duchess. Plants of this group have received Best of Show Award several times since first introduced. All are very hardy, compact, and dense growing; they flower heavily starting at two to three years from cuttings. All show slight but not appreciable indumentum.

Tony rates his favorite hybrids in the following order: Elie Pink Flair, Tony's Sham's Candy, Pinnacle, King Tut, Sham's Juliet, Ice Cube, Scarlet Glow, and all of the Yaku group with Yaku-Prince being a slight favorite.

Briefly, this is the story of Shammarello's rhododendrons. Mine has been a case of love at first sight. They are the finest and most compact growing group of plants that I have. Initially, I was attracted to them by their apparent sun hardiness, since the Shammarello Nursery is completely exposed to the elements without shade or protection of any kind. All of them have grown beautifully for me through long periods of drought without benefit of shade or water. Their only protection has been a fairly heavy covering of mulch. I would be the first to admit that other hybrids have more exotic blooms. Given a choice between an exotic bloom accompanied by rank or spindly growing plants requiring extraordinary thumbnail application to maintain any semblance of order, I would unhesitatingly cast my lot with foliage and habit, sun hardiness, as well as drought and winter resistance.

The Shammarello Azaleas

The Shammarello azaleas are not as widely known as his rhododendron hybrids, but they certainly are steadily becoming more popular. Over the years, Tony has worked with and named a wide variety of azaleas; currently he is marketing primarily eleven evergreen hybrids from crosses made between 1955 and 1968. Six of these plants are patented. All of them bloom between May 10 and May 25. In making the crosses that produced these excellent hybrids, it is safe to say that Tony certainly followed his own dictum of stirring up the genes.

One of the earliest group of crosses utilizing such diverse parentage as *poukhanense*, Indica Alba, Hino Crimson, *kaempferi*, and Gable hybrids produced Shammarello hardy evergreen azaleas. All are exceptionally hardy semi-dwarfs possessing good clear nonfading color. Maximum height of most varieties should be about 30 inches with a 4-foot spread.

Azalea Desiree was the first plant patented. This good midseason single white originated from an F_2 seedling selected from a sibling pairing of *poukhanense* x Indica Alba seedlings during 1955. This plant has always been hardy for me, and it has reached a height of 5-6 feet, with a compact spread of 4 feet.

The injection of Desiree into later crosses produced Marie's Choice, Hino White, Helen Curtis, and Elsie Lee. Marie's Choice, a large flowered single white, blooms May 20 and has a better growth habit and darker foliage than Desiree. Hino-White is a medium dwarf growing about 2 feet high and 3 feet wide. Its beautiful dark green foliage is all the more valuable as it is among the most leaf-persistent of all the white azaleas.

The patented Helen Curtis is my favorite of the Shammarello azaleas. The heavy white flower is hose-in-hose, almost double, blooms midseason, and makes a good compact medium dwarf plant 3 feet high and somewhat over 4 feet in width. Elsie Lee came from the same cross but grows somewhat less compact and has a semidouble bluish lavender flower.

Azalea Red-Red is a patented plant. The flower is single, brilliant blood red—certainly the darkest red color of the hardy evergreen azaleas—and blooms about May 20. This is a very hardy plant. In growth, Red-Red is a medium dwarf. May Belle, a patented plant, is a medium dwarf, almost double pink midseason bloomer and, again, is a good hardy evergreen azalea.

Tony rates his azalea favorites as Hino-Red, Helen Curtis, Red-Red, and May Belle.

Widespread Acclaim

During the last few years, recognition has come Tony's way. In 1967 he received a citation from the American Horticultural Society "for development, production and distribution of Rhododendron and Azalea varieties improved in flowering characteristics, habit of growth and hardiness." The Ohio Nurseryman's Association presented him with their Distinguished Contribution Award in 1972, and in 1973 the American Rhododendron Society awarded Tony the Gold Medal at the annual meeting in Pittsburgh.

His plants are both national and international in range. Complimentary comments on various hybrids have come from such diverse spots as Kansas, Georgia, South Carolina, New Hampshire, Minnesota, California, Oregon, Michigan, Washington, D.C., Illinois, New York State, Wisconsin, Nova Scotia, and British Columbia. Shammarello plants are also found in New South Wales, Korea, Japan, France, England, Scotland, New Zealand, and West Germany.

The achievements of this remarkable and modest man must be an example and inspiration for all of us. Without his patient work over a long period of time and his rigid, uncompromising standards, our garden possibilities would be so much the poorer.

APPENDIX A

Persistent Leaved Azaleas Raised and Introduced by A.M. Shammarello

Azalea Desiree. Plant Patent No. 2068 Hardy to −10°F; Parentage (*poukhanense* x Indica Alba, sib.) F₂ seedling. Flower: white, single, midseason-May 20. 5' high—4' wide.

Azalea Elsie Lee F. Hardy to −20°F; Parentage (Desiree x Rose Bud) Flower: bluish lavender, almost double, midseason-May 25. 4' high—4' wide.

Azalea Helen Curtis. F Patent No. 2837. Hardy to −20°F; Parentage (Desiree x Rose Bud). Flower: white, almost double, midseason-May 25—medium dwarf, 3' high—4' wide.

Azalea Hino-Pink. Hardy to −15°F; Parentage (Hino-Crimson x *poukhanense*) x (Fedora x Louise Gable). Flower: pink, single, midseason-May 10—medium dwarf. 30" high—4' wide.

Azalea Hino-Red. Plant Patent No. 2507 Hardy to −20°F; Parentage (Hino-Crimson x *poukhanense*) x (*kaempferi* hybrid unnamed seedling x James Gable). Flower: blood red, single, midseason-May 10—medium dwarf. 30" high—4' wide. Exceptional, hardy, flower does not fade in sun.

Azalea Hino-White. Plant Patent No. 2508 Hardy to −15°F; Parentage (Hino-Crimson x *poukhanense* x Desiree). Flower: white, single, midseason-May 10—medium dwarf, 30" high—4' wide. Olive green foliage; bud-hardy to −15°F.

Azalea Marie's Choice. Hardy to −20°F; Parentage (Hino-Crimson x *poukhanense* x Desiree). Flower: white, single, midseason-May 20—medium tall, 3½' high—4' wide. Outstanding, large glistening flowers.

Azalea Red-Red F. Plant Patent No. 3465. Hardy to −15°F; Parentage (Hino-Red x Wards Ruby) Flower: brilliant blood red, single, midseason-May 20—medium dwarf, 3'high—4' wide. The darkest red of the hardy red azaleas.

Azalea Sparkle. Hardy to −15°F; Parentage (*kaempferi* hybrid x James Gable). Flower: blood red, single, midseason-May 20—medium tall, 3½' high—4' wide.

Azalea Winter Green. Hardy to −15°F; Parentage (Hino-Crimson x *poukhanense* x Desiree). Flower: ivory-white, single, midseason-May 10—medium dwarf, dark green foliage. 2' high—3' wide. The most leaf persistent of the White Azaleas. Bud-hardy to −10°F.

May Belle. Plant Patent No. 3827. Hardy to −15°F; Parentage (Hino-Red x Helen Curtis) Flower: pink, almost double, midseason-May 25—medium dwarf, 2½' high—4' wide.

For Ratings of these plants, see Appendices to Chapter VII.

SUMMARY OF PARENTAGES OF AZALEA HYBRIDS

Not listed in other sections

1945—Apricot Glory. (Azalea Mollis Apricot x Mollis Apricot)
 Red King. (Azalea Mollis Large Orange Red x Mollis Dark Red)
 Yellow Bouquet. (Azalea Mollis Yellow x Mollis Yellow)
1950—Apricot Glory. (Azalea Mollis Apricot Glory x Mollis Apricot Glory)

1950—Red King. (Azalea Mollis Red King x Mollis Red King)

1951—Visco-Molle. (Azalea Viscosum x Mollis)

1951—Pink Gem. (Azalea Kaempferi Fedora x Gables Flame)

1951—Semidouble Light Lavender Pink Mucronulatum. (Azalea R. Conewago x Azalea Rose Greely)

1951—G 2-R-Sparkle and Sham's Flame. (Azalea Kaempferi Sd. Fire Ball x Gables Flame)

1951—H 4-P. (Azalea Louise Gable x Kaempferi Sd. Fire Ball)

1952—Seedlings Like Sherwood. (Azalea No. 114 Azalea Hino Crimson x Poukhanense)

1953—B 10-W Desiree and Cascade. (Azalea 1950-Sib. Seedlings of Poukhanense x Ledifolia Alba)

1954—Orange Red Seedlings. (Azalea Cumberlandense x Azalea Red King)

1955—Yellow Bouquet. (Azalea Yellow Bouquet x Azalea Yellow Bouquet)
Red King. (Azalea Red King x Red King)
Apricot Glory. (Azalea Apricot Glory x Apricot Glory)

1960—Helen Curtis P.P. No. 2837 and Elsie Lee. (Azalea Desiree x Rose Bud)
Flesh Pink. (Azalea Sparkle x Rose Bud)

1967—Seedlings Tender (Azalea Hino Red x Red Poppy)

1968—May Belle (Double Pink) and Century (Double Red). (Azalea Hino Red x Helen Curtis)

APPENDIX B_____

A.M. Shammarello Rhododendrons

Descriptive materials taken directly from A. Shammarello and American Rhododendron Society check list and registration information.

Belle Heller. (Catawbiense Album x white *catawbiense* seedling) Vigorous tall grower, good width proportion; leaves—dark green, 5″ x 1³/₄″. Flower: good white with conspicuous yellow blotch. Floret: 4″ wide, truss globular large. Blooms about May 25; bud hardy to −10°F. A.R.S. 00057 Synonym B-6-W.

Besse Howells. (Boule de Neige x red *catawbiense* seedling) Compact medium dwarf; leaves—dark green,

4″ x 1³/₄″. Flowers: burgundy red, ruffled with dark red blotch. Floret: 2¹/₂″ wide, truss globular. Blooms about May 25; bud hardy to −20°F. Frequently sets multiple buds, extremely floriferous. A.R.S. 000063 Synonym A-2-R

Cheer. (Cunningham White x red *catawbiense*) Compact medium dwarf; leaves-medium green, 4″ x 1³/₄″ slightly curved. Flower: light shell pink, conspicuous scarlet red blotch. Floret: 2¹/₂″ wide, conical truss. Blooms about May 5; bud hardy to −10°F. A.R.S. 000139 Synonym C-17-P.

Elie. (Cunningham White x red *catawbiense*) Medium height; leaves-lustrous dark green, 4″ x 1³/₄″. Flower: vibrant deep pink cerise with red blotch. Floret: 2¹/₂″ wide, conical truss. Blooms about May 10; bud hardy to −10°F. A.R.S. 000238 Synonym B-15-P.

Holden. (Cunningham White x red *catawbiense*) Compact semi-dwarf; leaves-glossy dark green, 4″ x 1³/₄″. Flower: luminous red with dark red blotch. Floret: 2¹/₂″ wide, conical truss. Blooms about May 18; bud hardy to −15°F. A.R.S. 000350 Synonym C-1-R.

Ice Cube. (Catalgla x Belle Heller) Tall compact plant, good width proportion leaves—dark green, 5″ x 2″. Flower: ivory white with good lemon yellow blotch. Floret: 2¹/₂″, truss large conical. Blooms about May 30; bud hardy to −20°F. A.R.S. 000356 Synonym B-53-W.

King Tut. (*smirnowii* x America) x (red *catawbiense* seedling) Compact medium dwarf; leaves—medium green, 5″ x 2¹/₂″. Flower: deep to light shades of pink with yellowish-brown blotch. Floret: 2¹/₂″ wide, truss semi-conical, larger than average. Blooms about May 30; bud hardy to −20°F. A.R.S. 000410 Synonym B-13-R.

Lavender Queen. Excellent medium height foliage plant, very compact; grows in tiers with lustrous dark green foliage. Flower: bluish lavender with minimum of magenta, truss smaller than average, slightly ruffled. Sister plant to early group but blooms approximately May 20.

Pink Cameo. (Boule de Neige x red *catawbiense* seedling) Medium dwarf plant; compact leaf—medium green, 4¹/₂″ x 1¹/₂″. Flower: clear pink with pinkish yellow blotch. Floret: 2¹/₂″ wide, conical truss. Blooms about May 20; bud hardy to −20°F. A.R.S. 00605 Synonym A-4-P.

Pink Flair. (Boule de Neige x red *catawbiense* seedling) Medium dwarf compact; leaves—excellent dark green, 3¹/₂″ x 1³/₄″. Flower: pastel pink with conspicuous red blotch. Floret: 2¹/₂″ wide, truss globular. Blooms about May 20; bud hardy to −20°F. A.R.S. 00616 Synonym A-31-P.

Pinnacle. [pink *catawbiense* seedling (Ignatius Sargent x Mrs. C.S. Sargent) x pink *catawbiense* seedling] Medium height; leaves—medium green, $4^1/_2''$ x 2″. Flower: pure pink with citron yellow blotch. Floret: $2^1/_2''$ wide, truss conical. Blooms about May 25; bud hardy to at least −20°F. A.R.S. 000633 Synonym B-7-P.

Prize. (Boule de Neige x red *catawbiense* seedling) Vigorous medium size plant; leaves-green, 4″ x $1^3/_4''$. Flowers: shrimp pink with light yellow brown blotch. Floret: 2″ wide, truss globular. Blooms about May 20; bud hardy to −20°F. Being discontinued in favor of *yakusimanum* hybrids because of some susceptibility to stem blight. A.R.S. 000645 Synonym A-1-P.

Rocket. (Cunningham White x red *catawbiense*) Compact tall plant; leaves dark green, 4″ x $1^1/_2''$. Flower: luminous vivid pink, slightly ruffled, scarlet red blotch (conspicuous at a distance). Floret-$2^1/_2''$ wide, conical truss. Blooms about May 18; bud hardy to −15°F. Upright habit limits use in landscaping. A.R.S. 000685 Synonym C-18-R.

Romeo. (red *catawbiense* seedling x America) Vigorous tall grower; leaves—leathery dark green, 4″ x 2″. Flower: blood red with large dark red blotch. Floret: $2^1/_2''$ wide, truss globular. Blooms about May 25; bud hardy to −20°F. A.R.S. 000690 Synonym B-22-R.

Scarlet Glow. (scarlet *catawbiense* seedling x red *catawbiense*) Compact upright plant of medium height, almost symmetrical. Leaves—dark green, well proportioned, slightly crinkled. Flower: dark red void of magenta. Bud hardy in approximate range of −10°F to −15°F.

Sham's Candy. (Pinnacle x Pink Cameo) Compact plant, medium height; leaves—good pea green, $4^1/_2''$ x $1^3/_4''$. Flower: deep pink with brown blotch, truss conical. Blooms about May 25; bud hardy to −20°F. A.R.S. 1973 Registered Synonym A-43-P.

Sham's Pink. (Boule de Neige x red catawbiense seedling) Medium dwarf compact plant with good rose pink color; being discontinued because stiff branches make shipping difficult. A.R.S. 000734 Synonym A-10-P.

Sham's Juliet. (Boule de Neige x red *catawbiense* seedling) Compact medium dwarf; leaves—pea green, $3^1/_2''$ x 2″. Flower: deep pink bud opening to apple blossom pink. Floret: $2^1/_2''$ wide, truss conical. Blooms about May 25; bud hardy to −20°F. A.R.S. 000733 Synonym A-16-P.

Sham's Ruby. (Kettledrum x America) Medium height, current year stems turned red; leaves—olive green, slightly convex, $4^1/_2''$ x $2^1/_4''$. Flower: blood red, dark red blotch. Floret: $2^1/_4''$ wide, truss conical. Blooms about May 25; bud hardy to −20°F. A.R.S. 1973 Registered Synonym B-31-R.

Spring Glory. (Cunningham White x red *catawbiense*) Dwarf compact plant; leaves: lustrous green. Flowers: light rosy-pink, large crimson-red blotch. Blooms about May 5; bud hardy −10°.

Spring Parade. (red *catawbiense* seedling x Cunningham White) Medium tall, very compact; leaves: dark green, vary from 3″ to 4″ long by 1″ to $1^1/_4''$ wide, recurved. Flower: scarlet red, clear. Florets: 2″ to $2^1/_2''$ wide, truss globular. Blooms about May 18; bud hardy to −20°F. Magnificent foliage plant also easy to force. A.R.S. 000763 Synonym C-26-R.

The General. (red *catawbiense* seedling x red *catawbiense* seedling) Compact medium height; leaves—dark green. Flower: brilliant crimson red with dark red blotch. Blooms about May 25; bud hardy to −20°F.

Tony. (Boule de Neige x red *catawbiense* seedling) Compact medium height plant; leaves—dark green, 4″ x $1^3/_4''$. Flowers: bright cherry red. Floret: $2^1/_2''$ wide, truss conical. Blooms about May 25, bud hardy to −20°F. A.R.S. 00810 Synonym A-7-4.

SUMMARY OF PARENTAGES OF RHODODENDRON HYBRIDS

Not listed in other sections

SYMBOL:
Sd: SEEDLING
Cat: CATAWBIENSE HYBRID

1940—Sham's No. 1-2-3-4-5. (Ignatius Sargent x America)
1942—Red Cat. 50 Sd. (Red Cat. Sd. x Red Cat. Sd.)
1945—Red Cat. Sd. (America x Kettledrum)
1945—Red Cat. Sd. (Kettledrum x America)
1945—Pink Maximum and Red Maximum. (Sefton x Maximum)
1953—Campy. (Campylocarpum x B11 R Red Cat. Sd.)
1953—Pink Brachycarpum. (Red Cat. Sd. x Brachycarpum)
1953—Spring Dainty (discarded). (Fortunei x America)

APPENDIX C

Yakusimanum Hybrids

These hybrids have been recently introduced; all are dwarf in habit with excellent foliage and branches snug to the ground. The silvery new growth, of course, makes a very interesting display of contrasting foliage. The slight indumentum on the leaf tends to repel insects and the plants do not seem to be easily infected with leaf or stem blights and are tolerant to root rot diseases except under very severe conditions.

All plants will tend to be about 2½' high and 3' wide in ten years. Flower buds are all hardy from −10°-−15°F. All come into bloom about May 20 and tend to set buds at about two to three years from cuttings.

The parentage of all these hybrids is King Tut x *Yakusimanum* F.C.C.

Yaku-Duchess. Flower buds, brilliant red open to a good red gradually blending to a lighter red.

Yaku-Duke. In juvenile stage not bushy, attains compact form at ages three to four years—Flower bud darkest red of the group opening to vibrant red and remains this color for some time eventually fading to white.

Yaku-King. Flower buds, a vivid red—deep pink gradually fading to rose pink.

Yaku-Prince. Foliage olive green—flower buds open to red-flowers chiffon rose pink gradually fading to apple blossom.

Yaku-Princess. Flower buds open light pink—Flowers good sparkling white.

Yaku-Queen. Flower buds open to a vivid pink—flowers good apple blossom pink gradually fading to white.

CHAPTER VI

Contemporary Hybridizers

The five hybridizers who are the subjects of the first chapters in this book were selected as representative pioneers who created rhododendrons and azaleas suited to the climate of eastern North America. Today, instead of the "lonely few" of a half-century ago, there are scores of dedicated hybridizers—many with a list of varieties already registered and appearing in commerce. Material is widely exchanged, and new breeders are encouraged.

To identify these hybridizers, a questionnaire was sent to approximately 120 people whose names were found, in large part, among contributors to the A.R.S. seed exchange during the years 1968 through 1975. The response was amazing; over 60 replies were received within two weeks, and more than 30 new names were added to the list. A great many completed questionnaires have been received with information on new hybrids.

The five pioneers have encouraged and inspired others to follow in their footsteps. The primary objective of almost every one of these hybridizers is to develop new, more attractive plants which are hardy in his or her particular locale. Although hardiness is often closely related to a resistance to low winter temperatures, the responses to the survey indicated an interest in resistance to heat, drought and poor soils in the hardiness category. The characteristic desired by these hybridizers might be better designated as that of a "good-doer."

Because growing conditions in most of the eastern United States are more severe than the milder areas of the British Isles and Pacific Northwest, rhododendron hybrids developed by these eastern hybridizers are likely to be suitable for use in more extreme growing conditions, although there can be exceptions. For example, hybrids developed and evaluated in sandy coastal areas may not be "good-doers" on heavier soils farther inland. Similarly, plants selected from shady growing conditions may not perform well when exposed to higher levels of light, even in milder climates. However, it should be anticipated that a goodly number of the new hybrids described here will be adapted to broad latitudes of temperature, light, and growing conditions. As these new hybrids are more widely grown, those cultivars which consistently perform well will eventually become better known, appreciated and further propagated.

Active eastern hybridizers are located from Nova Scotia southward to Florida, and westward to Illinois. Temperature zones are only an approximate indication of winter climate severity, as climatic influences can be highly localized, depending greatly on air drainage, wind, humidity and heat radiation (exposure). Gardens just a few miles apart can vary more than 10°F. in temperatures.

Most of the currently active hybridizers have become active since 1955 and many of their plantings are just reaching the evaluation stage. A few began hybridizing before 1940, and their selected cultivars have the advantage of a longer, more severe testing period.

Many of these hybridizers have well-defined objectives in their breeding programs, including dwarfness, clearer colors in the yellow, orange, and red range, an extended blooming season, fragrance, flower substance, and so on. It is especially notable that some hybridizers living in Zones 7, 8, and 9 are striving to develop rhododendrons and azaleas that are more resistant to heat. Detailed descriptions of the work of a few of the more active hybridizers are presented in Contemporaries and Their Work, a section of this chapter.

As part of the information requested in the survey, each hybridizer listed what he considered to be his best new hybrids. Those who furnished this information provided the names and/or parentage of more than 280 selected cultivars (page 187), of which only 35 have been registered. Many of these cultivars are still under test and observation as some hybridizers feel that 15 or more years is a minimum time to evaluate new hybrids. As more recent plantings mature and new clones are selected, it may be that some of those on the "best" list will be displaced by newer, better hybrids. However, even those eventually displaced, as well as the other cultivars listed which continue to be available, can be recognized as valuable "superparents" for further hybridizing.

Credit for this information belongs to those many dedicated hybridizers who have so generously shared their knowledge and work. Through years of study, planning, and devoted attention to the needs of their plants, they have given the genus *Rhododendron* a giant stride forward in history, and provided the opportunity for many more of their fellow men to enjoy the flowers of more "growable" cultivars.

Finally, we regret the omission of any eastern rhododendron hybridizer who may not have been reached by this survey, and whose name and contributions may have been inadvertently omitted in this study.*

---

*Any such hybridizer should contact George W. Ring, 11400 Valley Road, Fairfax, Virginia, 20030, so that they and their work may be included in future publications.

For a separate listing of hybrids registered by eastern hybridizers, see page 192.

Summary of the "Best" New Hybrids

Listed by Each Eastern Hybridizer Responding to this Survey. Arranged by Climatic zone.

ZONE 4

Clone	Hybridizer
R. keleticum (R58) x *R. carolinianum*	Barber
R. keleticum (R58) x PJM	Barber
R. glaucophyllum x *R. carolinianum*	Barber
Mary Fleming X PJM	Barber
Nodding Bells x *catawbiense hybrid*	Barber

ZONE 5

Clone	Hybridizer
Acadia (To be renamed Fundy) (*R. fortunei* op.)	Craig
Balta (*R. carolinianum var. album* x PJM)	Mezitt
Bellafontaine (*R. fortunei* x *R. smirnowii*)	Craig-Pike
Christina (*Catalgla x* Mrs. W. C. Slocock)	Delp
(*R. carolinianum var. album* x *R. keiskei* x *R. racemosum*	Winkler
Comet (*R. yakusimanum* x ?)	Skonieczny
Dark Red #1 (King Tut x Cm #7)	Robinson
Dorothy Macklin (*R. smirnowii* x *R. thomsonii*) x ?	Hancock
Evangeline (To be renamed Cornwallis) (*R. fortunei* x *R. smirnowii*)	Craig-Hancock
Evening Sky (Blue Diamond x *R. carolinianum*)	Hancock
R. fortunei x *haematodes* (F_2)	Angelini
Fox Fire (R. *smirnowii* x *R. haematodes*)	Foster
Front Yard Rhododendron (?)	Angelini
Gabriel (Dr. Dresselhuys x *R. smirnowii*)	Craig-Swain

ZONE 5

Clone	Hybridizer
Gaywink (*R. pubescens* x *R. keiskei* x *R. racemosum* x Blue Diamond)	Winkler
Grand pre' (To be renamed, Minias) (*R. catawbiense compactum* x *R. Williamsianum*	Craig-Swain
Harrisville #268 (Newport F_4)	Delp
Jenny (Pink Carolinianum x Calostrotum Rose)	Delp
Laurie (*Carolinianum var. album* x PJM	Mezitt
R. ledum groenlandicum x *R. yakusimanum*	Paden
R. ledum groenlandicum x *R. Elizabeth*	Paden
Little Boy Blue (Blue Diamond x *R. carolinianum*)	Hancock
Llenroc (*R. Carolinianum var. Album* x Cornell Pink)	Mezitt
Lola (Ignatius Sargent x Robert Allison)	Skonieczny
Mary Kittel (White hybrid x Mrs. P. den Ouden)	Mezitt
Millstream Maiden (Fox Fire F_2)	Foster
Millstream Red (*R. fortunei* x Catawbiense Rubra)	Foster
Nefretti x America	Angelini
Olga (*R. dauricum* x *R. mucronulatum*) x *R. minus*	Mezitt
R. pemakoense x Rose Elf	Foster
Peppermint Frills (Skyglow x Nova Zembla)	Skonieczny
Pink Pompon (*R. carolinianum* x *R. racemosum*)	Hancock
P.J.M. hybrid	Angelini
Polar Cap (*R. yakusimanum* x Jock)	Winkler
Pygmey (Boule de Niege x *R. yakusimanum*)	Skonieczny
Robby (*Pink R. Carolinianum* x *Mucram*)	Delp
Rose Pink (*R. yakusimanum x R. catawbiense*) x Mrs. C. S. Sargent	Robinson
Slippery Rock #174 (Newport F4)	Delp

ZONE 5

Clone	Hybridizer
(*R. smirnowii* x *R. haematodes*) x Mayday (double flowers)	Winkler
Timmy Foster (*R. racemosum* x *R. keiskei*)	Foster
Tony x (Scintillation x America)	Angelini
Vallya (*R. Carolinianum var. Album* x Cornell Pink)	Mezitt
R. wardii x America	Angelini
Wax Red (America x Mars)	Skonieczny
Wendy Lyn (Harrisville x Purple Splendour)	Delp
Weston (Dexter seedling)	Mezitt
Weezie	
Yellow Discolor (*R. fortunei* x Golden Bell)	Case

ZONE 6

Clone	Hybridizer
Alice Swift (*R. carolinianum* x (*R. mucronulatum* x *R. racemosum*) F$_2$)	Yavorsky
(America x Brittania)	Emerson
Anna Baldsiefen (Pioneer x Pioneer)	Baldsiefen
Anna Lise (unknown)	Prycl
Atrosanguineum x Medusa	Fetterhoff
Bermuda (Anna H.Hall x Nestucca)	Leach
Az. Betty Ann Voss (Lady Louise x Shinnyo No Suki)	Gartrell
Big Mac (*R. catawbiense var. Album*, La Bars White x *R. macabeanum*)	Knippenberg
Blondie (*R. maximum* x *R. catawbiense*) x Neried	Pride
Brookville x Mary Garrison	Miller
R. carolinianum x *R. keleticum*	Emerson
R. carolinianum x Pioneer	Fetterhoff
R. catawbiense x *R. Smirnowii*	Prycl
R. catawbiense var. album x Caroline	Emerson
R. catawbiense var. album, La Bars White x *R. yakusimanum*	Mehlquist

ZONE 6

Clone	Hybridizer
R. catawbiense var. album, "Glass" x County of York	Prycl
Consolini Red x America	Emerson
Copper (*R. yakusimanum* x Sir Charles Lemon)	Knippenberg
Cornell Pink x *R. lutescens*	Mehlquist
David Forsythe (*R. catawbiense compactum* x Mars)	Baldanza
(*R. discolor* x *R. wardii*)	Rachinsky
Doc Tolstead (*R. fortunei* x)	Prycl
Dom Perigon #1	Heyderhoff
Dom Perigon #2	Heyderhoff
Dorothy Amateis (America x Purple Splendour)	Amateis
Edith (*R. maximum* hybrid)	Pride
(Fabia x Catalgla) x (*R. decorum* x *R. campylocarpum*)	von Wettberg-Hardgrove
Firepink (*R. catawbiense var. album*, La Bars White x Kluis Sensation)	Knippenberg
Gibbon (Kluis Sensation x *R. yakusimanum*)	Reese
Goldfort x Ivisa Pekin	Miller
Goldfort x Mariloo	Miller
Goldsworth Yellow x *R. yakusimanum*	Rachinsky
Hardy Giant (*R. fortunei* x *R. fictolacteum*)	Knippenberg
Harold Amateis (*R. maximum* x *R. strigillosum*)	Amateis
Hereford *R. yakusimanum* x Jock)	Reese
Idealist x *R. yakusimanum*	Winkler, G.
Kathrina ?	Smith
Laurel Pink (Boule de Niege x *R. williamsianum*)	Knippenberg
Maletta (*R. auriculatum* x *R. discolor* x *R. ungernii* x ?)	Yates
Mars x *R. yakusimanum*	Winkler, G.
Mary Belle x *R. yakusimanum*	Miller
Matilda (Watchung x *R. carolinianum var. album*)	Yavorsky
R. maximum x (Crest x Caroline)	Rachinsky
R. maximum x *R. griersonianum* F$_2$	Emerson

ZONE 6

Clone	Hybridizer
R. maximum x *R. wardii*	Fetterhoff
R. minus x *R. racemosum* x *R. ciliatum*	von Wettberg
Mirelle Vernimb (selected *R. hemitrichotum*)	Vernimb
Mrs. Erna Heyderhoff	Heyderhoff
Mrs. Furnival x *R. yakusimanum*	Winkler, G.
Mrs. J. G. Millais x *R. catawbiense var. album,* La Bars White	Fetterhoff
Az. Nancy of Robin Hill (Vervaeneana x Lady Louise)	Gartrell
Nodding Bells [America x (*R. forrestii* var. *repens* x *R. griersonianum*)]	Amateis
Nuance (*R. catawbiense var. album*) x (*R. neriiflorum* x *R. dichroanthum* x *R. discolor*)	Leach
Olive Egan (Pioneer x Lady Alice Fitzwilliams)	Egan
Osfriesland x *R. yakusimanum*	Winkler, G.
Party Pink (Mrs. Furnival x *R. catawbiense var. album*)	Leach
Phyllis (*R. catawbiense var. album,* Powell Glass x *R. yakusimanum*)	Shanklin
Pink Mango (*R. maximum* x *R. catawbiense*) x Nereid	Pride
Professor Amateis Everestianum x Van Nes Sensation)	Amateis
Purple hybrid x Purple Splendour	Fetterhoff
Radnor (Red Cloud x *R. yakusimanum* F.C.C.)	Reese
Redberth (Mars x *R. yakusimanum* F.C.C.)	Reese
Red Brave (America x Mars)	Pride
Az. Redmond (Lady Louise x Hei Wa)	Gartrell
Rik (*R. racemosum* x *R. keiskii*)	Yavorsky
Robert Forsythe (*R. catawbiense var. compactum* x Mars)	Baldanza
Robin Leach *R. catawbiense var. album* x (Adriaan Koster x *R. williamsianum*)	Leach

ZONE 6

Clone	Hybridizer
Roman Candle (America x Mars)	Pride
Royal Star x Lackamas Sovereign	von Wettberg
Scintillation x Avalanche	Miller
Serendipity (*R. yakusimanum* x *R. chrysanthum*)	Potter
Shazaam (Pink Twins x Mars)	Yates
R. smirnowii x *R. yakusimanum*	Mehlquist
Snowden (*R. decorum* x *R. yakusimanum*)	Reese
Sumatra (America x Gertrude Schäle)	Leach
Susy (America x Mars) x (America x Blaze)	Ring, T. L.
(Tally Ho x Margaret Dunn) x Meadowbrook	von Wettberg-Hardgrove
Tiffany (Anna Baldsiefen x *R. keiskei*)	Baldsiefen
Az. Tonga (Ilam hybrid)	Baldsiefen
Tree Plant ?	Prycl
Virginia Delito ((*R. carolinianum* x (*R. mucronulatum* x *R. racemosum*) F$_2$)	Yavorsky
Vulcan x America	Mehlquist
Vulcan x *R. coriaceum*	Mehlquist
Vulcan x *R. fortunei*	Mehlquist
Vulcan x *R. yakusimanum*	Mehlquist
Vulcan x *R. yakusimanum*	Winkler, G.
Az. Welmet (Amagasa x Lady Louise)	Gartrell
Az. White Moon (Glacier x Gama Giku x Getsu Toku)	Gartrell
Az. W. W. McCartney (Maxwelli x)	Egan
Yatton (Goldsworth Yellow x *R. yakusimanum*)	Reese

ZONE 7

Clone	Hybridizer
Az. Alexander (*R. nakaharai* x Kin-no-sai)	Hill
America (selfed)	Yuskus
Anne Hardgrove (C. P. Raffil x Moser's Maroon)	Hardgrove
Anthony Wayne (Scintillation x Atrier)	Herbert

Clone	Hybridizer
Arctic Dawn (*R. carolinianum var. album x R. dauricum,* white form)	Lewis
Barbara Hardgrove *R. fortunei* x (*R. wardii* x *R. dichroanthum*)	Hardgrove
Blue Peter x *R. metternechii*	Mason
Bowie (*R. chapmanni* x *R. minus*) F$_2$	Skinner
Camps Red (cultivar of *R. bakeri*)	Skinner
Carita x *R. fortunei*	Yuskus
Caroline x America	Ring
Caroline x Champagne	Kehr-Ring
R. carolinianum var. album x *R. mucronulatum,* white form	Kehr-Ring
R. carolinianum x *R. dauricum* (L-2-6)	Lewis
Clara Raustein (*R. decorum* x *R. discolor*) x (*R. dichroanthum* x *R. fortunei*)	Raustein
Connie H. (*R. calendulaceum* x Klondyke)	Hollowell
Copper Cloud (Ilam seedling)	Wells
Cornell Pink (selected pink form of *R. mucronulatum*)	Skinner
Dexters x *R. fortunei* (group)	Emmerich
R. dichroanthum x *R. wardii* x *R. fortunei*	Murcott
Disca x Autumn Gold	Goodrich
Disca x Gloxineum	Goodrich
Donna Hardgrove *R. fortunei* x (*R. wardii* x *R. dichroanthum*)	Hardgrove
Az. Dorsett (Winter blooming form of *R. kaempferi*)	Hollowell
Epoch (Tetraploid form of *R. carolinianum*)	Kehr
Everstianum x Jan Dekens	Yuskus
Fortunei #1 (*R. fortunei* x Caractacus)	Reiley
Fortunei #2 (*R. fortunei* x Caractacus)	Reiley
Gary Herbert (*R.* vernicosum, Aff. Rock 18139 x)	Herbert
Golden Star (*R. fortunei* x *R. croceum*)	Hardgrove

Clone	Hybridizer
Goldsworth Orange x (*R. wardii* x Fawn) WCM #313	Marley
Gretchen Medlar (Boule de Niege x Henrietta Sargent)	Skinner
Hardy Splendour (Purple Splendour x Purpureum Grandiflorum)	Shapiro
Hawk x Idealist	Hyatt
Az. Linwood Pink Giant (A-3) x (Rose Greeley x K-28)	Reid
Az. Linwood Lustre (K-18) x (A-3)	Reid
Az. Jean C. (*R. calendulaceum* x Klondyke)	Hollowell
Joe Brooks Caractacus x *R. fortunei*	Yelton
Az. Joseph Hill (*R. nakaharai* x W. Leith)	Hill
June Fire (*R. catawbiense* x *R. discolor*) x (*R. fortunei* x *R. griersonianum* x *R. discolor*)	Wister
June Maid (*R. maximum* x *R. discolor*)	Wister
Katja (*R. catawbiense var. album* x *R. discolor*) x Mdm. de Bruin)	Raustein
Knaphill #10	Hardy
Knaphill #12	Hardy
Knaphill #20	Hardy
King Red (deciduous azalea seedling)	King-Kehr
La Bar's White x King of Shrubs	Martin
Leo x Nestucca	Yelton
Az. Linwood Blush (Salmon Spray x Jean Haerns)	Reid
Az. Linwood Salmon (A-3) x (Rose Greeley x K-28)	Reid
Louisa (Chinyeyi x W. Leith)	Hill
Az. Mabel H. (*R. calendulaceum* x Klondyke)	Hollowell
(Madonna x *R. fortunei*) x Nearing's Purple	Miller-Todd
R. makinoi x (Doncaster x *R. yakusimanum*) WCM #102	Marley

ZONE 7

Clone	Hybridizer
Mars x (*R. yakusimanum* x Etta Burroughs)	Marley
R. maximum x *R. arboreum*	Purdy
(*R. maximum* x *R. haematodes*) x Fire Music	Murcott
Meadowbrook x Pink Symphony	Murcott
Az. Michael Hill (Chinyeyi x *R. nakaharai*)	Hill
Millard Kepner (Decatros x *R. yakusimanum*)	Byrkit
R. minus x *R. dauricum* (L-4-4)	Lewis
Mrs. A. T. de la Mare x Madfort	Goodrich-Miller
Mrs. Betty Hager (*R. decorum* x *R. discolor)* x (Mdm. de Bruin)	Raustein
Mrs. G. W. Leak x Naomi, Exbury (WCM #205)	Marley
Mrs. P. D. Williams x *R. fortunei* (group)	Shapiro
Mrs. R. S. Holford x Red Hardgrove seedling	Shapiro
Mt. Joy (Pink twins x (*R. forrestii repens* x))	Herbert
Nodding Bells x (*R. haematodes* x)	Shaw
Northern Lights (*R. carolinianum var. album* x *R. dauricum*, white form)	Lewis
Az. O-My-O Hino-Crimson xSalmon Elf	Pryor
Az. Opal (A-3) x (K-28)	Reid
Owens-Dexter x Nancy WCM #5	Marley
Painted Star (Meadowbrook x Anita)	Hardgrove
Peach Brandy (Scintillation x *R. haematodes*)	Wister
Peachy Keen (Ilam seedling)	Wells
Peach Sunset (Ilam seedling)	Wells
Penny B. (*R. calendulaceum* x Klondyke)	Hollowell
Pikeland (*R. campylogynum* x *R. keiskei*)	Herbert
Az. Pink Pancake (Chinyeyi x *R. nakaharai*)	Hill
Pink William (Ilam seedling)	Wells

ZONE 7

Clone	Hybridizer
Pioneer x *R. mucronulatum,* pink	Ring
Primrose (Ilam seedling)	Wells
Purple Splendour x *R. fortunei*	Ring
Red Letter (Ilam seedling)	Wells
Rufus (Ilam seedling)	Wells
Scintillation #1 (Scintillation x)	Reiley
Scintillation x *R. metternichii,* Aff.	Goodrich-Kehr
Scintillation x Temple Belle TT21	Murcott
Scintillation x Temple Belle TT38	Murcott
Az. Sekidera x Glacier	Emmerich
Az. Sekidera x Rosette	Emmerich
Sparkler (Essex Scarlet x *R. fortunei*)	Shapiro
Sparkling Jewel (*R. discolor* x *R. fortunei*)	Wister
Spring Song (*R. racemosum* x *R. keiskei) R. keiskei*	Hardgrove
Sunrise (Ilam seedling)	Wells
Terry Herbert (*R. carolinianum* x *keiskei*)	Herbert
Tintoretto (Ilam seedling)	Wells
Tom Everert x Naomi #1	Todd
Tommy x	Goodrich
Trilby x *R. fortunei*	Yuskus
Vulcan x Purple Splendour	Hyatt
Vulcan x White *R. fortunei* hybrid (3 selections)	Hyatt
(Wada's *R. metternichii,* Aff. x)	Todd
Wedding Cake (Purple Splendour x (*R. fortunei* x Purple Splendour))	Shapiro
White Cap (Ilam seedling)	Wells
White Mucronulatum (*R. mucronulatum* x)	Kehr
Az. White Rosebud (Vervaneana Alba x Rosebud)	Kehr
Yaku#14 (*R. yakusimanum* x Mars)	Hardy
R. yakusimanum x Damosel	Yuskus
R. yakusimanum x Honeydew	Martin
R. yakusimanum x Janet Blair	Reiley
R. yakusimanum x King of Shrubs	Martin
R. yakusimanum x Mars	Purdy

ZONE 7

Clone	Hybridizer
R. yakusimanum x Scintillation	Todd
R. yakusimanum x Sir Charles Lemon	Yelton
R. yakusimanum x Vulcan	Yelton
Yellow Carolinianum	Kehr
Yellow River (*R. austrinum* x *R. canescens* x *R. alabamense*)	Skinner

ZONE 8

Clone	Hybridizer
Az. *R. alabamense* x *R. calendulaceum* (54 x 11)	Galle
Az. Alfred H. Holbrook (Treasure x Nuccio's Pink Champagne)	Early
Az. Anne Perry (Rose Gumpo x Okina-nishiki)	Pennington
Az. *R. arborescens* x *R. prunifolium* (54 x 3)	Galle
Az. *R. austrinum* x *R. atlanticum* (71)	Galle
Az. Beth Bullard (Eikan x Heiwa)	Pennington
Az. Hugo Koster x *R. speciosum* (58 x 11)	Galle

ZONE 8

Clone	Hybridizer
Az. Hugh Wormald x *R. austrinum*	Early
Az. K.J.P. (Kongo x)	Pennington
Az. Mike Perry (Hershey's Red x Okina-nishiki)	Pennington
Az. Mrs. L. J. Comer (Mrs. Hearns x *R. kaempferi*)	Early
Az. Nancy Bullard (Pink Gumpo x Okina-nishiki)	Pennington
Az. Narcissiflora x *R. alabamense* 54 x 5	Galle
Az. *R. prunifolium* x *R. serrulatum*	Early
Vulcan x Caroline	Early

ZONE 9

Clone	Hybridizer
Az. Carol Anne (Glenn Dale group x Satsuki group)	Caldwell
Az. Leigh Anne (Glenn Dale group x Satsuki group)	Caldwell
Az. Jamie (Glenn Dale group x Satsuki group)	Caldwell
Az. Strawberry Swirl (Glenn Dale group x Satsuki group)	Caldwell
Az. Sweet Ruth (Glenn Dale group x Satsuki group)	Caldwell

RHODODENDRONS AND AZALEAS REGISTERED BY EASTERN HYBRIDIZERS, 1959-1975

Abbreviations used: P.A.=Preliminary Award   A.E.=Award of Excellence

1975—RHODODENDRONS

Name	Parentage	Hybridizer
Helen Everitt	Dexter hybrid x Dexter hybrid	Everitt-Fuller
Kathryn Reboul	*R. spinuliferum* x *R. recemosum*	Hardgrove-Reboul
Millard Kepner	Decatros x *R. yakusimanum*	Schumacher-Byrkit
Sham's Candy	Pinnacle x Pink Cameo	Anthony Shammarello
Sham's Ruby	Kettledrum x America	Anthony Shammarello
Spellbinder	[Russell Harmon x (*R. calophytum* x *R. sutchuenense*)]	David Leach

Geisha   West   67

Silver Mist   B.S. Harding

Futurity   West

Spring is welcomed by the early Glenn Dale
azaleas, Geisha (66) and Dayspring (70). Also
widely grown are Silver Mist (67), Futurity (68),
Martha Hitchcock (69) and Grace Freeman
(71).

Martha Hitchcock   Suggs

Dayspring   West

71   Grace Freeman   West

Carmel's luminous claret red benefits from part shade (72); other Glenn Dale beauties: Epicure (73); Coral Sea (74); Zephyr (75); Pied Piper (76) and Bacchante (77).

72   *Carmel*   Living

75   *Zephyr*   B.S. Har

73   *Epicure*   B.S. Harding

76   *Pied Piper*   B.S. Har

74   *Coral Sea*   B.S. Harding

77   *Bacchante*   B.S. Har

Orange Flair   B.S. Harding

79   *Marion Lee*   B.S. Harding

Miss Jane   B.S. Harding

The Back Acres hybrids were Morrison's retirement achievement: Orange Flair (78); Marion Lee (79); Miss Jane (80); St. James (82). B. Y. Morrison at work in 1956 (81).

B.Y. Morrison in 1956   J.R. Dunlop

82   *St. James*   B.S. Harding

83   *Spring Dawn*   Leach

84   *Ice Cube*   Le

Shammarello's rhododendrons were bred for compactness and hardiness in the Great Lakes region: Spring Dawn (83); Ice Cube (84); Besse Howells (85); Holden (86) and Candystick (87).

86   *Holden*   Le

85   *Besse Howells*   Leach

87   *Candystick*   Le

King Tut   Leach

89 Yaku Prince   Shammarello

Sham's Ruby   Leach

Yaku Prince (89) is representative of
Shammarello's "Yaku Royalty" series; King
Tut (88); Sham's Ruby (90) and Pinnacle (91)
are popular hybrids.

Pinnacle   Leach

92   *Shaazam*   Yates

Flowers of the future: Shaazam (92) and
Maletta (93), both by Yates; Christina (94) by
Delp; Scintillation x Avalanche (95) from
Miller; Clara Raustein (96) by Raustein;
Royal Pillow (97), one of Mezitt's azalea
hybrids.

93   *Maletta*   Y

94   *Christina*   Delp

95   *Scintillation X Avalanche*   Miller

96   *Clara Raustein*   Raustein

97   *Royal Pillow*   M

Sumatra   Leach

103   *Connie Yates*   Yates

Nuance   Leach

More rhododendrons by contemporary breeders: Sumatra (98) and Nuance (99) by Leach; Sunburst (100) and Redder Yet (101), Leach-Pride hybrids; Pink Icing (102) by Pride; Connie Yates (103) by Yates.

Sunburst   Pride

Redder Yet   Pride

102   *Pink Icing*   Pride

104   *Scintillation X yakusimanum*   Goodrich

105   *White Rosebud*   H

106   *Wheatley X Crinigerum*   Good

More new eastern hybrids. From the Raymond Goodriches: Scintillation x *yakusimanum* (104) and Wheatley x *crinigerum* (106); from Dr. August Kehr: White Rosebud (105); from the Knippenbergs: Hardy Giant (107); from John C. Wister: June Fire (108).

107   *Hardy Giant*   Knippenberg

108   *June Fire*

1975-AZALEAS

Name	Parentage	Hybridizer
Elsie Lee	Desiree x Rosebud	Anthony Shammarello
Girard's Crimson	(Boudoir x Aladdin) x (Boudoir x Corporal)	Peter Girard, Sr.
Girard's Hot Shot	(El Capitan x Aladdin)	Peter Girard, Sr.
Girard's Rose	[(Fedora x El Capitan) x Boudoir] x Boudoir	Peter Girard, Sr.
Girard's Scarlet	(Aladdin x El Capitan)	Peter Girard, Sr.
Helen Curtis	Desiree x Rosebud	Anthony Shammarello
John Chappell	Knaphill azalea seedling	Boree-Chapman
Joseph Hill	*R. nakahari* x W. Leith	Rokujo-Hill
Leslie's Purple	Elizabeth Gable x Boudoir	Peter Girard, Sr.
Michael Hill	*R. nakahari* x W. Leith	Rokujo-Hill
Pleasant White	Kathy x Clara Marie	Peter Girard, Sr.
Renee Michelle	Boudoir x Gumpo Pink—chance seedling	Peter Girard, Sr.
Sparkle	Red *R. kaempferi* seedling x Gable's Flame	Anthony Shammarello
Suzannah Hill	W Leith x R. *nakahari*	Rokujo-Hill

1974-RHODODENDRONS

Name	Parentage	Hybridizer
Bellvale	*R. carolinianum* x *R. dauricum* (white form)	Warren Baldsiefen
Cary's Red	?	Edward Cary
Ethel V. Cary	*R. metternichii* x Mrs. Charles S. Sargent	Edward Cary
Finlandia	*R. catawbiense*, var. *album* x (Adrian Koster x R. *williamsianum*)	David Leach
Flair	*R. catawbiense*, var. *album* x (Adrian Koster x R. *williamsianum*)	David Leach
Halesite Maiden	?	Dorothy Schlaikjer
Mrs. Betty Hager	(*R. decorum* x *R. discolor*) x Mdm. de Bruin	Alfred Raustein
Rowland P. Cary	*R. metternichii* x Van der Hoop	Edward Cary
Shalimar	Dexter seedling	Vossberg-Schlaikjer
Shalom	Anna x Antoon Van Welie	Lem-Hess
Stockholm	Catalgla x *R. decorum*	Hobbie-Leach

1974-AZALEAS

Name	Parentage	Hybridizer
Alexander	*R. nakahari* x Kin-no-sai	Rokujo-Hill
Fragrant Gold	Knaphill seedling	Rolande DeWilde
Landon	?	R. W. Pennington
Louisa	Chenyeyi x W. Leith	Rokujo-Hill
Marilee	*R. nakahari* (open pollinated)	Rokujo-Hill
Spring Melody	Goldie x J. Jennings	Pride-Baldsiefen
Tropic Sun (pat.)	Bud sport of Hino Crimson	C. M. Akehurst
Wintergreen	*R. nakahari* (open pollinated)	Rokujo-Hill

1973-RHODODENDRONS

Name	Parentage	Hybridizer
Azonea	Azor x Catanea	Guy Nearing
Bangkok	*R. catawbiense* var. *album* x [*R. dichroanthum* x (R. griffithianum x *R. auriculatum*)]	David Leach
Besse Howells	Red *R. catawbiense* hybrid x Boule de Niege	Anthony Shammarello
Big Girl	C. O. Dexter x Avocet	Howard Phipps
Boulades	Boule de Niege x "Loderi" seedling	Guy Nearing
Cairo	(Catalgla x *R. fortunei*) x Eidam x *R. williamsianum*	David Leach

1973-RHODODENDRONS (cont.)

Name	Parentage	Hybridizer
Clara Raustein	(*R. decorum* x *R. discolor*) x [(*R. wardii* x *R. dichro-anthum*)x *R. fortunei*]	Alfred Raustein
Decalgla	Catalgla x *R. decorum*	Gable-Nearing
Dexanea	Catanea x white Dexter hybrid	Guy Nearing
Elsie Whipple	Vulcan x Boule de Niege	Ray Kruse
Elizabeth Sidamon-Eristoff	?	Howard Phipps
Epoch	*R. carolinianum* seedling (open pollinated, tetraploid form created with colchicine)	August Kehr
Gigi	Dexter seedling	Dexter-Burns
Golden Salmon	Atrier x Atrier	Gable-Nearing
Guy Nearing	R. detonsum x Gilian	Nearing-Raustein
Ice Cube	Catalgla x Belle Heller	Anthony Shammarello
Magna loss	(*R. wardii* x *R. discolor*) x unknown	Guy Nearing
Martha Phipps	?	Howard Phipps
May Time	*R. catawbiense* var. *album* x *R. yakusimanum*	David Leach
Mountain Flare	Boule de Niege x Loderi King George	Guy Nearing
Nathan Hale	Dexter seedling	Mrs. Hugo Schlaikjer
Nuance	*R. catawbiense* var. *album* x [(*R. nerriflorum* x *R. dichroanthum*) x *R. discolor*)]	David Leach
Parker's Pink	Dexter seedling	Dexter-Parker
Party Pink	Mrs. Furnival x *R. catawbiense* var. *album*	David Leach
Peking	(*R. catawbiense* var. *album* x Hawk) x LaBar's White x Crest)	David Leach
Pink Flair	Red *R. catawbiense* hybrid x Boule de Niege	Anthony Shammarello
Pink Globe	*R. catawbiense* (Gable's red selection) x *R. griersonianum* x *R. fortunei*	Guy Nearing
Pinkie Price	(Meadowbrook x *R. Fortunei*) x sibling	Howard Phipps
Rangoon	Fanfare x Gertrud Schäle	David Leach
Red Lion	Tally Ho x *R. catawbiense* (Gable's red selection)	Guy Nearing
Red Puff	Golden Horn x Catanea	Guy Nearing
Romeo	Red *R. catawbiense* hybrid x Red *R. catawbiense* hybrid	Anthony Shammarello
Roslyn	Purpureum Elegans x Everestianum	Paul Vossberg
Scarlet Glow	Red *R. catawbiense* hybrid x Red *R. catawbiense* hybrid	Anthony Shammarello
Scintillation	Dexter x	Dexter-Vossberg
Sham's Juliet	Red *R. catawbiense* hybrid x Boule de Niege	Anthony Shammarello
Sham's Pink	Red *R. catawbiense* hybrid x Boule de Niege	Anthony Shammarello
Shanghai	Mrs. Furnival x *R. catawbiense* var. *album*	David Leach
Singapore	Fanfare x Gertrud Schäle	David Leach
Signal Horn	Atrosanguineum x Golden Horn	Guy Nearing
Trumpeter	[Red *R. catawbiense* hybrid x (*R. griersonianum* x Romany Chal)] x Mars x *R. catawbiense rubrum*	David Leach
Wheatley	Westbury x Meadowbrook	Howard Phipps

1973-AZALEAS

Name	Parentage	Hybridizer
Henry Allanson	Mollis seedling (open pollinated)	John Keshishian
White Rosebud	Vervaeneana Alba x Rosebud	August Kehr

1972-RHODODENDRONS

Name	Parentage	Hybridizer
Applause	Catalgla x (Adrian Koster x *R. williamsianum*)	David Leach
Ballad	Dexter L-1 x America	David Leach
Bombay	[(*R. scyphocalyx* x *R. kyawi*) x Catalgla] x (Catalgla x *R. wardii*)	David Leach
Calcutta	(*R. scyphocalyx* x *R. kyawi*) x Catalgla	David Leach
Dolly Madison	*R. catawbiense* var. *album* x [*R. fortunei* x [(*R. arboreum* x *R. griffithianum*)]	David Leach
Inca Chief	Mars x (Mars x *R. catawbiense* var. *rubrum*)	David Leach
Poppinjay	(*R. maximum* x *R. catawbiense*) x [(*R. dichroanthum*) x (*R. discolor* x *R. campylocarpum*)]	David Leach
Robin Leach	Catalgla x (Adrian Koster x *R. williamsanum*)	David Leach
Scarlet Blast	Mars x (Mars x *R. catawbiense* var. *rubrum*)	David Leach
Small Wonder	Fanfare x Prometheus x *R. forrestii repens*	David Leach
Spring Frolic	*R. catawbiense* var. *album* x *R. yakusimanum*	David Leach
Virginia Leach	[(*R. maximum* x *R. catawbiense*) x [*R. dichroanthum* x (*R. discolor* x *R. campylocarpum*)] x (*R. catawbiense* var. *album* x *R. dichroanthum* x *R. griersonianum*)]	David Leach

1972-AZALEAS

Name	Parentage	Hybridizer
Colossus	Selected form of *R. calendulaceum*	David Leach

1971-RHODODENDRONS

Name	Parentage	Hybridizer
Ananouri	Brittania x *R. discolor*	Howard Phipps
Arctic Pearl	selected form of *R. dauricum* (white form)	Warren Baldsiefen
Big Savage	(Catalgla x *R. fortunei*) x Cadis	Henry Yates
David Forsythe	*R. catawbiense compactum* x Mars	Samuel Baldanza
Dorothy Amateis	America x Purple Splendour	Amateis-Baldsiefen
Erchless	C.O.D. x Mrs. Furnival	Howard Phipps
Francesca	Brittania x 202 Dexter	Consolini-Savella
Henry R. Yates	*R. litiense* x ?	Joseph Gable
Joe Gable	Catalgla x *R. wardii*	Joseph Gable
Joe Kruson	Vulcan's Flame x Mars	Henry Yates
Madame Pompidou	?	Kordus
Maletta	(*R. auriculatum* x *R. discolor*) x (*R. ungernii* x ?)	Henry Yates
Mamie Dowd Eisenhower	?	Kordus
Mini-White	*R. maximum* x *R. chrysanthum*	B. C. Potter
Mrs. Howard Phipps	Seedling 45 ? x Naomi	Howard Phipps
Pink Punch	Catalgla x *R. fortunei*	Henry Yates
Prof. Louis Amateis	Everestianum x Van Nes Sensation	Amateis-Baldsiefen
Robert Forsythe	*R. catawbiense compactum* x Mars	Samuel Baldanza
Serendipity	*R. yakusimanum* x *R. chrysanthum*	B. C. Potter
Tiffany	Anna Baldsiefen x *R. keiskei*	Warren Baldsiefen

1970-RHODODENDRONS

Name	Parentage	Named by
Betty Arrington	Dexter hybrid	G. A. Arrington

1969-RHODODENDRONS

Name	Parentage	Hybridizer
Big Mac	*R. catawbiense* var. *album* Le Bars White x *R. macabeanum*	Mrs. John Knippenberg
Mirrelle Vernimb	Selected form of *R. hemitrichotum*	Bryan Vernimb

1969-AZALEAS

Name	Parentage	Hybridizer
Frostburg	Desiree x Rose Greeley	Henry Yates

1968-RHODODENDRONS

Name	Parentage	Hybridizer
April Blush	*R. carolinianum v. album* x *R. mucronulatum*	Guy Nearing
Cliff Garland	Bric-a-brac x *R. mucronulatum*, pink form	Guy Nearing
Cliff Spangle	Bric-a-brac x *R. mucronulatum*, pink form	Guy Nearing
Connie Stanton	Princess Elizabeth x Boule de Niege	Ernest Stanton
Edmond Amateis	*R. catawbiense* var. *album* x Dexter seedling (Hess)	Amateis-Leach
Lady Rae	*R. souliei* x Robert Allison	Gable-Andrews
Mountain Aura	Dorothea x Red Hybrid	Guy Nearing
Mountain Glow	Dorothea x Red Hybrid	Guy Nearing
Mountain Queen	Dorothea x Red Hybrid	Guy Nearing
Pink Parasol	Selected form of *R. yakusimanum* (# 59-2)	David Leach
Summer Snow	*R. maximum* x (*R. ungernii* x *R. auriculatum*) F_2	David Leach
Tom Koenig	(*R. racemosum* x *R. keiskei*) x *R. keiskei*	Guy Nearing
Tow Head	*R. carolinianum* var. *album* x *R. ludlowi*	David Leach

1968-AZALEAS

Name	Parentage	Hybridizer
Garda Joy	Gable's H-12 G Beni-Kirishima seedling	Gable-Griswold

1967-RHODODENDRONS

Name	Parentage	Hybridizer
Harold Amateis	*R. maximum* x *R. strigillosum*	Amateis-Baldsiefen

1966-RHODODENDRONS

Name	Parentage	Hybridizer
Blush Button	C.O.D. x Honeydew	John Knippenberg
Caroline Gem	Elizabeth x Caroline	John Knippenberg
Hardy Giant	*R. fortunei* x *R. fictolacteum*	John Knippenberg
Laurel Pink	Boule de Niege x *R. catawbiense* x F. C. Puddle	John Knippenberg
Wayne Pink	?	John Knippenberg

1966-AZALEAS

Name	Parentage	Hybridizer
Hino-Pink	(Hino-crimson x R. *poukhanense*) x (*R. kaempferi* seedling x Louise Gable)	Anthony Shammarello
Hino-red	(Hino-crimson x *R. poukhanense*) x (*R. kaempferi* seedling x James Gable)	Anthony Shammarello
Hino-White	(Hino-crimson x *R. poukhanense*) x Desiree	Anthony Shammarello
O-My-O	Hino-crimson x 528 Salmon Elf	Robert Pryor

1965-RHODODENDRONS

Name	Parentage	Hybridizer
Pale Perfection	?	Wyman
Swansdown	*R. catawbiense* var. *album* x Belle Heller	David Leach

1964-RHODODENDRONS

Name	Parentage	Hybridizer
Anna Baldsiefen	"Pioneer" selfed	Warren Baldsiefen
Anna Hall	*R. catawbiense* var. *album* x *R. yakusimanum*	David Leach
Blaze	Mars x *R. catawbiense* var. *rubrum*	David Leach
Chesterland	?	Pot-Leach
Ivory Tower	*R. catawbiense* var. *album* x (*R. wardii* x *R. fortunei*)	David Leach
Lodestar	*R. catawbiense* var. *album* x Belle Heller	David Leach
Mount Mitchell	*R. maximum* seedling from seed of red flowered *R. maximum*	Baldsiefen-Leach
President Kennedy	*R. maximum* x Pink Pearl	Richard Fenicchia
Rococo	Boule de Niege x *R. fortunei*	Gable-Leach
Serenata	Russell Harmon x [(*R. dichroanthum* x (*R. discolor* x *R. campylocarpum*)]	David Leach
Sphinx	?	Carl Luenenschloss

1964-AZALEAS

Name	Parentage	Hybridizer
June Bride	*R. arborescens* x *R. bakeri*	David Leach
Maid of Honor	*R. cumberlandense* x *R. arborescens*	David Leach
Maori	Ilam hybrid x Ilam hybrid	Yates-Leach
Ruth May	Pink Pearl x Indica Rosa	Oliver & Simson Nurseries
Spring Party	selected form of *R. vaseyi*	LaBar-Leach
Spring Salvo	Ilam hybrid xScarlet Salute x Red King	David Leach
Tang	Scarlet Salute x Red King	David Leach

1963-RHODODENDRONS

Name	Parentage	Hybridizer
Dark Eyes	Kettledrum x (*R. detonsum* x. *R. griersonianum*)	Guy Nearing
Elam	Chance seedling of Chesapeake	Guy Nearing
Elsmere	Chance seedling of Chesapeake	Guy Nearing
Lisa	Catalgla x Madonna	Joseph Gable
Macopin	Chance seedling of *R. racemosum*	Guy Nearing
Mary Belle (P.A.)	Atrier x Dechaem	Joseph Gable
Pink Frosting	*R. catawbiense* var. *album* Glass x *R. yakusimanum*	David Leach
Ramsey Tinsel	Chance seedling of Chesapeake	Guy Nearing

1963-AZALEAS

Name	Parentage	Hybridizer
El Capitan	Aladdin x hardy red R. Kurume seedling	Peter Girard
Kathy Ann	white seedling x white seedling	Peter Girard
Lavender Bouquet	*R. poukhanense* x hardy *R. poukhanense* seedling	Peter Girard
Pink Plush	(*R. bakeri* x *R. arborescens?*)	David Leach
Pink Ripples	Little Beauty x *R. poukhanense*	Peter Girard
Purple Robe	*R. poukhanense* x "Purple Triumph"	Peter Girard
Scarlet Glory	Aladdin x red seedling	Peter Girard
Villa	*R. poukhanense* x Kathleen	Peter Girard
White Princess	(hardy white R. Kurume seedling x *R. poukhanense*) x Orchid Lace	Peter Girard

1962-RHODODENDRONS

Name	Parentage	Hybridizer
Betty Hume	*R. fortunei* hybrid (Dexter)	Baldsiefen-Efinger
Edwin Beinecke	*R. fortunei* hybrid (Dexter)	Everitt-Beinecke
Limelight	*R. catawbiense* var. *album* Glass x (*R. wardii* x *R. fortunei*)	David Leach
Pink Flourish	*R. catawbiense* var. *album* Glass x (*R. decorum* x *R. griffithianum*) x red *R. catawbiense* hybrid	David Leach
Spring Parade	Red *R. catawbiense* hybrid seedling x Cunningham's White	Anthony Shammarello

1962-AZALEAS

Name	Parentage	Hybridizer
Canterbury	Flashbrick x Darkie	Yates & Leach
Chamois	*R. bakeri* x *R. arborescens*	David Leach
Coloratura	*R. bakeri* x *R. arborescens*	David Leach
Cream Puff	*R. bakeri* x *R. arborescens*	David Leach
Pink Puff	*R. bakeri* x *R. arborescens*	David Leach
Scarlet Salute	*R. cumberlandense*—selected form	David Leach

1961-AZALEAS. Not formally registered—listed in A.R.S. bulletin only

Name	Parentage	Hybridizer
Alpine	(*R. indica* x *R. kaempferi*) selfed	U.S. Dept. of Agriculture M. W. Parker
Casablanca	*R. indica* x Snow	"
Flash	Flash Mobile x Flame Sport	"
Flirtation	Maxwelli x Snow	"
Green Eyes	Kurume, Maxwelli and *R. indica* parentage (2 seedlings)	"
Northland	*R. kaempferi* hybrid x Snow	"
Sanguinaine	Pride of Mobile x Flame Sport	"
Shocking Pink	Kurume, Maxwelli and *R. indica* parentage (2 seedlings)	"
Whitecap	Indica Alba x Snow	"
Dwarf Azaleas		
Boutonniere	(Maxwelli x Snow) x (*R. kaempferi* x Snow)	"
Dainty Rose	(*R. kaempferi* x Snow) x sibling	"
Flower Girl	(*R. kaempferi* x Snow) x sibling	"
Lavender Elf	(Maxwelli x Snow) x (*R. kaempferi* x Snow)	"
Leprechaun	*R. kaempferi*, Kurume and *R. indica* parentage	"
Little White Lie	(*R. kaempferi* hybrid x Snow) x Firefly x sibling	"
Orchid Belle	(*R. kaempferi* hybrid x Snow) x Firefly x sibling	"
Pequeno	(*R. kaempferi* hybrid x Snow) x Firefly x sibling	"
Ping Pong	(Maxwelli x Snow) x (*R. kaempferi* x Snow)	"
Pink Elf	(Maxwelli x Snow) x (*R. kaempferi* x Snow)	"
Pinkette	Kurume, Maxwelli and *R. indica* parentage (2 seedlings)	"
Purple Cushion	(*R. kaempferi* x Snow) x sibling	"
Rose Elf	(Indica Alba x Snow) x Salmon Beauty	"
Salmon Elf	[(*R. kaempferi* x Snow) x Firefly)] x sibling	"
Snow Drop	(Maxwelli x Snow) x (*R. kaempferi* x Snow)	"
Snow Flurry	(Firefly x Snow) x (*R. kaempferi* x Snow)	"
White Doll	Kurume, Maxwelli and *R. indica* parentage (2 seedlings)	"
White Elf	Kurume, Maxwelli and *R. indica* parentage (2 seedlings)	"
White Squall	*R. kaempferi* hybrid x Snow	"

1960-RHODODENDRONS

Name	Parentage	Hybridizer
Annie Dalton (A.E.)	*R. decorum* x *R. griersonianum* x America	Joseph Gable
Beechwood Pink (A.E.)	Atrosanguineum x *R. fortunei*	Gable-Herbert
Betty Breene	*R. smirnowii* x Dexter hybrid	David Leach
Blaze	Mars x *R. catawbiense* var. *rubrum*	David Leach
Catalode (A.E.)	Catawbiense Album x Loderi	Joseph Gable
County of York	Syn. for "Catalode"	
David Gable (A.E.)	Atrosanguineum x *R. fortunei*	Joseph Gable
Duet	*R. catawbiense* var. *album* x (*R. dichroanthum* x *R. griffithianum*) x *R. auriculatum*	David Leach
Fanfare	Red *R. catawbiense* hybrid x red *R. catawbiense* hybrid	David Leach
Great Lakes (P.A.)	*R. catawbiense* var. *album* x *R. yakusimanum*	David Leach
Janet Blair	Dexter hybrid x ?	David Leach
Pink Flourish	*R. catawbiense* var. *album* x ((*R. decorum* x *R. griffithianum*) x red *R. catawbiense* hybrid)	David Leach
Powell Glass	5th generation *R. catawbiense* var. *album*	Edmond Amateis
Tahiti	(*R. maximum* x *R. catawbiense*) x (*R. dichroanthum* x (*R. discolor* x *R. campylocarpum*)	David Leach
Vernus	Red *R. catawbiense* hybrid x Cunningham's White	Shammarello-Leach

1960-AZALEAS

Name	Parentage	Hybridizer
Desiree (P.A.)	*R. poukhanense* x Ledifolia Alba	Anthony Shammarello
Tang	*R. bakeri* x Red King	David Leach

1959-RHODODENDRONS

Name	Parentage	Hybridizer
Catanea	Clone of *R. catawbiense* var. *album*	Gable-Nearing
LaBar's White	Clone of *R. catawbiense* var. *album* (from West Va.)	LaBar's Nursery
Mary Fleming	(*R. racemosum* x *R. keiskei*) x *keiskei*	Guy Nearing

Rhododendron and Azalea Hybridizers in the eastern United States and Canada —1975

Listed by Climatic Zone.

Zone 4 (−30° to −20°F.)

Dean Barber, Rt. 1, Contoocook, New Hampshire 03229

Zone 5 (−20° to −10°F.)

Anthony Angelini, 87 Alvord Park Road, Torrington, Connecticut 06790

J. Brueckner, M.D., Regional Labor, Castle Street, Saint John, New Brunswick, Canada E2L 3B8

L. C. Case, 14 Lockeland Road, Winchester, Massachusetts 01890

John C. Cowles, 745 Washington Street, Wellesley, Massachusetts 02181

D. L. Craig, Head, Research Station, Kentville, Nova Scotia B4N 1J5

Zone 5 (cont.)

Weldon E. Delp, Box 434, Harrisville, Pennsylvania 16038

H. Lincoln Foster, Falls Village, Connecticut 06031

Leslie Hancock, 2151 Camilla Road, Mississauga, Ontario, Canada L5A 2K1

D. L. Hinerman, M.D., 6800 Scio Church Road, Ann Arbor, Michigan 48103

David G. Leach, 1894 Hubbard Road, North Madison, OH 44057

Edmund Mezitt, Weston Nurseries, East Main Street, Hopkinton, Mass. 01748

Walter Ostrom, Box 14, Site 28, Tanfallon, Nova Scotia, Canada

Donald W. Paden, 2112 South Race Street, Urbana, Illinois 61801

Newton W. Robinson, 34 Sayles Street, Alfred, New York 14802

Eugene A. Skonieczny, 100 Church Street, Kensington, Connecticut 06037

Lloyd C. Spear, 8 Chestnut Hill South, Loudonville, New York 12211

Captain R. M. Steele, Bayport, Rose Bay R. R. 1, Lunenburg Co., Nova Scotia, Canada

Mrs. Phillip E. Taylor, 10 Hillside Circle, Storrs, Connecticut 06268

W. L. Tolstead, Davis & Elkins College, Elkins, West Virginia 26241

Walter F. Winkler, Cundys Harbor, R.D.2, Brunswick, Maine 04011

James E. Wright, 156 Doty Street, Waltham, Massachusetts 02154

Zone 6 (−10° to 0°F.)

Edmond Amateis, 1620 Fifth Street, Clermont, Florida 32711 (formerly Brewster, New York)

Samuel Baldanza (deceased), Benton Harbor, Michigan

Warren Baldsiefen (deceased)—Bob Otterbien, Box 88, Bellvale, New York 10912

Walter J. Blyskal, 102 Hempstead Road, Spring Valley, New York 10977

Emil V. Bohnel, 245 North Lincoln Street, Pearl River, New York 10965

Ernest K. Egan, 40 Pease Road, Woodbridge, New Haven, Connecticut 06525

Gordon Emerson, 1850 Rt. 45, Rock Creek, Ohio 44084

William M. Fetterhoff, 5279 Richland Road, Gibsonia, Pennsylvania 15044

Robert D. Gartrell, 754 Birchwood Drive, Wyckoff, New Jersey 07481

Henry Heyderhoff, 348 Glenwild Avenue, Bloomingdale, New Jersey 07403

Mrs. John F. Knippenberg, 736 Pines Lake Drive West, Wayne, New Jersey 07470

Gustav A. L. Mehlquist, The University of Connecticut, Storrs, Connecticut 06268

George T. Miller, Lark Avenue, Hanover, Pennsylvania 17331

B. C. Potter, 167 Lampman Avenue, Port Ewen, New York 12466

Orlando S. Pride, 523 Fifth Street, Butler, Pennsylvania 16001

Otto Prycl, R. D. 1, New Stanton, Pennsylvania 15672

Michael R. Rachinsky, 21 Ludvigh Road, Nanuet, New York 10954

W. A. Reese, M.D., 579 Main Street, Pennsburg, Pennsylvania 18073

T. L. Ring, R. D. 3, Box 16, Bellaire, Ohio 43906

A. F. Serbin, M.D., 365 Simsbury Road, Bloomfield, Connecticut 06002

Robert G. Shanklin, Hillwood Road, Old Lyme, Connecticut 06371

W. David Smith, Box 123, R.D.3, Spring Grove, Pennsylvania

Dorothy G. Swift, P.O. Box 213, 164 Fleetwood Drive, Saunderstown, R. I. 02879

Robert P. Stockmal, 371 Leavenworth Road, Shelton, Connecticut 16484

Bryan Vernimb, R.D. 2, Box 250, Howell, New Jersey 07731

Bishop von Wettberg, 53 Quaker Farms Road, Oxford, Connecticut 06483

Gunther H. Winkler, 2 Converse Road, Bolton, Connecticut 06040

Harry L. Wise, 1830 Loudon Heights Road, Charleston, West Virginia 25314

Henry Yates (deceased), Frostburg, Maryland

Leon Yavorsky, R.D. 2, Bennett Road, Freehold, New Jersey 17728

Zone 7 (0° to 10°F.)

E. Reid Bahnson, 2725 Windsor Road, Winston Salem, North Carolina 27104

M. E. Byrkit, M.D., 28 West Potomac, Williamsport, Maryland 21795

Robert R. Emmerich, 11 Hildreth Avenue, Huntington, New York 11743

Robert A. Furman, 148 Willow Street, Garden City, New York 11530

Col. and Mrs. R. H. Goodrich, 10015 Saddle Road, Vienna, Virginia 22180

Charles R. & Velma Haag, Rt. 1, Box 89, Brevard, North Carolina 28712

Donald Hardgrove, (deceased)

Judson Hardy, 9006 3rd Avenue, Silver Spring, Maryland 20910

Charles Herbert, 1601 Country Club Road, Phoenixville, Pennsylvania 19460

Leon Heuser, Robbinsville, New Jersey 08691

Louisa B. Hill (Polly), 1106 Greenhill Avenue, Wilmington, Delaware 19805

Dr. E. A. Hollowell, 24 Acacia, Scientists Cliffs, Port Republic, Maryland 20676 (deceased 1977)

Donald W. Hyatt, 1948 Lorraine Avenue, McLean, Virginia 22101

August E. Kehr, 10202 Green Forest Drive, Silver Spring, Maryland 20903

G. David Lewis, Ph.D., 52 Glenwood Road, R.D.#1, Colts Neck, New Jersey 07722

Wallace C. Marley, 418 South Main Street, Waynesville, North Carolina 28786

Alfred S. Martin, 8106 Lincoln Drive, Philadelphia, Pennsylvania 19118

Howard W. Mason, RFD #3, Cedar Lane, Huntington, New York 11743

Elmer J. Morris, 2353 Hwy. #34, Wall, New Jersey 08736

Richard Murcott, Linden Lane, East Norwich, New York 11732

Robert L. Pryor, U.S. National Arboretum, Washington, D.C.

D. C. Purdy, 8 Mannetto Hill Road, Huntington, New York 11743

Alfred Raustein, 230 Union Avenue, Holbrook, L.I., New York 11741

G. Albert Reid, Box 243, Blackman Road, Linwood, New Jersey 08221

Harold E. Reiley, Rt. 1, Woodsboro, Maryland 21798

George W. Ring, 11400 Valley Road, Fairfax, Virginia 22030

Jacob Rosenthal, 86-52 Pinto Street, Holliswoods, New York 11423

Daniel H. Rumple, Jr., Rt. 4, Box 501, Kannapolis, North Carolina 28081

Benjamin & Marion Shapiro, 64 North Drive, East Brunswick, New Jersey 08816

Jonathan Shaw, Box 123, Sandwich, Massachusetts 02563

Henry T. Skinner, 2817 Bosworth Lane, Bowie, Maryland 20715

James R. Todd, Jr., Deerfield, Tremont Park, Lenoir, North Carolina 28645

David E. Wagner, 14701 Blackburn Road, Burtonsville, Maryland 20703

James S. Wells Nursery, Inc., 474 Nut Swamp Road, Red Bank, New Jersey 07701

Franklin H. West, M.D., 1045 Waverly Road, Gladwyne, Pennsylvania 19035

John C. Wister, 735 Harvard Avenue, Swarthmore, Pennsylvania 19081

Ernest H. Yelton, Rutherfordton, North Carolina 28139

Victor Yuskus, 21 Matinecdek Avenue, East Islip, New York 11730

Zone 8 (10° to 20°F.)

S. Chris Early, 4341 Harris Valley Road, Atlanta, Georgia 30327

Fred C. Galle, Callaway Gardens, Pine Mt., Georgia 31822

Larry Nixon, 1001 Athens Drive, Raleigh, North Carolina 27606

Ralphe W. Pennington, 3125 Rebecca Street, Covington, Georgia 30029

Zone 9 (20° to 30°F.)

Hugh A. Caldwell, Jr., 187 Brickyard, Doctor's Inlet, Florida 32030

W. E. Hamm, P.O. Box 966, High Springs, Florida 32643

Note: Dexter, Gable, Nearing, Morrison, and Shammarello are not included in the above listing since each is covered in a previous chapter.

Contemporaries and Their Work

EDMOND AMATEIS

No longer actively hybridizing, Edmond Amateis (a noted sculptor) nevertheless has developed some of the most unusual and attractive rhododendron hybrids suitable for commercial production. When in Brewster, New York, a frost pocket in Zone 6a, he successfully crossed many tender Asiatic species with hardier American natives and ironclads. In 1958, he received first prize at the International Flower Show in New York for Dora Amateis, a cross of (*R. carolinianum* × *R. ciliatum*). Other noteworthy selections include Louis Amateis (*R. carolinianum* × *R. bullatum*); Mildred Amateis (*R. carolinianum* × *R. edgeworthii*); Harold Amateis (*R. maximum* × *R. strigillosum*) and Nodding Bells (America × (*R. forrestii* var. *repens* × *griersonianum*)). In addition to his contributions of new plant material, Mr. Amateis is especially recognized for his illustrations in RHODODENDRONS OF THE WORLD by David Leach.

MAX E. BYRKIT

An avid hybridizer since 1967, Max Byrkit (with the help of his sons) raises about 2,500 seedlings anually and is now beginning to select new and better elepidote rhododendrons for his area—south of Hagerstown, Maryland. "Millard Kepner", a cross of (Decatros × *R. yakusimanum*) which is fragrant, has been registered. Just recently, he developed what is apparently a tetraploid form of *R. fortunei* from seeds treated with colchicine. The flower texture of this new form has exceptional substance. He is especially looking for luminosity in flowers, indumented foliage, and yellow and orange tones.

WELDON DELP

Weldon Eugene Delp began hybridizing rhododendrons in 1949 in Harrisville, Pa., where it is not unusual for winter temperatures to go below −25°F. His main objective is to combine the desirable traits of Asiatic species with hardier plants in order to improve the character of cultivars suitable for cold areas in the United States. To assure a supply of pollen of the more tender exotic types, and also to enjoy their plant and flower character, Mr. Delp has constructed a 40′ diameter geodesic dome of wood and fiberglass in which he protects from 250 to 300 varieties of rhododendrons, including species such as *R. edgeworthii* and *R. fictolacteum*. In addition to hardiness, he is striving to develop plants having flowers with full double florets. He grows over 5,000 seedlings annually, representing as many as 200 crosses. His interests range from deciduous azaleas to lepidote and elepidote rhododendrons. He often uses a super hardy form of *R. carolinianum* selected for his breeding program. Only a few seedlings have been named, although there are hundreds selected for further observation. "Christina", with white flowers tinted orchid and with a yellow eye, is reported to be one of his most outstanding cultivars. Christina (plate 94), is a hybrid of Catalgla × Mrs. W.C. Slocock.

S. CHRIS EARLY

Working since 1961 with azaleas and elepidote rhododendrons in Atlanta, Ga., Mr. Early's breeding goals have been to develop late summer and fall blooming native azalea hybrids, later blooming evergreen azaleas and heat-tolerant elepidotes. In the evergreen azaleas, parentage includes Belgians, Satsukis, Treasure and *R. kaempferi*. Gable's Caroline and *R. griersonianum* hybrids are being used to develop more heat-tolerant elepidotes. Some of his native azalea hybrids are fragrant. Mrs. L. J. Comer and Alfred H. Holbrook are two named evergreen azaleas.

ERNEST EGAN

Mr. Egan has been raising up to 7,000 seedlings per year since 1963. He is especially interested in resistance to insects and disease, as well as fragrance. Only two hybrids have been named, "Olive Egan", an unusual cross of Pioneer × Lady Alice Fitzwilliams which is slightly fragrant, and "W. W. McCartney", an Az. Maxwelli seedling with linear leaves and petals. In the author's opinion, more hybridizing effort is needed in the area tentatively explored by Mr. Egan in his "Olive Egan."

WILLIAM FETTERHOFF

Crossing the ironclads with cultivars having better flowers and plant habit, Mr. Fetterhoff has been able to select 12 or more new rhododendrons showing improvements over the limited number previously growable in his −20 to −25°F winter temperatures in western Pennsylvania. Raising from 1000 to 5000 seedlings per year beginning in 1960, he notes that he loses most of them before they become mature enough to flower. From those remaining, he now has a *R. maximum* × *R. wardii* of light yellow color and compact plant habit, an Atrosanguineum × Medusa, a pinkish orange color; and a white-flowered clone with yellow blotch, which he obtained from the cross Mrs. J. G. Millais × La Bar's White *catawbiense*. This last took Best-in-Show at the 1972 Great Lakes Chapter meeting. He recommends further hybridizing with lepidotes because of their desirable small stature.

H. LINCOLN FOSTER

Long known as a rock garden enthusiast, "Linc" began hybridizing rhododendrons in 1965, growing from 300 to 500 seedlings a year. Because of his location in Falls Village, Connecticut, his selected plants have a high resistance to low winter temperatures (−20°F.). Early efforts were with elepidotes. More recently he has directed his hybridizing toward small-leaved lepidotes suitable for the rock garden. Seven cultivars have been named but not yet registered. Two of them, "Foxfire" and "Millstream Maiden" are from the cross *R. smirnowii* × *R. baematodes*. "Timmy Foster" is a peach-colored cultivar of *R. racemosum* × *R. keiskei*. An unnamed seedling of *R. pemakoense* × Rose Elf is compact with a large flower.

FRED C. GALLE

As curator for the Callaway Gardens, Pine Mountain, Georgia, Mr. Galle has been making intraspecific crosses of native deciduous azaleas since 1954 in an effort to develop new color forms which are heat resistant and easy to root. He is also interested in developing elepidote rhododendrons adaptable to southern conditions. A number of the intraspecific hybrids have been selected for further observation and are being carried under number only. Parentage includes *R. arborescens, prunifolium, alabamense, calendulaceum, narcissaflora, speciosum, austrinum, atlanticum* and Hugo Koster. Some cultivars are fragrant.

ROBERT D. GARTRELL

By 1965—after 25 years' labor—Robert Gartrell had made over 1,000 evergreen azalea crosses and raised some 25,000 seedlings in Wyckoff, New Jersey. During his hybridizing, he has gradually identified clonal forms imparting a large degree of hardiness to their

offspring and eventually used these in combination with many of those classed as Satsukis. The resulting seedlings have had a high percentage of hardy, attractively flowered plants. From these, over 200 have been selected for further observation, and most have been distributed to 18 growers and nurserymen in the eastern U.S., as well as in New Zealand, Switzerland, and Australia. Many of these new plants, called Robin Hill Azaleas, have large, heavy-textured flowers. Parentage of many of the most successful crosses include Louise Gable, Oakland, Glacier, Heiwa, Eikan, Shinnyo-No-Tsuki, Tamagiku and others. Mr. Gartrell's selection of his five best include "Nancy of Robin Hill," "Betty Ann Voss," "White Moon," "Redmond," and "Welmet." Many other cultivars are just as desirable.

PETER E. GIRARD

A long-time nurseryman whose operation extends east of Cleveland along Lake Erie, Girard has developed some very fine evergreen azaleas with brilliant colors, especially in the red spectrum. A number have been registered, such as Girard's Hotshot, Girard's Scarlet, and Pleasant White, the last a lower growing form. His deciduous azalea creations are excellent. Some are hybrids of "Homebush" and therefore have well formed truss configurations in a wide range of colors. All of his hybrids are quite hardy. Most can stand −15°F and some exceed this; all were selected for aesthetically pleasing flowers.

COL. AND MRS. R. H. GOODRICH

Although beginning as recently as 1968 in Vienna, Virginia, the Goodrichs have been blooming plants in just 3 years from seed because of superior treatment of seedlings. They raise about 1,000 seedlings a year, and are looking for, among other characteristics, late bloom, heat resistance and attractive flowers. *R. maximum* is being used for lateness of bloom, and many difficulties normally associated with hybridizing with *R.*

maximum have been overcome by Ray Goodrich through study and observation. The Goodrichs are also charter members of the Gable Study Group, and have accumulated a wide knowledge of both the man and his plants. Some of their seedlings which are promising include a superb white, a cross by A. Kehr of Scintillation and *R. metternichii,* Mrs. A. T. de la Mare × Madfort (Miller cross), and Disca × Autumn Gold, this last a group cross, nicknamed DAUG, ranging in color from pale yellowish buff to apricot. Wheatley × *crinigerum* (plate 106) is a 1969 hybrid raised from G. Ring's seed. Scintillation × Yak Exbury (plate, 104) is a Todd cross from the A.R.S. seed exchange in 1969 (A.R.S. #469).

CHARLES AND VELMA HAAG

Long admirers of Joseph Gable and other hybridizers, the Haags began hybridizing in 1958 in New Jersey, growing up to 1,500 to 2,000 seedlings per year. After getting the Union County Rhododendron Display Garden underway, the Haags moved to a mountain aery near Brevard, North Carolina, a few years ago taking a great number of their rhododendrons with them. Those plants which became acclimated are now growing in partially cleared woodland. Gable and Dexter hybrids, as well as other hybridizers' cultivars are well represented along with their own. About 35 Haag cultivars have been selected from over 6,000 mature seedlings, with 6 or 8 considered worthy of naming and registration.

DONALD HARDGROVE

No longer active in hybridizing rhododendrons, Don Hardgrove began in 1945, taking full advantage of work by previous hybridizers, especially Gable and Nearing. Using the hardiest and best forms for parents then available, he kept excellent records on the performance of his seedlings, and by 1964 was able to write a paper outlining his successes and failures. This paper provided sound advice to prospective hybridizers, making plain the great depth of study he had put into achieving

new plants through carefully planned crosses. Some of his best hybrids resulted from crossing a hardy form of *R. fortunei,* from Nearing-Gable, with other hybrids and species having yellow genes. Golden Star, Painted Star, Glow Lite, Donna Hardgrove, Anne Hardgrove, and others are available (Tom Burns, L.I.) and make exciting additions even to the most complete gardens.

JUDSON HARDY

Judson Hardy's major objectives have been to develop deciduous azaleas resistant to powdery mildew. Beginning in 1956 in Silver Spring, Maryland, he has grown a large population of Knaphill seedlings, plus 30 cultivars, from which he has selected a total of about 25 forms that have a strong resistance to both mildew and insect damage. After crossing a large number of native azaleas with these cultivars, he has found that *R. bakeri* × Royal Lodge and *R. bakeri* × Medford Red seedlings have the best resistance to mildew and insects of any he has tried. Mr. Hardy is also working to develop truly miniature evergreen azaleas, using dwarf forms of *R. indicum, R. kiusianum* and *R. serpyllifolium.* His Knaphill #10, #12, and #20 are mildew resistant and fragrant.

CHARLES HERBERT

"Charlie" has been hybridizing in Phoenixville, Pennsylvania since 1945 on a limited scale, often using Joseph Gable's seedlings and cultivars as parents. In fact, he was a regular visitor to the Gable nursery, and as the story goes, often placed a rock on a low hanging branch of plants at Gable's that he admired. The next year he would then find "layers" of the best Gable cultivars which would otherwise have been unobtainable. Herbert has registered 18 cultivars and named many more. His five best are listed as Gary Herbert, Mt. Joy, Anthony Wayne, Terry Herbert and Pikeland. More recently he has concentrated on smaller plants, including lepidotes and *R. yakusimanum* hybrids.

MARY LOUISA B. HILL (POLLY HILL)

In 1957, "Polly" Hill began importing seeds of evergreen azaleas from Dr. Tsuneshige Rokujo in Japan, particularly of low growing types. The hybridizing by Rokujo, and growing and selection by Louisa B. Hill has been a happy combination. Many of the crosses involved the low growing species, *R. Nakaharai* with a Satsuki, while others were chiefly crosses to two Satsuki azaleas. By growing these seedlings, considerable progress has been made toward Polly's goal of prostrate evergreen azaleas with clear colors and hardiness in Zone 6. Ten have been registered and several others named. She considers Joseph Hill, Michael Hill, Pink Pancake, Alexander, and Louisa some of her best, with Alexander the most hardy. Her hybrids are available from the Bovees, Carlson's Gardens, and the Don Smiths.

E. A. HOLLOWELL

After he retired to Scientists Cliff, Port Republic, Maryland, E. A. Hollowell encouraged neighbors to make extensive plantings of rhododendrons and azaleas. The community maintains a complete collection of the Beltsville dwarf hybrids (evergreen azaleas), while Hollowell had a large collection of unnamed Glenn Dale and other azaleas from those which were replaced by quinine plants during World War II, at the Agricultural Experiment Station, Beltsville, Maryland. Primarily interested in developing a buttercup yellow elepidote rhododendron, he began hybridizing in 1947. Other interests included deciduous azaleas of which he selected and named at least four. One of his selections of *R. kaempferi,* named Dorsett, blooms during the winter each time temperatures rise enough to break dormancy.

AUGUST E. KEHR

Staff scientist in the U.S. Department of Agriculture, Dr. Kehr has been hybridizing rhododendrons and azaleas since 1961. He is especially interested in the development of a yellow evergreen azalea, double flowers and low growing types. In elepidotes, he is looking for disease resistance, dwarf hardy reds and yellows. A particular goal is a large flowered deep red deciduous azalea. Dr. Kehr has registered a fully double white azalea (White Rosebud) and a colchicine induced tetraploid form of *R. carolinianum* (Epoch). At this writing, he is president of the American Rhododendron Society. Under his leadership, a Breeders Roundtable has been an important part of the last four annual meetings, and a number of research projects have been sponsored by the A.R.S.

MRS. JOHN F. KNIPPENBERG

Mrs. Knippenberg began hybridizing rhododendrons in 1955 and continues to strive for plants with new interests and improvements, such as hardy large-leaved sorts, with indumentum if possible, more flower substance and later blooming periods. Five hybrids, including Laurel Pink and Big Mac, have been registered, while more than 25 others have been named while they continue under observation. Hardy Giant, a cross of *R. fortunei* × *R. fictolacteum; R. yakusimanum* × Sir Charles Lemon; La Bars White; *R. catawbiense* × Kluis Sensation are among those identified as their best.

Hardy Giant (plate, 107) is a *R. fortunei* x *R. fictolacteum* cross by D. Hardgrove in 1952; raised by Mrs. Knippenberg. Flowers are creamy white, with a raspberry blotch; plant grows upright, 7'x7'; blooms early May.

The Knippenbergs operate two nurseries, one in Wayne, New Jersey and a second on the Virginia eastern shore. Laurel Pink is also available from the Baldsiefen Nursery in Bellevale, N.Y.

DAVID GOHEEN LEACH

Dave Leach is often referred to as a hybridizer's hybridizer, with a major objective of producing hardy new cultivars for the Northeastern United States. He is trying to grow plants with the same range of flower colors, flower sizes, stature, growth habit, and foliage textures, seasons of bloom, etc., as found in those normally only adaptable to growing conditions in the United Kingdom and the West Coast of the United States. Since beginning in 1942, Leach has registered 67 new hybrids and has 24 more named but not yet registered. His earlier selections were made at Brookville, Pa., the "icebox" of the northeast. At present, he is continuing to grow and select improved plants in North Madison, Ohio, where conditions still provide a severe test. His nominations for his own best hybrids include "Nuance," "Party Pink," "Robin Leach," "Sumatra," and "Bermuda," all elepidotes. Nuance (plate, 99), defies accurate photo reproduction. A cross of (*catawbiense var. album x (neriiflorum x dichroanthum) x discolor*)). It has a full truss, dark buds. The flowers age through shades of pink with orange yellow, and it has dense plant habit with bud hardiness to −18°F and is very floriferous. Sumatra (plate, 98), (America x (*forestii var. repens* x Prometheus) is a dense, semi dwarf, scarlet early season bloom. A 1956 seedling, it is bud hardy to −15°F, and will be introduced in 1978. In addition, he has selected several noteworthy Ilam azalea hybrids, including Tang, a brilliant orangish red. Leach has authored numerous articles on rhododendrons and azaleas, and is noted for his RHODODENDRONS OF THE WORLD, the comprehensive book for everyone from the beginning collector to the advanced hybridizer. He is past president of the American Horticultural Society and was instrumental in obtaining a bequest which enabled the establishment of a permanent headquarters for the A.H.S. near Mt. Vernon, Virginia.

GUSTAVE A. L. MEHLQUIST

A backyard project in 1957, Gustave Mehlquist's rhododendron hybridizing quickly outgrew the available space until eventually the University of Connecticut allocated field space on a cold, windy hill for the plantings. Presently there are about 40,000 blooming size plants and an equal number of smaller seedlings to be evaluated. As a source of the cold-hardiness needed in southern New England, Mehlquist has used white forms of *R. catawbiense*, *R. smirnowii*, and *R. yakusimanum*. Many desirable hybrids have resulted from using Vulcan and some ironclads with these species. He has also used *R. mucronulatum*, pink extensively. No cultivars have as yet been named. At any meeting of rhododendron hybridizers, "Gus" is able to explain in simple genetic terms, why unexpected results ofter occur when two rhododendrons are crossed. He is also an expert in orchids, delphinium, and dianthus. In 1975, he received the A.R.S. Gold Medal for his guidance, enthusiasm, and above all, his abundant generosity. In the next few years, the world can expect to see real advances in rhododendrons from Dr. Mehlquist's planned breeding program and careful evaluation methods.

EDMUND V. MEZITT

The Weston Nurseries, Inc., in Hopkinton, Massachusetts, is one of the few commercial nurseries which hybridize and grow rhododendron seedlings in addition to their normal production of time-tested ironclads and many other types of plant material. The practice, started by Peter J. Mezitt and continued by his son, has resulted in the selection of a number of outstanding lepidote hybrids from thousands of seedlings lined out on part of the 350 acres of rocky slopes. P.J.M., a cross of *R. carolinianum* x *R. dauricum v. sempervirens* named after Peter J. Mezitt, is probably the best known, and several forms are in cultivation, most of a rosy-lavender color. P.J.M. cultivar "Elite" is probably the pinkest form. Other notable plants include Balta (*R. carolinianum* v. *alba* x P.J.M.); Vallya and Llenroc (*R. carolinianum* v. *alba* x Cornell Pink) and Olga, (a pink *R. dauricum-mucronulatum* hybrid x *R. minus*). Royal Pillow (plate 97) is an azalea hybrid (*R. poukhanense* x Vuyk's Rose Red) with vivid reddish purple, heavily textured petals. It grows as a low mound. Hybridizing continues and many seedlings are still under observation. The nursery also grows many seedling forms of *R. carolinianum* and kalmia which can be selected for flower color and plant character in the spring.

GEORGE T. MILLER

Greatly influenced by his proximity to Joseph Gable, George Miller in Hanover, Pennsylvania, began hybridizing in 1963 to develop the perfect yellow rhododendron having indumented foliage. Many of his primary crosses have been aimed at developing good, hardy yellows to use in subsequent breeding. A number of seedlings have fulfilled this first need notably Brookville x Mary Garrison, Goldfort x Mariloo, Goldfort x Ivisa Pekin, and others. Miller contends that Dexters make good parents for eastern hybrids. *Scintillation x Avalanche* (plate 95) is a cross made in 1967 by Jim Todd of North Carolina. It is hardy to 0°F. has large flowers and leaves, truss full and does not hold well in shows. Foliage is wind resistant, flowers have good fragrance, plant is 3' high and 4' across, and is open growing. He is also interested in large-leaved hybrids hardy enough for his area. To take full advantage of the pioneer work by Joseph Gable, George has assembled an extensive collection of the best Gable hybrids and has used many of them to develop new, and sometimes better, cultivars.

RICHARD MURCOTT

Richard Murcott is very active in the rhododendron society and arranged for the Breeder's Roundtable at the A.R.S. 1976 Annual Meeting at Valley Forge. Since 1964, he has been raising up to 500 seedlings a year, often building on Don Hardgrove's previous work. He is especially interested in trying to obtain *R. boothii* and *R. maddenii* hybrids hardy on Long Island. Other objectives include the development of densely clothed, indumented, hardy red flowered cultivars. Selected hybrids are based on Scintillation,

Meadowbrook, Temple Bells, [(*R. dichroanthum x R. wardii*) x *R. fortunei*], and other parentage.

RALPH W. PENNINGTON

Primarily interested in evergreen azaleas, Ralph Pennington has used the Glenn Dale and Satsuki races to improve the flowers and plant habit. Some of his cultivars are fragrant, and work on further developing this desirable trait is being carried forward by Bruce Hancock, Social Circle, Georgia. Ralph W. Pennington died suddenly in 1976; however, many of his cultivars are available from Mr. Hancock. Pennington's choices for his best include Beth Bullard, Nancy Bullard, K.J.P., Anne Perry, and Mike Perry. All are apparently hardy to Zone 6 even though developed in Georgia.

BASIL POTTER

In one of the colder sections of the Northeast, Basil Potter began hybridizing in 1962 to create several strains of dwarf and semi-dwarf elepidote rhododendrons hardy at his home in Port Ewen, New York. One of two hybrids registered is named Serendipity, a cross of *R. yakusimanum* x *R. chrysanthum*. He is growing a large collection of *R. chrysanthum* from three seed sources collected in China and Japan and reports that the degree of compactness is highly variable. Blooming times vary from late April to July 10. He likes those forms best which have been grown from seed provided by K. Wada.

ORLANDO S. PRIDE

A general nurseryman in the cold, cold regions of western Pennsylvania, Orlando Pride's first love has always been rhododendrons and azaleas. Another hybridizer who obtained much help from Joseph Gable, Pride has been growing up to 20,000 seedlings a year since 1928, the more vigorous always lined out in open fields to "take the test" of −25°F. Many of the seedlings were sold as specimen plants; however, a few were retained for further observation. A significant accomplishment of Pride's has been the development of a hardier race of persistent-leaved evergreen azaleas grown from crosses of seedlings obtained from Mr. Gable. About 20 of these have been named and are only now being recognized for their potential in extending the range of evergreen azaleas to much colder regions than any previously experienced. Mr. Pride also has developed a race of deciduous azaleas, largely based on the red parent, J. J. Jennings. Many of these do not set seed and as a result, maintain their vigor and floriferousness year after year. Of his many elepidote hybrids, Edith, Blondie, Pink Mango, Red Brace and Roman Candle are some of his best. "Lanny," as he is affectionately called by his friends, has also evaluated many hybrids for David Leach, who respects his opinion highly. Recently, Pride has reduced his hybridizing and is concentrating on propagating cultivars selected over the years. Hybrids illustrated include: Pink Icing, (plate 102) (*R. catawbiense* x County of York); Redder Yet, (plate 101) unknown parentage, one probably America—a Leach-Pride; Sunburst (plate 100) parentage (Nereid x *R. discolor*) x (*R. catawbiense* x *R. maximum*) also a Leach-Pride.

OTTO PRYCL

Another of the "ice-box" hybridizers, Otto Prycl has been growing and selecting rhododendrons in New Stanton, Pennsylvania, since 1962. Three cultivars have been named: Anna Lise, Doc Tolstead, and Tree Plant, the last name an interesting and descriptive name of a rhododendron of unknown parentage. Prycl's hybrids generally include *R. fortunei*, *R. smirnowii*, *R. catawbiense* and some Gable cultivars for hardiness.

ROBERT LEE PRYOR

Beginning in 1936, Robert Pryor worked with Guy Yerkes at the Agricultural Experiment Station in Beltsville, Maryland. One of their goals was to develop a yellow flowered, evergreen azalea. This goal has not yet been attained, but many other useful cultivars,

including a race of dwarf azaleas, have been produced in their breeding program. These dwarfs and other cultivars were released in the 1960s to nurserymen who took little note of their importance. In these days of smaller yards and gardens, there has been a new interest in slower growing, more compact cultivars and a few nurserymen are now beginning to propagate them. Many of the crosses were with the azalea Snow, *R. kaempferi* and Maxwelli. Others, not dwarf, which have proved themselves are Eureka, Polar Bear, H. H. Hume, and Guy Yerkes. Only one, named O-My-O, a cross of Hino Crimson and Salmon Elf (spinel red), has been registered. Just recently, seven new evergreen azaleas, induced tetraploids using colchicine, were released to nurserymen primarily for the forcing trade.

ALFRED RAUSTEIN

Another long-time hybridizer, Alfred Raustein began his work in 1960, on Long Island, to develop better rhododendrons for his area, with an emphasis on early blooming reds. Three cultivars have been named, Clara Raustein, Mrs. Betty Hager, and Katja. R. Clara Raustein (plate, 96), is a hybrid of (*R. decorum* x *R. discolor*) x early Gable hybrid) x (*R. wardii* x *R. dichroanthum* x *R. fortunei*). About 35 other selections are under observation but have not been named.

G. ALBERT REID

Chief propagator for Fischer Greenhouses in Linwood, New Jersey, from 1953 to 1967, G. Albert Reid worked with Charles Fischer, Jr., to develop hardy forcing evergreen azaleas comparable to those in the trade which needed winter protection. In 1967, Fischer kept the Linwood varieties best suited to the commercial florists' needs while Al Reid has continued to concentrate on plants better suited to outdoor planting. Colors of selected plants range from lavender through white to salmon and red. Many have double or partially double flowers and most are characterized by heavy textured, long lasting flowers. About 20 cultivars have been named, others are still under observation. These "Linwood Hardies" were the hit of the show at the 1976 Annual Meeting of the A.R.S. held at Valley Forge, Pennsylvania. According to Al, his best are Linwood Lustre, Linwood Pink Giant, Linwood Blush, Linwood Salmon, and Opal. These and other plants are available in 3- and 4-year sizes each spring at the Reid Nursery in Linwood, New Jersey.

GEORGE W. RING

From about 1964, August Kehr and George T. Miller were instrumental in generating and sustaining George W. Ring's interest because of the early seedlings that were the result of their plant crosses. In a few years, Ring was making his own crosses and growing up to 2,000 seedlings annually in Fairfax, Virginia. Those of his plants with vigorous root systems have given the best performance. Parentage includes Ironclads, Gables, Dexters, West Coast hybrids, and species. Most successful crosses have been those using Gable's Caroline and Cadis; *R. fortunei,* and *mucronulatum.* Both evergreen and deciduous azaleas have also been included in the breeding program. No cultivars have been named, although several have been selected for further testing.

A. F. SERBIN

Some years ago, A. F. Serbin made a special trip to the island of Yakushima off southern Japan to collect seeds of the rhododendron *R. yakusimanum.* Since then, he has made over 400 crosses involving *R. yakusimanum* as one parent. More recently, he has been using *R. chrysanthum,* another species native to Japan (the northernmost part) for early branching, early flowering, and dwarfing capabilities. With special cold pits, Serbin maintains one of the most comprehensive species collections in the northeastern United States. For a number of years he has also had a large collection of Exbury and Knaphill

deciduous azaleas. Although he has raised an average of 1,000 seedlings a year since 1959, Serbin has named only two. He believes in thorough testing before registering new hybrids.

BENJAMIN AND MARION SHAPIRO

The Shapiros are no longer active in hybridizing but have selected a number of seedlings from their work which began in 1958 in East Brunswick, New Jersey. Named cultivars are Sparkler, Wedding Cake, and Hardy Splendour. Purple Splendour, *R. fortunei* and well-known English hybrids are the major parents. Many unbloomed seedlings have yet to be evaluated.

HENRY T. SKINNER

Now living in Maryland, Henry T. Skinner has tried to develop more care-free rhododendrons and azaleas. After leaving Wisley, England, he earned his doctorate at Cornell University, largely as a result of a comprehensive study of American deciduous azaleas in their native habitat from Texas all the way to the north-eastern United States. As director of the Morris Arboretum in Philadelphia and later, of the National Arboretum in Washington, D.C., he endeavored to develop new hybrids of *R. atlanticum, viscosum, arborescens, oblongifolium, prunifolium* and *bakeri,* with interest currently centering upon a seemingly new race of multicolored deciduous dwarfs. Only a few cultivars have been named, such as Camp's Red, a selection in the wild of *R. bakeri;* Cornell Pink, a selected pink seedling of *R. mucronulatum;* "Yellow River," a natural hybrid of *R. austrinum x canescens x alabamense;* and "Gretchen Medlar," a cross of Boule de Niege x Henrietta Sargent. A compact form of *R. chapmanii x minus* is named Bowie. Many unnamed seedlings of his deciduous azalea crosses are resplendent in the Morris and National Arboretums, and should possibly be selected and propagated. In 1972, Skinner received the Liberty Hyde Bailey Medal for building the National Arboretum into a place of international prominence in the plant world.

EUGENE A. SKONIECZNY

Eugene A. Skonieczny began rhododendron hybridizing in 1960, aiming for purer colors of flowers hardy enough to withstand central Connecticut winters. Other objectives include more compact plant habit with longer leaf retention. Parent plants include *R. yakusimanum*, Dexter, and Gable cultivars as well as many of the ironclads. Even though he raises over 500 seedlings annually, only 7 have been named to date. None will be registered until thoroughly tested. Some of those named include Lola, (Ignatius Sargent x Robert Allison); Wax Red, (America x Mars) and Peppermint Frills (Skyglow x Nova Zembla).

CAPT. R. N. STEELE

Although "Dick" has plant collections in southern Virginia and Florida, his real-testing area is on the windblown flats of Nova Scotia. He has been hybridizing since 1958, growing from 800 to 2,800 plants per year—and has yet to name a single plant. A few have been placed in a 10-year trial program. Would that more hybridizers were as diligent in proving the worth of their selections. Dick is also an avid collector of Gable plants and has for long been one of Joseph Gable's most ardent admirers. Both Dick's enthusiasm and his ability to help and inspire others has contributed much to improve the genus *Rhododendron*.

JAMES TODD

To obtain rhododendrons tolerant of both heat and cold for North Carolina, James Todd has been using pollen he received from England, the west coast of the U.S.A., Phipps, Hardgrove, and other sources of Dexter and Gable cultivars, *R. metternichii*, Aff. and certain *yakusimanum* hybrids. He is also working toward extending the blooming season by including *R. diaprepes*, Lodauric,

Maryke and others in his breeding program. Selected cultivars include (Tom Everitt x Naomi); (Madonna x *R. fortunei* x Nearing's Purple); and (*R. yakusimanum* x Scintillation).

W. L. TOLSTEAD

Deep in the mountains of West Virginia, in 1957, W. L. Tolstead started hybridizing and selecting rhododendrons and azaleas which would be adaptable to the cold winters and short growing season in Elkins, West Virginia. He found that most evergreen azaleas either bloomed too early for the late spring, or too late to set buds and harden off for the early fall frosts. *R. nakaharai* hybrids seem to be more successful, as have been a few strains of *obtusum* selected from large populations of seedlings. A most important feature of Tolstead's work is his selection of hardy strains of some of the species, such as *R. racemossum*, *triflorum*, *augustinii*, *russatum*, *minus* and *carolinianum*. He has also worked with the Exburys, *R. japonicum*, *calendulaceum* and *nudiflorum*. Tolstead is now growing large numbers of seedlings from parents that have survived in Elkins over the past 10 to 15 years.

W. VON WETTBERG

W. von Wettberg always manages to send outstanding crosses to the A.R.S. seed exchange for general distribution. Many of his crosses are a continuation of Donald Hardgrove's work, involving both lepidote and elepidote rhododendrons. Since he began hybridizing in 1962, von Wettberg has selected a few plants for observation and will probably register those which prove their worth. In Zone 6, cold hardiness is a prime requisite for his plants. An interesting cross is his (*R. minus x R. racemosum*) x *R. ciliatum* numbered D-27. W. von Wettberg has also selected some of Don Hardgrove's seedlings which appear to be promising for propagation. One is numbered DH-8, a glowing, deep pink, and another DH-10, a light, yellow Fabia hybrid. Some 50 of the Hardgrove seedlings in his garden were budded for 1976 bloom for the first time. We have no reports on these yet.

WALTER WINKLER ·

Walter Winkler has a favored site close to the shore near Brunswick, Maine, and has been growing and hybridizing rhododendrons since 1940. He grows up to 1,000 seedlings a year and has selected a few lepidote and elepidote rhododendrons which are most attractive. One, 56-2 (*R. smirnowii* x *R. haematodes* x Mayday) has red, double flowers. Others include hybrids of *R. pubescens*, *R. keiskei*, *R. racemosum*, Blue Diamond, and *carolinianum v. album*. Gaywink and Weezie are two named cultivars.

JOHN C. WISTER

John C. Wister "played the horticultural field" over a long and enthusiastic career during which he has served as an officer in the American Rose Society, the Daffodil Society, the American Holly Society, and directed both the Scott Foundation at Swarthmore College and the Tyler Arboretum at Lima, Pennsylvania. In 1949, he served on the Dexter Selection Committee, a group of men who had a profound influence on the eventual identification and propagation of the finest Dexter seedlings growing in arboretums and gardens in the eastern United States. Many of the selected Dexter clones were propagated and planted by John at the Tyler Arboretum. From 1953 to 1963, with the help of Joan Higginbottom, Mary Green, Fairman Jayne, and George Hewitt, he made crosses of late blooming rhododendron hybrids and species in order to develop cultivars which would bloom at Commencement time—June 1 to June 20. He was most successful; the crosses of *R. maximum*, *R. discolor*, the Dexter #12506 group, and some of the Ironclads resulted in a new race of large-flowered rhododendrons with blooming periods ranging from the last week in May to early July. Some of the best, including June Fire, High Hope, Sparkling Jewel, Snow Shimmer, and Peach Brandy, have been propagated for private gardens. Further selections and propagations should be made.

HENRY YATES

Henry Yates was another who followed in the footsteps of Joseph Gable, beginning in 1955 by growing and sharing seedlings of Joe's crosses. Later, Henry made his own crosses and was highly selective in seeking superior plant habit. That his seedlings have been truly tested can be deduced from his location: Mt. Savage just outside of Frostburg, Maryland. Although Henry died in 1970, his best hybrids are just beginning to be recognized and grown; Maletta, Shazaam, and Big Savage in the elepidotes are examples. Connie Yates (plate, 103) is a Mars x *R. yakusimanum* FCC. Buds are red, opening to rose with white centers, fading to pink. Maletta (plate 93) (*R. auriculatum* x *R. discolor* x *R. ungernii*) is a large plant. Flowers are beautiful shades of pink with yellow. Shaazam (plate 92), (Pink Twins x Mars), selfed is compact, has a good habit, and dark green leaves. Flowers are pink with shades of yellow. Frostburg is a superior white azalea, and some of his Ilam azalea seedlings are outstanding.

LEON YAVORSKY

Leon Yavorsky's successes in rhododendron hybridizing have come from working with the lepidotes and with evergreen azaleas. About 12 have been named—including lepidotes Alice Swift, Virginia Delito, Rik and Matilda. Parentage of his hybrids includes the species *R. carolinianum*, *R. mucronulatum*, *R. racemosum*, *R. keiskei* and Watchung. Most bloom early. Selected evergreen azaleas are reported to be hardy to −10°F. Some plants are available from Lake Louise Nursery, RD 2, Box 235-A, Lanes Pond Road, Howell, New Jersey 07731.

ERNEST YELTON

Ernest Yelton has grown seedlings at

Rutherfordton, North Carolina since 1955. His major objective is to develop new compact, indumented rhododendrons of fine quality. One hybrid of (Caractacus x *R. fortunei*) has been named Joe Brooks. Others selected as promising include *R. yakusimanum* x Sir Charles Lemon; *R. yakusimanum* x Vulcan; and Leo x Nestucca.

CHAPTER VII

Ratings and Recommendations

In the late winter of 1973-74 the Eastern Book Committee of the American Rhododendron Society sent an eight page questionnaire to all members east of the Rocky Mountains. The purpose of the survey was: (1) to ascertain how successful the hybrids of Dexter, Gable, Morrison, Nearing, and Shammarello have been in adapting to conditions in a particular locale; and (2) to determine quality ratings for the plants of the five pioneers, and in addition, numerous other varieties of rhododendrons and azaleas for purposes of comparison.

For too long rhododendron ratings had been the product of small committees, usually West Coast nurserymen who had only scattered data on rhododendron performance in the East. The book committee desired to establish quality ratings based on the actual experiences of eastern growers, and to prepare lists of dependable varieties best suited for each eastern region. The replies from 199 respondents have helped to achieve these goals.

The questionnaire asked each grower to record his United States Department of Agriculture hardiness zone, average minimum temperature, and the prevailing growing conditions in his garden. The replies to these questions have been the basis for rating each rhododendron and azalea for its hardiness, and adaptability.

The grower was asked to register the number of years that each variety had been grown, to give it both bloom and plant ratings, to comment on it, and to give it a mark of xxx if that particular variety was truly outstanding in every respect.

Listed were 28 Dexter rhododendrons, 21 Gable rhododendron hybrids, 14 Gable evergreen azalea hybrids, 43 Morrison Glenn Dale azaleas, 12 Nearing rhododendrons, 23 Shammarello rhododendron hybrids, and 4 Shammarello evergreen hybrid azaleas. Ample space was provided in each category for growers to name and assess other plants of these hybridizers.

Finally, each respondent was requested to list his ten best plants in each of four categories: (1) Evergreen Azaleas (hybrids or species), (2) Deciduous Azaleas (hybrids or species), (3) Rhododendron Species and (4) Ironclad or Standard Rhododendron Hybrids (other than those of the five pioneer hybridizers).

The compiler thought that it might be helpful to indicate the number of recommendations that a plant received in addition to the number of growers reporting on that variety. Therefore, under *Reports* in the tables, the *first numeral* represents the number of people who recommended the hybrids as outstanding, while the *second numeral* represents the total number of reports. In the ratings for unlisted plants, the numeral under *Nominations for Best 10* indicates the number of times that particular plant was listed as one of the ten best in its category.

Quality of bloom and plant habit were rated from 1 to 5; 1 = unsatisfactory, 2 = fair, 3 = good, 4 = very good, and 5 = excellent. These ratings are expressed as "fractions": the numeral above the line (numerator) indicates flower quality while the numeral below the line (denominator) indicates the plant habit quality. In interpreting these ratings, we are using a concept similar to one employed by the American Rose Society, namely that of stating averages correct to the nearest tenth. A quality rating of 3.5 would be the average of all ratings received.

Hardiness is indicated by the minimum temperature in Fahrenheit degrees (in intervals of 5) that a plant will withstand with negligible damage to it and its flower buds. An * after the temperature numeral means that this particular plant has withstood this low temperature satisfactorily but has not been reported from a colder region. It may be possible that the plant is hardier at a somewhat lower temperature. An example of a rating follows.

Let us consider Amethyst from the Dexter rhododendrons:

Amethyst   1-10   3.7/2.5 $-5°*$

Of the 10 growers reporting on this clone, one person rated it outstanding. The 3.7 reflects flower quality slightly better than good, and the 2.5 represents a fairly good plant habit. Amethyst is hardy at least to $-5°F$, and the * indicates that it may be hardy at even lower temperatures.

If the reader questions the high quality ratings resulting from the survey, he must take into account that a gardener tends to consider anything that he grows to be at least good in quality; and if it is a favorite of his, it will be rated even higher accordingly. Then too, at times, the typical gardener subconsciously gives the plant quality a better rating if he likes the flower extremely well, or vice versa.

In anticipating the results of the survey, the committee was of the opinion that several of the varieties would have varying quality ratings from region to region. This was not the case. As a matter of fact, there were no significant differences for any plant rating from region to region, or from one region to the general rating for the entire East.

Resume by Regions

The Midwest Great Lakes Region

Perhaps the most varied and challenging of all areas for growing rhododendrons occurs in the Midwest. This region—comprising Illinois, Indiana, Iowa, Michigan, Minnesota, Missouri, Ohio, and Wisconsin—runs the gamut of 100°F. summers, −50°F. winters, severe winds, and 8.5 pH soil. However, with careful choice of plant material, sheltered planting sites, and proper cultural practices satisfactory results are possible. At present, the grower in this region is limited by the choice of superhardy rhododendrons available, but the work of modern day hybridizers gives us assurance of greater expectations.

In Minnesota, where −50°F. occurs occasionally, deciduous azalea *roseum* and hybrids of it have performed capably even above the snow line. *R. canadense* and *R. mucronulatum* have generally been satisfactory. Of the named varieties attempted, Nancy Waterer is the only deciduous azalea that can be labeled reliably hardy. P.J.M. ranks as the only evergreen rhododendron that can be recommended without reservation for this state. As for evergreen azaleas, only the hardiest Pride hybrids should be tried.

In Toledo, Ohio, where soil is of 8.5 pH, one enthusiast has grown Persil for ten years. The Gable azaleas Campfire, Elizabeth Gable Herbert, Louise Gable, and Purple Splendor have all survived 15-20 years in his region. He recommends Persil and Purple Splendor for their quality. Everestianum, *R. metternichii,* Mrs. Charles S. Sargent and Nova Zembla have all been beautiful over this 15-20 year period. Brown Eyes, Caroline, County of York, Disca, Elie, Rocket, and Romeo have also done well in his garden over a shorter period of time.

The Shammarello hybrids are popular and do well throughout the midwest in less severe exposures. The same is true for Nearing's Ramapo, Windbeam, and Wyanokie.

Deciduous azaleas generally thrive here if they have sufficient moisture. The exception is the Mollis hybrids, which do not respond well to extreme heat. Evergreen azaleas are restricted to the milder regions and must be chosen with care.

Varieties Recommended for the Midwest—Great Lakes Region

28 REPLIES RECEIVED.

THE NUMERAL AFTER EACH PLANT NAME REPRESENTS THE NUMBER OF RECOMMENDATIONS IT RECEIVED.

I(a). Listed Rhododendrons
1.	Scintillation	9
2.	Windbeam	6
3.	Pinnacle	5
4.	Ramapo	4
5.	Cadis	3
	County of York	3
	Ice Cube	3
	Pioneer	3
9.	Spring Parade	3

I (b). Deciduous Azaleas
1.	Cecile	7
	vaseyi	7
3.	Gibralter	6
4.	*schlippenbachii*	5
5.	*calendulaceum*	4
6.	Persil	3
	roseum	3
8.	*canadense*	2
	Nancy Waterer	2

II(a) Species
1.	*mucronulatum*	12
2.	*carolinianum*	8
	yakusimanum	8
4.	*catawbiense*	6
5.	*maximum*	5
	smirnowii	5
7.	*dauricum*	4
8.	*fortunei*	3
	hippophaeoides	3
	metternichii	3

II(b) Evergreen Azaleas
1.	Helen Curtis	5
2.	Hino Pink	4
	Hino Red	4
	Stewartstonian	4
5.	Boudoir	3
	Elizabeth Gable	3
	poukhanense	3
	Rosebud	3

III. Ironclads
1.	Nova Zembla	15
2.	Catawbiense Album	13

III.   Ironclads (cont.)
   3. Roseum Elegans   8
   4. Boule de Neige   7
   5. English Roseum   6
      Roseum Pink   6
      Mrs. Charles S. Sargent   6
   8. Lee's Dark Purple   4

IV.   Unlisted Varieties
   1. P.J.M.   11
   2. Blue Peter   3
      Candy   3
      Dora Amateis   3
      Janet Blair   3
   6. Cunningham's White   2
      Lodestar   2
      Mars   2
      Vernus   2

Upper New York State Region

In the northern part of New York, temperatures regularly reach −20°F. and frequently dip to −30°F.; winds are strong, and the soil is not as acid as it should be for growing rhododendrons. However, moisture is usually sufficient and deciduous azaleas do very well here. On the other hand, most evergreen azaleas are not very satisfactory, but some growers have had success with Boudoir, La Roche, Mildred Mae, and Springtime. In a slightly less severe location, one respondent reported satisfaction with Reward, the only survivor of eight Glenn Dale azaleas attempted.

Scintillation, Westbury, and Janet Blair have done well throughout most of this area, and all have bloomed satisfactorily after −20°F., when grown in sheltered locations. *R. yakusimanum*, Mist Maiden has come through −30°F. well and is recommended as "The Best." Macopin, Ramapo, Windbeam, and Wyanokie flourish throughout the whole area and are heartily recommended. Besse Howells is perfectly hardy here, and Holden does as well as Scintillation. Caroline, Conewago, and Pioneer thrive everywhere, while County of York does well in the more temperate and sheltered spots.

Varieties Recommended for Upper New York State

17 REPLIES RECEIVED.
THE NUMERAL AFTER EACH PLANT NAME REPRESENTS THE NUMBER OF RECOMMENDATIONS IT RECEIVED.

I(a). Listed Hybrids
   1. Scintillation   6
   2. Windbeam   5
   3. Ramapo   4
   4. Holden   3
   5. Conewago   2
      Wyanokie   2

I(b). Deciduous Azaleas
   1. Klondyke   5
   2. *schlippenbachii*   4
      vaseyi   4
   4. Brazil   3
      Cecile   3
      Gibralter   3
      roseum   3
   8. *arborescens*   2
      calendulaceum   2
      Daviesii   2
      japonicum   2
      narcissiflora   2
      Persil   2

II(a). Species
   1. *yakusimanum*   7
   2. *carolinianum*   5
      catawbiense   5
      maximum   5
      smirnowii   5
   6. *brachycarpum*   3
      dauricum   3
      fortunei   3
      mucronulatum   3
  10. *keiskei*   2

II(b). Evergreen Azaleas
   1. Springtime   3
   2. Rosebud   2
   3. *kaempferi*   1
      poukhanense   1

III. Ironclads
   1. Boule de Neige   9
      Nova Zembla   9
   3. America   7
    . Catawbiense Album   7
   5. Mrs. Charles S. Sargent   5
   6. Ignatius Sargent   4
   7. Caractacus   3

III. Ironclads (cont.)
    English Roseum   3
    Roseum Pink   3

IV. Unlisted Varieties
    1. Janet Blair   4

New England (excluding southern Connecticut)

Climatic conditions in the New England States are just a bit more conducive to growing rhododendrons than those in upper New York, and it is therefore possible for rhododendron enthusiasts to enjoy some plants that New Yorkers cannot.

Deciduous azaleas grow lustily but evergreen azaleas are still a gamble. One respondent stated that Amoena was the only azalea that survived the 1957-58 winter, when he lost 75% of his roses. Two growers replied that *R. kaempferi* and *R. poukhanense* grown from seed were the only survivors in their gardens. Others stated that only the hardiest Gable or Pride azaleas, especially Joe Gable and Nadine do well. Mildred Mae was reported satisfactory at −20°F.

Apple Blossom and Westbury join Brown Eyes and Scintillation as satisfactory Dexter rhododendrons. Wheatley, closely related to the Dexter rhododendrons, is a good variety here. Gable's Conemaugh and Kentucky Cardinal do well, and Cadis is satisfactory if the temperature does not drop below −10° or −15°F.

Besse Howells and Ice Cube are reported as good-doers, and several people name Belle Heller and Holden as being good varieties to grow. A number of the Shammarello rhododendrons are bothered somewhat by blooming in the fall and then suffering bud damage due to the ensuing cold of winter. This affliction of the Shammarello's becomes more common in milder regions.

Of the species, *R. brachycarpum* and *R. smirnowii* are perfectly hardy, and *R. fortunei* and *R. metternichii* will succeed except in the coldest sites. The Nearing hybrids Macopin,

Ramapo, Windbeam, and Wyanokie are joined here by Rochelle as a satisfactory hybrid in the milder areas.

Varieties Recommended for New England

24 REPLIES RECEIVED

THE NUMERAL AFTER EACH PLANT NAME REPRESENTS THE NUMBER OF RECOMMENDATIONS IT RECEIVED.

I(a). Listed Rhododendron Varieties
  1. Scintillation   11
  2. Cadis   3
    County of York   3
    Pink Twins   3
    Ramapo   3
    Windbeam   3
  7. Ice Cube   2
    Mary Fleming   2

I(b). Deciduous Azaleas
  1. Gibralter   8
  2. Cecile   7
  3. *luteum*   5
  4. *calendulaceum*   4
  5. Klondyke   3
    schlippenbachii   3
    Strawberry Ice   3
    vaseyi   3

II(a). Species
  1. *carolinianum*   9
    yakusimanum   9
  3. *catawbiense*   8
  4. *mucronulatum*   7
  5. *smirnowii*   4
  6. *racemosum*   3
    metternichii   3

II(b). Evergreen Azaleas
  1. Stewartstonian   11
  2. Louise Gable   8
  3. Rosebud   6
  4. Delaware Valley White   5
  5. Carol   4
    Fedora   4
    Hino Crimson   4
    Ledifolia Alba   4
    Palestrina   4

III. Ironclads
  1. Boule de Neige   12
  2. Nova Zembla   11

III. Ironclads (cont.)

	3.	Roseum Elegans	8
	4.	Catawbiense Album	6
		Mrs. Charles S. Sargent	6
	6.	America	5

IV. Unlisted Hybrids

	1.	Dora Amateis	7
	2.	P.J.M.	6
	3.	Blue Peter	5
	4.	Wheatley	4
	5.	Vulcan	3

The Long Island Region

The Long Island region, (southern Connecticut, northeastern New Jersey, and the suburban area of New York City) is one of the best areas in the east in which to grow azaleas and rhododendrons.

The Dexters thrive here and Mrs. W. R. Coe, Parker's Pink, and Wyandanche Pink are beautiful shrubs that rival Scintillation in the estimation of some gardeners. The Gables do well; Cadis, David Gable, and Mary Belle are much prized. All of the Gable azaleas flourish; Louise Gable, Rosebud, and Stewartstonian are especially beautiful.

The Nearing hybrids are very satisfactory and popular in this area; Mary Fleming and Rochelle are highly recommended. This should surprise no one, as Guy Nearing hybridized most of his rhododendrons in and for this area.

Shammarello hybrids are not seen very much throughout the Long Island region, but Cheer is one that is grown along with Belle Heller, Holden, and Pinnacle.

Most of the Glenn Dale azaleas would be satisfactory here, but the Gable hybrids mentioned earlier are more popular, probably because they are more consistent bloomers. Dora Amateis is used by some gardeners to replace white azaleas in the landscape. Deciduous azaleas create no special problems; they are being grown in increasing numbers and greater variety than heretofore.

Of the species, *R. fortunei* will be found in most gardens, and any gardener with dwarf rhododendrons is sure to include *R. keiskei* and *R. racemosum*. Some enthusiasts are trying large-leaved rhododendrons such as *R. calophytum, R. fictolacteum,* and *R. sutchuenense.*

Album Novum is an Ironclad that is very popular because many growers use it to blend brighter colored varieties into the gardens.

Many of the H-3 English and Dutch hybrids are found in sheltered sites. These would include Azor, Bonfire, Damozel, Goldsworth Yellow, and Vulcan.

Varieties Recommended for the Long Island Region

21 REPLIES RECEIVED.

THE NUMERAL AFTER EACH PLANT NAME REPRESENTS THE NUMBER OF RECOMMENDATIONS IT RECEIVED.

I(a). Listed Hybrids

	1.	Scintillation	12
	2.	Mary Fleming	6
		Windbeam	6
	4.	Mrs. W.R. Coe	3
		Wyandanche Pink	3
	6.	Cadis	2
		David Gable	2
		Mary Belle	2
		Parker's Pink	2
		Pioneer	2
		Rochelle	2

I(b). Deciduous Azaleas

	1.	*vaseyi*	8
	2.	*schlippenbachii*	7
	3.	*calendulaceum*	5
		Cecile	5
		Gibralter	5
	6.	*bakeri*	4
	7.	*canadense*	3
		narcissiflora	3
	9.	Berryrose	2

II(a). Species

	1.	*fortunei*	10
	2.	*carolinianum*	7
	3.	*yakusimanum*	6
		racemosum	6
	5.	*keiskei*	5
	6.	*degronianum*	4

II(a). Species (cont.)

metternichii	4
mucronulatum	4

II(b). Evergreen Azaleas

1.	Louise Gable	6
2.	Stewartstonian	4
3.	Purple Splendor	3
	Rosebud	3
	Rose Greeley	3
6.	Delaware Valley White	2
	Fedora	2
	kiusianum	2
	Springtime	2

III. Ironclads

1.	Boule de Neige	10
2.	Catawbiense Album	5
	Nova Zembla	5
4.	Roseum Pink	4
5.	Album Elegans	3
	Roseum Elegans	3

IV. Unlisted Hybrids

1.	Janet Blair	4
	P.J.M.	4
	Wheatley	4

The Middle Atlantic Region

The Middle Atlantic region (Delaware, Maryland, southern and central New Jersey, Pennsylvania, and West Virginia) is another section of eastern U.S.A. that is generally very satisfactory for azalea and rhododendron enthusiasts.

In western Pennsylvania, where winter temperatures drop below −10°F. regularly, growers have had success with Dexter hybrids Ben Mosely, Brown Eyes, Scintillation, and Tom Everitt. Albert Close, Beaufort, Caroline, Conemaugh, Conewago, and Pioneer are the only Gable rhododendrons tough enough for the rigorous winters here. County of York is borderline hardy, and Cadis barely fails to be satisfactory.

Ramapo, Windbeam, and Wyanokie are good Nearing plants both in the Alleghenies and west of them, as are Shammarello's Besse Howells, Ice Cube, King Tut, Pink Flair, and Pinnacle.

The Pride azaleas are the only evergreen azaleas suitable for this particular climate; many deciduous azaleas thrive here.

The region east of the Alleghenies poses no problems for the Dexter rhododendrons. Most of the Gable plants do well; Atroflo, Cadis, David Gable, Mary Belle, and Pink Twins are very popular. Pioneer and *R. mucronulatum* bloom so early that frequently they get nipped by frost. However, P.J.M. blooms just late enough to usually miss these spring frosts. All of Nearing's hybrids are well represented here, especially Mary Fleming, Ramapo, Windbeam, and Wyanokie.

Besse Howells, Cheer, Holden, Ice Cube, and Rocket seem to be the best Shammarello rhododendrons for this locale. Belle Heller frequently blooms in the fall and as a result is erratic in its spring performance. Many of the Shammarello hybrids have this same habit.

In evergreen azaleas, the Gables are preferred where temperatures go down to 0°F. and slightly below. South of Philadelphia, the Glenn Dale hybrids are the mainstay. This is to be expected, because Morrison developed his azaleas for the Washington, D.C., area. Deciduous azaleas do well throughout the region and are gaining in popularity.

Around Philadelphia and south of it, many of the better English and Dutch rhododendron hybrids are satisfactory. These would include A. Bedford, Blue Peter, Christmas Cheer, Goldsworth Yellow, Gomer Waterer, Mrs. Furnival, and Vulcan. Jean Marie de Montagu and Unique are among those that can be grown in sheltered sites.

Dora Amateis, Janet Blair, and Wheatley are eastern American hybrids that will be seen in gardens where the "rhododendron buff" lives.

Varieties Recommended for the Middle Atlantic Region

48 REPLIES RECEIVED.

THE NUMERAL AFTER EACH PLANT NAME REPRESENTS THE NUMBER OF RECOMMENDATIONS IT RECEIVED.

I(a). Listed Hybrids
1. Scintillation	25
2. Windbeam	11
3. Cadis	6
County of York	6
David Gable	6
Mary Fleming	6
7. Conewago	5
8. Caroline	4
Holden	4
10. Atroflo	3
Parker's Pink	3

I(b). Deciduous Azaleas
1. Gibralter	12
2. Cecile	11
3. *calendulaceum*	9
4. *vaseyi*	8
5. *nudiflorum*	7
schlippenbachii	7
Strawberry Ice	7
8. *bakeri*	6
narcissiflora	6
roseum	6

II(a). Species
1. *carolinianum*	14
fortunei	14
yakusimanum	14
4. *keiskei*	11
racemosum	11
6. *maximum*	10
7. *metternichii*	9
mucronulatum	9
9. *catawbiense*	5
impeditum	5
makinoi	5

II(b). Evergreen Azaleas
1. Delaware Valley White	14
2. Louise Gable	12
Stewartstonian	12
4. Springtime	9
5. Martha Hitchcock	8
Herbert	8
Rosebud	8
8. Rose Greeley	7
9. Geisha	6
Hershey's Red	6

III. Ironclads
1. Boule de Neige	19
2. Nova Zembla	18
3. Catawbiense Album	15
4. Roseum Elegans	10
5. Roseum Pink	9
6. America	7

III. Ironclads (cont.)
7. English Roseum	5
8. Mrs. Charles S. Sargent	4

IV. Unlisted Hybrids
1. Blue Peter	9
2. Mrs. Furnival	7
3. Gomer Waterer	6
P.J.M.	6
Vulcan	6
6. Janet Blair	5
Jean Marie de Montagu	5
8. Wheatley	4

Virginia Region

Offsetting weather conditions in Virginia alter the picture as to what plants have to tolerate. While the winters are milder and shorter than they are northward, the summers are hotter and longer. In addition, the rapid fluctuations between cold and warm spells in winter create problems, especially for early season blooming rhododendrons. As a result, plants such as Conemaugh, Mary Fleming, Pioneer and P.J.M. are not as satisfactory as they are north of the Potomac. Root rot is another condition that has to be contended with, but the Dexter and Gable hybrids seem to be resistant to it.

The Dexter hybrids are generally very reliable in Virginia. The same is true for the Glenn Dale azaleas, especially Glacier and Treasure. However, it must be mentioned that Sagittarius is still an exception. Virginia is too cold for it.

All of the Gable azalea and rhododendron hybrids are very satisfactory except for the early blooming varieties mentioned previously. Caroline, County of York, Cadis, David Gable, and Disca, along with Mary Belle are fine plants here.

The Nearing "Guyencourt" hybrids and Mary Fleming get nipped by frost too often to be recommended; Ramapo is a little difficult to please, but other Nearing hybrids are satisfactory.

The Shammarello hybrids that do best here

are: Besse Howells, Rocket, and Holden. The latter is recommended as the best of this group for Virginia. Most of the others bloom in the fall. Were it not for this, Belle Heller and Cheer would also be included in the list of recommendations.

Of the species, *R. fortunei* and *R. vernicosum* are beautiful here. The same is true of the Ponticum series in general.

Some of the most beautiful hybrids in the world grace many of the Virginia gardens. These include: A. Bedford, Anna Rose Whitney, Cynthia, Jan Dekens, Jean Marie de Montagu, Loder's White, Mrs. Furnival, Sappho, and Vulcan's Flame.

Varieties Recommended for Virginia

15 REPLIES RECEIVED.

THE NUMERAL AFTER EACH PLANT NAME REPRESENTS THE NUMBER OF RECOMMENDATIONS IT RECEIVED.

I(a). Listed Hybrids
1.	Scintillation	6
2.	Cadis	5
3.	David Gable	3
	Holden	3
	Windbeam	3
6.	Caroline	2
	County of York	2
	Disca	2

I(b). Deciduous Azaleas
1.	*calendulaceum*	5
2.	Gibralter	4
	viscosum	4
4.	Cecile	3
5.	*nudiflorum*	2
	Toucan	2
	schlippenbachii	2

II(a). Species
1.	*carolinianum*	5
2.	*fortunei*	4
3.	*mucronulatum*	3
	vernicosum	3
	yakusimanum	3
6.	*hyperythrum*	2
	maximum	2

II(a) Species (cont.)
	makinoi	2
	metternichii	2
	racemosum	2

II(b). Evergreen Azaleas
1.	Gumpo (various forms)	7
2.	Rosebud	5
3.	Stewartstonian	4
4.	Big Joe	3
	Corsage	3
	Delaware Valley White	3
	Glacier	3
	Treasure	3
9.	Ambrosia	2
	Buccaneer	2
	Coral Bells	2
	Glamour	2
	Hershey's Red	2

IV. Unlisted Hybrids
1.	Jean Marie de Montagu	7
2.	Vulcan	5
3.	Gomer Waterer	4
	Wheatley	4
5.	Anna Rose Whitney	3
	Blue Peter	3

Southern Region

The Southern region—Arkansas, Tennessee, North Carolina, and all states to the south of them—have three different climates to consider.

The coldest region is in the mountains, and the following are recommended for these cold locations: Besse Howells, Caroline, County of York, Holden, Ice Cube, Ramapo, Scintillation, and Windbeam. Hybrids recommended although not listed on the questionnaire are: Anah Krushke, Blue Peter, Cynthia, Dora Amateis, Janet Blair, and Wheatley. Only the tougher evergreen azaleas should be considered for the mountain areas. These would include *kaempferi, poukhanense,* and hybrids of these species. Native rhododendrons and deciduous azaleas do superbly here as do the old Ironclads.

In the Piedmont sections where temperatures do not go down to 0°F, plants need not be as winter hardy but they must be able to withstand the rigors of summer. Champagne, Scintillation, and Tom Everitt are very good here, but Sky Glow and Wissahickon are not. Most of the other Dexter hybrids do rather well.

In addition to Caroline and County of York, Annie Dalton, Cadis, and Disca are fine for the Piedmont. David Gable is subject to frost, and Pink Twins does not do well. Conemaugh and Conewago are rather difficult to grow, and Pioneer, along with *R. mucronulatum* and P.J.M., is just not suited for the South. It should be noted that Gable hybrids with either *R. fortunei* or *R. maximum* in their parentage are fine. This holds true for most hybrids of these species. *R. decorum, R. discolor, R. fortunei,* and *R. maximum* all withstand the heat very well.

Shammarello hybrids developed for the north generally are not suited to the long, hot summers; however, Besse Howells and Holden are very satisfactory; Rocket is satisfactory; and while Belle Heller is erratic in its blooming, some growers recommend it.

Most of the Nearing hybrids are unsatisfactory in the Piedmont; however, Rochelle is an exception, and Windbeam is a fringe plant.

Evergreen azaleas grow well in the Piedmont. The Gables tend to be a bit thin of leaves in the winter. Glenn Dale azaleas are generally satisfactory in this area and to the south of it. Sagittarius and Treasure do extremely well; Glacier is not always dependable, and Martha Hitchcock tends to be very leggy. The Kurumes are the best evergreen azaleas grown here.

The native azaleas indigenous to this region are superb, and their hybrids do better than any other deciduous hybrid azaleas. The same can be said of the American rhododendron species: *carolinianum, catawbiense, chapmanii, maximum,* and *minus.* It must be pointed out however, that *carolinianum* and *catawbiense* do poorly at lower elevations.

The Ironclads: America, Catawbiense Album, Caractacus and Lee's Dark Purple are fine; Roseum Elegans grows like a native. Boule de Neige does not do well, and Nova Zembla is very susceptible to root rot in the Piedmont.

Except in the coldest parts of the Smokies, A. Bedford, Anna Rose Whitney, Betty Wormald, Jan Dekens, Jean Marie de Montagu, Loder's White, Marchioness of Lansdowne, Vulcan, and Vulcan's Flame are good doers. The yellow flowering rhododendrons are not.

In the hottest regions of Alabama, Georgia, Louisiania, and Mississippi the evergreen azaleas are the only plants recommended. The Belgian hybrids and the Kurumes are especially suited for this area.

In summary, wherever rhododendrons can be grown in the South, the Dexters are fine, especially Scintillation; Gable's Caroline, and to a lesser degree, Cadis and County of York also do well. The value of Nearing's Windbeam and Wyanokie diminish as we get further south; however, Rochelle is worthwhile. Besse Howells and Holden are the most satisfactory of the Shammarello hybrids.

Varieties Recommended for the Southern Region

36 REPLIES RECEIVED.

THE NUMERAL AFTER EACH PLANT NAME REPRESENTS THE NUMBER OF RECOMMENDATIONS IT RECEIVED.

I(a). Listed Hybrids
1.	Scintillation	17
2.	Caroline	6
3.	Windbeam	5
4.	Besse Howells	3
5.	Belle Heller	2
6.	Cadis	2
7.	Mary Fleming	2

I(b). Deciduous Azaleas
1.	*prunifolium*	8
2.	*vaseyi*	8
3.	*austrinum*	7
4.	*calendulaceum*	7
5.	*canescens*	6
6.	Gibralter	5

I(b). **Deciduous Azaleas** (cont.)

7.	*atlanticum*	4
	nudiflorum	4
9.	*alabamense*	3
	bakeri	3
	Cecile	3
	speciosum	3

II(a). **Species**

1.	*fortunei*	9
2.	*catawbiense*	8
	carolinianum	8
	maximum	8
5.	*yakusimanum*	7
6.	*minus*	4
7.	*chapmani*	3
	racemosum	3
9.	*decorum*	2

II(b). **Evergreen Azaleas**

1.	Coral Bells	8
	Stewartstonian	8
3.	Gumpo (White)	7
	Louise Gable	7
	Rosebud	7
6.	Fashion	6
	Hino Crimson	6

II(b). **Evergreen Azaleas** (cont.)

8.	George Lindley Tabor	5
	Martha Hitchcock	5
	Purple Splendor	5
	Treasure	5

III. **Ironclads**

1.	Nova Zembla	14
	Roseum Elegans	14
3.	America	10
4.	Catawbiense Album	7
	English Roseum	7
6.	Caractacus	3
	Everestianum	3
	Lee's Dark Purple	3

IV. **Unlisted Hybrids**

1.	Cynthia	12
2.	Jean Marie de Montagu	10
3.	Blue Peter	8
4.	Anna Rose Whitney	6
5.	Purple Splendor	5
6.	Gomer Waterer	3
	Madame Masson	3
	Mars	3
	Vulcan	3

APPENDIX A

Ratings for the Entire Eastern United States

An asterisk (*) after the temperature in the following tables indicates this particular plant has withstood low temperature satisfactorily, but has not been reported from a colder region. All temperatures are reported in degrees Fahrenheit.

Table 1. DEXTER RHODODENDRONS

Variety	Reports	Quality	Hardiness	Comments
Amethyst	1-10	3.7/2.5	− 5°*	
Apple Blossom	4-13	3.6/3.3	−10°	
Ben Moseley	0-20	3.7/4.1	−15°*	
Betty Arrington	0-10	3.2/3.0	−10°*	
Betty Hume	2-15	4.2/4.1	− 5°*	Needs light; A show in late May.
Brown Eyes	2-11	3.9/3.4	−10°*	
Champagne	3-12	4.5/3.0	− 5°	
Dexter's Brandy Green	0-7	3.3/2.0	− 5°	

Table 1.   DEXTER RHODODENDRONS (cont.)

Variety	Reports	Quality	Hardiness	Comments
Dexter's Orchid	2-7	3.9/3.4	− 5°	
Gigi	1-7	4.3/4.2	− 5°*	Best of his reds.
Gloxineum	1-16	3.6/3.2	−10°	
Mrs. W. R. Coe	5-32	4.0/3.6	−10°	Large leatherlike leaves.
Parker's Pink	6-23	4.3/3.5	− 5°*	
Scintillation	86-121	4.4/4.3	−15°	Requires some shade.
Sky Glow	1-17	3.7/2.4	− 5°	Pale foliage.
Todmorden	1-13	4.2/3.2	− 5°*	
Tom Everitt	3-17	4.3/4.1	−10°*	Large foliage.
Warwick	0-21	3.3/3.3	−15°*	Shy bloomer.
Westbury	3-26	3.9/3.8	−10	
Wissahickon	1-40	3.5/2.7	− 5°	
Wyandanche Pink	5-18	3.6/4.2	− 5°*	Shy bloomer; Beautiful plant.

Table 2.   GABLE RHODODENDRONS

Variety	Reports	Quality	Hardiness	Comments
Albert Close	4-42	3.0/2.8	−15°	Shy bloomer.
Annie Dalton	1-14	3.7/2.9	− 5°	Least hardy of group.
Atroflo (Group)	3-49	3.4/3.3	− 5°	Heavy buff indumentum; Needs sun.
Beaufort	1-18	2.6/3.6	−20°	Needs sun.
Cadis	21-68	3.8/3.9	−10°	Give some sun.
Caroline	20-79	3.5/3.8	−20°	Good-doer everywhere.
Conemaugh (Group)	1-25	3.1/3.1	−15°	
Conewago (Group)	11-43	3.7/3.1	−25°	Easy.
County of York	18-79	3.7/3.3	−15°	Give some shade.
David Gable	13-43	4.1/3.7	−10°	Early bloomer.
Disca	4-31	3.8/3.6	− 5°	Late bloomer.
Henry R. Yates	3-14	3.9/4.2	− 5°*	Shy bloomer; Dark foliage.
Kentucky Cardinal	1-18	3.1/2.9	−10°*	
Mary Belle	2-13	4.1/3.8	− 5°*	His triumph.
Maxhaem Salmon	0-17	3.1/3.4	− 5°*	
Pink Twins	5-52	3.3/3.1	−10°	Hose-in-hose flowers.
Pioneer	6-77	3.2/2.9	−15°	Frequently frosted; P.J.M. better; Somewhat difficult.
Red Head	1-29	3.2/2.5	0°	
Robert Allison	0-26	3.4/3.2	−10°	Late bloomer.
Strawberry Swirl	1-23	3.6/3.1	− 5°	Not easy; quite early

Table 3.   NEARING HYBRID RHODODENDRONS

Variety	Reports	Quality	Hardiness	Comments
Brandywine	1-16	3.6/2.7	− 5°	
Chesapeake	0-14	3.3/3.0	− 5°	
Delaware	0-14	3.0/2.5	− 5°	
Hockessin	0-12	3.2/2.5	− 5°	
Lenape	0-16	3.1/2.5	− 5°	

Table 3. NEARING HYBRID RHODODENDRONS (cont.)

Variety	Reports	Quality	Hardiness	Comments
Macopin	1-8	3.4/3.0	−20°*	
Mary Fleming	18-59	3.9/3.8	−10°	Needs some shade.
Montchanin	0-16	3.0/2.6	−10°	
Ramapo	15-86	3.5/3.9	−20°	Sometimes difficult.
Rochelle	7-20	4.1/3.7	−10°	
Windbeam	39-105	3.9/3.8	−25°	Good-doer.
Wyanokie	6-51	3.6/3.7	−25°	Good-doer.

Table 4. SHAMMARELLO HYBRIDS

Variety	Reports	Quality	Hardiness	Comments
Belle Heller	4-51	3.8/2.9	0°	Inconsistent performer.
Besse Howells	8-32	3.6/3.7	−15°*	Easy doer everywhere.
Cheer	2-44	3.0/3.1	−10°	Blooms in fall.
Elie	3-35	3.3/3.4	−10°	
Holden	14-40	3.7/3.9	−15°	Good-doer
Ice Cube	5-26	3.7/3.3	−15°*	
King Tut	3-39	3.5/3.1	−15°	Not always easy.
Lavender Queen	0-32	2.3/3.8	− 5°	
Pink Cameo	1-15	3.6/3.5	−15°	
Pink Flair	4-12	3.6/3.4	−15°	
Pinnacle	7-32	3.7/3.2	−15°	
Rocket	3-41	3.2/3.6	−10°	Handsome foliage.
Romeo	1-12	3.3/2.9	−15°*	
Sham's Juliet	2-9	3.0/3.4	−15°*	
Sham's Ruby	0-22	3.2/3.1	−10°	
Spring Dawn	1-15	3.3/3.4	−10°	
Spring Glory	1-20	3.0/3.3	−10°	Blooms in fall.
Spring Parade	4-19	3.3/3.6	−10°	
The General	1-26	2.9/2.9	−10°	
Tony	4-34	3.3/3.3	−10°	Low plant.

Table 5. RHODODENDRON SPECIES

Species	Nominations for Best Ten	Quality	Hardiness	Comments
adenopodum	6	3.8/3.8	−10°*	Indumented
brachycarpum	11	3.4/4.1	−20°*	Handsome plant.
carolinianum	55	3.7/3.5	−25°	Requires sharp drainage.
catawbiense (Lavender)	34	3.1/3.3	−25°	Grows best in the Mts.
(White forms)	9	3.5/2.9	−25°	
dauricum	15	3.2/3.4	−20°*	First to bloom.
degronianum	12	3.5/4.0	−15°	
fortunei	45	3.9/3.7	−15°	Resists root rot and insects.
hippophaeoides	7	3.4/3.7	−20	Easy.
impeditum	8	3.4/3.7	−15°	
keiskei (Taller)	11	3.1/3.4	−10°	

Table 5.   RHODODENDRON SPECIES (cont.)

Variety	Reports	Quality	Hardiness	Comments
(Dwarf)	11	3.8/4.0	−10°	Early, good yellow.
maximum	34	2.3/3.5	−25°	Very easy.
makinoi	13	3.0/4.1	−10°	Give some shade.
metternichii	23	3.8/4.1	−15°	Good-doer.
mucronulatum (lavender)	23	3.4/3.2	−25°	Very good-doer.
(Pink forms)	16	3.7/3.2	−20°	
minus	9	3.1/2.9	−15°	June bloomer.
racemosum	27	3.8/3.6	− 5°	Some variation.
russatum	7	3.8/3.6	−15°	
smirnowii	17	2.7/3.1	−20°	
vernicosum	10	4.2/4.2	− 5°	Varies a great deal.
yakusimanum	55	4.5/4.8	−15°	Varies a bit; Not the easiest.
'Mist Maiden'			−20°	A little larger plant.

Table 6.   IRONCLAD RHODODENDRONS

Variety	Nominations for Best Ten	Quality	Hardiness	Comments
America	36	3.6/3.0	−20°	Popular red.
Boule de Neige	62	3.7/4.2	−25°	Give some shade.
Catawbiense Album	59	3.4/3.4	−25°	Sturdy, dependable.
Catawbiense Boursault	13	3.1/3.7	−25°	
Caractacus	11	3.3/3.3	−20°*	
English Roseum	26	3.6/4.2	−20°*	
Everestianum	12	3.1/3.1	−15°*	Easy.
Ignatius Sargent	10	3.6/3.9	−20°*	
Lee's Dark Purple	12	3.2/3.1	−15°	
Mrs. Charles S. Sargent	23	3.9/3.6	−25°	Top "Ironclad" flowers.
Nova Zembla	74	3.6/3.3	−25°	Perhaps best red on fine plant.
Roseum Elegans	44	3.4/4.2	−25°	Great doer, widely planted. Handsome plant.
Roseum Pink	25	3.2/4.0	−15°	

Table 7.   OTHER RHODODENDRONS RECOMMENDED

Variety	Nominations for Best Ten	Quality	Hardiness	Comments
A. Bedford	7	4.0/3.7	− 5°*	Tall truss.
Anna Rose Whitney	10	4.3/4.4	0°*	A western hybrid doing well here.
Blue Peter	32	4.1/3.4	−15°	Floriferous; beautiful truss.
Chionoides	9	3.2/3.7	−10°*	
Cunningham's White	7	3.3/4.3	−15°	Very compact; blooms in fall.
Christmas Cheer	6	3.5/4.0	− 5°*	Early season bloomer.
Cynthia	18	4.3/3.5	− 5°	Finest truss.
Dora Amateis	17	4.3/4.0	−10°*	Give some shade.
Gomer Waterer	18	3.7/3.9	−10°	Floriferous; fine foliage.
Janet Blair	19	4.2/4.2	−15°	Give some shade.
Jean Marie de Montagu	27	4.4/3.6	0°	Long lasting bloom.
Laetivirens	5	2.2/4.0	−15°	Syn. Wilsoni.
Madame Masson	7	3.1/3.9	− 5°	

Table 7. OTHER RHODODENDRONS RECOMMENDED (cont.)

Variety	Reports	Quality	Hardiness	Comments
Mars	10	4.2/3.0	−10°	Somewhat difficult.
Mrs. Furnival	11	4.8/3.7	− 5°	Exquisite bloom.
Myrtifolium	6	3.0/4.1	−15°	Very late lepidote.
P.J.M. (Group)	32	3.4/4.2	−30°	Perhaps hardiest of all?
Purple Splendor	12	4.4/3.6	0°*	Best purple; foliage vulnerable.
Vulcan	19	4.1/3.7	− 5°*	Floriferous; good-doer.
Wheatley	23	4.5/3.8	−15°	Exceptionally fine truss.

Table 8. MORRISON'S GLENN DALE AZALEA HYBRIDS

Variety	Reports	Quality	Hardiness	Comments
Ambrosia	2-13	4.6/3.2	+ 5°	Unique color.
Angela Place	1-9	4.0/3.7	0°*	
Aphrodite	6-16	4.2/3.9	− 5°*	
Buccaneer	6-34	3.9/3.7	0°	Shade.
Copperman	4-28	4.0/3.6	0°	Fades in sun.
Dayspring	8-21	4.3/3.5	− 5°*	Earliest.
Delos	3-16	4.1/3.5	0°	Best double.
Dragon	2-6	4.0/4.0	0°*	Brilliant rose red.
Dream	8-16	4.5/3.6	− 5°*	Best of *Simsii* hybrid group.
Driven Snow	0-7	3.3/3.5	+ 5°	
Everest	2-8	3.9/3.9	0°	Fine late white.
Fashion	9-31	4.1/4.1	0°	
Gaiety	6-21	4.3/3.9	− 5°	
Geisha	9-30	3.9/3.5	−.5°	Brightly striped, early.
Glacier	12-45	3.9/4.1	0°	Shelter; inconsistent.
Glamour	7-23	4.2/4.1	− 5°	
Greeting	2-14	3.8/4.1	− 5°*	
Martha Hitchcock	17-54	4.3/3.3	−10°	Vigorous; hardiest Glenn Dale?
Prudence	0-9	3.8/4.1	0°*	Excellent foliage.
Sagittarius	1-22	3.4/4.1	+10°	Fine plant; only for south.
Sarabande	0-8	3.2/3.0	0°	
Swan Song	0-6	4.0/3.2	0°	
Treasure	13-37	4.1/3.7	0°	
Zulu	0-12	4.0/3.2	− 5°*	

Table 9. EVERGREEN AZALEAS

		Gable Hybrids		
Variety	Reports	Quality	Hardiness	Comments
Big Joe	6-15	4.3/3.2	− 5°*	Good-doer; big show.
Carol	3-12	4.0/3.7	− 5°	
Elizabeth Gable	5-30	4.0/3.1	−10°	Long lasting bloom.
Herbert	21-46	3.7/3.5	−15°	Excellent-doer.
Louise Gable	36-76	4.1/3.7	−10°	Give some shade.
Mary Dalton	3-15	3.6/3.4	− 5°*	Give shade.
Mildred Mae	3-26	3.6/3.5	−10°*	Easy.
Polaris	4-13	4.4/4.2	− 5°	Floriferous.
Purple Splendor	14-63	3.8/3.4	−10°	
Rosebud	34-85	4.1/3.7	−10°	Semi-dwarf.

Table 9. EVERGREEN AZALEAS (cont.)

Variety	Reports	Quality	Hardiness	Comments
Rose Greeley	19-58	4.1/3.6	− 5°	Frost sensitive.
Springtime	16-35	4.3/3.6	−20°*	Very hardy.
Stewartstonian	43-85	4.0/3.8	−10°	Fades in sun.

Shammarello Hybrids

Variety	Reports	Quality	Hardiness	Comments
Desiree	1-25	3.7/3.6	− 5°	Varied results.
Helen Curtis	9-20	4.0/4.1	−10°	Superior White.
Hino Red	12-34	3.9/3.8	−10°	
Hino White	0-13	3.7/3.7	−10°	

Table 10. OTHER EVERGREEN AZALEAS

Variety	Nominations for Best Ten	Quality	Hardiness	Comments
Blaaw's Pink	5	4.4/4.2	0°	
Boudoir	8	4.2/4.1	−15°	See note 1 below.
Campfire	2-6	4.3-3.7	− 5°	See note 1 below.
Coral Bells	16	4.3/3.9	0°	
Corsage	3-11	3.8/3.9	−10°	Vigorous; See note 1 below.
Delaware Valley White	28	4.3/3.8	−10°	Best white azalea; a hardy *mucronatum*.
Fedora	8	4.5/3.5	−10°	
George Tabor	7	4.8/4.1	0°	Surprisingly adaptable southern Indian.
Gumpo White	11	4.6/4.7	0°	Protect from rabbits.
Hershey's Red	9	4.3/4.1	− 5°	
Hino Crimson	19	4.1/3.7	− 5°	Does not fade.
Hinodegiri	8	4.0/4.0	0°	
James Gable	9	4.2/3.6	− 5°	See note 1 below.
kaempferi (Species)	7	4.0/3.7	−10°	Almost deciduous.
Ledifolia Alba	8	4.1/3.7	− 5°	
Palestrina	12	3.9/3.6	−10°	Tall, sturdy, dependable.
poukhanense (Species)	8	4.2/3.5	−10°	Scented.
Sherwood Red	6	4.2/4.2	− 5°	

Note 1. Campfire and James Gable were not listed under Gable Hybrids in the questionnaire even though they are. Boudoir and Corsage were not named by Gable and hence they were not listed either.

Since Campfire and Corsage were both write-ins they appear in this list. For these varieties the 2-6 and 3-11 under first column represent recommendations out of total reports respectively for these azaleas.

Table 11. DECIDUOUS AZALEA SPECIES

Species	Nominations for Best Ten	Quality	Hardiness	Comments
austrinum	9	3.9/3.5	0°	
arborescens	9	3.3/3.7	−20°	Fragrant.
atlanticum	7	3.3/3.5	−20°	Scented.
bakeri (Cumberlandense)	13	3.8/3.8	−20°	

Table 11. DECIDUOUS AZALEA SPECIES (cont.)

Species	Nominations for Best Ten	Quality	Hardiness	Comments
calendulaceum	35	3.9/3.2	−20°	Variable.
canadense	7	3.1/3.3	−30°	
canescens	6	4.2/4.0	0°	
japonicum	6	4.7/4.2	−20°	
luteum	7	4.4/3.8	−15°	Very fragrant.
nudiflorum	15	3.6/3.3	−10°	Scented.
pruniflorum	16	3.7/3.8	− 5°	Stands heat.
roseum	15	3.7/3.3	−35°	Very fragrant.
schlippenbachi	29	4.1/3.8	−20°	Clones vary from white to pink to rose.
vaseyi—Pink Forms	28	4.4/3.3	−20°	
White Find	9	3.9/3.3	−20°	
viscosum	10	3.6/3.6	−20°	Fragrant.

Table 12. DECIDUOUS HYBRID AZALEAS

Variety	Nominations for Best Ten	Quality	Hardiness	Comments
Brazil	10	3.9/4.0	−20°	
Berry Rose	5	4.0/3.2	−20°	
Cecile	39	4.5/3.7	−20°	
Coccineum Speciosum	8	3.8/3.8	−15°*	
Daviesii	12	3.9/3.6	−15°*	Fragrant.
Fawley	5	4.0/3.2	−10°*	
Gibralter	43	4.4/4.2	−20°*	Great-doer.
Golden Dream	9	4.4/3.4	−20°*	
Golden Oriole	5	4.2/4.0	−20°*	
Klondyke	16	4.0/3.3	−20°*	
Marian Merriman	7	4.3/3.6	−15°*	
Nancy Waterer	7	4.0/3.7	−30°*	Hardiest hybrid?
Narcissiflora	13	3.7/3.7	−20°*	Fragrant.
Old Gold	6	4.7/3.8	−20°*	
Oxydol	7	4.7/4.1	−20°*	
Persil	8	4.1/3.6	−20°*	
Princess Royal	6	5.0/3.8	−20°*	
Strawberry Ice	16	4.7/3.6	−15°*	
Tang	5	4.4/3.4	−20°*	
Toucan	7	4.3/4.0	−15°*	

APPENDIX B _____

Favorite Plants for the Entire Eastern States

199 REPLIES RECEIVED.

THE NUMERAL AFTER EACH PLANT NAME
REPRESENTS THE NUMBER OF RECOMMENDATIONS
IT RECEIVED.

I. Rhododendrons

(A) Varieties listed in survey (Gable, Dexter, Nearing, Shammarello)

1.	Scintillation	86
2.	Windbeam	39
3.	Cadis	21
4.	Caroline	20
5.	County of York	18
	Mary Fleming	18
7.	Ramapo	15
8.	Holden	14
9.	David Gable	13
10.	Conewago	11
11.	Besse Howells	8
12.	Pinnacle	7
	Rochelle	7
14.	Parker's Pink	6
	Pioneer	6
	Wyanokie	6
17.	Mrs. W. R. Coe	5
	Ice Cube	5
	Pink Twins	5

(B) Species most often recommended

1.	*carolinianum*	55
2.	*yakusimanum*	55
3.	*fortunei*	45
4.	*mucronulatum*	39
5.	*catawbiense*	34
	maximum	34
7.	*racemosum*	27
8.	*metternichii*	23
9.	*keiskei*	21
10.	*smirnowii*	17
11.	*dauricum*	15
12.	*makinoi*	13
13.	*degronianum*	12
14.	*brachycarpum*	11
15.	*vernicosum*	10
16.	*minus*	9

(B) Species most often recommended (cont.)

17.	*impeditum*	8
18.	*hippophaeoides*	7
	russatum	7
20.	*adenopodum*	6

(C) Ironclads most often preferred

1.	Nova Zembla	74
2.	Boule De Neige	62
3.	Catawbiense Album	57
4.	Roseum Elegans	44
5.	America	36
6.	English Roseum	26
7.	Roseum Pink	25
8.	Mrs. Charles S. Sargent	23
9.	Catawbiense Boursault	13
10.	Everestianum	12
	Lee's Dark Purple	12
12.	Caractacus	11

(D) Other unlisted varieties recommended

1.	Blue Peter	32
2.	P.J.M.	32
3.	Jean Marie De Montagu	27
4.	Wheatley	25
5.	Janet Blair	19
6.	Vulcan	19
7.	Cynthia	18
	Gomer Waterer	18
9.	Dora Amateis	17
10.	Purple Splendor	12
11.	Mrs. Furnival	11
12.	Mars	10
13.	Chionoides	9
14.	A. Bedford	7
	Cunningham's White	7
	Madame Masson	7
17.	Christmas Cheer	6
	Myrtifolium	6
19.	Laetivirens (Wilsoni)	5

II. Azaleas

(A). Deciduous varieties recommended for the East

1.	Gibralter	43
2.	Cecile	39
3.	*calendulaceum*	36
4.	*vaseyi* (All Forms)	35
5.	*schlippenbachii*	29
6.	Klondyke	16
	prunifolium	16
	Strawberry Ice	16
9.	*nudiflorum*	15
	roseum	15
11.	*bakeri*	13
	narcissiflora	13

(A). Deciduous varieties (cont.)

13.	Daviesii	12
14.	*austrinum*	10
	Brazil	10
	viscosum	10
17.	*arborescens*	‚9
	Golden Dream	9
19.	Persil	8
20.	*atlanticum*	7
	luteum	7
	Marian Merriman	7
	Oxydol	7
	Toucan	7

(B). Evergreen azaleas recommended by respondents

1.	Stewartstonian	43
2.	Louise Gable	37
3.	Rosebud	34
4.	Delaware Valley White	28
5.	Hino Crimson	19
6.	Rose Greeley	18

(B). Evergreen azaleas (cont.)

7.	Martha Hitchcock	17
8.	Coral Bells	16
	Springtime	16
10.	Herbert	15
	Purple Splendor	15
12.	Treasure	13
13.	Hino Red	12
	Palestrina	12
	Glacier	12
16.	Corsage	11
	Gumpo White	11
18.	Fashion	9
	Geisha	9
20.	Boudoir	8
	Dream	8
	Helen Curtis	8
	Fedora	8
	kaempferi	8
	poukhanense	8

CONTRIBUTORS TO THIS VOLUME _____

"Hybrids and Hybridizers" is entirely the product of a volunteer group, who have written and illustrated the book. They are identified in these brief biographies:

EMIL V. BOHNEL, retired Medical research biologist with Lederle Laboratories, his specialty is virus vaccine development and toxicological evaluation of new drug safety; has been active in Tappan Zee Chapter, A.R.S. as President and Director; member of Nearing Study Committee; awarded Bronze Medal of A.R.S. in 1977; lives in Pearl River, N.Y.

WELDON E. DELP, nurseryman owner of Crystalaire Nursery, Harrisville, Pa; a Charter member of the Great Lakes Chapter, A.R.S. and an A.R.S. member since 1949; has been breeding rhododendrons and azaleas for thirty years; his breeding objective is improved H-1 hybrids.

JAMES R. DUNLOP, professional photographer and President of Dunlop Photographic Center in Washington, D.C. Became interested in azaleas after meeting Stuart Armstrong and Ben Morrison in Washington; later visited Morrison in Pass Christian where he photographed him working on new hybrids.

CAROLINE GABLE, daughter of the late Joseph B. Gable, is a professional newspaper woman at York, Pa. An active member of the Potomac Valley Chapter, A.R.S., and the Gable Study Committee, she lives at the Gable homestead in Stewartstown, Pa., and keeps an expert eye on her father's original plants and newer ones under study.

RAYMOND AND JANE GOODRICH, raise their rhododendrons in northern Virginia after Ray's retirement from the Army. Charter members of the Potomac Valley Chapter, they have been key members of the Gable Study Group. Their special interest: study of Gable clones and improving late blooming hybrids, using *R. maximum* and others.

RUSS AND VELMA HAAG, charter members of the New Jersey Chapter, A.R.S., and responsible for the founding of the Union County Rhododendron Garden in Mountainside, N.J. Russ is a chemical engineer with Exxon, Velma is a professional cake decorator; both are now active in the Southeastern Chapter, A.R.S., members of the Gable Study Group, and have been rhododendron breeders for twenty years. Now living in Brevard, N.C.

EMIL V. HAGER, retired from the machine tool and packaging business, enjoys professional status as a photographer, and has presented exceptional programs to many A.R.S. Chapters. Emil and wife, Betty, have been very active in the New York Chapter. They plan to move from Albertston, N.Y., to North Carolina and continue collecting rhododendrons and azaleas there.

BETTY S. HARDING, professional librarian in Montgomery County, Maryland Public Libraries, is an amateur photographer, with special interest in her father's extensive azalea and rhododendron collection in Germantown, Maryland.

GEORGE W. HARDING, retired Chief of the Division of Horticulture and Maintenance, National Capitol Parks, National Park Service,

Department of Interior, living in Germantown, Maryland. He maintains an impressive evergreen azalea collection, travels widely to keep the collection current, and serves on the Evergreen Azalea Committee of A.R.S. He is a frequent speaker on azaleas at local Chapters. Contributor to the Morrison biography in this volume.

STEPHEN HENNING is a physicist at Bell Labs. in Reading, Pa. He and his wife, Darlene, are members of the Valley Forge Chapter, A.R.S. His photographic interests are combined with raising rhododendrons, Christmas trees, and boy scout work.

EUGENE A. HOLLOWELL, late agronomist who specialized in plant breeding and crop production, had worked in the Bureau of Plant Industry of the USDA; published over 100 scientific and popular articles on trifoliums, mehlotus, and other grassland crops. Breeding goals: to improve azaleas and rhododendrons for the D.C. area.

HEMAN A. HOWARD, is a retired career horticulturist. After forty years at Arnold Arboretum, he became Horticulturist to Heritage Plantation on the former Dexter estate at Sandwich, Mass.; chief instigator of project to return all the best Dexter clones to their original home; active in Massachusetts Chapter, A.R.S.; host of 1980 A.R.S. Convention on Cape Cod; now consultant to Heritage Plantation; living at Wellfleet, Mass.

JOANN S. KNAPP, of Locust Valley, N.Y. is staff photographer for Planting Fields Arboretum; she also teaches and serves as a guide for The Friends of Planting Fields. Active in Long Island Horticultural Society and the New York Chapter, A.R.S., where she was Secretary and Director; received the Bronze Medal of the A.R.S. in 1975.

JOHN AND DOROTHY KNIPPENBERG are long time members of the New York and New Jersey Chapters of A.R.S. They have done considerable hybridizing of rhododendrons and operate Laurel Wood Gardens, a wholesale nursery at Pine Lake, Wayne, N.J., and an outstanding display garden of azaleas and rhododendrons.

DAVID G. LEACH, distinguished horticulturist; author; past President of the American Horticultural Society; founder of the Great Lakes Chapter of the A.R.S.; vigorous hybridizer of rhododendrons for the Great Lakes region; lives at North Madison, Ohio and is currently preparing the second edition of his *Rhododendrons of the World,* the most important single book on the subject. He has also in preparation an updated edition of Lee's Azalea Book, and a symposium on rhododendron nomenclature in New York in May 1978.

PHILIP A. LIVINGSTON, ornithologist, horticulturist, conservationist, photographer, and retired publisher of books on natural history subjects. Member of Philadelphia and Valley Forge Chapters, A.R.S.; Fellow of R.H.S.; editor of this volume, and continuing student of azaleas, rhododendrons, and dwarf evergreens at Narberth, Pa.

ALFRED S. MARTIN, Chief Executive Officer of King Fifth Wheel Company and Subsidiaries of Mountaintop, Pa.; past President and Gold Medal winner of American Rhododendron Society; currently a Director of A.R.S. and Chairman of Trustees of Rhododendron Research Foundation, and Board member of Rhododendron Species Foundation.

EDMUND V. MEZITT, President of Weston Nurseries, Hopkinton, Mass. A founder and first President of the Massachusetts Chapter of A.R.S. Began hybridizing in 1939; first cross resulted in the grex *P.J.M.* Makes several hundred crosses a year, with goal of developing outstanding hardy commercial varieties.

GEORGE T. MILLER, of Hanover, Pa., has been hybridizing for fifteen years, with major goal toward indumented yellow rhododendrons. He has an extensive collection of Gable clones, and many of his crosses are based on Gable material. His photographs of new varieties appear in this volume.

ORLANDO S. PRIDE began his experimental nursery in 1928, at Butler, Pa.; specializing in selective breeding of rhododendrons, azaleas, and hollies of great hardiness; past President of the Great Lakes Chapter, A.R.S. He has bred deciduous Ilam-Rothschild azaleas and introduced fifty Pride evergreen azaleas. New rhododendrons are forthcoming.

ALFRED A. RAUSTEIN, retired professional decorator, has an ericaceous plant nursery at Holbrook, in central Long Island, N.Y.; active in New York Chapter, A.R.S., member of R.H.S., Bayard Cutting Arboretum, and German Rhododendron Society. Adds zest to his golden years by hybridizing yellow rhododendrons.

GEORGE W. RING, a highway research engineer for the U.S. Department of Transportation, is a peripatetic rhododendron enthusiast, hybridizer, eastern Chairman of A.R.S. Ratings Committee; Chairman of Gable Study Group which gathered much data for Gable chapter of this book; a Director and past President of Potomac Valley Chapter; is considering a book on rhododendron hybridizers of the U.S. Pacific Northwest. He lives in Fairfax, Virginia.

LUDWIG SCHIERENBECK, son-in-law of C.O. Dexter, was founder and President of Dexdale Hosiery Mills, Lansdale, Pa. He worked with duPont in 1938 in application of nylon to hosiery manufacture. His wife, Alice Elizabeth Dexter, died in 1941. Mr. Shierenbeck died in 1976, at age 88, leaving three daughters, one son, sixteen grandchildren, and three great grandchildren. (His recollections of his father-in-law are key features of the Dexter chapter of this book.)

FRANCIS J. SHOLOMSKAS, Assistant Professor of Mathematics at Temple University, in Philadelphia, past President and Director of the Philadelphia Chapter, A.R.S., and very knowledgeable judge of rhododendron shows. Contributed article to Quarterly, January, 1966, on Philadelphia area rhododendrons. Lent his skills to the analysis, tabulation, and presentation of our survey results in chapter 7 of this volume.

PAUL E. SLEEZER, a professed gardener

since age six, is now retired from a career in the pharmaceutical industry (Hoffman LaRoche). A past President of the New Jersey Chapter, living in Denville, N.J., he was a major contributor to the Nearing Chapter of this book. He is actively interested in rhododendron genetics and hardiness.

ALBERT M. SUGGS, his career in art and advertising, devotes his retirement years to photography and travel. He is an active member of Valley Forge Chapter, A.R.S., the Men's Garden Club of Delaware Valley, and a graduate of the arboretum of the Barnes Foundation at Merion, Pa.

FRANKLIN H. WEST, Philadelphia psychiatrist, teaches at Hahnemann Medical College where he is a professor; in practice at the Institute of the Pennsylvania Hospital; a Trustee and past President of Tyler Arboretum, Lima, Pa.; a Director of the American Rhododendron Society, Rhododendron Research Foundation, and The West Company, Phoenixville, Pa., makers of pharmaceutical closures.

JOHN C. WISTER, of Swarthmore, Pa., retired Director of the Arthur Hoyt Scott Horticultural Foundation of Swarthmore College; retired first Director of Tyler Arboretum; at both places responsible for assembling and planting outstanding horticultural collections. As a member of the Dexter Study Group, he helped identify and name the outstanding Dexter clones; contributed much of the information in this book's Dexter chapter. He is still evaluating his June blooming rhododendron hybrids at Lima and Swarthmore, Pa.

HENRY R. YATES, late of Frostburg, Md., was for many years a collaborator of Joseph Gable, grew many of his seedlings, developed a tried and proven method for starting seeds which he described in A.R.S. Quarterly, July, 1966. Using Gable materials, he developed a number of fine azalea and rhododendron hybrids which his widow, Maletta, watches over at Frostburg. She is a member of the Great Lakes Chapter.

BOOKS FOR READING AND REFERENCE

The following titles are recommended to the grower and student alike, and form a large enough reference collection for most purposes. Also, several of the titles listed have extensive bibliographies, which will suggest additional titles.

RHODODENDRONS AND AZALEAS, Clement G. Bowers; Macmillan

THE AZALEA BOOK, Frederick P. Lee; American Horticultural Society

RHODODENDRON INFORMATION, J. Harold Clarke; American Rhododendron Society

RHODODENDRONS OF THE WORLD, David G. Leach; Scribner

DWARF RHODODENDRONS, Peter A. Cox; Macmillan

RHODODENDRONS, Wisley Handbook No. 2; Royal Horticultural Society

HANDBOOK ON RHODODENDRONS and their relatives; Brooklyn Botanic Garden

RHODODENDRONS AND AZALEAS, a Sunset Book, Lane Books

THE GLENN DALE AZALEAS, B.Y. Morrison; U.S.D.A. Monograph No. 20

AZALEAS, Fred C. Galle; Oxmoor House

RHODODENDRONS IN AMERICA, Ted Van Veen; Sweeney, Krist and Dimm

GETTING STARTED WITH RHODODENDRONS AND AZALEAS, J. Harold Clarke, Doubleday

In addition to reference books, membership in one or more rhododendron societies is recommended to those readers interested in the newest developments in rhododendrons and azaleas. The Bulletins are interesting and informative:

The American Rhododendron Society
Executive Secretary
617 Fairway Drive
Aberdeen, WA 98520

The Australian Rhododendron Society
P.O. Box 21
Olinda 3788
Victoria
Australia

The Rhododendron Society of Canada
Dr. H.G. Hedges
4271 Lakeshore Road
Burlington, Ontario
Canada

The New Zealand Rhododendron Association
Mrs. J.S. Clyne, Editor
38A Seddon Street
Highfield, Timaru
New Zealand

Subject Index

The figures printed in boldface type refer to the number under each subject in the color pages.

Variety Index

This index does not attempt to list all varieties and crosses mentioned in the book. Cultivars described or treated at length, or printed in color, are indexed. Many hundreds of cultivars appear in the tables and lists, a list of which appears at the end of this Index.

The figures printed in boldface type refer to the number under each subject in the color pages.

List of Tables

SUPPLEMENT

The Letters from Gable to Nearing

The lengthy correspondence between Joseph B. Gable and Guy Nearing is notable for its wealth of rhododendron lore and for a high level of literary quality.

A limited sampling of the letters of Nearing to Gable appears in the Nearing chapter, but the reverse correspondence had vanished. As this book was going to press, the missing letters were found and rushed to our editors who have extracted a small sample of the 642 fascinating pages.

A copy of the entire file is available by arrangement with the publisher of Hybrids and Hybridizers.

May 15, 1930

Dear Mr. Nearing,

Am sending the seeds separately and hope they succeed with you. I cannot of course tell you much about them except that every number sent came from China so there is no possibility of their having taken on pollen of any *catawbiense* hybrids etc. One of the names of the seed from Rothschild I am not able to make out surely and I noted same on the envelope. On the packets containing Rock's numbers the first number starting in each case with '03'—are the numbers I received the seed under, (I suppose Rock's serial numbers) the number at the upper right hand corner being my own sowing number for this spring. Over 200 kinds! I wonder if I shall be able to care for them all?

I still have quite a few numbers to sow including these I send you. I have come through alright with June sown seeds but I think they never catch up to those sown in January. Did you get the article in Country Life on Dexter's methods of raising from seeds? According to the article many of his azaleas and rhododendrons flower in a year or two from seeds profusely. Beats me. Thought when two year seedlings bore a flower or two I was doing wonders. Some flowers of my *poukhanense* hybrids were of wonderful form and good size and some of the purple shades were at least infinitely better than "Yodogawa" or "amoena" varieties at present popular in the trade. Also in the very hot sun of last week the Hose in Hose flowers of some of my hybrids (*poukhanense* x "Hexe") stood up better than "Yodogawa" and the plants are and will undoubtedly continue to be of much better habit of growth and can be listed as being as evergreen as any azalea.

My old friend Mr. Fraser who has been in the hybridizing game for a *mere* fifty years says grafted plants are but little better as seed or pollen as parents than the stock species upon which they are grafted. So I guess I will use the *catawbiense* & *maximum* species and am mighty glad to have the plant above for its vigor and color as it is undoubtedly own rooted as it came from N. C. in a bundle of collected seedlings.

In English gardening descriptions of things we must allow for a different point of view. They regard *R. viscosum* as one of the very best azaleas and we don't do much with it in this country commercially as you well know. They have gardened long enough and successfully enough to produce and become familiar with so many rhodos and azaleas (as well as other plants of other genera) of so many brilliant colors that too much of it tires and the little modest fragrant flowers of a plant like *R. viscosum* rests the eye and is appreciated.

October 23, 1930

I have sat down three times to write you and am now writing with an apple buyer waiting on me. I hope you can come along with the truck for the *concolors* on Mon. and that you will have a little time to spend here. We will be glad to have you lunch with us.

I return Mr. Barto's letter which I read with much interest. From his name he is probably not American born and that may account for his spelling (which is considerably better than I imagine mine would be in French or German!) but he has that self assurance in his manner which is typically American and more typical in the West than the East I believe. However his intense interest will undoubtedly bring results of some sort and that is what counts.

Jan. 30, 1931

Sowed my first lot of rhododendron seeds today and saved what I could of the numbers you were interested in. In many cases I could not say for sure whether there was really a seed among the fragments or not—in one case I could count just five and so I did not attempt to divide those infinitesmal lots but in each case where I could see a couple of dozen seeds or so I am sharing with you. I no longer pollenate a whole cluster of flowers—I did at first—but now remove all but two or three and this season the capsules that did set filled very poorly in most cases.

My friend in Vancouver who has seedlings 10-12 ft. high and yet unnamed insists that to get good color in hybrid seedlings the plants from which the seed is taken must be own rooted. With a long life of experiments and experiences as a background I think some weight should be given to his advice. The few *catawbiense* hybrid seedlings that have flowered for me have been far from good. Fraser of Vancouver grows a hybrid that is so dark it is about black judging from the dried flowers he sent me. He claims it is the darkest rhodo he ever saw and calls it "Mrs. Jamie Fraser" I believe.

I have noticed with the pollen from England that pollen which has adhered to the envelopes or filaments seems to be dead and only that which is yet in the anther viable. But to be sure it is much older than pollen from Longwood would be and it might be alright to take it on a piece of paper or envelope.

Feb. 17, 1931

I wish to compliment you on your most excellent article in the Florists' Exchange. I think it is certainly well done in every respect. 'Horticulture' asked me for some notes and I wrote a little article mostly on *R. racemosum*. On reading yours I wish I had left it to you but then perhaps they won't publish my article anyhow. I have never before written for publication except a short note on *Kalmia latifolia* which was published in Gardeners' Chronicle (English). Several letters have found their way in print and the article in the 1930 Rhodo Yearbook was part of a letter to a member over there and if I had known it was to be published would have revised it much more carefully or what is more likely, I would have never found nerve to send it at all.

May 31, 1931

Taking advantage of a business trip to Towson, Md. Friday I took an hour off to view the 'Asiatic Rhododendrons.' A salesman at once promised to show me them when I told him in what I was interested. He showed me acres of hybrids, all of which by the way have been propagated by layering and on the whole they looked well, possibly from being on their own roots, but the plants are unsymmetrical, the smaller ones very much so. "Mme. Masson" a white flowered sort which is new to me had—in my opinion—the prettiest trusses I ever saw and possibly the largest flowers I have yet seen on an outdoor plant. . . . Every few minutes however I urged my salesman guide to not waste time showing me the hybrids etc. as I had but little time and wished to spend it looking at the 'Asiatics.' He paid little or no attention so when we reached the end of the field and he stopped I said "Now which way to see the Asiatic species?" "These are the Asiatics you have just been looking at!" he replied. Then I unloaded on him a little to be sure and I think he at least understood the main points.

It seems to me that this sort of advertising will eventually harm the sale of the true species. The average customer will believe he is looking at "Asiatic Rhododendrons" when such a nursery as Towson tells him he is.

And when he comes up to my little place sometime and I show him such things as *R. impeditum* or *R. racemosum* or the triflorums and tell him they are of the Asiatic species he is apt to become argumentative for "has he not seen them all at Towson?"

Admires Dexter

July 21, 1931

I am sending back Mr. Dexter's letter as I have made notes of the principal things I want from it.

This letter of his only confirms my opinion that Mr. Dexter is a great grower and an enthusiastic rhododendron 'fan.' From what he had written me I believe he has done much more with the azaleas than with the other rhododendrons. In your letter he speaks of the alpines but little but in a letter to me spring of 1929 he mentions having flowered 'some of Rocks' Nos.' belonging to the Lapponicum series with very small flowers purple or lavender and not very interesting though when they bloom more profusely they should be pretty." He also stated that they seemed perfectly hardy but he does not mention them in your letter.

Dec. 19, 1931

It is impossible here to give my outdoor plants such protection as you speak of and for the most part they are left alone. In the frames I cover with the Celo-Glass covers only when temperatures are very severe and when we have snow I try to get the beds full, then place the covers on to keep the snow covering about the plants as long as possible. Often in March I have succeeded by these methods in having a covering of solid ice about the small seedlings.

Dec. 20, 1931

I gave up writing yesterday morning and now my head feels much clearer though I admit somewhat of a dazed condition apropos an article in House & Garden by Herbert Durand concerning the Royal Botanic Garden, Edinburgh, in which he states in writing of the rhododendrons there, "The finest of them as a matter of course, were those that were all-American or had been blessed with a preponderance of American blood." (!) And, "And the crowning glory, not only of the Arboretum but of the entire garden, is the most superb Rhododendron I have ever seen or ever expect to see. 'It is known far and wide,' said Curator Harrow, 'as Old Apple Blossom and it has stood where you see it for over one hundred years. We give a sight of it,' he added smilingly, 'to visitors who show a real interest in the garden and don't ask foolish questions, as a special and final treat—and we never fail to inform them that it is a pure-blooded American plant.' Old Apple Blossom stands ten feet high by ten feet in diameter and on that day was covered as with a blanket by a multitude of rosy flowers. Hardly a leaf was visible between them. A fortunate hybrid between *R. maximum & R. minus its proud origin is not to be questioned.*" (!)

My one poor plant of this hybrid less than an inch high, a lone survivor of some hundred or hundreds of germinated seeds, which lived for a little over five years to attain that stature and three leaves lacked only another paltry century to become the peer of the "most superb" of rhododendrons! And I was *almost glad* when that last thankless seedling died little dreaming the tragicness of the catastrophe that had befallen my garden! I deem further remarks superfluous save to state that I am not to be coerced into making the cross again until more 'unquestionable' evidence becomes available.

I do not think forcing tends to suppress fertility unless it is done in such a manner as to supress vigor. Any loss of vitality or any condition of unhealthiness is as liable to cause barrenness in plants as it is in animals. Perhaps more so for animals have ideas of their own. It has been my experience that a plant collected roughly or that is hurt in transplanting even though it flowers, is neither a good seed parent nor a good pollen parent until after a season or two when they have recovered. I have known such plants to produce no pollen and I regard it as very likely that a plant too weak to produce pollen will also fail to produce seed. . .*R. decorum* last year produced pollen in only a few anthers. Also it set seed in only three capsules.

Climatic influence also has an effect on fertility. *R.*

auriculatum rarely seeds with Magor or at Edinburgh even when hand pollenated. It seems to grow well there and produces pollen so it can hardly be lack of vitality.

Mr. Fraser of B.C., an old hybridist—alas growing too old as we all must—says that many hybrids, not all, at first sterile, later become fertile. Perhaps only partially, perhaps normally so. My experience not being carried out over so many years I have nothing to corroborate.

Feb. 29, 1932

Towson Nurseries who staged the Asiatic Rhododendron display last season wrote me for a list of such things as were named in Farrington's Book on Wilson. I took the opportunity to tell them that if they were "not familiar with the Asiatic Rhododendrons they would find them quite different from the fine display of *Catawbiense* hybrids I saw at their nursery last season."

Mar. 8, 1932

Well winter has at last put in its belated appearance and forced the mercury down very close to the zero mark this morning. Tomorrow from present indications it will be even colder. However, all of my little rhododendrons are covered with snow—some places only a few inches, other places as much as four feet, and if they do not stand it will probably be on account of tenderness and I do not care to bother with too many plants of tender species.

These storms come suddenly here. Sunday morning was mild and fair when we left here and it was only raining when we left my wife's brother 7 miles southwest of Balto. No mail, no telephones, no railroads open and the main road out front only open a few miles to the north though now open to Balto. southwards.

A West Coast grower who is interested is Mr. Theodore van Veen of Portland, Oregon. He is acquainted with Barto and has been growing azaleas and rhododendrons etc. in a wholesale way for some years.

. . . .I have seen *R. racemosum* showing color unharmed by a heavy freeze and we see *R. mucronulatum* do it every year. A good point in favor of *R. mucronulatum* hybrids—as far as I am acquainted with them—is their ease and quickness of forcing. If better color can be bred into them they may take a place in this line as the forcing time is reduced from six weeks or so to not over two weeks. I would like to get *mucronulatum* crossed by *cinnabarinum* and if I am "old enough to give advice" let me insist that you lose no opportunity to make this cross if the chance presents itself.

Dec. 19, 1932

.... I am in perfect accord with all you say about the publicity of our ideas and though I have not always told everything I could to everybody who asked it was mostly because of lack of time for—well you know there are those whom you just know will never be able to absorb much and you don't feel like taking the trouble—and not because I have any desire to be secretive. Of course I understand about why you do not publish your cutting propagating methods. And really I don't think you hurt the popularity of these plants at all by keeping the secret. The only one I know of who spoke resentfully to me of your keeping your method a secret was Mrs. Mary G. Henry. And though I used all the tact I possess I was unable to make any perceptible impression in your favor. But I must not talk about her. She has been very good to me but I perceive that like dynamite she must be handled carefully.

I sent the copy of the symposium to Mr. Morrison and the other two copies are both out. One to How at Tacoma, the other to your friend Mrs. Mustin, but I have so far received no additions.

Feb. 26, 1933

Dear Mr. Nearing,

Joe has not been propped up one half dozen times. About 10 days ago he commenced to cough mostly in the evening and since has been able to get up a great deal of phlegm, and since he was weak when he started this he is not gaining strength fast. The Drs. say it is delayed pneumonia and caused fluid in the side. We are thankful he has had no fever for two weeks and has not much pain in his side, but it is going to take time for him to get back where he was. It is rather hard on his business, but we are ready to do without comforts etc. if we are able to keep him with us and have good health. I can never manage these four kiddies like he can.

Yours Truly,
Mrs. Mary Gable

June 28, 1933

'Chasing yourself around in circles' is just about the right expression for what I have been doing since I can get around better. The only trouble is I am too slow and don't complete the circles as quickly as I should in order to get to things at the right time.

.... We will soon be done moving old plants to larger pots and to the open ground and then I shall have to look around for some place to put this years seedlings. In moving I have so far found only one true *R. haematodes* and I am supposed to have three. Perhaps they will turn up yet and I hope so as I regard this one

of the most valuable species for us. If not as a true species at least as a parent of new hybrids. And another very valuable one judging from its behavior here is *R. discolor*. Standing out distinctly in my bed of *decorum* and *Fortunei* that were injured are 5 or 6 plants of *discolor*—or at least they have the typical foliage of *discolor*—that were not at all injured and neither these nor the two outdoor plants from the Arnold Arboretum nor my seedlings from Magor that are now in 6 in. pots (and should be in 10″s) lost a single bud from frost, whereas *decorum* and *Fortunei* suffer habitually in this respect here. And I believe that *discolor* is just a shade hardier than *auriculatum*. At least its leaves come through the winter in a rather more presentable appearance though *auriculatum* is thoroughly bud hardy.

Oak Hybridization

Oct. 23, 1933

Yesterday we walked out in a grove of oaks and persimmons near the 'Rocks' of Deer Creek and I noted a few Post Oaks (or Jack Oaks?) *Quercus marilandica*. The variation in them was astonishing and I took some time to studying them—casually of course. There were a few Pin Oaks, *Quercus palustris,* there also and after wandering over several acres I came to the conclusion that almost every oak in the grove was of hybrid origin between the two species. Only a few were typical *palustris* (or nearly typical) and only a few *marilandica* came near the type. The other 90 or 95% showed almost every possible variation between, the leaves, the nuts, the branches, bark and tomentum were combined in almost every conceivable combination. Indeed I can't think of a possible combination of characters that wasn't shown up somewhere among those oaks. I am bewildered when I think of rhododendron hybrids and their future when we bring so many species together instead of only two as in this grove of oaks. Records of their parentage can not be too carefully kept if we expect to know what we have after while. I know that I am unable to give the pedigree of some of my azalea hybrids now.

Dec. 31, 1933

There has been a week of real winter weather here—and I suppose with you also. Dec. 29 and 30th, 5 and 7 degrees below zero and just zero on the 28th. Mr. Halfdan Lem of Ketchikan, Alaska, reports that he much fears that his 'rhododendrons' will be badly injured by a temperature of 7 above—the coldest they have experienced in Ketchikan since 1915—and only 10 inches of snow! He also states that it rained all summer—only 10 sunshiny days in 1933. Is it any wonder that the Sitka spruce does not grow well here. I had a number of these, several thousand I think from an ounce of seed sown in 1920. Four survived until last winter— or more probably the spring of 1933—at least all were dead when I went out to get them last spring.

Feb. 22, 1934

Well how do you like this? 5 below again yesterday morning but we have considerable snow. In places the snow is 12-15 ft. in others the ground is quite bare. An examination of my azalea hybrids of the *Kaempferi* and *Poukhanense* crosses out in the fields shows that at least 90% of them are killed. And I was unable to find a single good bud on any *species* that I have of the obtusum subseries excepting on *Poukhanense*. On this the flower buds show little or no injury at present. . . . You notice I call *Poukhanense* a species. That just comes natural for it is hard for me to think of *yedoense* (yodogawa) as a species and *Poukhanense* as a variety though I know our systematists treat this species in that manner. It would be an exactly analogous case if *R. nudiflorum* were to be considered a variety and the double flowered form of it of which I have seen but one plant were considered the species.

April 7, 1934

It is very disheartening to find some species of which one may have a quantity as *decorum, auriculatum, neriiflorum,* etc. a total loss or nearly so but when one finds that other things as *discolor, Fortunei, haemetodes, vernicosum* aff. 18139 Rock etc. come through alright in full exposure not a plant being killed then we feel like we have some things that are really worthwhile and that we no longer need to worry about as to their hardiness or lack of it.

Dec. 17, 1934

I have just returned from seeing hundreds of acres, perhaps thousands of them, of rhododendrons and made some observations while on the hunt of whitetail deer, presumably. There is an area somewhere near the line of Cameron and Elk Cos. where over 90% perhaps 95 or 99% of the *Rhododendron maximum,* which constituted the main ingredient of acres of impenetrable thicket, is dead. From drought? Mostly so I think. Then 10 or 12 miles north is an area where although the inhabitants claim the drought was severe every stage of growth of this Rhod. from a quarter inch seedling to some that measure 32 feet are to be found and no dead plants.

. . . . the wonder to me is that *Rhod. maximum* has stood as well as it has. . . . . So we must add to the good qualities of this rhod. a great degree of drought

resistance which is I think quite a desideratum in this part of the country.

April 18, 1935

Mr. Rothschild wrote me for names of my hybrids and I sent him the names I first sent you. He replied that as far as possible they were discontinuing the combination of two specific names and I suggested Indian names. Hence the names in the year book.

June 7, 1935

Mr. B. Y. Morrison was here Sat. and looked things over and appeared to be much interested in the rhodos. He has taken a series of studio pictures of some of my hybrids and hopes to keep a continuous line of articles on rhodos. in his magazine.

July 24, 1935

Just had a communication from a New England firm, 'Cronamere,' telling me that someone in my locality was offering good size *racemosum* at 50ᵉ and wondering if I couldn't do better! I answered that I hoped my progress toward bankruptcy would be more nearly normal.

Sept. 2, 1935

Yesterday I just happened to see my one capsule of *Smirnowii* crossed by pollen of *Haematodes* was opening, so I lost a few seeds from it. Both *Smirnowii* and *Haematodes* ripen their seed very early and should be gathered before Sept. 1. Boule de Neige is another that ripens early and splitting the capsules to the very base all seed is lost unless one is on the watch for them.

Feb. 4, 1936

At last Dr. Bower's Book on Rhodos. Haven't had time to go over it thoroughly yet but I do think he has on the whole given us something worthwhile. I notice one very regrettable mistake. He has given me credit for the *Carolinianum* x *Kaempferi* hybrid which is yours. I am telling him about it but yet I feel guilty for I probably did not tell him that you produced the cross and he has taken for granted seeing it here that it was my product. If I may criticize I think he has taken too much 'for granted.' I have not corresponded with him to any great extent yet he has written a lot about my experiences with different rhododendrons and not always as I should write them. I think he must have taken some shorthand notes when here and then expanded on them at leisure as is the habit of some reporters. Another thing I might criticize is his copyright notes inside the title page where he has so evidently included in the work quotations and transcriptions from others who have given them freely to him.

Mar. 7, 1937

If bluebirds and robins make a spring, then spring is here but I fear that like prosperity it is yet 'just around the corner.'

R. Metternichii has finally flowered i.e. if what I have under that label is really *R. Metternichii* (or *Degronianum*). I noticed the bud on my plant swelling some weeks back so brought it in. The flowers are a fair pink or rose color with darker stripes down the medial lines as with *R. brachycarpum* but there is a dark red blotch breaking into profuse spotting on the inside of the corolla that greatly enhances the beauty of it. The shape of the flower however is much nearer Bowers No. 58 (*Fargesii*) than it resembles No. 54 (*R. Degronianum*). Two of the flowers in the cluster have 6 corolla lobes, the remainder 5. The inflorescence type is more like Bowers (6) than anything else but surely it is not near *Nuttalli*. I have tried to obtain a picture so perhaps can send you a print later.

R. mucronulatum x *R. spinuliferum* from pollen you sent from Longwood is also in flower but apparently there is nothing remarkable about it. It is a little better in color than *mucronulatum* and much more evergreen and has not yet opened its flowers near as widely.

I think that the elimination of some species i.e. a voluntary discarding, not the work of the weather, will be desirable here. Certain things after years of trial fail to do well and others are of so little value if they do succeed that it is almost a shame to put them on the market.

May 27, 1937

Well, I saw Arnold Arboretum or at least part of it. The crowd on Sunday was too great to see much so I went back on Monday morning and Mr. Rehder and Dr. Kobuski went around with me and I saw most of their plantings of the rarer species and hybrids of rhododendron. One of the loveliest *Smirnowii* hybrids was in flower and I think it very much like my cross with *Fortunei* but theirs is an enormous thing. There are also several *Smirnowii* hybrids labelled *Smirnowii* which helps to explain why my seedlings from there contain so many hybrid forms. *Smirnowii* x *Arboreum* is in flower here now and is uniformly good. Mostly pink but the color is pure and there is one bright red, very clear but not dark—something like a glorified Carvalho.

Dexter has the most wonderful lot of *Fortunei* hybrids. Personally I think there is little but *Fortunei* blood in most of them but his selections are certainly

outstanding. He does have a *Fortunei* x *haematodes* cross in which he has obtained a great variation in color from apricot pinks to white, some of them of the most lovely shadings imaginable. The plants of this are rather dwarf and are in full flower at 12 to 18 inches with huge clusters for the size of the plant—there were about 800 in bloom. But my plants of *haematodes* from the Arboretum, which Wilson told me came from Dexter, were certainly not pure typical *haematodes* and I feel sure it is this form and not the true species that Dexter has used for I saw his plant that he thinks is *haematodes*. Be this as it may he has some wonderful things flowering out there in the open on Cape Cod and I believe they would be hardy with us for his experience in the tests of hardiness of various other species seem to be about the same as my own.

Dexter by the way has great drifts of *muliense*, *chryseum*, *fastigiatum*, *impeditum* and *hippophaeoides* in the rock garden there and they look as much at home as the heather and brooms in the rocks of Scotland. One secret of his success in my opinion is the abundance of water he gives them. He has the whole place laid with pipes for irrigation and says he never has had any shortage of water so far.

The two *brachycarpum* hybrids that I have been waiting years to see bloom finally opened and I almost could wish they hadn't done it. The foliage was so good that I have hoped they would have at least moderately good flowers but they are a pale hopeless looking mauve that will likely remain friendless even in the garden of a rhodo fan. And this in spite of the fact that they have a very much elongated rhachis and 24 flowers of good size to the cluster. The pedicels are also some two to three inches in length making a large open cluster.

On Rooting Cuttings

July 9, 1937

I suppose you are thinking by this time that I am not very anxious to obtain the cutting information that you so kindly offered me. Writing is always sort of a bore to me so if I have the least excuse I find it very easy to 'postpone the evil day.' Any such information that you choose to give will be greatly appreciated and kept strictly confidential. The fact is, to be perfectly frank, I have been keeping a few things under my own hat concerning the raising of cuttings that I have learned in the course of my own attempts to propagate in this manner.

Four parts of granulated German peat moss to one part of Michigan peat is much better than pure German peat or sand or sand and peat in my experience for any ericaceous material. Concolor fir and Douglas fir rooted sparingly in this as against none in sand but juniper (*communis* var.) rooted better in sand.

Potassium permanganate 1 oz. to 5 gal. of water is applied to the cuttings with a watering can using enough to wet all the foliage thoroughly and saturate the top soil. This immediately after placing the cuttings. This is generally washed off in a few hours.

After a few days ferrous sulphate, also 1 oz. to 5 gal. of water is applied in the same manner and amount late in the evening and allowed to remain on the foliage over night. And if at any later time the leaves of the cuttings appear to be somewhat too yellow this application may be repeated. So treated very yellow leaves have been observed to turn dark green in 24 hours.

Just how much of this is generally known I do not know but the only thing I have heard of others using is the potassium permanganate. This has been recommended as a soil treatment before placing the cuttings but I never heard of anyone using it as above after they have been placed in the rooting medium.

Had I previously sent you a photo of the rhododendron Caroline picked to be named for her? It has flowers much like *R. Fortunei* but the foliage is more like a *catawbiense* variety. It is one of the things I would like to root.

July 26, 1937

It certainly was good of you to give me all that information on growing cuttings. Sure I'll keep it to myself. This season I hardly see how I shall even be able to put it into practice as it seems everything is trying to keep about one or two jumps ahead of me.

You place your cuttings much deeper in the medium than I. If the cuttings are too deep they do not root nearly so quickly or so well as they do if they are only ¼–½" deep in my conditions. Very often cuttings placed so shallow as that fall over on top of the peat and lie there quite exposed. It is not unusual to find these the first of the lot to root. Formerly the peat was covered with sand and I have also used sphagnum moss, rough leaf mould or other material in the bottom of the box but could see no advantage in my practice of these methods here. When sand was placed on top of the peat azalea cuttings invariably rooted quicker where the sand was lightest and a larger percentage of rooted cuttings were also obtained so the sand was discontinued with better results.

Mr. Morrison puts his azalea cuttings in three or four inches in the medium and is undeniably successful but his methods also differ from mine in other ways. What I am after is speed and as my azaleas put in June 25—27th are now ready to pot up with somewhere between 90 and 100% struck—and no Hormodin—I think I might do worse.

There is not the slightest doubt in my mind that your

method is much the better one for the broadleaf rhodos. I have never made a really serious attempt to root this class but while a few have rooted well—*Williamsianum* and *Wardii* never fail—I would feel beaten before I started were I to try the named hybrids on a commercial scale.

Your idea is reflected light—mine has been refracted light. Under the cel-o-glass with reasonable care and sufficient moisture I have yet to see either cuttings or the tiniest seedling hurt even in periods of hottest sunshine.

It requires a number of years to propagate any commercial quantity of a new thing even if it does as well as the azaleas, and the rhodos do not make as much wood so it will take much longer in their case. So perhaps it is better not to try to produce too many new things but rather to take better care of what one has already started and try to propagate the best of it until it reaches commercial proportions. Yet I must make some new crosses from time to time as the inspiration strikes me but I have abandoned the idea of making every new cross I can think of and try to make only those that would seem to promise the best results. There are so many things around here now that had better never been made and yet I do not like to destroy and they are ever requiring more and more room and work to take care of them. There must be an end to it somewhere.

July 22, 1938

Rain, rain and more rain but it hurts little here though I always think of your situation and whether you will have another flood. But we did have a tornado and I heard over the radio and read in the papers that my nursery was totally destroyed! Not that bad of course but my loss to crops and shade trees will be hard to estimate for a while. We have cut enough firewood from the trees that were blown down on the lawn to do us next winter and we still have five apple trees in the orchard blown over and hundreds of oaks in the woods. The loss to the apple crop will be about fifty per cent and corn and other things are also hurt very badly. However we fared well compared to some of our neighbors whose buildings were ruined and livestock all killed in addition to their crops. We had no damage worth mentioning to our buildings and we are seldom hurt much by high water up here so we are lucky I suppose even if only by comparison. Mr. Anderson next below me has over five hundred apple trees uprooted and seventy five or more per cent crop damage.

I did lose a few rhododendrons. The one I will miss most is the large plant of America. A great limb just missed the plant of Souldisclit that I sent you a flower of. Three plants in all of this cross flowered. They were much alike in general appearance and color except that the crimson spotting in the throat varied from conspicuous to absent and the seedling from which I sent you the bloom had the largest flower. It seems to be setting seed from pollen of *discolor,* as do many other things for I used *discolor* pollen on everything I could find in flower.

On *discolor* itself I used mostly pollen of the *Fortunei* hybrid that I call Caroline and a large flowered seedling of Decatros. And such seed pods I never saw on any rhododendron in my experience. They remind one of small green bananas.

I have not had time to look over everything that I tried to cross but I have noticed quite a number of them that have apparently 'taken'. One of the most interesting things to me is Atrosanguineum x *repens* and another is *Smirnowii* x *floccigerum,* pollen of this last from the Rock No. that flowered here blood red with a very thick fleshy corolla.

I never had that leaf pest here but saw it very bad at Gillin's place and he said arsenate of lead killed it for him.

December 27, 1938

At last I have gotten around to making a few copies of this years inventory and am sending you one herewith. Of course there are bound to be some errors and omissions but I think it is fairly comprehensive. No effort was made to include 1 & 2 years seedlings that are still in twos and this seasons cuttings. Anything you wish from this list to replenish your flood losses—or any other losses—is yours for the asking. And please ask.

(The inventory of 14 single spaced typed pages, approximately 56 lines to the page, contained rhododendron species & hybrids, numbered azalea hybrids, plus 84 lots of his 1938 seed crop.—Ed.)

January 26, 1939

Never again I think do I wish to sow another such list of collectors numbers as that from the U.C. BG, Rock expedition or the Magor hybrids. We already have by our own experience found out enough about the species and series to know what is hardy enough to be of any use to us, we have practically all the sorts that we can grow under such protection as we can give them without artificial heat either up to flowering size or nearly so. There are of course a few very desirable things that we would like to have but we know what they are and can select them.

My experience with *maximum* hybrids apparently does not coincide with yours. My only two tender crosses are with *Griersonianum* which is now long dead and with *haematodes* which I still have but which

seems to need heavy protection. Your *discolor* hybrid with *maximum* I consider one of the hardiest, and prettiest plants in foliage on the place. Also the cross with *campylocarpum* is a lovely hardy thing and several more promising matings with *maximum* as one parent are coming along. One in particular, *maximum* x Mrs. Jamie Fraser, which last is I think a *californicum* x *arboreum* hybrid by George Fraser, is a most vigorous thing with red stems and petioles but at four feet and sown in 1930 has not yet flowered. I doubt if the *maximum* x *Fortunei* from Hicks is true. It flowers too late and there are other characters that lead me to doubt it. I think at least that I could make a better cross between these two species—if I live long enough I may. Conceit? Maybe. Well at least it is honest conceit, and only failure to do it will take it out of me. I'll confess I do not know what the Hicks plant—it is one of Bowers' hybrids—really is, I thought too it was true at first. Flowering late in life is a *maximum* hybrid fault.

January 29, 1940

Conestoga died by the dozens for me the last two seasons but I think I have found the cause but whether I have or not that hybrid in its first generation is fully hardy here to winter cold, though it does start a little early in spring. The reason I lost so many plants seems to be an excess of soil acidity. I had a lot of testing done here last summer after losing several thousand of my rooted cuttings of the numbered azalea selections and found that the soil tested as low as 3.4 and that where the azaleas looked best it tested around 5.5 to 6.5. A heavy application of bone meal brought a lot of them back that were not too far gone but I moved my Conestogas to the woods where they have recovered and now look fine. . . . . *Racemosum* also showed a liking for soils around 6–6.5 but Conewago looked fairly well in the more acid spots and *discolor* and some various other broad leaf hybrids seemed to do better below 5—perhaps 4.5 to 5. I did not have any tests that showed lower than 4.5 from soils where these broadleaved sorts were growing but I do not think it would hurt them like it did Conestoga and some of the azaleas. An azalea that very definitely likes its soil neutral or nearly so is *Schlippenbachii*. In soils that are too acid the leaves turn before the summer is half over and they look like they are sunburnt but they are not for they will do the same no matter how shady.

. . . I also applied a heavy dose of bone meal to a number of potted Lapponicums of various species that had turned yellow and that seem to always pass out when they get that way here. Before the summer was over they seemed to show a much improved color or at least some of the plants did but it was so late when I tried it and with no tests to show what the soil was in the first place I would not want to make any definite statement.—I stopped typing right here and went out and looked at that bed and the half that had the bone meal still looks best.

March 21, 1940

I sure do wish you could have some of the acres of flood proof rhododendron ground that is doing nothing here but to sink me deeper in debt paying taxes on it. I dream sometimes of putting it into use but it will probably never all be used in my time for this is the 54th year for me.

Sometimes too I think we should form a partnership of some kind but I am so much embarrassed financially that it also embarrasses me to suggest anything of that sort. But there are at least 50 acres of potential rhodo nursery laying idle. The soil needs nothing but the bushes and small trees to be taken off.

June 10, 1940

I am glad that you 'cannot quite agree' with me concerning the triflorums and I hope in some other matters also for if we agreed perfectly on everything and did everything alike our results would be also monotonously parallel. Variety is desirable and thank God we still live in a country where we dare to differ with impunity but with so many nations getting imbued with the idea that they can't get to hell quite quick enough perhaps our freedom is imperilled also. Yet I shall boast while I may.

But the trouble with the triflorums is that there seem to be none quite hardy enough. Crosses outside the series of which I have several seem to do well provided the other parent possess a good margin of hardiness and the only 'other parent' possessing this margin of hardiness in my experience is *mucronulatum. Carolinianum* has not proven its worth but I have used it only once as far as I can remember. At least the only *carolinianum-triflorum* that I have flowered is the one with *Davidsonianum* and they have now all perished. Perhaps in some measure I confess from neglect for they were not nearly as good as *carolinianum* itself.

Mucronulatum x *ambiguum* is a close second to Conewago if indeed it rates second. In flower Conewago is just a shade superior. I have the original plants of each side by side and always have to call visitors' attention to the fact that there are two different plants growing there. Out of flower I would say that the mucr-amb cross is the best. It is more evergreen and has the better plant habit. Also cutting grown plants branch out into a nice shapely plant much earlier than Conewago. It may not be quite as hardy—but no injury has ever occurred to either here from winter cold. Conewago is one or two days earlier to flower.

After all the *Fortunei* hybrids are, considering everything, the best crosses that I have so far in my work here. They are growable, hardy, make nice plants, mostly fragrant, flowers and trusses of good size and shape, come before the new growth hides anything and indeed lack only one thing—deep colored forms. To offset this there are very few seedlings with really bad color; most all of them with the exception of some of the *Smirnowii* x *Fortunei* have very clear pale coloring.

March 17, 1941

*Dear Guy:

Mr. Powell Glass of Lynchburg, Va. the son and press agent of U.S. Senator Carter Glass sent me some seeds of seven white *catawbiense* rhododendrons that he found in the mountains in that section and has collected and moved to his home in Lynchburg. These are now in 3 & 4 inch pots, there are 117 of them and he is still to get half. If you will be interested to have some of these will be glad to let you have some. It is hard to say how many will be white flowered although Mr. Powell says that he made an effort in intercross between the white flowered plants, in producing this seed.

I think too that perhaps all the rhododendron species that will benefit us much are those that are now growing on the west coast. It seems just about impossible to grow to flowering size in the east many of the most desirable species that we need for hybridization purposes. Rhododendron culture is not uppermost in the minds of many Britishers at the moment and it will be years before the damage there can be repaired and apparently the end is far from being in sight yet. In any war that really gets serious it seems that about so many men must die before peace can come. It does not seem to matter if the instruments of death are bow and arrow or the more lethal modernities now in use, no country will submit until it has lost a certain, fairly constant percentage of its manpower. And only those countries that tried not to fight as Poland, Holland and Belgium have lost much manpower as yet. If history is to repeat itself Hitler must be put down and he is too strong for this to be accomplished for some time—some years in my opinion. There can be no peace with such as Hitler in power no matter if he may have some good things in his ideas. Peace to his type means only an opportunity to prepare for new conquests. And in the meantime our democracies and our rhododendrons will have to suffer.

---

*See Nearing-Gable letter of December 29, 1940. Page 156

Some time ago I wrote you that an application of bone meal seemed to be helping my ailing lapponicums. Now after three years of repotting in soil heavily mixed with bone meal some of those old sickly plants are as healthy looking as anything on the place. In fact they are all either dead or healthy—kill or cure. This season every lapponicum that was repotted was given a generous amount as indeed we did to most of them last year and my lapponicums apparently have taken on a new lease of life. In this same category I have placed all the dwarf lepidotes as *keleticum, saluenense* etc. with the same appearance of favorable reactions. Also the obtusum series of azaleas in general are so greatly benefitted by bone meal that I would no longer care to try to grow them without.

....*Racemosum* that had bone meal worked into the soil about the roots showed great improvement for the most part but I only used it on the plants that looked sickly. In fact excepting the azaleas of the obtusum group and the lapponicums and their kind general use has not been made of it for I see no use in using it where I have no trouble.

It is not the nitrogen alone that does this for at first and again this season I used the bone in comparison with cow manure on some old yellowed azalea plants with everything in favor of the bone.

January 21, 1942

I think I did tell you that the large plant of *R. Smirnowii*—so labelled—in the Arnold Arboretum, is undoubtedly a hybrid. Since it is the largest and perhaps oldest plant there under that name it is perhaps the plant upon which the Arnold Arboretum reputation for the species is built. It has been so often recommended in their bulletin and in other writings by the plantsmen there. Right beside this old plant there are growing—or were growing when I was last there in 39 I think—two or three small half killed out plants of the type that I regard as true *Smirnowii*. The best of these was also flowering one time I was there from buds which had many blighted florets. The large hybrid *Smirnowii* beside it had wintered perfectly.

By the way I may have never written you that Mr. Powell Glass told me last spring after visiting the Arnold Arboretum and a number of other rhododendron plantings in the north that now he could understand the almost universal criticism of the color of *Catawbiense* that he had been reading. He contends that the species as it grows in his native mountains—around Lynchburg, Va.—is much superior to the types he saw in cultivation in the north. The plant that I have selected and call on my lists of seeds etc. 'Catawbiense Red' he called good but not at all exceptional in that section. I would sure like to

investigate R. Catawbiense in his locality when in bloom and may for my daughter has been rooming at school for three years with a Lynchburg girl who is a friend and neighbor of the Glass family and we have had numerous invitations to visit in Lynchburg from both sources.

March 14, 1942

We are all very sorry to hear of your mother's going. The whole family remember her for they met her when we stopped at your place returning from New England and she was so thoughtful for the travel weary kids that they never forgot it. You will indeed have your hands full with your invalid father. Of my own mother only a few little scattered memories persist for she died when I was four.

I do suppose I had better give up the Lichen Book at least for the present because I am sure the background to understand it is missing here. There is just one thing I am curious about and ask it not at all in a critical spirit—you do not give the names of the author of the botanical names? Perhaps these are given elsewhere or perhaps these are your own?

In poring over Millais....I found some other information of interest to me. The illustration of *R. Sutchuenense* (two forms) facing page 246 shows in the lower picture almost an exact replica of the old plant back of the woodhouse that I have had labelled *oreodoxa* ever since I received it. And that was in the days of Prof. C. S. Sargent who gave me the first plants of rare species I own, perhaps in 1921 or '22. Of these there were a dozen plants and there are four survivors, *discolor, Fortunei, auriculatum* (in lathhouse) and this *oreodoxa* (?). Yes, and there are two more but sickly and periodically winter injured—*decorum* (the old plant once illustrated on a calendar) and a *decorum* hybrid. All of these have been in the open for years except *auriculatum* which was placed in the lathhouse some three or four years ago where it does very well indeed. Only *discolor, Fortunei* and this doubtful *oreodoxa* are really hardy and never injured.

I get more and more disgusted with *R. Smirnowii* with each passing year. This A.M. I went out to get a small budded plant of this species to force and possibly get it in bloom with *oreodoxa*. With perhaps a dozen plants in bud I could only find one that had solid buds and even these are doubtful. It has been quite a few years since I have had a good full truss on *Smirnowii*. Its hybrids however seem to do pretty well. And if *Smirnowii x arboreum* is hardy it would seem to possess some inherent hardiness. *Smirnowii x decorum* is bud tender but I always blamed that on *decorum*.

I have always tried to blame this losing of its flower buds on Smirnowii's tendency to start growth in the fall and not because of lack of inherent resistance to cold if fully dormant but I begin to be not so sure.

About the homeliest of rhododendron plants and the most colorful in flower that I am able to grow satisfactorily with no protection but an uncovered lathhouse is Essex Scarlet. I think I recall its foliage being browned a little once when in the open but it never loses a floret from its flaming trusses. In contrast with Cynthia which will evidently not set a single seed or produce a grain of pollen Essex Scarlet is a prolific parent and I sure hope it proves a good one. When it was out in the nursery it was side by side with Dresselhuys and was the less injured of the two.

My tires are not new but with normal usage both my truck and car should be O.K. for two years or more... I much suspicion that when we get all the planes and tanks into action and the Heinies subs get the bulk of our tankers there will be no gas for any of us anyhow, tires or no tires. In which case I still have two mules!

The War Years

January 8, 1942

Well our good old friend Mr. Magor has passed on and I am sure if rhododendron lovers had any share in building up his future reward in the life to come he would not want. Letters from Australia, New Zealand, Chile, Japan and Germany that I can recall, all praised him for his disinterested generosity in helping them to obtain their wants. That he appreciated a little of this in return I well know for he once wrote me that out of the hundreds of recipients of seeds etc. from him I was one of the few who not only thanked him but reciprocated in kind. Nothing was too much trouble for him it seemed. If he did not have the seed I wanted himself he would go fifty miles to a neighbor's garden or send to Edinburgh Botanic or to Ireland before he would abandon the effort—and then apologize—a true old English gentleman.

And I just had a Christmas note from Mr. Fraser of Ucluelet, Vancouver Island, who first introduced me—by mail—to Mr. Magor. So to these two men more than all others—almost to the exclusion of all others—I owe my acquisitions in the first few years of my rhododendron growing. My oldest plants of *discolor* and *Fortunei* are from his seeds and such old standbys as *Catawbiense* x *Fortunei*, Boule de Neige x *Fortunei* (*Orbiculare* x *Williamsianum*, (from seed),) *Smirnowii* x *Fortunei* are from pollen 'from England.'

One wonders in view of world conditions whether it will be advisable to sow any seed of ornamentals. If I

were able to enlist I know I would not sow any. But it would seem that practically all the demand during the duration of the war will be for food materials and food plants. In fact I have had practically no inquiries since the war started. But I think I'll just stick to my guns and try to keep my rhododendrons going for so many establishments will no doubt be destroyed that it may be impossible for a long time to get the cooperation from other countries that we have enjoyed in these last years of peace.

April 20, 1942, 2:10 a.m.

Am writing in an aeroplane observation post where I am having a heck of a time to keep warm without smoking myself out. We have had so many mornings in April when it just reaches the freezing point—enough to make the *mucronulatum* and *sutchuenense-oreodoxa* etc. look a little sad though it does not freeze enough to take the flowers altogether.

July 18, 1942

In working among the plants this year I have been noticing the locality of origin of the species that are proving hardy here, particularly those from China. No really definite work has been done but I have browsed through the Species of Rhododendron in the evenings some and find that most of the things that are fully hardy are from Western Szechuan and from not too high. From Hupeh where one would think the climate would resemble ours possibly more most things seem to be a little more tender. Thus *Houlstonii* is none too hardy from Hupeh and Eastern Szechuan in mixed woods at 4500-7000 ft. alt. while *discolor* also from Hupeh and Szechuan at 4000-7000 ft. alt. but which also extends into *Western Szechuan* is fully hardy. And not only the Fortunei series but *longesquamatum* of the barbatum section and *insigne* of the arboreums seem just as hardy as any other rhodo. here, both from Western Szechuan.

...Perhaps some species like *decorum* which is found in Yunnan and Szechuan may also be found in this region of Western Szechuan from which our hardy forms seem to come.... The better forms may have been met up with in Yunnan or in some milder clime, the inferior or mediocre forms that may occur in West Szechuan are passed up which if fine for English conditions but may be where we have lost out in getting the *hardiest* forms of these species for *our* part of the world.

...perhaps it would do no harm to catalogue our hardy Chinese species with the localities where they originated, if known, with a view, when again possible, to have some collector make a point of collecting every species possible from that section no matter how often it may have been sent home to us from some other parts of its habitat.

... My health has been excellent for quite a long time now but just at the present I am hobbling around with a mule kicked hip but it will be O.K. in a day or two. That old mule has kicked at me thousands of times in the last thirty years and this is the first time he ever landed square. I would have sold him years ago but I was afraid he would just kill someone and felt that I knew how to handle the old fool better than anyone else. He is the only animal I ever knew that *never* reacts favorably to kind treatment. I always liked to work with animals and if it was not for this one old mule I would say that you can win any of them to you.

May 17, 1943

This from the Observation Post again at 1 A.M. Today I again had opportunity to observe the *Fortuneis* planted on the campus of Western Maryland College at Westminster, Md. They were at their best which was the best I ever saw from that species around here.... these plantings are in fairly sunny situations which seems to cause both more profuse flowering and better denser plant growth. My own *Fortunei* are not yet in flower though about to open.

The occasion was the graduation exercises of my two older girls, Caroline and Elizabeth, from the College, which occasion also should relieve the strain on my finances considerably from that of the last four years. Louise is also in college and James is rapidly advancing toward that stage. He is several inches taller than I now.

June 27, 1943

At the moment *Auriculatum, arborescens, maximum, minus* and Camps' Red are in flower. And yes, the diminutive flowered *semibarbatum, micranthum* and *Tschonoskii* are all doing their bit. Except the first mentioned all of these are fully hardy and take no particular care except *semibarbatum*. In this species one is compelled to take particular care to watch for its blooming time or the flowers will pass all unnoticed. They are just that inconspicuous. However, I regard their coloring and markings as exquisite and am sure were the florets as large as *auriculatum*, rhododendron literature would be crowded with its praises. But aside from being so tiny the little florets are so retracted back beneath the foliage—but I suppose you have it too, my plant coming from you, so you already know all this.

You are quite right that the problem of deciding which plants to introduce is a 'perplexing' one. And the perplexity does not always cease even after one has decided. I have already discontinued some of my first azalea introductions. This is bad, very bad. But it is an extremely difficult thing to evade. The trouble seems to be that there is no ultimate in this business. It is an infinite thing.

No matter how outstanding the new variety, improvements will ever be made. The best selling—and best to grow varieties—of all plant varieties are never permanent.

It is a continuously progressive process and I still affirm that when I named an azalea it was an improvement on any thing on the market in its day and in its class. But I keep right on breeding. .... And so it happens that something that looked so good to me ten or fifteen years back that I named it—and some of these have had enough merit to be grown by the thousands to fill the demand—have been so much outdone by newer creations of my own in their same color class etc. that I would be untrue to my work if I did not discard them and introduce the better variety.

I do not believe in introducing everything that is pretty or just a slight improvement etc. I think a good bit of my trouble with the azaleas was that so little or no work had been done in breeding hardy sorts that I had the field too much to myself. Almost every new color that came from the *Kaempferi-Poukhanense* crosses was hardy and hence a new hardy azalea in a new color for a hardy type. Hence I did not hesitate to propagate it. I am still proud of them for I have seen a few gardens with hundreds—one with thousands of Gable azaleas now taller than an average person and I feel that my first ambition in azalea breeding—that of making it possible to duplicate the azaleas of Magnolia Gardens farther north—is perhaps more than an idle dream.

The little 'Rosebud' azalea of which I sent a flower or two is an altogether different type of such promiscuous parentage that it would take a stud book to explain it. It is very dwarf and floriferous and hardy through eight years of record. It roots readily from cuttings. Some of the best old plants of azalea do not root well. It may be introduced in a few years if it will produce wood enough to work up a stock. Have an absolutely blood Red *obtusum* hybrid now. Something that has been non-existent either hardy or tender.

As for *Fortunei* hybrids failing in popularity I do not think they have had a chance so far. I have yet to sell a clonally propagated plant or to name a variety unless 'Caroline' is partly *Fortunei* and this I have not sold, only named. I could have sold hundreds if I had them—I have just worked my stock up to 24! This old plant Andorra Nurseries offered me $200.00 for but I asked $500.00. Humphreys saw it in flower. A hired man said we were both 'd-n' fools. Maybe so. Mrs. du Pont declared 'Caroline' is 'better than White Pearl even if White Pearl were hardy.' .... One point concerning plant introductions. Ninety-nine times out of each hundred it takes the originator to introduce a new variety to the retail consumer. The commercial nurseryman is a hardheaded business man and not inclined to take chances. The variety must get in the gardeners' hands and a demand started before the average nurseryman shows any sign of interest.

Quest for Yellow

April 2, 1945

Personally I have so many fine white and pink hybrids now and a world of unproven seedlings coming along in these colors that I am working mostly towards better reds, orange and yellow if possible. The yellow is I concede the most interesting objective to the rhodo enthusiast but to the general public it certainly will not be. The reds, crimsons and scarlets will captivate the great bulk of the public's fancy. A hardy purple as good or better than Purple Splendour will sell like wildfire too. P.S. is growable here in the open but I would not call it entirely hardy. In fact though it has always come through I am still looking for the time when it will not.

June 24, 1945

The Rhododendron Year Book (American) has been received some time ago and I think fairly well scrutinized and on the whole it is a very good beginning. At least much better than I had expected. I had not realized how greatly the cultivation of rhodos has developed in the N.W. and how much experience some of these growers have acquired by now. It makes me think back to the days before the Jap beetle quarantine when over half of all the stock I shipped went to Washington and Oregon and Northern California. It may be that these are doing better out there than I know.

.... It is most fervently hoped that the plant of 'Brachycarpum' pictured opposite page 122 is not from a plant sent west by the Gable Nursery and so tagged but I am afraid it is possible. A Mr. Nottcutt of England, a rather noted grower of rhododendrons sent me seeds of *brachycarpum,* purportedly, that grew up to be *campanulatum.* That was in the days of the beginning and a little *campanulatum* just may have gone west and grown up with the country under an assumed name.

Nearly all the seedlings that I took the trouble to sow from the very tender—but also very choice—hybrids that Magor so faithfully sent year after year, were planted out and left to take their course which course was short and none too sweet. But a few of them do survive though they never got anywhere. The most notable of these is the large plant of *Aucklandii* x *Thomsonii* which opened three florets in all this year.

September 18, 1945

Your flood calamity must surely be terrible disheartening and of course if sympathy alone could help any you are already recovered. Of all the misfortunes that have befallen my work with the rhododendrons none has so much disheartened me as to receive the news of this latest of yours. The way it is raining here yesterday, all night and today you will be playing Noah again this morning. ... this wet summer has so adversely affected my farm crops that I am sure to be in the financial doldrums before the winter ends unless some unforeseen windfall bursts loose—which it don't with me. I have been out of debt for the third time in my 26 years of married life, since last June. Soon it is borrow again.

January 25, 1946

Mr. D. L. Hardgrove wrote me yesterday saying he had sent me some rhododendron seeds of your crossing along with some of his own. This has stirred up the hope that you are going on with your hybridizing in spite of the calamity of last summer. If something like that would happen to me the way I feel now I am afraid I would quit too.

The last letter I had from you—think I have written you twice since—you said Hardgrove was gone from Baldwin and quitting the game too. Through the years I have contacted so many very interesting persons who were interested in beginning to hybridize rhodos or azaleas or hollies or some interest that is also an obsession of mine, but who after a few seasons lost interest that I hesitate to pass on things that are *too* critical. But you are interested in Mr. Hardgrove and so if I hear nothing from you to the contrary I will send him some things too. This letter is the first direct contact I have had with him.

January 29, 1951

.... Caroline, though of unrecorded parentage, looks like it has *Fortunei* and *Catawbiense* blood and perhaps something else. But whatever, Caroline is proving a wonderful 'mama' and from its hybrids have come practically all the *hardy large* flowered seedlings that I have had such a hard time selecting the best from in late years, and I still wonder about some of my discards.

Two clones are being propagated, Disca (*discolor* x Caroline) and Cadis (Caroline x *discolor*), the first a white with florets over four inches, did you see this one? I think so. And the second a pink with florets little if any less in size and an exceedingly free bloomer. These might throw something *close* to your ideal, quicker.

No more reds of the Cat. hyb. group will enter into

anything of mine but Essex Scarlet when I am looking for red flowers. The only reason there are no seeds by it on the 1950 list is that Old Essex took a rest from flowers this season. .... Essex Scarlet would put red tints in a skunk cabbage and hurts hardiness not at all as far as my experience goes. The only thing is that awful plant habit but it is not too difficult to breed away from that it seems. .... I certainly would not want a plant of Essex Scarlet as a specimen in the border!

"Call Ramapo Yours"

February 19, 1951

Saturday, Mr. Orlando S. Pride of Butler, Pa. was here and spent several hours. He is a nurseryman and Landscape architect, just a young fellow but been in the business 22 years. Fifteen years ago he bought a truckload of those old azalea seedlings that I had out in the field mostly two-four foot sizes. They were *poukhanense* x *Kaempferi, poukhanense* x Ledifolia Alba, *poukhanense* x Hexe and possibly a few lesser sorts, he is not sure. But what interests me is that many plants of these—in fact he says all of the *poukhanense* x *Kaempferi*—have withstood these fifteen winters without plant injury and the only bud injury from late spring frosts. A fair percentage of that group were of clear pink and rose colors and he has selected a few plants of this color for propagation. Since he says his lowest this year was 'only' 23 below and it is not 'unusual' for it to go down to −30, well he really has me interested.

.... I would say his tested plants have been enduring at least 10 degrees more of frost than mine and I am much revived in azalea interest by his report. Most of these plants were planted out by him just as he got them from me and he speaks of fifty out of about sixty-five planted out in a very exposed park site that have *never* been hurt. At that time he was bidding on the Pymatuning Park project. Koster got the bid with his hybrids of *Kaempferi* and *Malvatica* and there is not one plant left where some of mine planted right across the drive on a lawn by Pride are huge things covered with flowers each spring.

I guess you kind of know how good that makes one feel. I believe he said Kosters planted about six hundred plants.

April 8, 1951

The story of your 'Guyencourt Rhododendrons' is very interesting both in your letter and the Flower Grower clipping you so kindly sent me. Of course I have not seen any of this cross in flower but those plants at Buck's certainly looked good. I would not have expected this cross to be hardy—just another instance of the good that may come from different individuals having their own ideas!

I can not give you any light on the origin of Ramapo. There is no record in my notes of any hybrid of *carolinianum* and *fastigiatum* and I think you had better call it all your own. ... you had better call "Ramapo" your child and save his reputation.

You wrote that Caroline just would not root for you. Cannon never rooted one and I got *one* out of maybe 500-1000 trys. Coplen got 98 plants out of his first 100 giving me half and he is averaging about that same by the thousand now.

So—when they will root—root 'em. And when they won't (and *only* when they won't) graft 'em, I say for I do not believe in keeping a good rhododendron down. "Layering is excellent but slow" so we continually hear but the more I do of it the better I like it. It is almost 100 per cent certain and when one can put down a limb of Conewago and get 64 plants growing in three and four inch pots in two years from these buried branches compared with about 10% a year from cuttings which is an optimistic estimate of my average on Conewago, well what do you think?

I am unable to propagate fast enough with *all three* methods.

Grafted plants on *maximum* get on their own roots quickly. I have seen roots on stems of Caroline grafts at the unwrapping stage and it's the stubbornest cutting of them all. I also looked at some 18-24″ Caroline and had to cut the ball of one of them all to pieces to find any trace of the *maximum* root.

Coplen is rooting some of my azaleas and going at it in a big way. He propagates around the clock i.e. perhaps four or five lots of cuttings are taken from the plants kept growing continually in his houses. There are now some 20,000 Rose Greeley (D-3-G) in his houses and he says he can increase it to 100,000 by December. .... I must have had a rabbit's foot in each pocket and my neck through a horse shoe to get this lovely, hardy, hose-in-hose with large white flowers, in two generations from a Ledifolia Alba x *Poukhanense* cross! I got only two other whites from 240 seedlings and they were poor.

January 10, 1952

Hybrids of *brachycarpum* with almost anything produce a percentage of dwarfs such as that with *decorum* which has grown into wide dense plants with fairly good white flowers. .... its hybrid with *Fortunei* has flowered as quite small plants but the leaves and flowers are large and the plants will probably be of fair size when mature.

There are some seedlings of *carolinianum* x *impeditum* F2, that were very dwarf but I suspicion I was not sufficiently meticulous to keep the tiniest ones coming along. When one raises something of this sort with the dwarf types as the objective I guess one should discard all the normal healthy ones and concentrate on the culls and weaklings.

. . . in nature these types are generally crowded out by the stronger types and we seldom find them developed and in nursery cultivation they are culled out and we never know just how many of these dwarfs and mutants are potentially present in plant types. Some species no doubt have very few but I suspicion that especially among species that have lived for a long time somewhere in their latter evolutionary period, at high altitudes or in extraordinarily exposed conditions the percentage might prove surprisingly high.

January 18, 1952

You say that a secondary cross needs at least a thousand seedlings to reveal its potentialities and I am sure you are conservative if anything but how is one to grow a thousand of all these things to maturity? I am sure it is too large an order for me, and I try to think of methods of circumventing the full program though I fear there is little chance.

In the first place practically all of my secondary crosses have enough tender 'blood' in them to lose a large percentage long before they need permanent room, from winter cold, and the sooner they are weeded out the better. Some have lost 90% and over and still paid off. Atrier lost about 97%, I believe. In others every plant has lived and flowered. The second generation of Catfort for example has produced nearly all salable seedlings but not a thing worth propagating. If 97% of these had been frozen out I would have been better off.

So in chaotic and rather total disregard for the Mendelian laws—and I believe them to be excellent laws—I follow along lines that have given results without raising the necessary thousand or ten thousand plants—not that I have attained the ultimate—for that is unattainable, though like perfection in this life it is a goal we dare not lose sight of if we are to do our best. And that too is a good law for if we attained the ultimate in our various lines what would be left for generations yet to come? Should they be allowed nothing but *absolute* leisure to enjoy the perfections we had created?

John Wister just called and is coming up today so I must get together what I can recall about Dexter. About all I know first hand is the four or five hours I once spent there with him. I had a wonderful time and saw a lot of things but the thing that impressed me most was the great number of species, tender here, that met one at every turn out there on Cape Cod and seemed to be quite happy about everything. He never wrote me afterwards and though he had written down quite a list of things to send me I never received any after my visit.

In fact I think he never wrote me more than a half dozen letters and I feel sure I wrote five times to his one at first.

Some of my very first things came from Dexter, however. Around 1920 or '21 Prof. Sargent sent me six tiny rhodos, three *Fortuneis* and three *decorums*. They were mailed by Dexter from Sandwich. I had written Prof. Sargent about some of the seed I had sown and he asked me to send certain seedlings to Dexter which I did. That opened up a (limited) correspondence and we exchanged tiny seedlings. Two or three inches was about the limit either of us had attained at that time. My oldest plants of *Fortunei, decorum* and *discolor* (and perhaps *Smirnowii*) originated there.

April 27, 1952

Schlippenbachii, it seems, will never quit growing on me. Of all the azaleas, species and hybrids that we can grow, it certainly gives more sheer loveliness with less labor than anything else on the place. In fact the more severely one leaves it to its own devices the better it appears to thrive. Where it is exposed to the azalea borer as it is in the woods here among thousands of native *nudiflorum*, it pays to go over the plants in September and get the infested tips before they go down the stem. Many nurserymen say they have trouble with this azalea and even the Arnold Arboretum have published that it is difficult to transplant—I just *cannot* see why? . . . Yet, in this part of the country it is not a common garden plant.

You have done me many a good turn, Guy, but if I could pick out the one I appreciate most I would say it was those three tiny plants of *R. adenopodum* you gave me. The one plant I raised is just coming into flower and as usual everyone who sees it would want one—many ask what I would take for the old plant.

May 30, 1952

I think I have told you of a plant of Maxhaem that has fine bronze new growth which lasts well through the summer that I have been waiting years to see. *Can you imagine it opening yellow?* I could not but that is exactly what has happened. *Haematodes* must be a most variable species indeed from my experience in crossing it with such well fixed species as *maximum* and *Catawbiense,* but a yellow. And another pale yellow occurred in a discolor hybrid. I think it is a *Wardii* x *discolor* seedling but the florets are long like *discolor* and do not open as widely. There are pronounced pink shadings too and the whole effect is very lily like. Also it is flowering as a very young plant.

On a table in the room I have trusses of sixteen new first showings. There is a cardinal red of the darkest shade with a very nice truss and flowers of unusual substance but a little on the small side. A red about like

America but slightly darker with a better truss and—this is what counts—good foliage and plant habit. A purple about the shade of Purple Splendour but *without* the dark blotch in the throat—which would help! It will no doubt be hardier than that border line variety. Then there is a *discolor* derivative (x Caroline) that has larger flowers and trusses than Disca and Cadis, intermediate in color and larger, more densely borne foliage. The flowers seem a little lacking in substance but so far have not wilted or fallen—in about a week. And there are a lot of new reds, a whole crop of them, mostly Essex Scarlet seedlings with the first truss or two, and it is hard to tell which is the better this season. Also a Brittannia x America which was earlier and of good color though not so deep as some of these. Perhaps you saw that one?

It is all very pleasing and very bewildering. The more fine things flower, the more difficult the choice, as one does not want to introduce too many varieties along any one line. And then it is hard to discard those which are already being propagated every time a new one comes along with a floret a quarter inch more in diameter, a color a quarter of a shade deeper but they keep growing on one and one grows older and more indifferent.

Sincerely,

Joe

April 16, 1944

It is too bad to hear of your misfortune with your lath house. I certainly hope that you will find your damages less than you anticipate and that you will be able to carry on. And if you could know just how I feel at the moment you would realize how much this sounds to me like the 'blind leading the blind.' My back is hurting so that I can hardly sit here but it hurts anyway I can get so I might as well sit here I figure and if it is impossible to write you a decent letter at least you will know I sympathize. I have been out all working days so far but unless something happens for the better I must send back all my orders—that I so laboriously made boxes for last winter—and refund the cash—that I have already spent.

As to the plants they are so far in the best shape as far as winter injury goes that I ever saw them. Everything that succeeded in growing a viable flower bud in last summer's drought still has it intact. So barring the possibility of a late frost—I saw everything frozen here once on the 10th of May, not an apple, grape, pear peach or anything of the kind anywhere—there should be some things that I never saw before. Practically all the triflorums that have managed to survive, though frozen back times innumerable, are bringing through what buds they managed to form. There are in all some dozens, perhaps even a hundred or more of these sticking around where I left them to fight their own

battles, and many of them have lost all means of identification. In the matter of flower buds dead from last year's drought, the obtusum azaleas are the worst offenders. One plant may have every bud dead and the next impossible to find a dead one on it and we discovered this condition last September.

But the lapponicums not only produced no buds but they have left the premises in entirety unless it be a plant of *hippophaeoides* that may be partly alive. This plant has stood in the open for quite a few years and generally flowers. The side that is yet alive promises to be completely covered with bloom this time. And as yet I never flowered a yellow lapponicum! They are now quite gone unless they may send up shoots from the base.

At the moment, *mucronulatum* is in full flower though many plants lost some buds from drought, others are covered. My 'rose' colored selection of this really stands out as a definite improvement in this. It is several days later to open than the typical form it seems. Conemaugh is opening and also *mucronulatum* x *spinuliferum* (or *spinulosum*?). Whatever; it is a hardy thing with perhaps the most lovely florets of any *mucronulatum* cross but a heck of a straggly unhealthy looking plant with twisted, distorted and diseased looking foliage.

Keiskei and *ambiguum* together with practically all the triflorums are swelling. There are no buds on *sutchuenense*—which shows drouth injury rather badly—or on *haematocheilum* which opened before *mucronulatum* last year. *Campanulatum* and *adenopodum* are showing color and the lovely little Conemaugh x *Keiskei* is going to be well worth one of my very scarce films if present promise is fulfilled. This is a real gem, the best dwarf I ever produced by far in my opinion.

My lath house is going 'east'. It would have fallen except for some props before this but I have so little of value in it and my experience with it so unsatisfactory that it makes little difference. Anything that is hardy in the lath house seems to be equally hardy among the oaks and hickories down in the woods so that is where I plant almost everything out now.

Loderi, at least so tagged, is in bud but this seedling so much resembles *Fortunei* with the exception of being more tender that I doubt if it will be much else when it blooms.Cat.album x Loderi is also in bud and this is an event I have long wanted to witness. The plant has always been of rather remarkable appearance.

Well I must go and lay down a while I guess. I do hope that you will not have to give up your work. If you must sell it will be almost tragedy for of course your plants are not worth anything like as much to others as they are to you.

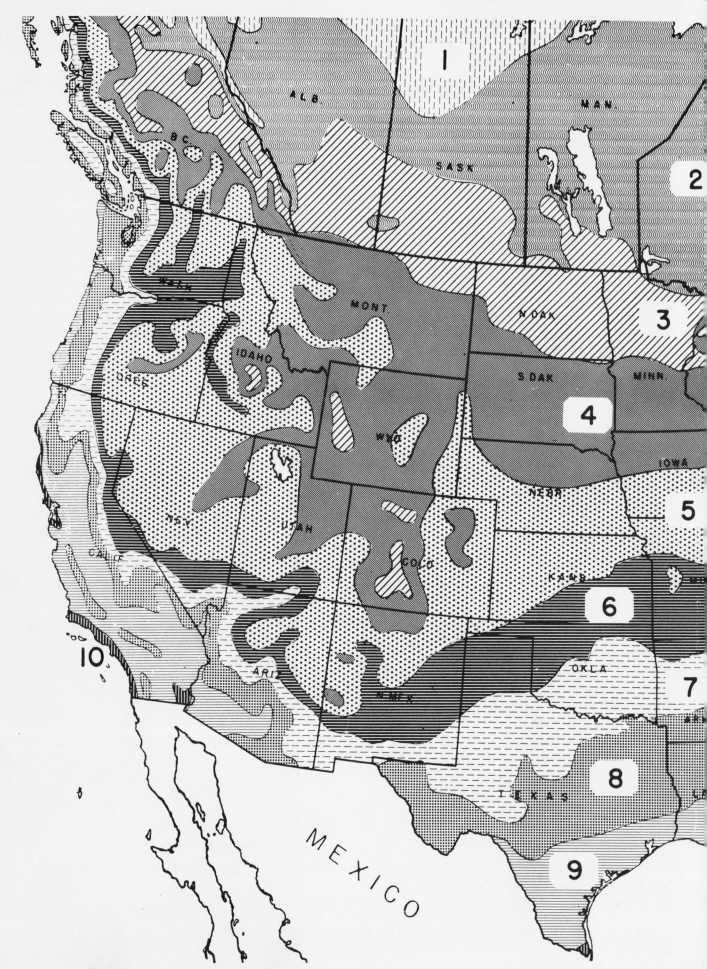